THE COMMONWEALTH EXPERIENCE

Volume Two: From British to Multiracial Commonwealth

By the same author

SURVEY OF BRITISH COMMONWEALTH AFFAIRS (2 vols)
SOUTH AFRICA 1906–1961: The Price of Magnanimity
THE IRISH QUESTION 1840–1921
CONSTITUTIONAL RELATIONS BETWEEN BRITAIN AND
INDIA: THE TRANSFER OF POWER 1942–47
  (10 vols published) (*editor-in-chief*)

THE COMMONWEALTH EXPERIENCE

Volume Two

From British to Multiracial Commonwealth

Nicholas Mansergh, F.B.A.

*Emeritus Smuts Professor of
the History of the British
Commonwealth and Fellow of
St John's College, Cambridge*

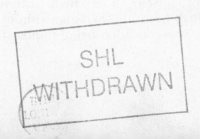

First edition published as one volume by Weidenfeld & Nicolson *1969*

Second edition published as two volumes 1982 by
THE MACMILLAN PRESS LTD
London and Basingstoke
Companies and representatives
throughout the world

ISBN 0 333 33160 5 (hardcover)
ISBN 0 333 33161 3 (paperback)
ISBN 0 333 33168 0 (hardcover two-volume set)

Printed and bound in Great Britain
at The Pitman Press, Bath

To
The Master and Fellows
of
St John's College, Cambridge

Contents

Contents of Volume One: The Durham Report to the Anglo–
Irish Treaty   viii
List of Maps   ix

PART ONE   THE BRITISH COMMONWEALTH OF NATIONS
          1921–47
  1 Status Seeking and Tariff Reform, 1921–36   3
  2 India: an Uncertain Goal   43
  3 Appeasement and War: the Commonwealth Rôle   71 ×
  4 India: the Tryst with a Divided Destiny   104 ×

PART TWO   THE COMMONWEALTH SINCE 1947
  5 Constitutional Transformation, Irish
    Republican Secession, Indian Republican Accession
    and the Changing Position of the Crown   135
  6 The Climax of Commonwealth and
    a Time of Disenchantment   163
  7 Men of Commonwealth: Smuts,
    Mackenzie King and Nehru   202

PART THREE   RETROSPECT 1838–1981
  The Historical Experience   236

Notes   258
Bibliography   274
Index   286

Contents of Volume One: The Durham Report to The Anglo–Irish Treaty

Contents of Volume Two: From British to Multiracial Commonwealth
Preface to the First Edition
Preface to the Second Edition

PART ONE   THE FOUNDATION MEMBERS AND THE NATURE OF THEIR
            ASSOCIATION
  1 The Commonwealth in History
  2 Commonwealth Origins, 1839–67; English Thinking and the
    Canadian Experiment
  3 South Africa; Races and Riches, War and Union
  4 The Pacific Colonies; Self-government and Consolidation
  5 'The Business May Seem Prosaic'; Co-operation by Confer-
    ence, 1887–1911

PART TWO   THE BRITISH COMMONWEALTH OF NATIONS, 1914–21
  6 The Catalyst of War
  7 Ireland; the Dominion Settlement

Notes
Index

List of Maps

1 The British Empire c. 1931   256
2 The Commonwealth 1981   257

PART ONE

The British Commonwealth of Nations
1921–47

'They are autonomous communities within the British Empire, equal in status, in no way subordinate one to another in any aspect of their domestic or external affairs, though united by a common allegiance to the Crown, and freely associated as Members of the British Commonwealth of Nations.'

REPORT OF THE INTER-IMPERIAL RELATIONS COMMITTEE,
IMPERIAL CONFERENCE 1926

'The Conference made clear, without doubt, that the predominant ideal and purpose of the British Commonwealth was peace, and that all efforts would be directed to the end of securing world appeasement and peace.'

THE RIGHT HON. J. A. LYONS, IN THE AUSTRALIAN
HOUSE OF REPRESENTATIVES, 24 AUGUST 1937

'It is true we have not, sitting in London continuously, a visible Imperial War Cabinet or Council. But we have, what is much more important, though invisible, a continuing conference of the Cabinets of the Commonwealth.'

THE RIGHT HON. W. L. MACKENZIE KING, ADDRESS TO
MEMBERS OF BOTH HOUSES OF PARLIAMENT
IN WESTMINISTER HALL, 11 MAY 1941

1 Status Seeking and Tariff Reform, 1921–36

Two fundamental questions of dominion status remained unresolved after the Imperial Conference 1921. The first, discarded but not disposed of by the Conference, was the necessity or otherwise of redefining British-dominion relations in terms that would bring law into line with conventional practice on a basis of equality, or near-equality. The second, entangled with the first but distinguishable from it, was the international status of the dominions. The answers to both questions were sought and found in the decade 1921–31 against a pattern of imperial relations determined for the most part in distant pre-war years. The nature of that pattern conditioned both the dominion demand for change and the formulae and statutory forms in which it was ultimately effected. The structure of the British imperial system, as it emerged from the first world war, is accordingly the appropriate starting-point for an enquiry into the reasons for, and the manner of its subsequent transformation. There was an imperial, as well as dominion–nationalist, premise to the Commonwealth conclusion.

The outline of the system was clear.[1] The king in Parliament was sovereign throughout the Empire. In theory he could act, and Parliament at Westminster could legislate, for the whole Empire. Laws extending to the dominions, it is true, were no longer enacted by the imperial Parliament, but the legal competence of that Parliament to do so was in no way impaired. The constitutions of all the dominions, including that of the Irish Free State enacted in 1922, were embodied in British Acts of Parliament and in the view of British and dominion governments, other than that of the Irish Free State, derived authority from them. By way of logical counterpart to this overriding British legislative competence went continuing British control over colonial and dominion legislation. In every case the assent of the sovereign's representative, the governor-general, was essential to the valid enactment of dominion legislation. In theory at least it was not to be thought of as

3

necessarily forthcoming, since the governor-general in each dominion remained entitled either to withhold such assent or to reserve a bill for the signification of the sovereign's pleasure by Order in Council. Furthermore, even when the assent of the governor-general had been given, it lay within the discretionary authority of the Crown to disallow a dominion Act. It is true, once again, that these powers were deemed obsolescent or even obsolete in practice, but dominion objection to their theoretic survival persisted. There were other relics of imperial control which if also obsolescent were evidently not yet altogether obsolete. There was the Colonial Laws Validity Act, 1865, which *inter alia* declared that any Colonial Legislation which conflicted with any of the provisions of a British Act of Parliament was to the extent of such repugnancy null and void and which, in so doing, expressly maintained the subordination of the former colonial legislatures to the Parliament of the United Kingdom. This subordination was by no means hypothetical. It was a matter of law and as *Nadan's case* was to demonstrate in 1926, the law had to be interpreted and should occasion arise, applied. In practice the Colonial Laws Validity Act also imposed limits upon dominion freedom of legislative action in respect of appeals to the judicial committee of the Privy Council, the conferment of honours and the determination of the national flag – though in the last instance the Irish Free State exceptionally was enabled to make its own unfettered choice – all being matters on which enactments by the Parliament at Westminster possessed overriding authority.

Subordination in law was paralleled by subordination in constitutional practice. The governor-general in a dominion was the representative of the Crown. But he was also the agent of the British government through whom formal communications were conveyed to dominion governments and from whom their communications to the Colonial Office were received. A governor-general, furthermore, furnished the home government with reports upon the political situation in a dominion, and should he feel so disposed or should occasion demand it, he was free to seek advice about the action he should take from the Colonial Office. In practice there was a strongly established convention that such advice should be sought only when matters of imperial interest were at stake, but it was the governor-general who remained the judge of what constituted such an interest. The dominions, other than New Zealand, disliked and had come to mistrust the duality implicit in the governor-general's rôle and sought to divest him of his politico-administrative responsibilities as an agent of the British government and so to leave him as a royally representative figure, fulfilling only the political and social duties performed by the sovereign in Great Britain. There was also the question of appointment. It had become established practice by 1921 that the government of a dominion should be consulted informally in advance about the appointment of a governor-general, so as to ensure at least that the nominee of the imperial government would not be unwelcome to them. But the initiative still rested with London. It was a reinsurance to dominion governments to have thus acquired something approaching an informal veto but it was not tantamount to possessing the right to advise. It was this on which their sights were set.

Externally it was not doubted that the first world war had brought about a significant advance in the international status of the dominions but the nature and extent of this advance remained debatable. The dominions were recognised as being completely self-governing within their own frontiers, they recruited and controlled their own armed forces, they had been brought into consultation on imperial foreign policy and they had received qualified international recognition in the making of peace and in membership of the League of Nations. But, the question remained, were they sovereign states? This was a question that could be (and was) debated in terms of international law. But it was also one to be considered in terms of international practice and it was this in which the dominions were the more immediately interested. What was their position in respect of the treaty-making power? Were they entitled to separate representation at international conferences? How was their membership of the League of Nations to be interpreted? India, also, was a member and was evidently not a sovereign state.

In 1919 the prime minister of Canada had obtained a signed Declaration from President Wilson, Clemenceau and Lloyd George stating that

> upon the true construction of the first and second paragraphs of Article 4 [of the League of Nations covenant] representatives of the self-governing dominions of the British Empire may be selected or named as members of the [League of Nations] Council.

This was intended to provide and was generally taken to represent international recognition of the dominions as separate political communities – a status which was also implicitly acknowledged in the assimilation of their position to that of all other League members in the International Labour Organisation and by the grant to them of the rank of distinct states, under the statute of the Permanent Court of International Justice in 1920.[2] But (other perhaps than by reasonable inference) such recognition registered no explicit advance in respect of sovereignty. Nor did it carry, as the Canadian government was to learn to its chagrin, any necessary consequences in respect of separate representation at international conferences. That was conditional upon the invitation or form of invitation issued by the Powers summoning the conference and the Powers in these years, the United States no less than the United Kingdom, were apt to be unmindful of dominion susceptibilities, interests and newly acquired status. The dominion response, New Zealand always excepted, was apt to be pained remonstrance and a patient resolve to establish dominion international identities in practice. Separate diplomatic representation in foreign capitals was one way in which this dominion purpose could be furthered, and in 1920 the Canadian government made the necessary arrangements for the appointment of a Canadian minister plenipotentiary to Washington. For a number of reasons (not the least of them being that no Canadian of sufficient wealth and appropriate qualifications was prepared to expend his resources on a diplomatic enterprise upon which the Canadian government saw fit to embark but not to provide for financially) the post was not filled until 1926 and in the meantime the Irish Free State had taken over the Canadian diplomatic pioneering rôle with the appointment of an Irish minister to Washington in 1924.[3]

Treaty-making proved a testing ground of status. Until 1919 dominion participation had been confined to consultation in respect of treaties in which their interests were likely to be involved, except – and it was an important exception – in the case of commercial treaties. Here the precedent established in the negotiation of the United States–Canadian Reciprocity Treaty 1854 was accepted, with the result that such treaties might be negotiated by and for any colonies that desired them even though the resulting agreement remained British in respect of formal ratification. The position was comprehensively defined in 1894, when in response to submissions from the colonial governments represented at the Conference then meeting in Ottawa, the secretary of state laid down certain principles which were in essence sustained till 1919. The colonies, Lord Ripon noted,[4] did not desire treaty-making power and it would not be possible to give it to them since that would result in the destruction of imperial unity. But separate treaties could be made with colonial co-operation for colonies that desired them, a condition of their negotiation however being that concessions from foreign states detrimental to the interests of other parts of the Empire should not be accepted and that concessions to foreign states should be extended to all other powers entitled by treaty to most-favoured-nation treatment and *gratis* to all other parts of the Empire. The application of these principles was variously tested before 1914 but always within the agreed framework of a single imperial treaty-making authority.

How much was changed in theory by the procedures adopted in the signing of the peace treaties in 1919? The United Kingdom delegates, it will be recalled, then signed for the Empire as a whole. In so far as their signatures were to be regarded as possessing overriding authority, it could reasonably be contended that while there had been concessions to dominion sentiment in practice, the principle of a single imperial treaty-making authority remained unimpaired. Sir Robert Borden would have preferred a different procedure, with the United Kingdom signatures limited to Britain and the dependent Empire and dominion signatures separately for each dominion, so as to signify the existence of separate dominion treaty-making powers. But all that he obtained was the deferment of United Kingdom ratification of the peace treaty, pending approval by dominion parliaments.[5] This was a concession which was significant in an imperial context without, once again, being conclusive internationally. There was, accordingly, carried over into the 1920s an unresolved British-dominion debate about the nature of dominion treaty-making power, behind which lay the larger theoretic questions of international status and more immediate practical issues of the making and control of imperial foreign policy.

In 1911 Asquith had declared that responsibility for foreign policy could never be shared. During the war years it came to be shared. But did dominion participation in the making of foreign policy in the imperial war cabinet mean that there had come into being a system of joint British-dominion responsibility for the making of imperial foreign policy? The procedures adopted for the negotiation of the peace treaties and for the signature of the Treaty of Versailles suggested (with certain qualifications) that such was the case. Furthermore, the notion of such joint responsibility survived the disappearance of the imperial war cabinet. So much was apparent from the argument of the Colonial Office paper on *A Common Imperial Policy in Foreign Affairs*[6] submitted to the cabinet in March 1921, preparatory to the Imperial Conference of that year. The paper noted the changes that had taken place during the war. 'Before the Great War,' it recalled, 'the direction of foreign policy was in theory and in practice vested in His Majesty's government.' Apart from occasional consultation on particular issues

> the general foreign policy of the Empire, while in fact largely influenced by consideration for the known policies and interests of the dominions and India, was still shaped and controlled by ministers whose only direct responsibility was to the Parliament of the United Kingdom.
>   The sudden outbreak of the Great War revealed the anomaly of this state of affairs. Effective consultation during the critical days of the negotiations in which His Majesty's Government strove to avert the catastrophe was impossible and was not attempted . . . It was clearly recognised from the very outset that such a situation could not be allowed to recur.

But how was this to be done? The Colonial Office felt that the answer was to be found in the Empire's experiences in the making of peace. The negotiations and the Treaty of Versailles were 'a landmark of the greatest significance in the constitutional development of the British Commonwealth', but of far greater practical importance was the fact that through the British Empire delegation 'effect was given to the views and wishes of every member of the British Commonwealth as a single co-ordinated imperial policy'. With the break up of the British Empire delegation, however, 'the control of the ever changing field of foreign policy has almost entirely relapsed into the hands of the United Kingdom'. In 1920 the imperial cabinet had not met; the international situation could not be left to itself and while the dominions had been kept informed far more fully than before the war they had not had any appreciable share in shaping the policy pursued, 'though that policy may have involved consequences of the greatest moment for the whole future of the Empire'. The conclusion to be drawn, argued the Colonial Office memorandum, was not that unity of policy had become less necessary but rather that the more complete the equality of status, the less tolerable was a state of affairs 'in which one member of the group should exercise exclusive control over a policy which may involve the most vital interests and even the existence of the others'. The outstanding need was, therefore, for unity in policy, and the chief practical problem to devise a satisfactory means by ministerial representation in London, improved communications, or in some other way, by which the acknowledged difficulties of continuity of discussion might be overcome.

At the Imperial Conference, Lloyd George lent his support to ideas of unity through joint control. 'There was a time when Downing Street controlled the Empire', he told the dominion delegations at the Imperial Conference; 'today the Empire is in charge of Downing Street.' Six months later in the debate on the Anglo–Irish Treaty he was more specific. A million men had come from the dominions to help the motherland in the hour of danger. But although they had come, their governments had had no share in the making of policies that had brought Britain into the war. They should not in the future be placed in the dilemma of supporting Britain in a policy that they might or might not have approved, or of deserting her in time of trouble. Therefore there must be consultation before the event. That was right; that was just; that was advantageous. There must be one instrument of policy and in the circumstances that instrument could only be the Foreign Office. But the dominions claimed a voice in the determination of future policy and that claim, Lloyd George recalled, had been gladly conceded. At the Imperial Conference general decisions were arrived at with 'the common consent of the whole Empire'. Then, warming to his theme, the British Prime Minister moved on to his eloquent climax:

> The sole control of Britain over foreign policy is now vested in the Empire as a whole. That is a new fact . . . The advantage to us is that joint control means joint responsibility, and when the burden of Empire has become so vast it is well that we should have the shoulders of these young giants under the burden to help us along. It introduces a broader and a calmer view into foreign policy. It restrains rash ministers and it will stimulate timorous ones. It widens the prospect.[7]

These were stirring thoughts. They invited, however, certain questions. Was not joint responsibility a mirage unless there was effective joint control? Was there effective joint control? If so, by what means was it exercised? Perhaps such questions would have been thought unreasonable, or unseasonable, at the time. Yet some nine months later Lloyd George himself, in an episode that has gone down in Commonwealth history as the Chanak incident, lent to these questions new point and dramatic urgency. The occasion was the repudiation by the young Turks, under Mustapha Kemal in 1922, of the near eastern treaty settlement. They rose up in arms and drove the Greeks headlong from Asia Minor. By early September that year the British were left at Chanak and on the Straits as the principal defenders of Constantinople against the onrush of the victorious Turkish advance. In this situation of military exposure and political peril Lloyd George decided to appeal to the dominions. On 15 September he sent a dispatch to their several prime ministers, asking whether dominion governments wished to be associated with the British stand in defence of the Straits and of the peace settlement and whether they would wish to be represented by a contingent. Even the announcement of dominion armed support, the message urged, would of itself exercise a most favourable influence on the situation and might help to prevent actual hostilities. The dispatch was followed by a statement to the Press disclosing that an appeal had been made to the dominions for contingents in defence of interests for which they had already made enormous sacrifices and 'of soil which is hallowed by immortal memories of the Anzacs'.

The response to the British prime minister's appeal was varied. New Zealand replied affirmatively and at once. The Australian reply was reassuring. So much, however, could not be said of the rejoinder from the new prime minister of Canada, William Lyon Mackenzie King. On Saturday 16 September 1922 King was in his constituency, North York, and the first he heard of the British appeal was an enquiry by a newspaper reporter about the response Canada proposed to give to it. Later he learned that the dispatch itself had in any case reached his office in Ottawa several hours after the Canadian newspapers had printed the public announcement from London. Nor had there been any information, still less the joint consultation which might have been thought of as a pre-condition of joint responsibility. The dispatch was the first and only intimation which the Canadian government had recieved, so King later told the Canadian House of Commons, from the British government about the impending crisis in the near east. It was all, King suspected (and throughout his life he was much given to such suspicions), an imperialist device to test out 'centralisation versus autonomy as regards European wars'. With this uppermost in his mind he decided on his reply. It had the merits of simplicity, democratic impeccability and complete impregnability. Parliament, he said, should decide. Parliament was not sitting. It would have, should circumstances demand it, to be summoned. That would take time – a circumstance as satisfying to Mackenzie King as it was frustrating to Lloyd George. There were further attempts at persuasion from London and a later protest from the Canadian Conservative leader, Arthur Meighen that the Canadian reply should have said 'Ready, aye ready; we stand by you', but Mackenzie King not only remained firm but if anything stiffened in negation. He did not stand alone; General Smuts was with him.[8] Nor was Australian opinion unanimously on the other side – Chanak was a party issue – and the government privately protested at the brusqueness of Lloyd George's appeal. Yet Chanak became a landmark in Commonwealth history, because Mackenzie King made it so.

In the immediately succeeding years there were two interpretations of the Chanak incident. The first was that it was a warning against thinking of joint responsibility without ensuring full, prior joint consultation. On this line it was argued that the Canadian prime minister was affronted because he had been neither informed nor consulted about British policy in advance. Had he been so, the argument proceeded, then the incident itself, in the form in which it actually arose could not have occurred. Furthermore, was it not possible that, had the Canadian prime minister and his cabinet colleagues been in full possession of the facts and the dangers of the situation in the near east, they would have proved more co-operative? What was required therefore, above all, was effective machinery. But was this the correct interpretation? What had Mackenzie King in fact said? He had told the Canadian Parliament that it was neither right nor proper 'for any individual or for any group of individuals to take any step which in any way might limit the rights of Parliament in a matter which is of such great concern to all the people of our country'.[9] He was, in fact, asserting the supremacy of Parliament. On that principle he took his stand. He might have done otherwise. He might have complained, as did the Australian government, at the failure to consult or at the breakdown of all semblance of joint responsibility for the making of policy but he did neither. The reason was clear. Had such been his chief grounds for complaint then the remedy would indeed have been more effective machinery to ensure that joint responsibility became a reality. But Mackenzie King did not want joint responsibility; he felt it was a device to commit the dominions to British policies. He wanted something quite different – the disentangling of dominion from British policies. He wanted separate dominion policies, not joint imperial policies, howsoever arrived at. There was no better means of advancing his aim than by appeal to the sovereignty of Parliament. He stood then upon a rock of principle. From that rock he was to be moved neither by the cajolings of

imperialists nor in subsequent years by the plight of the League of
Nations. King was under no misapprehensions about the wider
implications of his stand. The principle he had enunciated was one
that could be (and was to be) applied as effectively against
international as against imperial commitments or obligations.

In retrospect the aims of Canadian policy are apt to appear
deceptively clear-cut. At the time there was confusion about them,
certainly in London – a confusion more pardonable perhaps than
Canadian historians are apt to allow. As a result of experience
during the war the British government were convinced that the
dominions, Canada included, wished to participate in the making
of foreign policy. This was true, broadly speaking, in respect of
Australia and New Zealand and also, though with certain qualifications, of South Africa, so long as General Smuts remained in office.
But in respect of Canada under Mackenzie King's Liberal administration it was a conviction well calculated to foster misunderstanding. The Candian government desired control of foreign
policy, of Canadian foreign policy, but far from being anxious to
participate in the making of a common imperial or Commonwealth
policy, it was anxious at all costs to be dissociated from it. For
Canada the road to equality was deemed to lead not through equal
participation in the making of one policy but in the separate control
of several policies. Canadian emphasis was therefore consistently
upon the plural 'policies' and against the singular 'policy' for the
British Commonwealth of Nations, upon separateness and against
the unity advocated in the Colonial Office Cabinet paper of 1921. It
was this that successive British governments found difficult to
grasp, despite Mackenzie King's explanations and aggrieved re-
monstrances.

Chanak was followed by the Canadian–United States Halibut
Fisheries Treaty 1923, the Lausanne Treaty 1924, and the Locarno
Pact 1925, all of which raised points of principle and two of which
were the cause of Anglo–Canadian disputation. The first, the
Halibut Fisheries Treaty, was negotiated by the Canadian minister
of fisheries with the United States representatives, and Mackenzie
King advised the British government that since the proposed treaty
was of concern solely to Canada and the United States and did not
affect any particular imperial interest, the signature of the Canadian minister would suffice. This meant the deliberate by-passing
of the British ambassador, to test and establish a Canadian right to
make and sign a treaty of particular concern without the intervention of United Kingdom government authority. The British
government acquiesced with, and the British ambassador without,

grace and the treaty was signed in a tense atmosphere in Washington on 2 March 1923.[10] Mackenzie King had reason to be satisfied for he had established a precedent by which he set much store, namely that a Canadian minister acting alone might sign a treaty and that treaty might be subsequently ratified by the king, acting on the advice of the Canadian government. It was a precedent important for all dominion governments and one vindicated by the Imperial Conference 1923. It opened the way in a vital respect to separate dominion control over foreign relations. As such it was duly remembered. Thirty years later, on 2 March 1953, a commemorative ceremony was held on Parliament Hill in Ottawa in the presence of the American ambassador and the prime minister, Louis St Laurent, with television cameras duly recording the scene. One thing only was missing – a halibut.

The limits, however, as well as the extent of the Halibut Treaty precedent are to be noted. The treaty was a commercial treaty, and the dominions' right to negotiate their own commercial treaties was comparatively long-established. It is true that there had been a significant procedural departure from precedent since hitherto at each stage nominal British control had remained in the appointment of dominion negotiators by the king on the advice of the British government, in the formal signature of the treaty by a British representative and finally in ratification by the king acting on the advice of the British government, and all had been dispensed with. But what of the other side of the coin? Hitherto the British government had also possessed the right to conclude treaties for the whole Empire, including the dominions, without dominion participation in negotiation or ratification. Did that right subsist? Or had treaties affecting the whole Empire henceforward to be concluded by the British government on behalf of the United Kingdom and the dependent Empire and also by the dominions severally on their own behalf? What was at issue here, at root, was whether for treaty-making, and by necessary inference, for diplomatic purposes, the British Empire was or was not to be thought of as a unit. This was the crucial question and it was debated, once again in an Anglo–Canadian context, most notably in respect of the negotiation and conclusion of the peace treaties with Turkey.

The precedents of Versailles were all-important for the dominions as a point of departure in post-war peace-making procedures. But they were not all-sufficient. Neither the British government nor those of the dominions could decide alone upon the nature and composition of the British presence at an international conference. Other states also had opinions. They raised objections to dominion representation at the conference called at Lausanne to conclude peace between the allied Powers and Turkey. The British government acquiesced and the Versailles precedent of a British Empire delegation was thus discarded. Dominion governments were duly informed of the position in this respect and also of the general lines of British policy. They were further informed that in due course they would be asked to sign the subsequent treaty. The Canadian government thereupon raised certain questions of principle, about which they were in fact concerned, but from which the British government inferred Canadian disappointment at not being invited to the conference. They were seemingly encouraged in their belief by communications from General Lord Byng, the governor-general of Canada.[11] But in fact the Canadian government did not wish to be represented and were much relieved when the British government had first apologetically explained that their representation was impracticable. 'Thank God we weren't [invited]' was apparently the sentiment of all the members.[12] What Mackenzie King was concerned to do was to exact the highest possible price in terms of status from the non-invitation. In particular he had no intention of agreeing to sign, on behalf of Canada, a treaty about which he had not been consulted, in the negotiations for which Canada had not been represented and in which the dominion had no immediate interest. The consequence, as it appeared to him, of such non-participation was non-commitment. He was careful to distinguish between the Canadian position at Lausanne and as it had been at Versailles. At Versailles, Canada had immediate and direct interest. In such circumstances, so Mackenzie King recorded in a note reprinted by his biographer,[13] Canada should be represented with full powers, it should sign the treaty, Parliament should be given an opportunity to approve it, and assent to ratify it should be given by the governor-general in council. But where interest was not immediate or direct, as at Lausanne, then Canada did not need to be represented, and if not represented should not be expected to sign, and if not signing should be left to approve or not to become a party to any such treaty on the merits of the case, with assent to ratification conditional on approval. On these premises Canada, not being represented at Lausanne, should not be asked to sign nor Parliament be required to approve nor the governor-general to ratify the subsequent treaty.

The Canadian prime minister's exposition of the rôle and responsibilities of a dominion in treaty-making was approved in the detailed Resolutions of the Imperial Conference 1923 on treaty-making, it being laid down *inter alia* that, in respect of treaties negotiated at international conferences, 'the existing practice of signature by plenipotentiaries on behalf of all the governments of the Empire represented at the conference should be continued'. Practical affairs, however, are apt to be more complicated than logical analysis may suggest and not all eventualities were covered by the Resolution. In the particular case of the Turkish Treaty, Canada, not being represented at the Lausanne Conference, was under no obligation to sign the resulting treaty. But, and here was the rub, she remained technically at war with Turkey, unless and until she did so. The Canadian position had to be further refined. It was necessary after all to sign and ratify the treaty in order to end the war, though in so doing Mackenzie King was at pains to circumscribe narrowly the degree of responsibility incurred. It was one thing, he argued, to sign a treaty to end a state of war; another to enter thereby into actual or moral obligations for the future. King made it clear that Canada, unrepresented at the conference, was assuming no obligations of either kind.

The debates on treaty-making derive their significance from their bearing upon the international status of the dominions on the one hand and the extent of dominion responsibility for imperial international commitments on the other. King was concerned at once to enhance Canada's international status and to limit her obligations. On both counts he objected to dominion commitment, by treaty or otherwise, to the fulfilment of obligations entered into by Britain alone and he sensed that such would be the consequence in practice of any acceptance of ideas of a common imperial foreign policy.

A common foreign policy [warned his closest adviser, Dr O. D. Skelton, in 1923[14]] . . . offers a maximum of responsibility and a minimum of control. It commits a dominion in advance to an endorsement of courses of action of which it knows little and of which it may not approve, or in which it may have little direct concern. The real way in which the dominions may extend their power is the way in which such extension has come in the past – by reserving for their own peoples and their own parliaments the ultimate decision as to their course of action.

The argument was logical, the conclusion convincing, and in fact guided the course of Canadian policy. It is to be noted however that the extension of dominion freedom of action inevitably curtailed the range of Britain's imperial authority. If ultimately the dominions were to determine individually their own external policies in all respects, then Britain's ability to speak for the Empire as a whole would be conditional upon prior consultation with the dominions and their agreement in each individual case that she should do so. Mackenzie King understood that in critical international issues this represented a major practical problem of politics. He allowed specifically, in the notes already alluded to, that in high political treaties affecting peace and war, the Empire would act as one, though the extent of obligation imposed upon its self-governing members would be a matter of arrangement to be determined by each of them in the light of the merits of the issues at stake. But it was the direction that immediately mattered and it was not to be supposed that London would acquiesce in such a reinterpretation of imperial-international obligations without first testing the ground.

The Imperial Conference 1923 provided the occasion. The principal protagonists were Curzon as foreign secretary and Mackenzie King. King thought of Curzon as the archetype of the superior, overbearing, centralising imperialist, while Curzon found King 'obstinate, tiresome and stupid'[15], though he had reason also to note his remarkable persistence. As the major issues of the conference were reviewed one by one – foreign affairs, trade, defence – King considered what was said and analysed what was written lest inferences be drawn or precedents established by which common policies and centralised control might unobtrusively gain acceptance. Among British historians it has been widely assumed that Mackenzie King was tilting at windmills. But fuller evidence makes it clear that this was not altogether so. Whitehall, it may be allowed, was not in the hands of conspiratorial imperialists as King was only too apt to suppose – in point of fact it was itself divided, with the Foreign Office entertaining no wish to have their responsibility shared or their freedom shackled by the requirements of centralist consultative procedures – but there was a determination, and particularly in the Colonial Office, to preserve the diplomatic unity of the Empire so long as the price in terms of imperial relations was not too high. It was believed that the means existed to promote this end. The Imperial Conference was conceived to be a qualified albeit obviously second best peacetime substitute for the imperial war cabinet and as such it was thought the Conference could formulate at least the broad outlines of policy for the whole Empire. On that assumption there was the machinery and, it was hoped, there was also sufficient common will to ensure agreement on a single imperial foreign policy. But King was far from being interested in improved machinery; he was profoundly, indeed passionately, opposed to the end that machinery was intended to serve. He felt that in peace and also in war it was not for any central body, however composed, but for each autonomous government of the Commonwealth to determine its own course of action. His views passed neither unnoted nor unchallenged. One entry in his diary records how

> Lord Derby . . . rather tried to force my hand in the matter of how far the dominions might be expected to go with respect to the Empire being attacked at any point. I felt obliged to interrupt him and to point out that Canada's co-operation could not be taken for granted. I stated that had war arisen last year against the Turks it is extremely doubtful if Canada would have supplied any troops.
>   It was an unpleasant and somewhat trying experience. . . . However, it constitutes to my mind the most important of all the statements made at the present Conference.[16]

At the end, after rather more than the familiar flurry of last minute consultation and revision of drafts, Mackenzie King succeeded in securing the addition of a paragraph in the section of the Report on foreign relations, which stated that the Conference was a Conference of representatives of the several governments of the Empire, that its views or conclusions on foreign policy were necessarily subject to the action of the governments and Parliaments of the various portions of the Empire and that it hoped the results of its deliberations would meet with their approval. These words, in the opinion of King's biographer of this period, Professor MacGregor Dawson, signified the departure of the imperial cabinet from the scene, and at the same time let it be inferred that the earlier imperial Conference, with its non-committal conversations, had quietly resumed its place.[17] This gave to King the substance of what he wanted. But that is not to say he achieved it against all British odds. The technical problems of formulating 'centralist' policies had moved the British government, and especially the Foreign Office, towards a more accommodating position. They, too, for reasons very much of their own, were becoming 'decentralist'.

How important was the outcome of the Imperial Conference 1923, in the broader imperial setting? Professor Dawson has argued that it was this Conference and not its successor in 1926 that was decisive, on the ground that the 1923 Conference marked the point at which the Empire reversed the centralising tendencies of the war and post-war years and moved towards a more stable condition based on the nationalism and independence of the dominions. On this argument change was initiated in 1923, confirmed in 1926. This assessment Dr Wigley[18], in a detailed study of the British as well as the Canadian records, has subsequently endorsed, judging the 1923 Conference 'to be a critical point of departure for British-dominion relations', more significant than that of 1926 'in the development of practical dominion autonomy', because the failure to establish any collective policies in key areas of foreign policy 'represented an acknowledged major step forward for the supporters of devolutionary change'. But to this one reservation needs to be entered. The 1923 Conference to all seeming foreclosed the centralist road and by so doing left open the way to a recasting of imperial relations in terms of a dominion automomy extending to foreign, over and above domestic, policy but it did not ensure that there would be the necessary consensus of opinion to enable that road to be travelled in united company. That necessary measure of agreement remained to be achieved and its achievement was not to be lightly assumed. There 1926 retained its place.

The 1923 Imperial Conference certainly reflected the coming of a new spirit into Commonwealth relations. King was mainly responsible but it is well to remember that behind King stood Skelton, the biographer of Laurier, who was to become the chief artificer of a Canadian diplomatic service. No one who worked with him, thought Vincent Massey, could fail to recognise that he was anti-British. Lord Lothian more penetratingly observed in 1940 that relations with his Canadian colleagues in Washington would be better if 'Skelton did not regard cooperation with anyone as a confession of inferiority', while Professor Soward retrospectively, and after studying the official records, concluded that Skelton was essentially North American 'determined not to become involved in European power politics, hostile to the centralisation of Commonwealth policies in Downing Street . . .'[19] Those attitudes were shared by General Hertzog, the spokesman of renascent Afrikaner nationalism, who was to succeed Smuts as prime minister in 1924, and by the Irish administration of W. T. Cosgrave, which was resolved furthermore with the easing of its domestic problems, to seize each opportunity that offered to assert the international personality of the Irish Free State. In 1923 the Irish Free State, in the face of British discouragement, became the first dominion to establish a permanent delegate to the League: in 1924, the year in which it accredited a minister to Washington, it also registered the Treaty, despite British objection, as an international agreement with the League. Clearly the forces pressing for change were gathering momentum.

In November 1924 L. S. Amery was appointed colonial secretary in Stanley Baldwin's first administration. He made it a condition of his acceptance of office that at long last the Colonial Office should be broken up into its component parts and a separate department created responsible for relations with the dominions.[20] In 1925 this division took place and Amery became the first secretary of state for dominion affairs, though in fact he continued to combine this new office with that of secretary of state for the colonies throughout his tenure. Amery had his own views of the pattern of dominion development and he was not predisposed to notions of separate. dominion responsibility for foreign policy. In 1917 he had contemplated consolidation of the self-governing empire on the basis of establishing permanent machinery for the making of common imperial policies, and in 1921 he had responded to Smuts' proposal for a declaration of dominion rights with the suggestion that they should 'of course, include an affirmation not only of the complete independence and equality of the several partners, but also the indissoluble unity of all of them under King and Crown'.[21] But while Amery thought in terms of common loyalty, common policies and common action, he appreciated that such aims might be furthered by timely concessions to dominion sentiment more effectively than by grudging acquiescence in their demands. The all-important thing for him was the preservation of the unity of the Empire in a period of transition and while he was a man of tenaciously held ideas, his approach to Commonwealth constitutional, as distinct from trade, policies – he was a doctrinaire tariff reformer – was in the pragmatic Colonial Office tradition.

The negotiation and ratification of the Locarno Treaty in 1925 underlined the Commonwealth lessons that were to be drawn from Chanak and Lausanne. In this instance there was no search for a common imperial initiative in Europe because the co-ordination of separate policies through consultation between widely scattered governments appeared to present too many practical difficulties. It was impossible, said Sir Austen Chamberlain, publicly reaffirming a Foreign Office view that was familiar in the corridors of Whitehall, in the debate in the House on the Locarno Treaty, to wait on the dominions.

> . . . the affairs of the world do not stand still . . . I could not go, as the representative of His Majesty's government, to meeting after meeting of the League of Nations, to conference after confer-

ence with the representatives of foreign countries, and say, 'Great Britain is without a policy. We have not yet been able to meet all the governments of the Empire, and we can do nothing.' That might be possible for an Empire wholly removed from Europe, which existed in a different hemisphere. It was not possible for an Empire the heart of which lies in Europe . . . and where every peril to the peace of Europe jeopardised the peace of this country.

Accordingly the Locarno Treaty was signed by the United Kingdom government alone, with a proviso in Article 9 to the effect that 'the present treaty shall impose no obligation upon any of the British dominions, or upon India, unless the government of such dominion or of India signified its acceptance thereof'. None in fact did so. Their reasons were given at a meeting of the inter-imperial relations committee of the Imperial Conference 1926. For Canada Ernest Lapointe, minister of Justice, noted in a prepared statement that the treaty involved additional obligations in a European field which, though of interest to Canada, was not 'our primary concern', while Mackenzie King added that the fact that the United States had not assumed any obligations in European affairs placed the Canadian government in a somewhat difficult position. General Hertzog was equally clear that South Africa should not enter 'more deeply into matters concerning Europe and Great Britain, unless cause were shown'. The Irish Free State in reserving its position in effect adopted the same attitude, and the New Zealand prime minister commented that New Zealand while ready to assume them was very much concerned about becoming 'responsible for obligations to which she might find it difficult to give effect'. Stanley Bruce who 'felt very keenly that there should be common action' from the dominions underwriting the Locarno Treaty, received support from Newfoundland alone. It is important to note however that the countervailing majority dominion view did not indicate dissent from the policy of the British government, but rather the conviction that the treaty was the responsibility of the British government. This was coupled with a disposition on the Canadian and South African, and a positive wish on the Irish side, to underline their separateness in foreign policy. In no case, other perhaps than the Irish, did it mean that the dominions would necessarily dissociate themselves from consequences which might arise from the British signature of the treaty; on the contrary comments offered by dominion leaders at the 1926 Imperial Conference suggested that for the most part they would be

predisposed to support Britain in resisting any challenge to the
security system established at Locarno especially, Lapointe carefully noted, as it applied to frontiers in Western Europe only.[22]

The changing pattern of Commonwealth international relations,
important in itself, was furthermore a manifestation of deeper
forces at work. It was not Mackenzie King and his insistence upon
the supremacy of Parliament and the consequent logical necessity
of separate foreign policies within the Commonwealth who required a new exposition of the nature of Commonwealth relations,
it was the nationalists throughout the dominions, in Canada
certainly, but more particularly in South Africa and in the Irish
Free State. When General Hertzog came to office in 1924 he made,
so one of his biographers has told us,[23] a 'meticulous study' of the
minutes and documents of all the Imperial Conferences up to that
time, as well as various memoranda including that drafted by
Smuts in 1921. His first speech as prime minister was on the theme
of 'South Africa first' and South Africa's Commonwealth membership was implicitly made conditional upon national self-interest.

General Hertzog's immediate aim was to advance South Africa's
Commonwealth standing by securing international recognition of
her independent status, and he was correspondingly the more
sensitive to any failure on the part of foreign countries to recognise
South Africa's separate international identity. When Amery wrote
to tell Hertzog of the impending separation of the Dominions from
the Colonial Office, he sought also to give him some plausible
reassurance on this count.

> I think the real answer you seek [wrote Amery] lies in action
> which will enable foreign countries to grasp the essential,
> peculiar character of the British Commonwealth. But of course
> the fact that the nations of the British Commonwealth came into
> being through evolution has prevented their existence impres-
> sing itself upon the outside world and it will take a little time
> before foreign governments will remember at international
> conferences that all H.M.G.'s will be entitled to be present and
> are each entitled to the individual courtesies due to sovereign
> states.

But Hertzog was not prepared to give time. He wanted recognition
here and now. He came to the Imperial Conference in 1926 thinking in terms of an assertion of dominion sovereignty to be formally
communicated to foreign governments on the basis of the full equality
of the dominions with Britain within the Commonwealth and

resolved, if these ends were not obtained, to return home and set 'the Veldt on fire' with a demand for republican independence.

The balance of forces within the Commonwealth, together with her standing as the senior dominion combined to place Canada in the position of near-arbiter. South Africa and the Irish Free State, though not in agreement about means were insistent upon redefinition of relations, generally in the first instance and particularly and precisely in the second, in terms of equality. Australia and New Zealand were dubious of the wisdom of any such dialectical exercise, so Canada was left to fill her traditional mediatory role. The Canadian attitude however was the outcome less of her central position or of any theoretic preconception than of experience and circumstance, and it was these which persuaded the Canadian government, in the person of Mackenzie King, Ernest Lapointe and their advisers, to come down on the side of redefinition. Before the Canadian prime minister came to London for the Imperial Conference he had had cause to reflect that those forms, which W. M. Hughes had dismissed in 1921 as a few figments, might represent realities.

The 1925 Canadian general election had given no party a majority. Arthur Meighen and the Conservatives had swept English-speaking Canada, King himself being defeated, but the Liberals were enabled to remain in office so long as they enjoyed the support of the Progressives from the prairies. In this treacherous political situation news broke of a customs scandal of distressing dimensions. A motion of censure was tabled in the House of Commons. On defeat, though not on the censure motion itself, King asked the governor-general for a dissolution. The governor-general declined on the ground that Arthur Meighen, the Conservative leader, could form an alternative government. Meighen was invited to do so, formed his government and then in melodramatic circumstances was defeated in the House. Meighen asked for a dissolution and the governor-general acceded to his request. Mackenzie King campaigned on the constitutional issue. Did not the refusal of a dissolution to him in the first instance imply subordination of status? Would it be in accord with convention for the king to refuse a request for dissolution in similar circumstances by a British prime minister? He contended that the answer to the first question was in the affirmative and to the second in the negative, since no request for a dissolution had been denied in Britain for a hundred years. He enlisted the weighty support of Professor A. B. Keith, who believed the refusal of the dissolution to King to be a challenge to 'the doctrine of equality in status of the dominions and the United Kingdom and has relegated Canada decisively to the colonial status which we believed she had outgrown'. The Colonial Office however had not been consulted by the governor-general and Amery refused to express any opinion. Indeed, it is apparent from a letter from General Byng to King George V that the governor-general had acted on his own initiative and judgment.[24] But that did not qualify the fact that his judgment might have been mistaken or that his action might have carried with it the suggestion of the discretionary authority enjoyed by nineteenth- rather than twentieth-century British monarchs or colonial governors.

The King-Byng controversy was not the only experience stiffening Mackenzie King's resolve to insist upon equality of status. In 1926 the supreme court of Alberta dismissed appeals from a petitioner named Nadan against convictions by a police magistrate for carrying unbonded liquor in unlicensed transport on his way from Alberta to Montana. Nadan thereupon appealed to the judicial committee of the Privy Council. His appeal (subsequently dismissed) was allowed on the ground that Canadian legislation – Section 1025 of the Criminal Code of Canada – purporting to abolish Appeals in criminal cases was *ultra vires*, because it conflicted with nineteenth-century enactments of the British Parliament allowing appeals to Her Majesty in Council in all cases.[25] The Colonial Laws Validity Act remained on the Statute Book. That Act provided, it will be recalled, that any Act of a colonial legislature conflicting with an Act of the British Parliament was to the extent of such conflict null and void. Was not the judgment conclusive proof of continuing Canadian subordination?

While the Canadian prime minister came to London in 1926 with substantial reason to seek for the removal of remaining elements of subordination in British-dominion relations, not to mention a triumphant election campaign on the constitutional issue behind him, his approach was different from that of Hertzog and, while rather closer, still quite distinct from that of the Irish Free State representatives. The status seekers were of one mind in seeking to enhance their countries' status, but not about the means by which this should be done. The Irish listed the elements of continuing subordination with a view to their systematic elimination; the South Africans desired first and foremost a definitive declaration; while King, anxious to secure full equality and autonomy for Canada, was so opposed temperamentally to such abstract definition that he remained dubious of the advantages of it, especially in view of the almost certainly acrimonious debate to which the attempt would give rise.[26] His first inclination therefore was to avoid any such discussion and to concentrate upon particular reforms which would achieve the ends he had in mind. At the head of his list was the complete separation between the office of governor-general as representative of the Crown and as an agency of the British government. Such separation, earlier advocated by Smuts among others, would ensure on the one hand that a governor-general would henceforward fill the rôle of constitutional monarch alone and on the other, the development at the inter-governmental level, of the system of high commissioners representing their respective governments in other Commonwealth capitals. His proposals in fact commended themselves to the Conference, but in so far as King was sanguine enough to think that particular reforms of this kind might satisfy South African demands without the need for any formal declaration he was mistaken. It is true that neither Australia nor New Zealand desired a declaration and that at the outset Amery was not only averse to one, but further contended that such an unprecedented attempt to define the undefinable was beyond the authority of an Imperial Conference.[27] The South Africans, however, were not to be deflected.

The committee on inter-imperial relations set up by the Imperial Conference and comprising the prime ministers and principal delegates of the dominions held its first session on 3 October 1926. Lord Balfour, as chairman, opened the proceedings with a statement on imperial relations. Before 1914, he observed (rather questionably), the British Empire

> seemed to alien observers the frailest of structures. A state which (so far as its western elements were concerned) consisted in the main of six self-governing communities, bound together by no central authority, not competent to enlist a single recruit or impose a single shilling of taxation, might look well painted on the map but as a fighting machine is surely negligible.

But the war had refuted 'this plausible conjecture'. It had, however, also left the Empire unexplained and undefined. The peace brought not enlightenment but, if anything, added to the obscurities. Yet the general character of the Empire was easy to define. It might be conveniently divided, thought Lord Balfour, into elements of three different kinds: 1. Britain and the self-governing dominions, 2. India, 3. the dependencies of the self-governing states including mandated territories as well as colonies. Only the first was the particular business of the committee. They were concerned with the problems raised by 'the most novel and yet most characteristic peculiarity of the British Empire', namely the co-existence within its unity of six (or seven including Newfoundland) autonomous communities. 'The statement of fact,' Balfour proceeded, 'though very simple, is barely intelligible to foreigners and no doubt among ourselves has given rise to some secondary difficulties.' Their task was to enlighten the world outside and remove these 'secondary difficulties'.

Were they 'secondary'? Clearly General Hertzog did not think so. He followed closely upon Balfour with an address that set the tone of the committee discussions and settled the character of its Report. Hertzog made plain that he could speak for South Africa alone but he claimed that it would 'be monstrous, and certainly disastrous', if the freedom of one dominion were dependent upon the will of others. 'The dominions are all free and equal in status but no one has the right to claim, and I hope no one will claim, that the exercise of the rights and privileges inherent in that freedom and equal status shall be standardised for all with mechanical monotony. That would be the death of organic development within the Empire, a stagnation leading to decay.' As for South Africa it was 'imperatively necessary' that the nature of dominion relations should not remain uncertain either in the world or in the Commonwealth itself. Since 1921 there had been no longer any question as to the character or degree of dominion independence. The British government had assured the dominions that they were 'independent states', 'equal in status' and 'separately entitled to international recognition as independent states'. But the facts thus acknowledged had been neither publicised nor proclaimed. They should have been. 'We are not a secret society', and quoting very extensively from General Smuts' 1921 memorandum, Hertzog advanced to the conclusion that the nature of dominion status should be authoritatively declared to the world. Smuts had warned against the danger of always being too late. 'Much ill-feeling and unpleasantness would have been avoided if effect had been given to his advice at the time.' But it was still not too late and Hertzog ended with the anxious appeal: 'I implore that what should have been done in 1921, shall now no longer be delayed.' By his plea, he ensured it should not.[28]

General Hertzog was not only determined upon a declaration, but he had brought with him a first draft. He was invited to submit it to the committee and he did so, the draft being circulated on 28 October. It spoke of the prime ministers of the United Kingdom and of the dominions recognising that they were respectively the representatives of independent states, equal in status and separately entitled to international recognition, with governments and parliaments independent of one another, united through a common bond of loyalty to the king and freely associated as members of the Commonwealth of Nations, and acknowledging that any surviving forms of inequality or subordination were conditional solely upon the voluntary agreement of the associated state concerned, and deeming it desirable that the constitutional relation between Britain and the dominions should be made known and recognised by all other states. The somewhat ponderous drafting together with Hertzog's presentation, provoked mildly critical comment from Kevin O'Higgins, who wrote that Hertzog, while 'a very decent and likeable kind of man' talked a lot and none too clearly. This was borne out by Hankey, who in his end of the day *resumés* of proceedings to the prime minister thought fit to mention the length of Hertzog's speeches – one of them lasted three quarters of an hour – as well as his reiteration of argument. It has, however, to be remembered that Hertzog was engaged in something rather more than ordinary committee give and take. He was seeking to win a point of principle, one to which he attached great importance – namely the acceptance and public formulation of a statement on status – and on which at the Conference he had, despite a modicum of sympathy, no firm ally.[29] Therein lay the importance of his initial draft and his presentation of it. There were many succeeding drafts and suggestions, in the course of which Mackenzie King persuaded Hertzog to drop 'independent' with its disturbing (for Canadians) North American associations, Amery reintroduced the term British Empire, while the Irish rejected 'common bond of allegiance' and the South Africans 'common citizenship of the Empire'. What emerged, despite discarding as well as rephrasing, derived, however, from a South African initiative, which achieved its substantive purpose, though formal communication to foreign governments as Hertzog proposed was dismissed out of hand.

There were other initiatives on other matters – Canadian, in respect of the office of governor-general and of improved intra-imperial consultation especially through the appointment of high commissioners both in London and in dominion capitals – it was 'an anomaly and an absurdity', alleged Mackenzie King, that the British government should have no representative in Canada – and Irish, in respect of particular surviving inequalities which the Irish delegation listed in a memorandum and all of which they wished to see removed. Not least among Irish preoccupations were appeals to the judicial committee of the Privy Council which the Irish delegation urged should be dealt with upon 'principles of equality'. It is, an Irish submission on this subject contended, in strict accord with such principles that an appeal should lie to the judicial committee from the courts of any state in the Commonwealth which desires the continuance of such appeals but it would be 'a violation of such principles to deny the right of a state which desires that finality on judicial questions should be reached within its own area to determine that such shall be the case'.[30] The Irish achieved in this as in most other matters their particular purposes. They were concerned to dismantle piece by piece what remained of the British imperial structure, Kevin O'Higgins commenting (in discussion on Hertzog's proposals) that a declaration would be of little value if contradicted by the facts. But the Irish delegation having repudiated external association in 1921, and having embraced, as members of the pro-treaty party, dominion status as a means rather than an end, would seem to have thought on the longer term of filling the void left by the republic with an Anglo–Irish dual monarchy on early Sinn Féin lines. This may have added to the emphasis which they placed upon the importance of direct and equal Irish access to the Crown.

In the end the committee, over which Lord Balfour 'somewhat deaf, occasionally somnolent' but 'with intellectual powers unimpaired by the years', presided 'with a smile like moonlight on a tombstone', produced the Report, which bears his name.[31] It is a document to be considered as a whole, with particular attention to but without undue emphasis upon that section of it which was italicised because of a typist's misunderstanding – or so Amery records, though if so it may be thought the typist had a better sense of history than the assembled prime ministers – and which described the relations of the United Kingdom and the dominions in phrases, as well known as any in British constitutional history.[32]

The Balfour Report stated that the committee on Inter-imperial relations were of the opinion that nothing would be gained by attempting to lay down a constitution for the whole Empire but that there was in it one important element which from a constitutional viewpoint had reached full development. This element was composed of the United Kingdom and the overseas dominions. Their position and mutual relations might therefore be 'readily defined' 'They are autonomous communities within the British Empire, equal in status, in no way subordinate one to another in any aspect of their domestic or external affairs, though united by a common allegiance to the Crown, and freely associated as members of the

British Commonwealth of Nations.' In this sentence four important characteristics of membership of the British Commonwealth,
which comprised the United Kingdom as well as the dominions,
were identified. The dominions were 1. autonomous communities
2. within the British Empire 3. freely associated as members of the
British Commonwealth of Nations 4. united by a common allegiance to the Crown. There was deliberate variety in phrasing,
which enabled New Zealanders to place most emphasis on their
being within the British Empire and South African nationalists, by
contrast, on 'autonomous' communities. But it was of secondary
importance. So too were the questions of interpretation that arose
about the meaning of 'freely associated' – did it or did it not imply
that a dominion was free to dissociate if it so desired? – and
'common allegiance' – was it or was it not to a common Crown?
Henceforward these were questions that could be debated at least
within an accepted context. That is what made the 1926 Report so
significant. And in identifying the things deemed to be of fundamental importance in a new and experimental inter-state relationship it helped to shape the pattern of future development.

The setting in which the 1926 italicised definition was placed was
written by Lord Balfour, resting on his bed, on sheets of a loose-leaf
notebook he always used for his original drafts.[33] It observed that a
foreigner attempting to understand the true character of the
British Empire by the aid of this formula 'would be tempted to
think that it was devised rather to make mutual interference
impossible than to make mutual co-operation easy.'[34] But the
foreigner, it need hardly be said, would be mistaken. The rapid
evolution of the dominions, the Report continued, demanded an
adjustment to changing conditions. 'The tendency towards equality of status was both right and inevitable.' 'Geographical and other
conditions' made federation 'impossible' and the only alternative
was autonomy. Every dominion in 1926 was in fact if not always in
form master of its own destiny and subject to no compulsion
whatever. But the British Empire 'is not founded upon negations'.
It depended upon positive ideals. Free institutions were its life
blood. Free co-operation was its instrument. And 'while each
dominion is now and must always remain the sole judge of the
nature and extent of its co-operation no common cause will, in our
opinion, be thereby imperilled'. Equality of status, the Report
continued, was thus the root-principle governing inter-imperial
relations, not, be it noted, either common allegiance or free
association. But principles of equality did not extend to function.
Diplomacy and defence required more flexible machinery and for

a long time the United Kingdom would remain the predominant partner. This was certainly true. It was also a distinction which imperialists emphasised, nationalists discounted. It existed markedly in the transitional period and it made relations psychologically difficult in the years before the second world war.[35] Equality in principle is not easy to reconcile with continuing dependence in practice.

The Balfour Report was 'first and foremost, finely accurate description'. It described, noted Professor Hancock, 'not merely the form but the motion of a community'.[36] Professor Wheare, in his authoritative study on *The Statute of Westminister and Dominion Status*, observed that the importance of the Balfour Report was underestimated in 1926 and in consequence that of the Statute of Westminster overestimated in 1931, because the full implications of the definitions included in the former were not realised until the attempt was made to translate some of them into strict law five years later[37] – or to put the matter rather differently the Balfour Report had made explicit the principles on which the British Commonwealth rested and what remained to be done thereafter was the important but lesser task of giving them effect where necessary in law. Since equality was the 'root-principle', this involved first the removal of inequalities[38] – a point seized upon by the Irish from the outset and pursued by them with a rigorous logic that at times proved disconcerting in Downing Street. The inequalities included the power of reservation whether obligatory or discretionary, the power of disallowance, the sections of the Colonial Laws Validity Act of 1865 which declared that 'an act of Parliament or any provision thereof shall be said to extend to any colony when it is made applicable to such colony by the express words or necessary intendment of such Act ...' and that such colonial legislation (Section 2) as was repugnant to any provisions of an act of the imperial Parliament 'shall be to the extent of such repugnancy ... void and inoperative'. Even if it was at the time of enactment 'an enabling Act, not a restrictive or disabling Act', its provisions were clearly inconsistent with equality of status. There were also limitations on the power of dominions to enact extra-territorial legislation, implying inequality and causing practical inconvenience. All these were matters on which detailed and expert inquiry was necessary. It was carried out in 1929–30 by the Conference on the Operation of Dominion Legislation and Merchant Shipping Legislation[39] and the Imperial Conference 1930[40]. Where appropriate their recommendations were embodied in the Statute of Westminster.

The Imperial Conference 1926, in enunciating the root-principle of equality had itself either reinterpreted certain of the conventions of intra-Commonwealth relations or made recommendations to ensure the full application of this principle. Thus the Conference tendered advice to the effect that a small amendment be made in the king's title to take account of the status of the Irish Free State. This amendment contemplated the substitution of a comma for an 'and' between Great Britain and Ireland, so that the title would read, 'George v, by the Grace of God, of Great Britain, Ireland and the British Dominions beyond the Seas King, Defender of the Faith, Emperor of India'. King George v acquiesced with reluctance in this modification, for in such matters, we are told, he disliked change.[41] In respect of the office of governor-general the Conference recommended that the governor-general in a dominion should no longer act in any way as the representative or agent of the United Kingdom government and should in all essential respects hold the same position in relation to the administration of public affairs as the king in the United Kingdom. This general redefinition of function satisfied Mackenzie King, mindful of his controversy with General Byng about the discretionary authority of governors-general, while judiciously refraining from comment upon the exercise of the royal prerogative or the king's position. The Imperial Conference 1930 carried this reinterpretation of the rôle and functions of governors-general to its logical conclusion by stating that 'the parties interested in the appointment of a governor-general of a dominion are His Majesty the King, whose representative he is, and the dominion concerned . . . The ministers who tender and are responsible for such advice are His Majesty's ministers in the dominion concerned.'[42] The prime minister of Australia, J. H. Scullin, in the exercise of this exclusive dominion responsibility and to the embarrassment of Sidney Webb, improbably esconced as Lord Passfield at the Colonial Office, overbore King George v's wishes in 1929 in pressing and ultimately obtaining, despite every objection which it occurred to the sovereign to advance, the appointment of Sir Isaac Isaacs as the first Australian-born governor-general of Australia.[43]

Equality in the relationship of the dominions and the United Kingdom to the Crown was most significantly recognised by according to them an equal responsibility in determining the succession to it.

In as much as the Crown is the symbol of the free association of the members of the British Commonwealth of Nations, and as they are united by a common allegiance to the Crown, it would be in accord with the established constitutional position of all the members of the Commonwealth in relation to one another that any alteration in the law touching the Succession to the Throne or the Royal Style and Titles shall hereafter require the assent as well of the Parliaments of all the dominions as of the Parliament of the United Kingdom.[44]

This definition of dominion responsibilities in respect of the royal succession set out in 1929 was reproduced in the preamble to the Statute of Westminster. Amery entertained misgivings lest it should lead to a dominion relationship to the monarchy that amounted to no more than a purely personal union. General Hertzog on the other hand, and for precisely the same reason, was well contented until General Smuts argued that the new relationship precluded secession without agreement. Hertzog responded by moving an amendment in the House of Assembly adopting the Report of the 1929 Conference subject to the condition that the relevant section should not be taken as 'derogating from the right of any member of the British Commonwealth of Nations to withdraw therefrom'. This was duly noted by the Imperial Conference 1930.

The Preamble of the Statute of Westminster 1931[45] set out by way of historical record the conventions already agreed in respect of status and of succession to the Crown, and further declared that in accordance with the established constitutional position no law made by the Parliament of the United Kingdom 'shall extend to any of the said dominions otherwise than at the request and with the consent of that dominion'. The Act itself restated this fundamental principle so that, as a matter of law, the Parliament of the United Kingdom was thereafter precluded from legislating for a dominion without the request and consent of its government or Parliament. The Act also, by way of counterpart, clarified the powers of dominion Parliaments in accordance with the principles of the 1926 Imperial Conference by giving them authority to legislate on matters of dominion concern, hitherto within the competence of the imperial Parliament, to repeal legislation on such matters and to legislate with extra-territorial effect.

In conformity with the principles embodied in the Act it was at the request of some of the dominions that some continuing restrictions were left upon their powers. At Canada's request, section 7 expressly excluded the British North America Acts 1867–1930 from the operation of the statute; at the request of the

Pacific dominions section 8, likewise, excluded the constitutions of Australia and New Zealand; section 10, inserted again at the request of the dominion governments concerned, stipulated that the statute should not apply to New Zealand, Australia, and Newfoundland (whose dominion status was shortly to lapse), unless and until it was adopted by their respective Parliaments. More generally, it may be said that South Africa and the Irish Free State accepted the statute without reservation, though neither altogether relished the notion of an Act of the British Parliament as the charter of their freedom, that Canada adopted it subject to the reservation in respect of its constitution, but that neither Australia or New Zealand did so, not wishing to exercise the powers the statute proposed to confer upon them. These varied reactions throw much light upon the outlook and balance of opinion in the British Commonwealth at that time.[46]

It was not till 1942 and 1947 that the Statute of Westminster was adopted in Australia and New Zealand respectively. The reasons for the delay, ended because of practical inconveniences experienced in wartime, were those elaborated by Menzies in Canberra in 1937. 'I think that the business of devising the Balfour Declaration in 1926, and the business of devising and drafting the preamble of the Statute of Westminster . . . were both open to grave criticism.' The 1926 declaration was 'a grave disservice'; the 1926–31 process 'a misguided attempt' to reduce to written terms something which 'was a matter of the spirit and not of the letter'. W. M. Hughes, five years later, spoke of the 1926 Report as a 'wonderful document'.

> It took stock of everything. Nothing escaped it . . . Every prime minister went away perfectly satisfied – Mr Bruce because it altered nothing that affected Australia, Mr Mackenzie King because it taught Lord Byng where he got off, and General Hertzog because he was able to assure the burghers that the king of England was no longer the king of South Africa, although it was true that the king of South Africa was also king of England.

But to Hughes it was all a mistaken attempt to appease the unappeasable. These Australian views were to some extent reflected or shared by a section of Conservative opinion in Britain, *The Times*, dismissing the statute as a piece of 'mere pedantry', for which there was and could be no enthusiasm, but about which also there need be no great apprehension.

The attitude of the Canadian government to the Act was very different and advantage was immediately taken of its enactment to abolish Canadian appeals to the judicial committee of the Privy Council in criminal cases. There remained, however, what the Minister for Justice, S. G. Garson, in 1949, was to term two 'badges of colonialism' – the right of appeal to the Judicial Committee in civil cases and amendment of the constitution by Parliament at Westminster. The first was abolished that year by a Canadian Act declaring that the Supreme Court of Canada should exercise exclusive ultimate appellate civil and criminal jurisdiction in Canada; the second circumscribed by an Act of the Imperial Parliament, the BNA (No. 2) Act 1949 (No. 1 gave effect to Newfoundland's union with Canada), passed at the request of the Canadian Parliament, and enabling that Parliament to amend the BNA Act in all particulars other than matters coming within classes of subjects assigned exclusively to the Provinces or rights and privileges assigned to them. Mr Garson hoped 'the last essential of our complete autonomy, namely, the taking unto ourselves of the right to amend our own constitution' in these further and fundamental respects would soon follow. In fact, with federal and provincial authorities failing to reach a sufficient measure of agreement on an indigenous process for the amendment of a 'patriated' constitution, such as would at once mitigate the misgivings of Quebec and meet the newer concern of other, and notably the Prairie, provinces lest their control over energy and recently discovered resources be impaired, it was deferred until 1981 when after tense and fluctuating negotiations conducted by Canada's Prime Minister, Pierre Trudeau, the way to Canada's attainment in law of 'full independence and international sovereignty' was opened by agreement of all Provinces, other than Quebec, in a package deal. In December of that year, which marked the fiftieth anniversary of the enactment of the Statute of Westminster and as such was Trudeau's target date, the two Houses of the Canadian Parliament made formal request to Parliament at Westminster, to enact, for its part, a last amendment to the BNA Act.

In South Africa the Statute had important implications. For nationalists its substance was more satisfying than its origin. They deemed the assertion of a South African, as distinct from a United Kingdom source as hitherto, for the fundamental law of the Union to be a condition of equality within the Commonwealth. Accordingly they concluded that the substance of the Statute of Westminster should be enacted by the South African Parliament as a South African law so as to give its provisions indigenous authority. This could not be done without risk of complications, chief among them being the possibility that the entrenched clauses of the South Africa Act 1909 safeguarding existing voting rights in the Cape and equality of the English and Dutch languages, might no longer, should the South African Parliament so decide, be excluded from amendment by simple majority vote. Hertzog and Smuts, in requesting the enactment of the Statute of Westminster, had placed on record that their request was made on the understanding that the Act would not derogate from the entrenched clauses of the South Africa Act. Their statement however, while morally, was certainly not legally binding and the bearing of the Statute of Westminster upon the entrenched clauses of the South Africa Act remained legally untested and was to be the crucial question in a major constitutional crisis some twenty years later. Subsequent agreement between the two generals, resulting in a coalition and then in a fusion government, made possible the enactment of the Status of the Union Act in 1934.[47] Section 2 indicated its principal purpose. 'The Parliament of the Union shall be the sovereign legislative power in and over the Union.' As a corollary the position of the king as king of South Africa was emphasised and by implication there was enunciated the doctrine of a divisible crown. In all this Afrikaner legalism was seeking to find a way by which a separatist policy could – if or when occasion arose – be legally carried through.

The Irish reaction was rather different, but of a comparable complexity. At the Conferences of 1929–30 and in the drafting of the Statute of Westminster, the Irish played a very active part. As Patrick McGilligan, the Irish delegate to the Conference and a man for whom a distinctive place in the Commonwealth history of these years[48] has been reasonably claimed, told the Dáil he had 'brought forward definite things that we wanted rulings upon in accordance with the principles set out in 1926. We had limited terms of reference and within them we got the completest satisfaction.' With republican nationalism, however, once more in the ascendant and de Valera brought to power early in 1932, one consequence was that the period of Irish refashioning of the Commonwealth ended before its fulfilment.

The passage of the Statute of Westminster had brought out some of the ambiguities in the Treaty Settlement 1921. The first article of the treaty had declared that the Irish Free State should have the same constitutional status as the Dominion of Canada, the Commonwealth of Australia, the Dominion of New Zealand and the Union of South Africa, and the third Article had more particularly defined Irish status by reference to that of Canada. But was there not and had there not always been the possibility of conflict here? Canadian status was not fixed; it was changing, it was developing fast. Was it not the case that under the earlier provisions of the treaty, Irish status should likewise develop and advance? But what if such advances were in conflict with other provisions of the treaty? Was Irish status then to be regarded to that extent as frozen and immutable? English die-hard opinion took this view and sought to except the Irish Free State from the Statute of Westminster on that ground. President Cosgrave objected; the Irish Free State was not excepted. When de Valera came to office, he announced his intention of removing the Oath of Allegiance from the constitution. It was mandatory under the treaty – though President de Valera voiced his doubts even about that. But was it mandatory under the Statute of Westminster? President de Valera, it is true, did not pose this question; after all the statute was a British enactment. He deployed instead arguments grounded in national right. He told J. H. Thomas, the secretary of state for the dominions, on 22 March 1932, that the constitution was the people's constitution; that the government had an absolute right to modify it as the people desired. The people had declared their will. There was no ambiguity about their resolve to remove the oath. It was an intolerable burden and a relic of medievalism. It was the cause of all the dissension in Ireland since the treaty. It made friendly relations with Britain impossible. It was a test unparalleled in treaty relationships between states, and it had been imposed under threat of immediate and terrible war.[49] It had to go and it was clear it was going, whatever the British government or for that matter Irish lawyers might say.

Was President de Valera, in his assault upon the oath, challenging the sanctity of the treaty settlement as a whole? J. H. Thomas, after some increasingly acrimonious exchanges in which the area in dispute was widened both constitutionally and economically by the Irish government's decision to retain Irish land annuity payments, was convinced that this was so. Encouraged by the thought that there would be an early General Election in Ireland – in which he was right – and that de Valera would lose it – in which he was wrong – he took an uncompromising line, maintaining that the oath was mandatory under the treaty, that it was an integral part of the 1921 settlement and that the treaty as a whole was an agreement 'which can only be altered by consent'. President de Valera remained outwardly unmoved. 'Whether the oath was', he wrote on 5 April 1932, 'or was not an integral part of the treaty made ten years ago is not now the issue. The real issue is that the oath is an intolerable burden to the people of this state and they have declared in the most formal manner that they desire its instant removal.' They desired the removal of other things besides and their wishes were met. Following the abolition of the oath in 1933, there came a series of constitutional amendments culminating in the abolition of the office of the governor-general, the keystone as it were of the dominion constitutional arch, in 1936. The constitution of 1922 in consequence became a thing of shreds and patches and whatever validity the treaty continued to possess in contractual terms it had lost in law since the Removal of the Oath Act 1933 deleted the 'repugnancy clause' from the constitution.

Had the Irish acted unconstitutionally? There were two answers, conflicting and paradoxical to this question. The Irish courts, basing themselves on the constitution of 1922 and the fundamental authority it gave to the provisions of the treaty, as late as 1934 maintained that the Irish government were acting *ultra vires* in their constitutional reforms because no power had been conferred upon them by which they were entitled to repeal the repugnancy clause in the constitution. But the judicial committee of the Privy Council in a judgement delivered a year later concluded otherwise. They argued that the effect of the enactment of the Statute of Westminster was to remove the fetter that lay upon the Irish Free State legislature and that accordingly the *Oireachtas* had become free to pass legislation repugnant to imperial legislation – in which the treaty had also been embodied – and that they had in fact done so. In other words, in British law, though not in Irish, de Valera's revolution was not in a legal sense a revolution at all. He had done in the constitutional field what under British law he was entitled to do after 1931. It was J. H. Thomas who on this point had had the ground cut away from under his feet,[50] as some among his advisers had forewarned him might be the case.

The abdication of King Edward VIII in 1936 was the first major test of the new constitutional arrangements. All the self-governing members of the Commonwealth were concerned with the succession to the Crown. In the early stages of the crisis however, Baldwin alone advised the king as his 'counsellor and friend'. The king was the first to suggest that there should be consultation with dominion governments – on the question of a possible morganatic marriage with Mrs Simpson. Consultation followed, but between governments, and not (as might have been expected) between the king and his governors-general.[51] Dominion governments were united in opposition to marriage in any guise. The Australian prime minister, J. A. Lyons, spoke of 'widespread condemnation' if

Mrs Simpson became queen and of a morganatic marriage as 'running counter to the best traditions of the monarchy'.[52] Mackenzie King on second thoughts – his first were ambivalent – said that Canada would not approve whether Mrs Simpson became queen or not; General Hertzog that abdication would be a lesser evil than marriage. 'The one would be a great shock, the other a permanent wound.' The king abdicated. Because Australia and New Zealand had not adopted the Statute of Westminster, the Abdication Act merely records their assent thereto. Canada requested and consented to its enactment. The South African government maintained no legislation was necessary in the Union, whereupon King George VI succeeded under the relevant provisions of the Status of the Union Act on the signature of the Instrument of Abdication by King Edward VIII on December 10. This interpretation of the constitutional position served further to underline the separate position of the king as king of South Africa. The Irish Free State took the opportunity of removing all reference to the Crown in the constitution and of enacting the External Relations Act which specifically defined the functions that might be discharged by the Crown at the discretion of the Executive Council of the Irish Free State. This took two days, so that between 10–12 December there were, as Professor Wheare has noted, two kings in the Commonwealth.[53] This is a matter of interest to constitutional historians but of incidental importance. What was important and impressive was the measure of agreement among Commonwealth governments throughout the crisis. Because Baldwin's opinion that the Crown was the 'last link of Empire that is left' was widely endorsed, all who were anxious to preserve its unity exercised their responsibility with due regard to the magnitude of the issues at stake.

Yet the Commonwealth was more than a constitutional experiment; it was, in so far as it was anything, an historic association of peoples and governments. Their interests whether separate or held in common were manifold, and at the climax of the constitutional changes in the relations between Britain and the dominions in 1931, peoples and governments alike were preoccupied with the reality of twentieth-century international economics in their harshest manifestation.

The dominions valued their tariff personalities as they valued their political personalities. But in terms of trade there had been no centralised Empire since the commercial revolution of the mid-nineteenth century. There was no occasion, therefore, in the inter-war years for dominion dismantling of an imperial trading system. That had long since been done – by the imperial power itself. There was no possibility either, as Joseph Chamberlain earlier in the century had perforce to concede, of reestablishing a unitary trading system within the Empire. But while Empire free trade was beyond the bounds of practical politics a reciprocal imperial preferential system remained for many years precariously poised on the margin of them. There was one condition of its realisation, as Imperial Conference after Imperial Conference recognised, and that was a British retreat from her free trade principles. She continued to receive preferences from protectionist dominions, she gave nothing in return. Would she be prepared, in the light of wartime and later experience, if not to abandon, then at the least to allow an imperial exception to traditional trading doctrine or dogma?

In the twenties, the omens were not altogether unfavourable. The first world war fostered an upsurge of imperial economic sentiment. The emphasis was on economic defence but the goal was imperial self-sufficiency. The most extravagant hopes were entertained by a committee under the chairmanship of Lord Balfour of Burleigh appointed in 1917 to enquire into British commercial and economic policy after the war. It recommended *inter alia* that all new United Kingdom duties should be made preferential in favour of the Empire. The Imperial War Conference endorsed the recommendation with the result that dominion imports were accorded a modest preference in respect of duties levied by the British government for the raising of revenue or for wartime protective purposes on a small range of selected commodities. This was deemed not inconsistent with Free Trade principles and while too marginal in effect to afford any particular satisfaction to the campaigners for imperial preference, at their most 'visionary' – the description is that of Dr Drummond[54] – in those post-war years, advance along such lines commended itself to the favourably disposed but less ideologically committed. This was particularly so in that concessions of this kind would be the result not of intra-imperial bargaining, which the negotiation of imperial preferences would necessarily involve and which administrators feared would be more likely to impair than strengthen intra-imperial relations, but of each individual government's assessment of its own interests. Mackenzie King put the two points concisely at the Imperial Conference in 1923, observing that Canada granted preferences because of what she 'conceived to be her own best interests' and he had no desire to make them 'a matter for bargaining'.[55] Such, however, they were destined to become.

As the economic strains of wartime relaxed, enthusiasm for

economic, as for political, integration waned and the goal of imperial preference came to appear almost as remote as ever. But not quite. The Conservative Party was in the ascendant in Britain and among the Conservatives there were many converts to the cause. In 1923, abruptly and evidently without full consideration, the new Conservative leader Stanley Baldwin, in order, so Amery alleged, 'to dish Lloyd George', announced that he would fight the forthcoming election on the platform of preference. He was defeated. It was not an encouraging experience. When he returned to power in 1924, Baldwin sought to foster intra-imperial trade by institutional means, bringing into existence, despite dominion uneasiness, an Imperial Economic Council and an Empire Marketing Board, the former to achieve its end by consultation and advice, the latter by publicity – both 'pathetic efforts', as they have been aptly described, to create 'non-tariff preferences' for Empire goods.[56] Before the 1929 election Amery, a chief among 'the visionaries', tried to persuade Baldwin to make Empire development a plank in the party platform, but Baldwin confined himself to generalities supposedly under Treasury and Churchillian influence and his 'own laziness and love of peace'. Perceptibly none the less the party, and perhaps also the country, were moving away from earlier, often uncritical, faith in free trade.

It was not, however, tentative half-commitment but a world economic crisis that finally brought about the change. As world markets collapsed Empire statesmen sought refuge within imperial frontiers. Certainly there was the attraction of an idea but it was harsh necessity that impelled them to action. The Labour government in Britain, faced with near-desperate dominion appeals for co-operative action, were unable to offer any constructive response, because the Chancellor, Philip Snowden refused to contemplate any departure from Free Trade principle. That a conference should be held in Ottawa was agreed; but the preparatory work essential for it was delayed by the Cabinet deadlock in London and inadequate organisation in Ottawa.[57] With the fall of the Labour government in October 1931, the scene was transformed. Early in the following year, on 4 February, the succeeding National government introduced the Import Duties Bill. By allowing the imposition of tariffs the enactment of the Bill later that year at long last opened the way to imperial preference. Neville Chamberlain, with the process of political decentralisation that had culminated in the Statute of Westminster in mind and with the memory of his father's frustrated campaign to move him, spoke of renewed endeavours to promote imperial trade as 'an attempt to bring the Empire together again'.[58]

The Imperial Economic Conference assembled in Ottawa under the enthusiastic chairmanship of R. B. Bennett. He hailed the Conference as unique among all other assemblies of history. 'Faced with the need for unselfish and concerted action,' he said, 'the prospects of achievement were never more certain.' But behind the Ottawa Conference lay the shadow of falling prices, the ruin of countless primary producers in the dominions, among them the wheat growers of the Canadian prairies, New Zealand dairy farmers, and wool growers in Australia, faced with a fall of no less than 50 per cent between 1928 and 1931 in the export value of their wool. In such circumstances it is not surprising that the exhilaration which undoubtedly prevailed in Ottawa appeared to some as having an air not of natural spontaneity but of the enforced gaiety of a septuagenarian wedding.

At Ottawa the cry was for more trade within the Empire. Yet the welfare of the Empire was tied in with world trade. 'Anything tending to check the foreign exports in the United Kingdom', said Baldwin, 'must lessen the purchasing power of her people and so damage the market on which the dominions so largely depend.' The spokesman of an exporting manufacturing country could say no less. But Britain was prepared to continue to allow free entry of dominion primary produce. This was 'the greatest boon' that Britain was able to offer to the dominions. Since the enactment of the Import Duties Act it was an exclusive privilege, its value enhanced by the raising of tariffs against foreign competitors. This tariff barrier was reinforced in some instances by quantitative restrictions on a quota basis. In return British manufactured goods secured increased preferences in dominion markets. But the advantages that accrued both to Britain and to the dominions were secured chiefly by raising trade barriers against the foreigner. Imperial protectionists welcomed this and R. B. Bennett spoke of the 'new and greater Empire' which was coming into being. But liberals whose aim was the gradual freeing of world trade were affronted. Mackenzie King on 17 October 1932 professed himself dismayed at the great 'protectionist wall' which was being arranged around the frontiers of Empire, making trade with the rest of the world increasingly difficult. The protagonists of preference discounted the idea that they were engaged in economic warfare with foreigners. They were concerned to develop Empire resources and claimed that they were moved as much by an ideal as by necessity. Their economics were defensive, the economics of siege, and they neither intended nor desired to engage in economic warfare with others.

There was bargaining of the kind that had been foreseen with misgiving in Ottawa. The outcome of it was not an agreement but a multiplicity of agreements. Their range, variety and detail makes difficult any general assessment of the results of the Conference. In the immediately succeeding years statistics show an increase in Empire trade. But was this wholly due to Ottawa? Between 1932 and 1938 Canadian exports to the United Kingdom increased sharply. But they also increased sharply to the United States where there were no preferential arrangements. That did not in itself diminish the worthwhileness of the Ottawa agreements to Canada; after all they ensured the vitally important United Kingdom market for Canadian wheat. But the larger question remains as to whether the Ottawa agreements modified or even changed the direction of Canadian trade. Mackenzie King and Bennett were in agreement about the importance of keeping open to Canada and holding 'the most valuable market this dominion has ever known', but King, destined to return to office in 1935, was critical of anything that savoured of exclusive concentration upon the British and Commonwealth markets. Multilateralism was a distant objective but negotiating with the United States to restore trade to its former level led first to bilateral and then to triangular United Kingdom, United States, Canadian commercial agreements in 1938, the United Kingdom and Canada sacrificing advantages in their own markets and receiving compensation in United States markets. As a result by 1938, six years after Ottawa, 'the greatest triangular exchange of commodities in the world' had been frozen into patterns of reciprocal advantage by three commercial treaties, to two of which Canada was a signatory.[59] Australian experience ran roughly parallel with Canadian. It was, as Professor Hancock has observed,[60] that imperial preference was good but not enough. Britain's own agricultural protectionism, Japan's value as a market for wool (Japan took 13.2 per cent of Australia's wool exports in 1928–9, 20 per cent in 1932–4), as a good customer by bilateral standards and her expansionist policies, despite the disturbing element of the dumping of cheap textiles, had both to be taken into account. Imperial trade was only a part of Australia's general interests – an important part but still only a part, as is statistically shown with some 60 per cent of Australia's exports going to Empire countries in 1936. In 1937 Menzies pointed out that 'we are reaching a point in economic history when a rigid insistence upon the fullest measures of Empire preference may prevent the British countries from taking their proper part in a great movement of world appeasement through the revival of trade'. The same point was put more precisely when it was remarked that wool was too big a thing to be imperial in its trade outlets.

What was true of Canada and Australia and the other dominions was even more true in the case of Britain. It was essential for a great manufacturing nation dependent upon export markets to retain and develop the foreign markets for her goods. She could not afford to be cabined and confined within a constricting Commonwealth framework. Yet the figures suggest that the Ottawa agreements somewhat improved the position of the dominions in the British market and of British goods in dominion markets. Between 1929 and 1936 British imports from the Empire amounted to 29.4 per cent of total imports in the first year; 35.3 per cent in 1932 and 39.1 per cent in 1936. The percentage for 1932, the year of the Ottawa Conference, did not reflect the results of that conference. There was, therefore, a trend towards larger British imports from the Empire before the Ottawa Conference. The figures show that in respect of imports it was confirmed and developed after the Conference. But might not some of that development have taken place in any case? Analysis has revealed that at least some items in dominion export lists to Britain which enjoyed no preference showed a more marked increase immediately after the Ottawa Conference than those which had the benefit of preference. In sum, the very complexity and variety of the Ottawa agreements still induces a certain caution in judgment upon their consequences. The least that can be said is that at Ottawa the possibilities of increased Empire trade were examined and that as a result of the Ottawa Conference they were given opportunities for development more favourable than they would otherwise have enjoyed. But already in the 1930s the sufficiency of Commonwealth trade – especially for Britain – and its growth-potential, even under favourable stimuli, were becoming suspect. It was valuable but it was not enough, and even more important it was not likely to become enough.

This much, it is now clear from the records, was understood from the outset. The conferees at Ottawa were not blind to the need for a multilateral trading system, Bennett in 1933 contemplating a complementary agreement with the United States, while Walter Runciman, President of the Board of Trade thought of the Ottawa Agreements as 'a launching pad for a massive programme of trade bargaining with foreign countries'.[61] Despite superficial appearances, therefore, the United Kingdom and the dominions in their trading as in their international policies were perforce looking increasingly outwards. For Britain, Ottawa was a milestone on the road that led to but did not necessarily end in Brussels.

2 India: an Uncertain Goal

The dominions whose status was defined in the Balfour Report and whose names were listed in section I of the Statute of Westminster were predominantly European in respect of their population and wholly European in respect of their government. There were minorities of non-European origin in Australia, in Canada and in New Zealand; there was a large non-European majority in the Union of South Africa. But neither minorities nor majority were in a position to exert a decisive influence upon government. In Canada and even in South Africa it was the cultural tensions between peoples of European stock that hitherto had exercised a formative influence upon national policy, and possibly for that reason it was in the past by no means unknown, however much discountenanced by Canadian scholars, for the term 'race' to be applied to relations between English and French-speaking Canadians, while on the lips of South African politicians the terms 'race' and 'racial', until recent times, customarily referred to relations between British and Afrikaners.[1] That they did not warrant such a description if the term 'race' were to be precisely defined was in a sense beside the point; it was terminology that in South Africa at least was felt to have both traditional justification and an inner appropriateness, since the term 'cultural' seemed (and to a fast diminishing number may still seem) an anodynous description of the painful intensities of Anglo-Afrikaner antipathies at critical moments in their common history. Multi-racial membership of the Commonwealth in the strict sense, meaning the self-governing membership of states inhabited by peoples of different racial origin, dates only from 1947. For that reason in March 1954 the prime minister of Pakistan, Mohammad Ali, spoke of 1947 as a year in Commonwealth history in true line of succession from 1867 and 1926 and as important as either. It was from the British North America Act that the conception of dominion self-government derived; from the definition of dominion status in the Balfour Report that the contemporary Commonwealth might be dated; and while in the prime minister's opinion the pace of constitutional

43

evolution thereafter had been 'slow, painfully slow',[2] South Asia had attained self-government; and multi-racial Commonwealth membership thereupon became a political reality eighty years after the Dominion of Canada had come into being.

The association between self-government and Commonwealth membership, to which Mohammad Ali referred had proved to be the historical precondition of the enlarged Commonwealth, but on the British side at least it was by no means always assumed that this would be so. Radical imperialists like Joseph Chamberlain, famous proconsuls, Curzon, Cromer, Milner, had alike emphasised excellence in the art of government as the outstanding contribution by Britain to the Empire overseas. By government, however, they meant orderly and impartial administration of non-European dependent territories, not the government of them by their own peoples. That British settlers in Canada or Austrialia or New Zealand should believe that they inherited the traditions, and were therefore entitled to practise the art of responsible self-government, was a matter for acquiescence or welcome according to the viewpoint, but assuredly one neither for surprise nor for concern. It was a rather different matter when other Europeans, non-British in extraction, claimed corresponding rights. Neither Afrikaners nor Irish were considered well fitted to exercise them, the former largely because they were too paternalist in their notions of government as well as hostile to the British connection, the latter also on that second ground and because they were deemed politically too volatile. As for representative institutions and responsible self-government for non-Europeans, that for long seemed altogether inconceivable to the traditional British imperial ruling class. To a later age preoccupied with problems of race there seemed a simple explanation – racial prejudice. But this explanation is insufficient. The government of Empire in its higher reaches was as aristocratic as it was autocratic – this it was that gave point to James Mill's jibe, later to be quoted with relish by J. A. Hobson,[3] about imperial administration being a vast system of outdoor relief for the upper classes – but the great majority of its peoples, including all its non-European peoples – the 'lower races' – were not thought of as qualified to govern themselves on Darwinian notions of fitness rather than racial preconceptions, though indeed the two often merged. Curzon, noted Dr Gopal,[4] had no racial prejudice. But he proceeds – 'this was a mental blindness and not an ethical virtue. A man who was not really aware even of the lower orders in Britain could not be expected to register the full significance of the problem of race relations in India.' It was not tolerance but insensitivity that precluded discrimination on Curzon's part. Curzon as viceroy stood in lonely preeminence, but his insensitivity was shared for precisely that reason by many lesser men who on lesser heights but in corresponding isolation sustained the administration of Empire.

The outlook of the rulers, acclaiming at once the supreme virtues of the British system of government and refusing to extend its benefits to subject peoples, produced an Indian paradox. It was the Indian National Congress which from the day of its first session in Bombay in 1885 demanded the extension of British parliamentary institutions to India, while the British exponents of what Joseph Chamberlain once described as 'the best form of government', continued to express doubts about the wisdom of acceding to the Congress demand. Thus the oblique introduction of the representative principle in India in 1892 and its further extension in the Morley-Minto reforms of 1909 were widely regarded in Britain, and not only by conservative opinion, as a 'sop to impossible ambitions'. 'The notion', said Lord Kimberley, a former Liberal secretary of state for India in 1890, 'of a Parliamentary representation of so vast a country almost as large as Europe containing so large a number of different races is one of the wildest imaginations that ever entered the minds of men.'[5] 'We are no advocates of representative government for India in the western sense of the term'; wrote the viceroy, Lord Minto to Morley at the India Office in March 1907, 'it could never be akin to the instincts of the many races composing the population of the Indian Empire. It would be a western importation uncongenial to eastern tastes.' In reply Morley concurred in the repudiation of 'the intention or desire to attempt the transplantation of any European form of representative government to Indian soil' and two years later reassured the House of Lords by saying that he thought it neither desirable nor possible nor even conceivable that English political institutions should be extended to India.[6] 'If I were attempting to set up a Parliamentary system in India,' he told the House of Lords[7] in speaking of the reforms jointly associated with his name and that of the viceroy, 'or if it could be said that this chapter of reforms led directly or necessarily up to the establishment of a Parliamentary system in India, I, for one, would have nothing at all to do with it.' For the foreseeable future 'a Parliamentary system in India is not the goal to which I for one moment would aspire'. Not even with war and all the changes it brought did this note of scepticism disappear. The Simon Commission, friendless, boycotted and resented chiefly by reason of its wholly British membership, in a

Report published in 1929 exuded the depressing sort of wisdom that springs from doubt and misgivings.

> The British Parliamentary system ... has been fitted like a well-worn garment to the figure of the wearer, but it does not follow that it will suit everybody ... British parliamentarianism in India is a translation, and in even the best translations the essential meaning is apt to be lost.[8]

But while in common with others before and after them the Commission talked somewhat spaciously of forms of democratic government other than the British – the American presidential system, because of the strong, stable executive it was thought to provide, the Swiss, because of its non-party administration and, more exotically in the last phase, the Austro–Hungarian *Ausgleich* of 1867 by reason of its contrivances for duality in government, were apt to be the most favoured alternatives, the last named appealing particularly to L. S. Amery[9] and kindling momentary interest in Mountbatten – it remained doubtful whether the British rulers of India, or indeed Indians trained under the British system, would have been qualified to apply them. What is certain is that the British system was what self-conscious Indian opinion wanted and it was also the system which by a gesture of faith rather than by reasoned conviction was proclaimed in 1917 to be the goal of British policy in India.

The ambivalence in British attitudes to the future government of India was implicit in the nature of British rule. The *Raj* was strangely compounded of splendid assurance and inner uncertainties. The assurance came the more easily to the men on the spot, to the soldiers and the administrators, the governors and the viceroys of British India. They occupied the seats of power; they determined how it should be exercised; they were the heirs of Empire and in 1903 and 1911 (a trifle self-consciously perhaps) they organised Durbars in Delhi with a king-emperor in the second case making spectacular entry in person into the Red Fort so as to underline imperial succession from the Mughal rulers who preceded them; they were aware that behind them, sustaining their authority, were not only the indigenous instruments of power, but also, should the need arise, the resources of a world-wide Empire. Yet behind the sometimes formal and occasionally glittering façade of absolutism there remained the reality of divided responsiblity. The British rulers of India were subject to control. It was remote control, that of the secretary of state for India in London, of the cabinet (of which he was a member) and of the Parliament, to which that cabinet was responsible. Autocracy was thus subject to democracy. That subjection was in practice intermittent and apt on occasion to be irritating rather than effective. It could hardly, indeed, have been otherwise. Yet subjection there was and in principle and practice alike its ultimate reality was asserted and reasserted.

The form of Indian government and of imperial control over it was determined when the Mutiny sounded the death-knell of East India Company rule in India. 'India', it was stated succinctly in the Government of India Act 1858, 'shall be governed by and in the name of Her Majesty, and all rights in relation to any territories which might have been exercised by the said Company if this Act had not been passed shall and may be exercised by and in the name of Her Majesty . . .'[10] In addition the governor-general was invested by Royal Proclamation with the more resounding designation of viceroy, as was deemed appropriate for a representative who was at once to exercise the august responsibilities of government in India and to serve as counterpart to the new secretary of state for India responsible to cabinet and Parliament, not as the colonial secretary for a multiplicity of dependent territories but for an Empire as it had been and as it was soon to be known again. The viceroy was to be assisted in the discharge of his Indian duties by an Executive and Legislative Council, composed in the first instance of officials, but to the number of which was added in 1861 not less than six nor more than twelve unofficial members, for the discussion of legislative proposals.[11] These reforms somewhat broadened the basis of government but since the Legislative Council was limited to discussion, with members furthermore being debarred from the asking of questions or the moving of resolutions, and the viceroy retained the power to overrule his Executive Council, there was no effective restraint on vice-regal authority in India. The checks upon it existed not in India but in London, and for their efficacy in practice much depended upon the personalities of viceroys and secretaries of state and the relations between them.

There were some parallels but as many contrasts between Indian and Irish administration. Under the union, the highest executive officers in Ireland were the lord lieutenant and the chief secretary, but while it was customary for one or other of them to sit in cabinet, it was by no means uniformly the chief secretary who did so and Balfour was of the opinion that the real headship of the Irish government belonged to the minister who happened to be both in the cabinet and the House of Commons.[12] But in the case of India distance alone precluded any such alternation. The secretary of state, by virtue of his office, was securely entrenched in the cabinet, the viceroy resident in India for his period of office. There was, accordingly, clearer demarcation than in contemporary Ireland of status and function. The secretary of state had no executive duties to discharge in Calcutta or Delhi, as had the chief secretary in Dublin, while the viceroy far away had few opportunities of influencing the cabinet in the event of disagreement with the secretary of state, his ordinary channel of communication with the Cabinet being through the secretary of state. More generally the different responsibilities discharged by viceroy and secretary of state, and the sharply contrasted worlds in which they moved, tended to foster not personal rivalries but a sense of common participation in an historic undertaking. As communications with the east improved with the laying of the overland cable to India in 1868, the opening of the Suez Canal in 1869 and the completion of a British submarine cable in 1870, the possible direct influence in practice of the secretary of state over government in India increased.[13] But in principle there was no change. In contrast again with the continuing administrative confusion in Ireland from the time of union, the relationship between secretary of state and viceroy had been defined at the outset and was as need arose subsequently restated. Thus the secretary of state in a dispatch of 24 November 1870 to the government in India noted that

> the risk of serious embarrassment would become much greater than hitherto it has been found to be, if a clear understanding were not maintained as to one great principle which from the beginning has underlaid the whole system. That principle is, that the final control and direction of the affairs of India rest with the home government, and not with the authorities appointed and established by the Crown, under Parliamentary enactment, in India itself.
>
> The government established in India is (from the nature of the case) subordinate to the imperial government at home. And no government can be subordinate unless it is within the power of the superior government to order what is to be done or left undone, and to enforce on its officers, through the ordinary and constitutional means, obedience to its directions as to the use which they are to make of official position and power in furtherance of the policy which has been finally decided upon by the advisers of the Crown.[14]

This subordination which the secretary of state re-emphasised could be, and was, irksome to viceroys, not least, as may well be imagined, to Lord Curzon:

I have been thinking [wrote Curzon to the secretary of state, Lord George Hamilton, in May 1902] over the experience of the last 3½ years. . . . It seems to me to establish conclusively a desire upon the part of your advisers in the India Office to thwart and hamper me in the work which I am endeavouring to undertake here . . . I will ask you to try and put yourself in my position. Here I am working away the whole day long and a considerable part of the night, in the discharge of what I believe to be a serious and solemn duty. I am conducting the task in exile, in complete isolation from all friends or advisers, surrounded by forces and combinations against which it often requires great courage to struggle, habitually harassed, constantly weary, and often in physical distress and pain. If, in addition to all these anxieties, against which I am capable of holding up my head, I am also to be perpetually nagged and impeded and misunderstood by the India Council at home, I say plainly that I would sooner give up the task.

Hamilton replied with tolerant understanding.

The very magnitude of the work which the viceroy can do [he wrote] makes control of any kind the more obnoxious to him . . . But, after all, is the viceroy's position in this respect more trying than that of the other public servants and ministers of the British Empire? Look at the prime minister in this country, or the head of any one of the great departments of state who has to represent that department in the House of Commons. Take the position either of Salisbury, Balfour, Beach, or Chamberlain: they are subjected to a different form of check and interference far more annoying, and far more effective, than any to which a viceroy can be subject. Take the great men who have preceded you in your office: Warren Hastings, Cornwallis, Wellesley, Hardinge, and Dalhousie – they all had to carry on their work under the same conditions which you find irritating and dilatory, and I think I may fairly say that not one of those distinguished predecessors had as easy a colleague to deal with in this country as myself.[15]

Yet might not Curzon have retorted that the checks upon

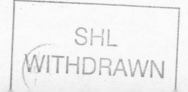

colleagues in London were the outcome of personal debate and discussion and that, as a matter of fact, his distinguished predecessors in India had been ridden on a looser rein?

There was more at issue in these exchanges than particular situation or personality. Behind them lay the question of final control. Curzon, in his dispatch, had challenged established tradition in expressing the view that 'the keys of India are not in England, nor in the House of Commons. They are in the office desk of every young Civilian in this country.'[16] He was, however, mistaken and it was important at the time and for the future that he was mistaken. It became the practice in subsequent years for reforms in Indian government to be known by the hyphenated names of secretary of state and viceroy – Morley-Minto in 1909, Montagu-Chelmsford in 1919 – the secretary of state's name coming first, in accord with appropriate constitutional usage. And usage in this case coincided with political reality. The keys of India were in the House of Commons in so far as they were in British hands at all. The secretary of state was necessarily responsive to the mood of the House and the House itself was responsive to the mood of the people. In the critical twentieth-century years both House and people were notably more disposed to change than were the viceroy, his advisers and the British administration in India and their disposition, intermittently or even negatively voiced, had greater influence than the government of India's aversion to it. As more radical members of the House of Commons well understood, a parliamentary question was a weapon of some potency. It had to receive an answer; that answer would be publicised in India, and for that reason the secretary of state would ordinarily consult the viceroy about its content. Such consultation in turn served to convey to the viceroy something of trends of opinion at home which he might well not find congenial, but to which he had perforce to pay some regard.

In the perspective of history the determining of policy assumes its decisive importance, but what was apt to loom larger in the eyes of contemporaries was the outlook and impact at the personal level of imperial government and administration in India. What manner of men were responsible for the administration of this vast eastern autocracy? The answer, in respect of all the higher reaches of administration, was Englishmen – carefully prepared, rigorously selected by public examination and, as a body of men, of higher calibre than administrators in any other part of the Empire. Gokhale, the Moderate, who guided the Congress in the early years of the century and who viewed politics 'as a lever for the regeneration of his country' noted with more than a touch of envy how well trained, well organised and free from vanity or self-advertisement the British bureaucracy in India was. Among constitutionalists such views were and continued to be widely entertained. But the members of the ICS were none the less for most of the period for the most part Englishmen. The queen's proclamation announcing the new order in 1858 had specifically admitted all, irrespective of race or creed, who were suitably qualified to offices in the administration. But in practice there was a wide gap, much resented by politically self-conscious Indians, between intention and fulfilment. That gap created, among other things, what was known as 'the service question'. Entry into the Indian civil service was by competitive examination. But the syllabus for that examination was based on the English school curriculum and the examination itself was held in England. Both inevitably discouraged Indian candidates whether Moslem or Hindu. For the latter there was additional discouragement in as much as Hindus travelling overseas were automatically deprived of their caste and obliged to seek readmission to it on return. In 1878, furthermore, the age of examination was reduced from twenty-two to nineteen – at which age Indian candidates had not had the teaching to enable them to compete with much hope of success against the products of English schools. In India there arose a demand for 'simultaneous examinations' in Britain and in India so as to relieve Indian candidates at least of the necessity to travel to Britain. It was accepted in principle in 1893, and a bill was introduced and passed in the House of Commons to give effect to it. But even this modest ameliorative measure was not acted upon until 1919. Truly was it remarked that Englishmen in the east acquired an oriental insensitivity to time.

The composition of the Indian administration was one question – a political question with racial overtones – the outlook of the administrators another. In so far as it was reflected in their idealised concept of their rôle, that outlook owed its distinctive quality to the historiography of the Empires of the ancient world as reinterpreted in the older English universities and transmitted by them to those who taught at Haileybury and other English public schools. The virtues these administrators prized were courage, independence, manliness, fair play and the even-handed justice enjoined upon rulers in the last words of David, king of Israel:

> He that ruleth over men must be just,
> Ruling in the fear of God.

> And he shall be as the light of the morning
>   when the sun riseth,
> Even a morning without clouds.

With these idealised concepts went a Virgilian bias in favour of the solid virtues of the countryman and against the unstable urban intelligentsia, combined with a reliance for their own part upon character, good sense and good judgment rather than ideas. Attachment to and detachment from those over whom they ruled were nicely blended, but Sir William Wedderburn, a former member of the ICS was not far from the mark in speaking of having experienced from the inside the working of an efficient but unfeeling bureaucratic machine. The more lasting achievements of British administration – the introduction of a unified system of law and justice, with a code of civil and criminal procedure such as India had not hitherto known, the organisation of administration, in the districts, the provinces and at the centre of British India – are themselves indicative of the outlook of the administrators as well as of the immensity of their achievement. Their memorialist has written a record of the men of the ICS in two volumes carrying the appropriately Platonic subtitles of *The Founders* and *The Guardians*. But the work as a whole carries the title, *The Men who Ruled India*.[17] They were 'the heaven-born', rulers who came from outside and ruled from above. The barriers that existed in practice against Indian recruitment heightened their isolation in their homes, their clubs, the residencies of governors and the palaces of viceroys. If they were insulated largely in self-protection against the ideas of those whom they ruled, with time and distance, movements of opinion at home also ceased to have much impact upon them.

James Bryce, when he visited India in November 1888, returned somewhat disappointed with the civil service. He recognised the quality of the men in the higher posts and noted that they were intelligent, very hard-working, with apparently a high sense of public duty and a desire to promote the welfare of the people of India. But he proceeded,

> they seem rather wanting in imagination and sympathy, less inspired by the extraordinary and unprecedented phenomena of the country than might have been expected, with little intellectual initiative; too conventionally English in their ways of life and thoughts to rise to the position . . . They are more out of the stream of the world's thought and movement than one was prepared to find.[18]

Fifteen years later Lord Curzon, confessedly in a mood of frustration, made sharper comment.

> How often have I not pointed out to you [he wrote to the secretary of state] that there are neither originality, nor ideas or imagination in the Indian Civil Service, that they think the present the best, and that change or improvement or reform . . . sends a cold shiver down their spine.[19]

This was unjust but it contained an underlying truth. If and when change was to come to India, from the British side the impetus would be from the House of Commons and from sections of public opinion at home, emphatically not from the general body of British administrators or soldiers in India. They were as little welcoming to the ideas of the Liberal, Edwin Montagu, at the close of the first world war, as they were to the cautious reformism of the Conservative, Lord Irwin, a decade later, while of their reception of Sir Stafford Cripps on his 1942 mission it may be remarked that it was as correct as it was constrained. The post-war Labour administration was regarded, as the author in the early weeks of the last viceroyalty had occasion to note, not so much with distaste, though that was pronounced, as resentful incomprehension at the British electorate for having put it in office. Yet ironically enough the greatest achievement of these men who were so averse to change was to provide the conditions without which change might have led to chaos. In this respect their work was without parallel in the British or in any other western European empire.

On the longer view and in a wider context there was about British attitudes to change in India a deeper ambivalence. There was on the one hand the firmly established tradition that British rule in India had a fixed term and purpose. The Mills among thinkers and Thomas Munro, Mountstuart Elphinstone, Sir Henry Lawrence and many others subscribed to it. They spoke, with Macaulay, of 'the proudest day' in British history when the British rulers of India, having equipped the peoples of India to govern themselves, would withdraw, their task accomplished. Nor was it chance that these sentiments of early thinkers and administrators were much favoured for quotation by those whose responsibility it was to transfer power in 1947. But it is not to be supposed for a moment that this view was universally or consistently entertained in the intervening years. For the greater part of what K. M. Panikkar wrote of as 'the Augustan age of European Empire in Asia',[20] which he dated from 1840 to 1914, most of the British rulers of India

were more disposed to think of the present hour of greatness than
of some future day of abdication as the 'proudest moment'. The
British Empire in India was, in Curzon's view, 'the miracle of the
world' and 'the biggest thing that the English are doing any-
where'.[21] Why should he, why should men who worked under or
after him, hasten the day of its eclipse? 'No one', wrote Curzon's
successor, Lord Minto, in 1907,[22] 'believes more firmly than we do
that the safety and welfare of India depend on the permanence of
British administration. . . .' To a sense of mission in the conscienti-
ous discharge of a great task laid upon Britain by Providence there
was allied the more realistic calculation, as Curzon phrased it, 'as
long as we rule India, we are the greatest power in the world. If we
lose it, we shall drop straight away to a third-rate Power.' This,
indeed, was part and parcel of the thinking of Empire; these very
words were to be echoed by Winston Churchill in the 1930s when
he was campaigning violently against plans of the predominantly
conservative National administration to bring into being a self-
governing Indian federation. Who, sharing Curzon's opinion,
would deliberately bring forward the hour of departure and so
precipitate the British decline from greatness? And for those who
questioned mission and *realpolitik* judgment alike, there were still
doubts and uncertainties. The subcontinent was not only vast; its
destiny was obscure. Even Roman history could provide no
satisfying parallel to British rule in India, nor all history point a way
by which it might reach its supposedly natural term. Macaulay had
found it difficult to form any conjecture as to the fate reserved for a
state which resembled no other, and acknowledged that the laws
which regulated its growth and decay were unknown. His successors a century later rarely claimed to have been able to define them.
Many were sanguine; some were filled with foreboding, that
staunch Gladstonian, John Morley, rather surprisingly among the
latter, and confiding to Gokhale that 'somehow or other he had an
impression that a terrible catastrophe was in store for England in
connection with India'. But almost all, including Curzon, allowed
that change there had to be and the question at issue accordingly
was what direction should it take? There was one answer, and one
answer only, that as the years went by acquired a reassuringly
familiar ring even to those who would have greatly preferred that
the Raj should continue undisturbed. It was that the peoples of
India should advance by way of representative to responsible
government and finally to dominion status. But however right it
may have appeared to a growing body of British parliamentary and
public opinion at home and for quite different reasons to the

majority of politically self-conscious Indians, it seemed for long inapplicable in such unfamiliar surroundings to the British rulers of India. In its Commonwealth setting the last half century of the British *Raj* in India is in one part the story of how these rulers of India and those associated with them in the India Office – where the Durham Report was not, as in the Colonial and Dominion Offices, at any time recommended reading for new recruits – were at last persuaded (though even then with qualifications) that the familiar road, even in an unfamiliar setting, was the one to travel, if only because no other was sufficiently known to them.

The strangeness and complexities of the setting are not in question. In the cities and the countryside of twentieth-century India, contrasts between great wealth and abject poverty, splendour and misery, self-sacrificing integrity and degrading corruption would have found much by way of European counterpart in pre-revolutionary France where, as Balzac remarked *'l'incessant concubinage du Luxe et de la Misère, du Vice et de l'Honnêté'* were of the essence of life. Politically India was no less evidently divided between the provinces of British India and the Indian princely states which comprised well over a third of the territory of the subcontinent and one quarter of its population. At the deeper level of religion and culture it was divided into several communities, there being at the time of the 1931 census some 239 million Hindus, 78 million Muslims, 4 million Sikhs and 6 million Christians in the subcontinent. So long as the alien imperial power remained, the positions of classes, provinces, princes and communities in relation one to another were fixed from above. They might seek for advantage here or betterment there but their appeal was to a final and external authority. Once the endurance of that authority appeared in doubt then there was bound to open (as there did) a struggle for succession or survival.

What placed it in doubt? Not recollections of Macaulayesque oratorical flourishes – they had a place, an important one, but only *after* doubt had been instilled. Psychologically it was a principal consequence of the Mutiny for Englishmen and of the Great Rebellion for Indians to apply the terminology of each to the events of a single traumatic year. It had happened – and what had happened once could happen again. When in August 1942 the viceroy wished to convey in a personal message to the prime minister the gravity of the situation resulting from the Quit India movement, the yardstick he applied was that of the Mutiny – 'I am engaged here in meeting by far the most serious rebellion since that of 1857.'[23] But for the long intervening years when the Raj

seemingly attained the pinnacle of power and assurance the
possibility of revolt, once demonstrated, in its latency was almost as
important cumulatively as the event itself.

The psychological background renders the more comprehensi-
ble the political foreground. The notion of freedom attained by
force had been given substance. It was for Indians thereafter, as for
other peoples sensitively aware of their subjection, to debate and
decide whether such means were necessary or desirable. The
Indian National Congress, founded in 1885, enunciating a
gradualist programme for modest constitutional reforms, discounted by silence even such a contingent possibility. The reliance
of their leadership was upon a responsive British government,
which they conceived of as a British Liberal government;
Campbell-Bannerman was 'the tried and and trusted friend of
freedom', while Morley (who went to the India Office) was said by
Gokhale to be one whose 'teachings next after John Stuart Mill have
been for years past largely moulding the thought of the new India'.
But the continuance of such an approach was implicitly conditioned by the imperial response to nationalist expectations. ' . . . if
this Liberal government', wrote R. C. Dutt in 1906, 'fails to give a
more representative character to the Indian administration we
shall never get anything by peaceful methods and England will be
teaching us to pursue Irish methods . . .'[24] But England in the
Indian case taught neither one thing nor the other, being neither
unresponsive nor yet, for the majority of Congressmen, sufficiently
responsive. It was accordingly, to oversimplify a complex historical
issue, left to the Indian nationalists to debate whether to seek
advance by means of greater constitutional pressure or to turn to
forceful means, the principal protagonists of these respective
viewpoints in earlier years being Gokhale and Tilak. It was Gokale
and the constitutionalists who prevailed – but what remains debatable in historical terms is the extent to which British concessions
were, as the British and the Moderates represented, the fruits of
Gokhale's persuasive eloquence or of British sensitivity to the risk
of violence, should sufficient concessions not be made. Or to put it
more directly, how far would Gokhale have got, had there been no
threat of 'Irish methods'?

Despite post-war disturbances in the Punjab, agrarian unrest in
the United Provinces, acts of terrorism in Bengal or of later
symbolic protests such as the seizure by young men of the arsenal at
Chittagong in 1930 – the last graphically commemorated in an
exhibition in the National Archives in Delhi fifty years later – it was
not until 1942 that recourse to physical force on a national scale

seriously occupied the minds of the Congress leadership, whatever rhetorical outbursts to the contrary might suggest. It was not violence, but the weapon of non-violent non-cooperation as enunciated by Gandhi, that dominated the intervening years. There was also, under Gandhi's inspiration, the transformation of the Congress from an élitist organisation into a mass movement, though recent analysis indicates that it might more properly be thought of as a congeries of local movements, rather than a nation-wide unified movement.[25] Either way the inner propulsions and outward manifestations of Indian nationalism were transformed. But with transformation came also the risk of dilution of aim. The declared goal was freedom, political freedom. But, as in pre-revolutionary Ireland, so in India in the thirties, there were other and potentially distracting preoccupations, notable among them Gandhi's deep concern for the poor in a country of countless impoverished villages and for the outcastes, or Harijans, whose cause he was making peculiarly his own. To the young Jawaharlal Nehru, one of Gandhi's most ardent disciples, Congress commitment, or even serious involvement, in social questions of so far-reaching a nature before freedom was won seemed to risk division in Congress ranks and, worse still, the possibility of the Congress, or some of its members, being drawn by ineluctable stages into cooperation with imperial authorities at ground level. Political freedom 'first and foremost' was for him not only the chief but the only object of Congress' existence. All else, however deserving or important, must await attention when freedom was won. Gandhi, slow to sense what was deemed to be at issue, in the end conceded the case for concentration upon the overriding political aim. And that, in cruder terms, for Congress meant concentration upon securing control for itself of the instrumentality of power, that is of the government of India.

The claims of the Indian National Congress for succession to the Raj appeared to its own members, and indeed to many outside, to be conclusive. 'Congress alone', Gandhi told the Round Table Conference in London in 1931, 'claims to represent the whole of India . . .'[26] and to it, and to it alone, should power be transferred. That claim was disputed by the princes – British officers in Indian dress the Mahatma termed them – and began first to disquiet and then ultimately to alienate the great majority of the Muslims. The reason was clear. The Congress not only demanded independence from the British but looked forward to an independent India, democratically governed by a people exercising their will through representative institutions. In a land in which community commanded a first allegiance, such institutions were bound to place ultimate power in the hands of the majority community. Unrestricted exercise of that power, which electoral arithmetic thus conferred, might be mitigated by constitutional devices of one kind or another, but no amount of constitutional ingenuity could alter the balance of numbers or deprive the majority of the final authority which numbers conferred upon it. For this reason there existed, below the superficial complications of the Indian political scene, an underlying simplicity which left none of the parties concerned with power or the succession to it – the princes, the Congress, the Muslim League, the British – with much ground for manoeuvre.

The princes, from the greatest among them in Travancore, Hyderabad, Kashmir and the Rajput states, down to the smallest rajahs exercising sway over some few thousand acres, were dependent for survival against the rising tides of nationalism, democracy and a hostile Congress, upon their association by treaties with the Paramount Power. They were insistent, therefore, upon the sanctity of those treaties, from which they derived the essential reassurance for their continued status and privileges. Down to the accession to office of the Labour Government in 1945 and more particularly until the coming of the Cabinet Mission in the spring of 1946, the greater princes at least could count upon sympathetic backing from an imperial power grateful for their loyalty in time of war and well content for the most part to see these islands of stability (not to say reaction) standing seemingly secure, as bulwarks against the assults of popular and left-wing nationalist revolution, though the more percipient among the princes could not but be aware how different things might look when the time of British departure from India became imminent.

The Muslims, it is true, as the second largest community in India, enjoyed a somewhat wider freedom of action. Nonetheless the Muslim leaders, from Sayyid Ahmad in the last quarter of the nineteenth century, to the Aga Khan early in the twentieth century, to Mohammed Ali Jinnah in the inter-war years, were compelled, sooner rather than later, in each case to concern themselves with the question of what would be the position of this large and therefore potentially disruptive minority community in an India from which the British *Raj* had withdrawn. There were two possible answers. The first was submergence of the smaller community in a national movement before independence and thereafter in a nation-state in which inevitably the majority community, the Hindus, would play the dominant part. Such merging, or submerging, of community interest implied first, confidence in the goodwill and sense of justice of the majority and secondly, acceptance of a national before a communal allegiance. There were periods of Muslim-Hindu *rapprochement*, most notably the so-called Lucknow Pact of 1916, when it seemed as if the first condition was to be fulfilled. But the periods of such understanding proved intermittent and in each case they were followed by a more prolonged and more intense expression of mistrust and finally of open antagonism. However these movements in opinion are to be interpreted historically, the Muslim leadership had little choice in the end. Once there was insufficiency of trust, the minority had to seek safeguards. They did so in 1906–7 and they secured them in the Morley-Minto reforms of 1909, with communal electoral rolls and voting weighted in their favour. Subsequently the aim of the Muslim leadership was defensive, holding the British to the concessions they had made and seeking in the inter-war years to strengthen still further their position against the day of majority rule. Step by step they advanced from a position of special voting rights to insistence upon a federal as against a unitary state, from a federation with a strong centre to a federation with a weak centre and finally to partition. Each advance remained conditional upon a British willingness to concede.

The Indian National Congress for its part had every reason to press the simple claim of majority rule in a unitary state. The Congress High Command demanded representative institutions on the British model without distinction of class or creed, a unitary form of government with a cabinet responsible to an elected lower House and ultimately an independent India in which the fragmentation of princely states and divergent communities, would be erased from the political map. The nature of their demand presupposed their hostility to the princes and British backing for them and while, in 1916, they accepted electoral discrimination in favour of the Muslims, their later demand as formulated, notably in the draft constitution prepared in 1929 under the chairmanship of Motilal Nehru, was for a unitary state with minimal minority concessions. Therein lay the natural interest of the Congress, and it might reasonably by argued that they could not in the circumstances think or act otherwise. But the hard question that lay before its leadership in the critical years was the extent to which they should or should not modify their aims in the interests of national unity.

British purposes in India, down to the outbreak of the second world war, were to all outward appearances the least narrowly circumscribed. The initiative in respect of enunciation of policy rested in their hands. They were well placed, especially in view of the always latent and ultimately open conflict for the succession to power, to hasten or retard the time of their withdrawal. It was widely credited by the Congress that the British government used this freedom of action to strengthen the position of the princes against democratic India and to entrench Muslim minority against Hindu majority, on the well-established imperial principle of divide and rule. The first is hardly open to dispute; the second, while less easy to determine, is certainly true to the extent that the allegation can be supported by reference to particular policies or actions, the more important of which were the partition of Bengal, the concession of separate electorates and of weightage to the Muslims in the Morley-Minto reforms and the opening of the way under the Government of India Act, 1935 to responsible government in the Provinces in advance of the Centre. Both raised issues which in changing situations down to 1947 retained their essential character and significance.

The first partition of Bengal was the work of Lord Curzon, who, industrious as always, had stated in 1902, his intention of 'looking into the question of political boundaries generally' and on so doing found those of Bengal 'antiquated, illogical and productive of inefficiency'.[27] 'I should like to fix the boundaries for the next generation', he told Sir Alexander Godley. The purpose of the Bengal partition was twofold. The first, an administrative object, was to free the governor-general from responsibility for the government of the province, which had been considered too large by Lord Dalhousie in 1853 and which in his opinion had placed upon the governor-general 'a burden which in its present mass is more than mortal man can fitly bear'. The second was political, at least in its effects, namely to create a new province of East Bengal including all districts in which the Muslims were in a majority. This meant the creation of a Muslim majority province out of an area where the Muslims had hitherto been in a permanent minority. The Muslims were not unitedly in favour, many of the landed classes especially being opposed to the partition of the province, and the Hindus were violent in their denunciation. Thousands of articles were written and speeches made against it. Lord Curzon read them. He did not find in them 'one single line of argument, there is nothing but rhetoric and declamation'. The partition was effected in 1905. It was undone at the Delhi Durbar in 1911. But its consequences were great. It served as a sharp stimulus both to Indian nationalism[28] and to Muslim separatism. Neither, and most certainly not the former, was part of the viceroy's intention. His opinion, expressed in a dispatch to the secretary of state in November 1900, was that 'the Congress is tottering to its fall, and one of my great ambitions while in India is to assist it to a peaceful demise'.[29] But the Congress, despite the division between constitutional moderates and extremists, emerged from the viceroyalty, not weakened but strengthened.

One important cause of the revival of the Congress was the resentment at a partition which was thought to indicate a deliberate British policy of building up Muslim minority consciousness as a counterweight to nascent Indian nationalism. That suspicion was heightened by the concession in the Morley-Minto reforms of weightage and special electorates to the Muslims. In the inter-war years it was all pervasive in the Congress ranks, drawing sustenance from these past experiences and present force from the supposed bias of many British administrators in favour of Muslims as against Hindus. Supposition, however, even with an air of probability about it, is not tantamount to conclusive historical evidence. But politically it can be, and in this case almost certainly was, of first importance. It presumed a deliberate British purpose, not of early withdrawal, but of the extension of the period of British rule by the accentuation of India's domestic divisions. Such an interpretation of British governmental policy in so far as it rested upon an equation of the actions and words of particular British leaders at varying times with settled governmental policy over an extended period of time, was an oversimplification even though evidence now available confirms the correctness of some at least of contemporary Congress suppositions. There was no consensus in British opinion about India. On the contrary at the critical time informed opinion in Britain was much exercised and divided about British policy in India. Nor could it be determined in isolation. No British government could pursue for long a policy in India inconsistent with the general pattern of British imperial policy and of a kind not generally acceptable at home. The more important limiting factors upon British freedom of action in India in the inter-war years were, therefore, compounded of Indian nationalist pressures and the reaction of public and parliamentary opinion at home to those pressures. In India the second was apt to be unduly discounted.

It was against this pattern of varied Indian and British interests that the advance to responsible government and dominions status proceeded. The Morley-Minto reforms had increased Indian representation in the legislative councils at the centre and in the provinces and in so doing had served to heighten the Congress demand for a crossing of the line that divided representation from responsibility. But the British government had remained uncommitted about ultimate purpose, and when challenged about them Morley (as earlier noted) had taken refuge in philosophic agnosticism. The first commitment was that given by the secretary of state for India, Edwin Montagu, in 1917 when on behalf of the government he declared that responsible government was the goal of British rule in India. Once the goal was proclaimed the debate henceforward became one of form and timetable, not of purpose. Both were important. The form of government was bound to touch closely on majority-minority relations as well as on the future rôle of the princes, while in respect of time there was not likely to be any departure from the tradition of imperial powers doing too little too late. But far more important was the self-imposed limitation upon British freedom of action. After 1917 they were formally committed to responsible government for India. That implied an Indian constitution on the dominion model. The Indian nationalist leaders were quick to grasp the signifiance of the weapon which the British cabinet, only half-comprehendingly, had placed in their hands. A promise had been made and the Indians were resolved that Britain should be kept to it. Adolf Hitler addressing the German chiefs-of-staff in the Reich Chancellery in November 1937 put this aspect of the situation in a nutshell when he remarked that Britain's half-measures in India 'had given to the Indians the opportunity of using later on as a weapon against Britain the non-fulfilment of her promises regarding a constitution'.

The Montagu declaration was made in the third year of the first world war, after the collapse of tzarist Russia and before the entry of the United States, when German fortunes were once more in the ascendant and when the presence of dominion statesmen ,and Indian representatives in London for the meetings of the Imperial War Conference and cabinet served as a constant reminder of the critical importance of wartime aid from the Empire overseas. Was it not at once right and reasonable, in view of the massive Indian contribution to imperial forces, to seek to conciliate rising national sentiment with assurances of greater Indian participation in the government of the subcontinent? And was it not natural in the circumstances to think of that greater association developing on a dominion pattern, all the more so in view of the great advances in dominion reputation during the war? The answers to both questions, as authorised by members of the war cabinet, were in the affirmative. But it was left to their successors to formulate practical policies on the basis of this broad definition of aims. It was not an easy assignment.

The language of the Montagu declaration was the language of the Durham Report and, at one remove, of dominion status. But what were its actual implications? The war cabinet was too preoccupied to ponder them. But one day they had to be faced. First to be considered was the question of area. The Montagu declaration spoke of India, not of British India. The distinction was not without importance. The gradual development of self-governing institutions, to quote the words of the declaration, 'with a view to the progressive realisation of responsible government in India as an integral part of the British Empire',[30] was to be the goal of British rule. Since India meant the whole of the subcontinent, this in turn meant the inclusion of the Indian states, and since the representative element was altogether lacking in the government of the great majority of them, it implied of necessity slower advance towards the goal than conditions in British India of itself might have been felt to justify. In the context of international and even of British Commonwealth relations any alternative was probably impracticable, as indeed the constitutional advisers to the viceroy concluded in 1929[31] when reviewing this among other related questions, while in domestic terms any distinction in respect of the goals for British and princely India would have been interpreted, and not unreasonably, as a classic example of an imperial essay in the tactics of 'divide and rule'. But the price of common advance was the familiar one of the more backward slowing down the more forward.

There were larger issues. Responsible government implied dominion status but was not synonymous with it. The Government of India Act 1919, giving effect to the Montagu-Chelmsford reform programme, established a diarchical system of government in the provinces of British India, with control of selected subjects transferred to Indian ministers responsible to Indian elected legislatures and, at the centre, an Assembly and a Council of State, both with a majority of elected members though neither having power of control over the viceroy and his executive, together with a Chamber of Princes as a consultative body. These reforms were intended to be steps (albeit more modest than Indian opinion hoped for) along the road to responsible government. But they had no bearing upon status. They served indeed to underline the fact that India's status in the Commonwealth and internationally had outstripped her government. At home there could be no question about India's continuing dependence: abroad she wore at least the trappings of autonomy. India was represented with the dominions at the Imperial War Conference 1917 and in the imperial war cabinet; she was a signatory to the Treaty of Versailles and a founder-member of the League of Nations. It is true that her representatives were nominated by the secretary of state but, it could be argued, this in itself did not diminish the status accorded externally to the country. On any reckoning India's international personality had thus developed further than her domestic self-government. Yet it was responsible government, not dominion status, that was the proclaimed goal of British rule. Was it conceivable then that the status of a dominion might be accorded to India without, or in anticipation of, the acquisition and practice of responsible government? Technically it was not impossible, as subsequent developments in the Commonwealth were to demonstrate, but politically it was precluded if only because the British *Raj*, startled by the pace of the advances in dominion status, was concerned to delay rather than to hasten the date of the coming into existence of an Indian dominion and, therefore, predisposed to insist responsible government as a pre-condition of it.

In April 1929 the viceroy, Lord Irwin, asked his advisers for a note on 1. dominion status showing what it would mean in practice as applied to India, 2. how far the British government had ever given any undertaking to work up to it and 3. how far Indian opinion had demanded it.[32] The posing of the questions in itself reflected the ambiguities of British policies subsequent to the Montagu declaration and the difficulties of the British position as seen from Delhi. Both stemmed from a single source. In 1917 responsible government, while carrying a dominion implication, had been of itself reassuring. It had a fixed and static meaning. Dominion status, however, had not. The decade that followed the Montagu declaration witnessed the transformation of the old system of British-dominion relations, with its assurance of British predominance, into the new Balfourian association with equality as its fundamental doctrine. Not surprisingly, the advisers to the *Raj* sought reassurance in the fact that it was responsible government that had been specifically promised to India in 1917. It was also what had been reaffirmed in the Montagu-Chelmsford Report and in expositions of it by the viceroy, Lord Chelmsford, and the secretary of state, Edwin Montagu. The duke of Connaught, however, at the inauguration of the new Council of State and Legislative Assembly on 9 February 1921 had delivered a message from the king-emperor referring to the 'beginnings of *Swaraj* within my Empire' and to the 'widest scope and ample opportunity

for progress to the liberty which my other dominions enjoy' – a
phrase open to more than one interpretation – but then Lord
Reading, as viceroy, once more retreated to safer ground in
speaking of 'the high destiny' which awaited India as a partner in
the British Empire. The first Labour secretary of state, Lord
Ollivier, was predictably more forthright, saying in 1924 that His
Majesty's government had themselves the same ultimate aim as the
Indian *Swaraj* party, namely, 'a responsible Indian dominion
government'. In substance this was reiterated by Stanley Baldwin
on 24 May 1927 when he spoke of India 'in the fullness of time'
being in 'equal partnership with the dominions'. While these later
statements were indicative of the trend of British thinking, they
were not tantamount to formal commitments. Some of them
understandably were seized upon by the Congress, despite contrary and controversial interpretation by the Home Member, Sir
Malcolm Hailey, on behalf of the government of India[33] in 1924, as
evidence that responsible government necessarily implied dominion status.

The Indian National Congress, constitutional in membership
and conceptual aim, unlike Sinn Féin, positively embraced the idea
of a dominion goal. In 1906 it had adopted as its objective 'the
attainment of a system of government for India similar to that
enjoyed by the self-governing dominions of the British Empire'. In
1916 the Congress and the Muslim League jointly proposed that
India should 'be lifted from the position of dependency to that of
an equal partner in the Empire with the self-governing dominions'.
In 1924 the alternatives for India were spoken of by Gandhi as
Swaraj within the Empire on terms of equality or outside if the
British government did not concede self-rule within. The first
recommendation of the All-Parties Conference 1928, under the
chairmanship of Motilal Nehru, based on article 1 of the Anglo–
Irish Treaty read:

> India shall have the same constitutional status in the comity of
> nations known as the British Empire as the Dominion of Canada,
> the Commonwealth of Australia, the Dominion of New Zealand,
> the Union of South Africa and the Irish Free State, with a
> Parliament having powers to make laws for the peace, order and
> good government of India, and an executive responsible to that
> Parliament, and shall be styled and known as the Commonwealth
> of India.

It was, and was intended to be, an article which firmly associated responsible government with dominion status. Motilal Nehru did not regard dominion status as a final goal; he declared in favour of 'Complete Independence', but not against full dominion status 'as full as any dominion possesses it today'.[34] What mattered in other words for the Congress leadership was the conquest of power. It was by that criterion dominion status was to be judged, though Gandhi in greater depth thought of it not as a constitutional objective but rather as a frame of mind in which acceptance of equality was the essence.[35]

The viceroy's constitutional advisers observed that what had prompted an attitude of greater caution on the part of the British government was the fact that while the Indian demand for the same status as the dominions remained constant, this status changed and so altered the nature of the demand. Two particular developments were uppermost in mind, the first – the 1926 Balfour Report on Inter-Imperial Relations and the second the Indian claim that dominion status after that date carried with it the power to secede. But disturbing in some of its aspects though the prospect of dominion status in its redefined and developing manifestations might appear to the British *Raj* in Delhi, there were also counter-balancing and more reassuring considerations. There was the distinction which the Balfour Report had drawn between status and function which might, so it was suggested to the viceroy by his advisers, enable a relationship to be established between Britain and an Indian dominion which would concede equality of status but permit of a continuing functional inequality in its turn leaving open the way for a continuing British exercise of responsibility in special fields. More important still was the obverse of the Congress insistence upon dominion status as a necessary corollary of responsible self-government – namely British insistence upon responsible self-government as a necessary corollary and precondition of dominion status.

What had prompted the viceroy to make enquiries in the first instance were controversies stirred not by statements but by silence. The Simon Commission, highly sensitive as it showed itself to be to the manifold difficulties of adapting a system of responsible government to India, had avoided all reference to a dominion status goal in its Report. In the face of indignant Indian reaction at such omission, the Viceroy, Lord Irwin, decided that he should seek publicly to repair it.[36] On 31 October 1929 he did so saying that dominion status was implicit in the 1917 declaration on responsible government and that its attainment was therefore to be regarded as the natural issue of India's constitutional progress. But despite the criticisms that had prompted and the protests by diehards that followed upon the viceroy's essay in interpretation, was it tantamount to a new departure? Was it conceivable that a British government could have stood firm on the letter of responsible government and rejected dominion status as its natural sequel?

The memorandum the Home Department had submitted to the viceroy before his statement (and in response to his April enquiries), throws some light on the answers as seen by his advisers in Delhi. The argument of the memorandum was to the effect that in practical terms the significance of the distinction between responsible government and dominion status was of little importance. The relevant passage read as follows:

. . . are the implications of dominion status now so wide that the imperial government could not feel itself able honestly to assert that dominion status is the goal of its policy equally with responsible government? The answer might seem to be in the negative, since the implications of dominion status need to be considered conjointly with the implications of responsible government. In each case whether the goal of Parliament be responsible government or whether it be dominion status, the problem is essentially the same, namely the extent to which government in India can be released from external control. In neither case can the consummation of the policy be reached by a stroke of the pen. The reality of dominion status cannot be obtained until the goal of responsible government has first been reached. If we assume for the moment that the immense obstacles in the path of full responsible government have been successfully removed, that the entire executive and legislative authority in India has been made to accord with the will of Indian electorates, and that Parliament has ceased to be responsible even that there shall be a government in India, it would seem to follow that the imperial government, even if it so wished, might then be unable to deny to India a status equal to that of the other autonomous units of the Empire, which also reached dominion status through the same channel of responsible government. If there be anything in this argument, the difficulty of accepting dominion status as the goal of British policy may be little, if at all, greater than the difficulty involved when responsible government was adopted as the declared policy of Parliament; and the connection between the two may be found to be so intimate that the final consummation of full responsible government may automatically involve the realisation of dominion status.

In the 1930s the correctness of this analysis was underlined. The British government, assailed at every stage in the country and in the House of Commons by the diehards, proceeded by way of Round Table Conferences in London in 1930–1, through a Parliamentary Select Committee, to the Government of India Act 1935, condemned with Churchillian gusto as 'a monstrous monument of sham* built by the pygmies'. The advance was towards responsible government in British India, and an all-India federation comprising British India and the princely states with no suggestion that the coming into being of the federation should be conditional upon responsible or even representative government in the states.

The Government of India Act 1935, in all its length and complexity was a major state document. In the fullness of time it was to serve a larger purpose, as a means whereby a transfer of power might be effected with speed and in constitutional order. But in its immediate objectives it was only partially successful. It suffered from one considerable and one fundamental disadvantage. The Preamble, describing the Act as one 'to make further provision for the government of India' contained no reference to dominion status nor did the Act itself make any provision for its attainment. But the fundamental liability lay in the fact that the Bill was drafted and debated in London. The constitutions of other dominions had been home-made. Mahatma Gandhi was insistent that the constitution of a free India should follow that precedent. Since the Government of India Act did not do so, he had no use for it and declined, despite encouragement from Pandit Nehru, to read its provisions. In such circumstances it was not surprising that the Act failed to win the confidence or to appeal to the sentiments of nationalist leaders whether in the Congress or the League. It was in fact a highly conservative document. The federation of India which it contemplated was not to come into existence until two-thirds of the princes had agreed that it should do so, and then, if and when they had done so, the position of the princes was to be strongly entrenched within the federation. A calculation made for

---

* Churchill insisted that this and not 'shame' was the word he had used. The following exchange about it took place in the House on 11 February 1935:
Mr Foot: The Right Hon. Gentleman broadcast the other day, and he told the people of this country . . . that we had erected 'a monstrous monument of shame built by the pygmies'.
Mr Churchill: Not 'shame' but 'sham'.
Mr Foot: I was quoting from the *Listener*.
Mr Churchill: I am quoting from the speaker.

the viceroy in 1937 indicated that should the minimal number of princes accede there would be a Federal Lower House of 346 members and that on the basis of the provincial election returns, the Congress, despite its impressive showing in them, was not likely to secure more than a hundred seats in it. 'A Congress strength of 100 in a House of 346', commented the secretary of state on receiving this assessment, 'is not unduly alarming . . .'.[37] As objectionable to Congress sentiment as the electoral system with its inbuilt checks and balances, was the extent and range of the reserve powers vested in the viceroy and the provincial governors. Nor were they alone in this. Jinnah spoke of the Act as consisting of 98 per cent safeguards.

The federal provisions of the 1935 Act never came into force, because a sufficient number of the princes did not accede to the proposed federation. They received tentative, intermittent encouragement to do so from a viceroy who had received no directive from the secretary of state to give it – a fact which has cast renewed doubt upon the authenticity of the government's proclaimed purpose of bringing into existence an Indianised centre. Provincial elections under the Act were, however, held in 1937. They demonstrated the formidable organisation and popular backing for the Congress and were followed, after protracted exchanges between the Congress leaders and the viceroy about the exercise of the governors' reserve powers, by the formation of Congress ministries in the Congress-majority provinces. Jawaharlal Nehru, so his biographer tells us, while viewing acceptance of office as primarily a means of fighting against the imposition of federation, was fearful lest the Congress as a result would become involved in 'petty, reformist activities' and emerge a 'responsivist, constitutional organisation'. He 'hated it all'.[38] None the less with the formation of provincial governments a new page in Indian history had opened. Its dominant feature was constitutional advance in the provinces: constitutional stagnation at the centre. That boded well for the future of parliamentary government by bringing it close to the immediate interests of the people: ill for unity, by strengthening the provinces against the centre.[39]

In terms of responsible government, dominion status and partition, the decade 1937–47 had a unity of its own. At its opening the British government had conceded an extension of the area of responsible government while reserving their position on dominion status and reposing their faith in federation; the Congress and the League were preparing efficiently in the first case, inefficiently in the second[40] to exploit the political possibilities of mass electorates; and the Congress made ready to repudiate the dominion status-Commonwealth goal in favour of *Purna Swaraj*, or complete independence. At the close of the decade responsible government was a. reality; federation had died without ever coming to life and India was divided, no longer between British India and the Indian states but between Pakistan and Hindustan; and dominion status, mistrusted by more conservative British opinion because of its capacity for development and by the Indian National Congress – which over the years had paid too much attention to the weighty volumes in which Professor A. B. Keith with unrivalled learning expounded the still continuing inequalities in the status of the dominions[41] and too little to what Mackenzie King was actually doing – because it was thought to fall too far short of independence, came into its own at last as the one means by which power might be effectively and speedily transferred. Upon the principal participants there was thus exerted at a time of imperial retreat, domestic division and national revolution, the pull of Commonwealth experience with a persistence that few of them recognised and posterity is unlikely to credit.

3 Appeasement and War: the Commonwealth Rôle

We accepted in this motherland [Winston Churchill told the House of Commons in the debate on the Statute of Westminster in November 1931] the view of those who wish to state the imperial obligation and imperial ties at their minimum; we abandoned the whole apparatus of sovereignty and constitutional law to which our ancestors, and even the later Victorians, had attached the greatest importance. Remembering that, and remembering the atmosphere of those days, not long gone, and the spirit of those days, I cannot think that we were wrong, and I do not think that we are wrong now. I feel that we are bound, where the great self-governing dominions of the Crown are concerned, boldly to grasp the larger hope . . . [1]

In isolation these words might suggest that on the British side the whole process of redefinition had been an act of faith. Faith there was certainly and it was the more easily sustained in years when the prospect of world war appeared remote or, to the more ardent believers in the League, nonexistent. It was powerfully reinforced by an idealised concept of Commonwealth, to which much contemporary writing, not least Lionel Curtis's *Civitas Dei*, bears heady witness, as well as by cooler appraisal which saw in the new relationship an escape from imperialism by way of an experiment in free and equal association between nations. Did not this last, alone, provide sufficient cause to proceed with magnanimity, courage and vision?

Had there been some practicable alternative to Commonwealth, in the form of imperial federation or other centralising system, there might have been no very assured British, as distinct from dominion, answer.

I had misgivings [said Churchill speaking of 1926] that we were needlessly obliterating old, famous landmarks and signposts, which although archaic, have a historic importance and value. I remember that that great statesman, the late Lord Balfour, with whom I talked this matter over very often, answered me, and to some extent reassured me, by saying, 'I do not believe in wooden guns.' I thought that a very pregnant remark. He saw no advantage in preserving an assertion of rights and powers on which, in practice, we should not find it possible effectively to base ourselves. I still repose faith in the calm, lambent wisdom of that great man in his later years.[2]

But had the guns not been wooden, Churchill might well not have been so easily reconciled. Those who thought of the twentieth century as the age of democratic progress and of the common man in all his natural goodness regarded the dismantling of Empire with facile optimism, while those who feared the century was likely to be dominated by wars on the greatest scale were troubled about the looseness of Commonwealth ties and the consequent undermining, as it seemed to them, of British power. Governments, and especially British governments, in the 1930s were compelled by unfolding dangers to ask themselves, and others, what dominion status, as redefined between 1926 and 1931, implied in terms of the Commonwealth willingness and capacity to wage war. The framers of the Balfour Report had expressed their belief that no common cause would suffer as a result of the full autonomy of the dominions in external as in domestic affairs. In the 1930s that conviction was put to an earlier and more severe test than they can have foreseen.

As the threat of war re-emerged, certain fundamental considerations about the rôle of the dominions were bound to occupy the mind of any British government. Dominion advances in status in the 1920s and early 1930s, while not the by-product of a sense of security, were more widely and more readily acceptable in many circles because of the supposed safeguard against war offered by the League of Nations. Once that safeguard began to appear inadequate, official (and unofficial) opinion in London began to realise for the first time the new element of uncertainty in British planning and thinking introduced by separate dominion responsibility in external policy. This realisation was accompanied by a new appreciation of the variety of dominion interests and of the factors that were likely to influence their policies. Canadian preoccupation with national unity; South Africa's concern to keep European warfare out of the continent of Africa; Australia's anxieties about a two-ocean war and sense of exposure to attacks from her near-

north; Irish resentment at continued British occupation of the
Treaty ports, not merely on the grounds of infringement of
national sovereignty but as a limitation in practice upon Irish
freedom of action – all of these were factors to be taken into
account. It was not enough for the government of the United
Kingdom to seek in general terms, and as a United Kingdom
interest, to give substance and effective being to the new concept of
equal dominion partnership within a Commonwealth of Nations,
but it had further to reckon with the fact that henceforward unity
of Commonwealth policies, even in face of grave dangers, could no
longer be assumed but had in each instance patiently to be worked
for. There were questions of critical importance to be asked. Under
what circumstances could the United Kingdom count on dominion, or majority dominion, backing in war? Was it, to be more
specific, certain that the dominions would fight in a war for the
enforcement of the authority of the League of Nations, or in a war
for the maintenance of the peace treaties which so many of their
leaders had condemned and continued to denounce, or in a war for
the safety and survival of the Empire? These were questions the
answers to which were open, or partially open, in the early 1930s
and they were only to be made explicit by a process of actual
confrontation. Later commentators, so mindful of pre-war errors
in judgment, are apt to overlook the questions and consequently to
ignore the achievement. A substantially united Commonwealth
entered the war in 1939 and emerged victorious from it in 1945.

The testing phase for the Commonwealth internationally
opened in 1931, the year of the Japanese attack upon Manchuria.
The moment for the attack was well chosen. There was confusion
and disorder in China and preoccupation with the application of
near-desperate remedies to prop up collapsing markets in the
British Commonwealth and the United States. Of the dominions,
Australia and New Zealand were regionally the most concerned.
Other countries, far from the Pacific, thought the time had come to
enforce the authority of the League, but even after Japanese naval
action against Shanghai, the attitude of the Australian government
remained reserved. Public opinion was said to regard military
action as 'unthinkable' and the Australian government, mindful of
the 'vulnerability of our empty north' and Australia's almost
exclusive reliance on the Royal Navy, waited on Britain and on the
United States. In Canada, also, caution was the keynote. The
government was prepared to accept the conclusions of the League
but felt that it was not for a small power to give strong, positive
direction. In the debate at Geneva on the Lytton Report on events

in Manchuria, the Canadian delegate, owing to the absence of adequate instructions from home, was said (it may be thought with commendable prudence in the light of a later incident) to have spoken 'strongly on both sides of the question'. South Africa and the Irish Free State were more forthcoming. But they were also further away. In sum, the outcome of the Manchurian incident served to underline the difficulty of concerted action in the far east without active United States participation, and to drive home the lesson that the writ of a non-universal League could not, and did not, run in the Pacific. What of the Mediterranean?

In September, 1935, Mussolini resolved to invade Abyssinia 'with Geneva, without Geneva or against Geneva'. This time there was no occasion for procrastinating enquiry into what had taken place. On 7 October 1935 Italy was branded as an aggressor by the League of Nations. All the dominions endorsed the declaration. It was shortly followed by a speech at Geneva by the British foreign secretary, Sir Samuel Hoare, indicating in forthright terms British support for the League and for sanctions. How far were the dominions themselves prepared to go? The autumn election in Canada returned Mackenzie King to office. His government issued a statement saying that the absence of three of the Great Powers from the League, its failure to secure disarmament and the unwillingness of members to enforce sanctions in the case of countries distant from Europe had increased the difficulty of assuming obligations in advance. Canada accordingly 'did not recognise any commitment to adopt military sanctions and only Parliament could decide upon them'. On 2 November 1935 the Canadian delegate, Walter Riddell, misinterpreting his inadequate instructions and carried away by his own zeal, proposed the addition of sanctions on petroleum, coal and iron and steel against Italy. In Rome these sanctions were branded as 'the Canadian proposals'. In Ottawa Mackenzie King read his Monday morning newspaper 'with amazement' while in Quebec the reaction was sharp and unfavourable. In due course Riddell was disowned in a statement issued by Ernest Lapointe, the minister of justice, the leading French–Canadian member in the cabinet and Mackenzie King's life-long political ally, while the Canadian prime minister was away in Washington.[3] Canadian repudiation did not imply opposition to sanctions of this kind but that Canada did not wish to take the initiative. 'It was only from the fame of leadership that the government backed with such rapid steps' a Canadian diplomatic historian has written.[4] But Mackenzie King had been genuinely alarmed. 'What a calamitous act was that of Riddell's at Geneva!' he wrote to Vincent Massey. 'Had we not made clear that it was Riddell speaking for himself . . . Canada might for all time have come to be credited with having set Europe aflame . . .'[5] Later he went so far as to tell the House of Commons that but for his rapid retreat from the Canadian delegate's imprudent initiative, 'the whole of Europe might have been aflame today'.[6] The lesson drawn in Ottawa was that of the need for cautious reserve as dangers in Europe and the far east intensified.

In Canberra reservations were more precise and particular. They were that enforcement of sanctions would lead to naval warfare in the Mediterranean, which in turn, by reason of the heavy commitment of the Royal Navy, would leave Australia dangerously exposed to attack from Japan. These were not passing but continuing fears and as the Australian records amply confirm,[7] Australian governments were consistently in favour of negotiations and, if necessary, appeasement of Italy to avert any such eventuality right down to Italy's entry into the war in 1940. But it was the events of 1935–6 that led to their first forthright formulation.

Likewise South African policy was firmly grounded upon South African interests. Chief among them was avoidance of war in Africa. That meant strong support for League action. At Geneva the Union's eloquent spokesman, C. te Water, spoke of the danger to the adventuring nations of the black peoples of Africa, who never forgave and never forgot an injury, and to 'our own white civilisation' through the attempted advancement of European ambitions in Africa by force. The New Zealand Labour government also and zealously supported the League and sanctions. Its ideal was social security within and international security overseas. In the Irish Free State the imposition of sanctions against Italy was materially of no importance but psychologically of controversial moment because sanctions, even if only nominal in their effect, by a Catholic country against the homeland of the Papacy, disturbed the minds of many of its people. Nor was the fact that their imposition meant close cooperation with Britain at Geneva calculated to afford psychological compensation. On the contrary, stung by opposition taunts on this score, de Valera was moved to retort: 'If your worst enemy is going to heaven the same way as you are, you don't for that reason turn around and go in the opposite direction.' But it was also apparent that, short of the negotiation of a defence agreement on the basis of the ending of partition, not then quite so remote a possibility as it later became, any such Anglo–Irish co-operation in international affairs was possible only under the umbrella of the League. The cover it could offer never looked reassuring again after December 1935 when the British stand for sanctions collapsed amid the indignities of the Hoare-Laval Pact. At one blow, faith in Great Power leadership and in the League itself was gravely undermined. 'Where are the Great Powers leading us, who have not the faith to persevere?' enquired te Water, when later sanctions were lifted.[8] Others asked the same question and received no reassuring answer.

The interaction of Anglo–dominion policies in the Abyssinian crisis allow of no large conclusions. British policies followed a course that was not easy to comprehend, let alone to predict, whereas for dominion governments they were lacking the resources and, in some instances, the experience with which to formulate policies that might be at once realistically and consistently applied. Much was said at meetings of dominion High Commissioners with the Secretary of State for Dominion Affairs, which were initiated at this time, but a good deal of it reflected the views of individual High Commissioners as well as or as much as, those of their governments. To quote the Irish High Commissioner, Mr Dulanty, as though he were at all times voicing the views of Mr de Valera, is manifestly misconceived. And much the same would have applied to Vincent Massey and Mackenzie King, had not King discouraged Vincent Massey's attendance. The meetings, moreover, were for exchanges of view not statements of policy, which ordinarily would be conveyed in an official communication. It has indeed been inferred from detailed analysis of Anglo–dominion exchanges during the crisis that 'no British government was prepared in any matter affecting its own assessment of its vital interests to defer in the least to the views of dominion governments'. But since the dominions were themselves much divided in their attitudes in the unfolding crisis, all it could reasonably be deemed to demonstrate was that the British government was unlikely to heed dominion views when they were themselves divergent.[9] The reactions of the dominions to the failure of the League in Abyssinia were, broadly speaking, twofold – greater reliance on imperial defence, coupled with a policy of appeasement. In the circumstances both were prudent, even if the second was not heroic. Without a League resolutely supported by the majority of Great Powers there was a risk that attempts on the part of the British Commonwealth alone or in association with France to maintain peace on the basis of the European *status quo* might overtax their combined resources or fail to enlist their combined effort. The first counselled a realistic assessment of war potential, the second a restrained approach, especially where the aggression was in some way qualified or capable of an exculpatory, as well as a censorious, interpretation.

The first (and, as it subsequently came to be regarded, the critical) step in the Nazi career of aggression, the militarisation of the Rhineland in March 1936, elicited no forthright condemnation from Britain or from the dominions, partly because it was susceptible of just such varying interpretations. Their governments did not support the French, still less the Polish view, that this open defiance of the Versailles Treaty and of the freely-negotiated Locarno Pact should be resisted by force. Lord Halifax later recalled defensively, but correctly, that 'there was no section of British public opinion that would not have been directly opposed to such action in 1936. To go to war with Germany for walking into their own backyard . . . at a time moreover when you were actually discussing with them the dates and conditions of their right to resume occupation, was not the sort of thing people could understand'.[10] This incomprehension would have been enhanced in Britain because of the views widely entertained that the Treaty of Versailles was in many of its provisions illiberal, even vindictive, whilst in the Commonwealth overseas and notably in South Africa, many judged it iniquitous. Indeed for that very reason the South African government, mindful of the 'unequal terms' of the Treaty of Versailles, asked their High Commissioner to inform the British government of 'the most serious consequences of any participation in a war [on the Rhineland issue] . . . which . . . the Union Government could not but condemn in the strongest manner and from which it would feel compelled to withhold its support'.[11] More generally, if such action were not going to be understood and supported in Britain with its direct interest and formal obligations, what hope was there of its being understood in distant dominions? General Smuts, far from voicing criticism of Britain's inaction, expressed unqualified appreciation of Britain's restraint. 'We are tremendously proud', he said,[12] 'of the way she has stood in the breach.' The tribute was perhaps the more appreciated because totally unmerited, the one thing that the British government had declined to do being to stand 'in the breach' with its French ally. But that was as the dominions desired.

Mackenzie King drew a more far-reaching conclusion, noting in his Diary in March 1936 that the Ethiopian and Rhineland crises had made it 'apparent to all that Europe is becoming a maelstrom of strife, and that we are being drawn into a situation that is none of our creation by membership in the League of Nations'.[13]

In the shaping of the Commonwealth policies between 1936 and the outbreak of war there were three landmarks. The first was the Imperial Conference 1937, the second the Czech crisis of September 1938 and the third the Anglo–French guarantee to Poland in March 1939. The Imperial Conference meeting in late May-early June 1937, devoted seven sessions to the discussion of foreign affairs. The principal preoccupation of delegations was the formulation of their respective responses to the failure of the League and, arising from it, of their attitudes henceforward to collective security. Fear of being committed by obligation to an ineffective and discredited international organisation was predominant. The covenant, argued Hertzog, had been dealt so heavy a blow that the sanctions provisions (Articles 10 and 16) – which anyway had come to be regarded as part of the Treaty of Versailles and as a means by which those who wanted to keep what they had got might be enabled to do so – would have to be looked upon as non-existent. The League itself, he proceeded, would have to be reduced to something that corresponded with the realities of the situation, namely to a moral force rather than one to be relied upon by small countries in the case of aggression, because any such reliance would be 'like relying on a piece of wood which had already proved rotten and which broke every time a strain fell on it'. Chamberlain and, in view of his conclusions on the Rhineland crisis, it need hardly be said, Mackenzie King, warmly concurred. It was impossible, argued King, to restore Abyssinia or redress the wrong that had been committed and any further attempts to do so might hasten the risk of a conflagration in Europe. It was necessary to avoid such a calamity. Nor with the substance of the League's authority gone, could King see any merit in clinging to the form. It would serve only to enhance the risk that Canada might become embroiled in a League war. 'In Canada', he told his colleagues, 'the people had been much disillusioned by what happened at the League. In Canada the people were saying that membership of the League constituted a real risk of their becoming involved in war'. For his part 'he did not want to base Canadian policy on the League of Nations. If the covenant remained as at present, that meant supporting collective security which he did not believe in'. He was prepared to base Canadian policies on the ideals but not on the principles of the League. Hertzog specifically agreed, while Bruce speaking for the Australian government, in reaching the same conclusion, commented that experience 'had shown that the failure of the League to realise universality had completely altered the position ... particularly in regard to the employment of sanctions ... in a League which was not universal the application against a powerful aggressor of force of any kind had been shown to be in fact impracticable'.[14] Most of all his words reflected Australia's now constant concern lest the Japanese situation should be reopened. Only New Zealand challenged these general assumptions, Savage declaring that he could not subscribe to anything which had the appearance of destroying the League of Nations. As long as the gun was unloaded, he said with the Canadian delegation clearly in view, there were those who were willing 'to support the League but the moment the gun was loaded they would not have anything to do with it'. The majority of the delegations, however, were not to be moved, Hertzog observing that 'it was surely very illogical to want to give to an institution which had failed satisfactorily to make use of much smaller powers, the greater powers' which Savage contemplated[15], while in the closing stages of the Conference Mackenzie King showed himself furthermore concerned about possible commitments to the Empire over and above the League. In Canada, he said, there was 'a great dread lest the country should be committed at the Imperial Conference to some obligation arising out of the European situation'. It must accordingly be made clear that the Conference was not laying down a policy, only reflecting a consensus of opinion with the right of individual parliaments to decide fully recognised.[16]

The published Report of the Conference reflected the balance of opinion, as expressed in these private exchanges of view, and duly underlined the predominant dominion desire for dissociation from European problems and freedom from European commitments. New Zealand's unsupported advocacy of continued and unqualified support for the League was consigned to a footnote – for which the chief credit, or otherwise, goes to Mackenzie King[17] though the Australians, particularly Bruce, were pleased to have it so – while the consensus of remaining opinion was expressed in non-committal phrases about the basing of policies on the aims and ideas of the League. Resolved at all costs that their countries should not enter into nor accept obligations to a moribund institution, British and dominion representatives expressed their faith in the settlement of differences 'by methods of co-operation, joint enquiry and conciliation'. They declined to be drawn into ideological divisions and, while themselves firmly attached to the principles of democracy, registered their view that differences between political creeds should be no obstacle to friendly relations. Behind the easy, complacent phrases, it is true, there were certainly misgivings. But the hopes of the great majority of the Commonwealth leaders, whether from the United Kingdom or the dominions, were in 'international appeasement' both in political relations and in trade. The aim of the Conference was best summed up by General Hertzog, who concluded that 'in the attainment of this high object of world appeasement ... the mission of the Commonwealth stands clearly defined'.

One thing at least was made clear beyond all question by the Imperial Conference, namely, that a united Commonwealth would not fight or run the risk of being involved in a war to uphold or enforce the authority of the League of Nations. By 1937, in other words, collective security on a League basis was a non-starter in the Commonwealth. That narrowed the field and it became at once more important, and more difficult, for Great Britain to ensure that the conditions of dominion cooperation in wartime were fulfilled. What were they? They were summed up in the word 'appeasement' which the Imperial Conference had accepted as describing the approach which offered the best chance of preserving world peace. The conclusion (except for New Zealand) was common but it derived from varied premises. This is frequently overlooked. Even in foreign policy the overseas dominions were thought of at the time, and apt to be written of later, as a category or species of state with shared outlook and shared interests. This was far from being the case, as may best be indicated by a brief recapitulation of dominion preoccupations.

In 1931–2 Australia had reason to recognise that the writ of the League did not run in the Pacific and it caused little surprise in Australia when some three years later it was found not to run in the Mediterranean either. There were then Australian fears lest a head-on clash between the Royal Navy and the Italian Navy, might so damage the Royal Navy as, among other things, to alter the balance of power in the Pacific. In the Abyssinian crisis, noted a contemporary,[18] for the first time the faith of the Australian public in British naval supremacy was severely shaken. When Italy's adventure in East Africa was followed within a year by German reoccupation of the Rhineland, the vulnerability of Australia, should Britain be heavily engaged in the west, was further brought home. The Australian government's reaction militarily was to increase defence expenditure, with the Labour opposition demanding first priority for air defence, and diplomatically, so far as lay within Australia's influence, to limit the geographical extent of war. With these aims and considerations in mind the Australian government would seem never to have entertained misgivings about the wisdom of seeking to appease Italy and detaching her from Germany. At all costs, in their view, must the Mediterranean lifeline be kept open. Nor did the Australian government favour an agreement with the Soviet Union, because Japanese membership of the anti-Comintern pact meant that Russian participation in war was likely to extend that war to the Pacific. Towards Japan, Australian policy was variable, but in the last years of peace it moved perceptibly towards appeasement, as evidenced by the export to Japan of scrap metal from Port Kembla. Towards Germany, however, Australia's attitude was more robust and there was no doubt at any time of Australia's solidarity with Britain in the event of her being forced into war by the European dictators. It was war in two hemispheres that was the Australian nightmare – and not without reason.

In Canada, Mackenzie King walked delicately. After the Imperial Conference he visited Berlin and gave to Hitler (who appears to have listened courteously though he may not have been greatly interested) a lucid résumé of recent developments in Commonwealth relations. He delivered, to judge by his own record, which alone would seem to have survived,[19] a warning that if the time

> ever came when any part of the Empire felt that the freedom which we all enjoyed was being impaired through any act of aggression on the part of a foreign country, it would be seen that all would join together to protect the freedom which we were determined should not be imperilled.

And while, like many visitors to the German chancellor at that time, King concluded that Hitler was at once patriotic and essentially pacific,[20] he grasped that expansion of some sort in eastern Europe was in Hitler's mind. At home the Canadian government strengthened national defences, while the prime minister continued to emphasise that Canada was not committed to any particular course of action. Only Parliament could decide what Canada would do in the event of a world war. This dismayed the protagonists of Empire, the protagonists of the League and the protagonists of Canadian neutrality. Against each in turn he deployed the same argument. He could not commit Canada to a war in which the Empire was engaged, or to a war sanctioned by the League, or to neutrality, because each and all would deprive Parliament of its rightful freedom of choice. His policy was directed towards two ends – preservation of Canadian unity and the strengthening of ties with the United States. The second was notably advanced when on 18 August 1938, President Roosevelt visited Canada and said at Kingston: 'The Dominion of Canada is part of the sisterhood of the British Empire. I give to you assurance that the people of the United States will not stand idly by if domination of Canadian soil is threatened by any other Empire.'[21] Both considerations – of national unity and closer association with a still isolationist United States – led Mackenzie King to detach Canada more and more from day-to-day issues in Europe, and both seemingly served to strengthen the argument in favour of appeasement. Before Canada went to war King felt he had to convince all Canadians from Quebec to Vancouver that there was no honourable alternative. He even hoped that with time he might be in a position to persuade the United States likewise.

Unity, unattainable but long sought, was also the goal in the Union of South Africa. The Fusion government, with Hertzog as prime minister and Smuts as deputy prime minister, was founded upon an agreement to differ on controversial and still unresolved politico-constitutional questions, notably secession and neutrality. In foreign policy, the Fusion government could remain united only in inaction once the unifying bond of the League was fraying. The formula was 'South Africa first'; the test, how it was to be interpreted. General Hertzog attributed most of the evils of the time to the iniquitous Treaty of Versailles – the 'monster treaty' which, in his view, had murdered its own offspring, the League, and which by provoking German attempts to remedy the injustices it had inflicted upon them, was the main cause of the threat to European peace. The next war, he prophesied, not once but many times, would be 'the child of Versailles'. Responsibility for Hitler's aggressive actions was to be attributed not so much to Hitler as to the peace treaties and the actions of the victorious allies, who had been responsible for imposing them in 1919 and upholding them since. 'If war did come because England continued to associate with France', he said at the Imperial Conference in 1937,[22] 'in a policy in respect of central and eastern Europe calculated to threaten Germany's existence through unwillingness to set right the injustices from the Treaty of Versailles, South Africa cannot be expected to take part in the war ...' Smuts was in no strong position, even if he had so wished, to dissent from his prime minister's general opinion for had he not himself protested at the time and subsequently at the vindictiveness of some of the provisions of the Versailles Treaty? More positively it is clear that he agreed with Hertzog on the more particular point that South African interests did not demand South African participation in a war to defend the post-war territorial settlement in eastern Europe. Where he differed was in thinking and later in saying, that if

England were attacked or threatened South Africa would fight. In the actual circumstances of the time, the survival of the Fusion experiment thus became conditional upon either a policy of appeasement or, in the event of war, upon a *casus belli* which Hertzog and Smuts were agreed in regarding either as involving or not involving South African interests.

As the Czech crisis loomed in the spring and summer of 1938, the British government were made aware that the three larger dominions favoured a policy of appeasement, that the Irish Free State was edging towards neutrality and that by the New Zealand government alone was the wisdom of concession likely to be seriously questioned.

In May 1938 while Smuts sought for some encouragement in Chamberlain's despatch of the improbable person of Walter Runciman, President of the Board of Trade, on a peace mission to Prague in the reflection that 'the Lord sometimes uses indifferent instruments to show His power',[23] Mackenzie King, who was at his most uncommunicative for most of the Czech crisis, hoped that the Czechs would yield to Hitler's demands, because he believed, almost certainly correctly, that the alternative was a war in which Canada would do, and he thought should do, 'all she possibly could to destroy those Powers which are basing their action on *might* and not on *right*',[24] despite the price of war on such an issue in terms of Canadian unity, about which he had the gloomiest of forebodings.

On 25 May at a meeting of the Dominion High Commissioners, other than the Canadian, absent at his Prime Minister's behest, but reinforced in respect of Australia by two Ministers, Sir Earle Page and Robert Menzies, who were in London to discuss revision of the Ottawa Agreements, the views of the other dominions were restated on lines that were already and were soon to become more familiar, in response to the Foreign Secretary, Lord Halifax's assessment of the crisis as seen from London. There was the South African preoccupation with Versailles – in the view of the Union Government, so Mr te Water reported, the separation of the Sudeten Germans from Germany was one of many blots on the Treaty, and 'an indefensible one', and it was the firm conviction of the South African Minister in Berlin that 'Germany would never stop until the Sudeten Germans had been absorbed into the Reich'. Sir Earle Page indicated that the Australian government desired 'a politically satisfied Germany which would be ready to take her share in the peaceful development of the World. 'Would', he enquired, 'the German Government be satisfied if they got the Sudeten Germans, and if they would be satisfied, would it not be

wise to give the Sudeten Germans to them?' Lord Halifax indicated
there were other German objectives, including Dantzig and the
former German colonies. Menzies wondered if Germany would
even stop short of the rest of Czechoslovakia, but Page was
supported by te Water – 'Germany', he said, 'must be satisfied before
there could be any real détente in international relations.' When
asked by Bruce what exactly was the Union Government's view he
replied that 'if war broke out and first France and then the United
Kingdom was involved over Czechoslovakia it was very doubtful if
the Union would come in'.[25]

In August, the Australian Attorney General, R. G. Menzies
following in the footsteps of Mackenzie King to Berlin, commented
to his Prime Minister upon the very high reputation Chamberlain
and Halifax enjoyed there, upon the qualities of the British
Ambassador, Sir Nevile Henderson, 'an extremely clear-headed
and sensible fellow', came to the conclusion that the actual
absorption of the Sudeten into the German Reich is not in the
immediate programme and was 'more than ever impressed with the
view that this problem requires a very firm hand in Prague,
otherwise Benes will continue to bluff at the expense of much more
important nations, including our own'.[26] On 31 August the Acting
British High Commissioner, Percivale Liesching, reported that the
Australian Prime Minister, J. A. Lyons was 'conscious that a war
involving Great Britain will, in fact, see the Commonwealth
committed to active participation, but is more anxious that the
views of this Government should be made clear and that His
Majesty's Government in the United Kingdom should not overestimate the ultimate moral support obtainable here in a conflict over
the Czechoslovakian issue'. On 2 September Lyons cabled Chamberlain that the Australian Government viewed 'with regret and
alarm' President Benes' delay in making a public announcement of
the 'most liberal concessions' he can offer to the Sudeten Germans,
while on 14 September Liesching was reporting after a meeting
with Lyons that he was satisfied that the Commonwealth Government 'remain strongly of the opinion that almost any alternative is
preferable to involvement in war with Germany in the event of the
latter forcibly intervening in Czechoslovakia'.[27] This, as may be
seen from the Australian records, was a just appreciation of
Australian views.

Meanwhile in London the dominion high commissioners, Vincent Massey (Canada), Stanley Bruce (Australia), te Water (South
Africa), J. W. Dulanty (Irish Free State) – New Zealand's representative W. J. Jordan remained throughout in Geneva – individually

or collectively pressed their point of view upon the secretary of
state for the dominions affairs, Malcolm MacDonald, upon the
foreign secretary, upon the prime minister himself when opportunity offered, and by no means least upon the editor of *The Times*,
Geoffrey Dawson. A few extracts from the entries in the diary of
the Canadian high commissioner, Vincent Massey,[28] suffice to
indicate dominion feelings in the interval between Neville Chamberlain's second visit to Hitler at Godesberg on 22–3 September
when, in his words to the House of Commons, he 'bitterly
reproached the chancellor for his failure to respond in any way to
the efforts which had been made to secure peace', and Munich –
the period, that is to say when it seemed that even Chamberlain's
patience might also be exhausted.

September 24th. A meeting with the H.C.'s and Malcolm
MacDonald at the Col. Office. All four of the H.C.'s (Jordan of
N.Z. is at Geneva) take a view on the basic issue rather different
from MacDonald's emphasis. We are all prepared to pay a higher
price for peace than he. The difference is because the dominions
are removed further away from Europe, not because our sense
of honour is less acute. Bruce . . . feels very strongly that the
German proposals can't be allowed to be a *casus belli* and says so
on behalf of his Govt. Te Water and Dulanty speak with great
vehemence as well . . .

September 25th. Greatly perturbed at the mood of the
morning papers on the crisis. Extreme condemnation of German
proposals given to Chamberlain. . . . Little or no appeal to calm
judgment . . . I had an hour's talk with Geoffrey Dawson at his
house and he and I agreed that something must be done. I
suggested that he see Halifax and also get Bruce who having
been prime minister had special influence among the H.C.'s in
such matters – to do all he could . . . Bruce delivered to Chamberlain a helpful message on behalf of his government – which is
a record. I wish mine would act!

September 26th. 10.30 meeting of H.C.'s with MacD. at the
Col. Office. Things look worse and worse. All four H.C.'s – N.Z.
is still absent – feel that the German proposals should not be
allowed to wreck peace . . .

September 27th . . . A talk with Te Water at my house in
evening – then a H.C.'s meeting at Dom. Office with Malcolm
MacD. – then after the officials had retired we talked until 2 a.m.
on the general subj. of dominion opinion on the present issue.
We all made it clear for ourselves (and some spoke for their

governments) that there might be a dangerous reaction in the dominions to a decision to plunge the Empire into war on the issue of how Hitler was to take possession of territory already ceded to him in principle ... surely the world can't be plunged into the horrors of universal war for a difference of opinion over a few miles of territory or a few days one way or the other in a time-table! That thank God is I believe Chamberlain's view and that of his cabinet ...

It was indeed. In view of the strong official and personal pressures from the dominions in favour of the appeasement of Hitler in the Czech crisis of September 1938, and the generally enthusiastic dominion response to the Agreement, it has been alleged that the dominions had a direct responsibility for Munich. But this is not substantiated by the records. It is true that the dominion governments both wanted and welcomed the avoidance of war on the Sudeten question at almost any price. When the Australian government was challenged in the House of Representatives with having done nothing effective, Menzies replied: 'We kept in touch with the British prime minister. We said: "This is a great work you are doing ... We are completely behind what you are doing to avoid war." '[29] But it was Chamberlain who was doing the work, the Australian and other dominion governments who were behind him. It could hardly have been otherwise. None of the dominions had either treaty obligations or commitments in Europe. Had the British government contemplated a course other than the appeasement of Hitler at this time, then indeed they would have met with strong dominion representations and would thereafter have had to face the prospect of a war with a divided Commonwealth. Ireland would have been neutral and South Africa non-belligerent, since Smuts and Hertzog had signed a secret compact, the existence of which was not known to the British High Commissioner, Sir William Clark, early in September 1938, agreeing that in the event of war South Africa's interests demanded non-belligerency.*

---

*Controversy later arose as to whether the agreement related specifically to the 1938 Czech crisis, or applied generally and without time limit to a war arising in Eastern Europe. Smuts sought to sustain the limited, Hertzog the broad interpretation. The text of the compact was consistent with the latter but, as the sequel made clear, the issue at stake was not a matter of consideration at the time, no doubt because of the differences it would have brought to the surface. There is, curiously enough, nothing in the published *Smuts Papers* on this: on the contrary a gap of several weeks.

For Smuts this would not have been a welcome conclusion and his enthusiasm on 30 September for Chamberlain – 'a great champion has appeared in the lists, God bless him' – reflected his relief at escape from a painful predicament. There would have been New Zealand, Australian and Canadian cooperation, but in the case of Australia and Canada there would have been, at the very least, strong minority reservations about the *casus belli.* 'The probability of having to meet Parliament with Europe at war was a nightmare', Mackenzie King told Malcolm MacDonald on 1 October 1938, but he was prepared to advocate Canadian participation. Had the British government, therefore, contemplated resolute rejection of Hitler's demands and had that policy led to war, then they would have been confronted with the failure of their long-term aim to preserve substantial Commonwealth unity. This the Munich settlement averted. If war came later and after the western powers had made sacrifices even if principally at the expense of another, in the interests of peace, then, as J. A. Lyons, the prime minister of Australia, said 'at least our hands are clean'. The phrase in the circumstances has its irony. But 'clean hands', meaning hands free from the stain of responsibility for starting a war, were, it is not to be doubted, a condition of Commonwealth unity in war. Had the Czechs at all times stood firm on principle and declared that they would rather go down fighting than discuss with allies or enemies the unity and integrity of their country, then other aspects of the situation would have been driven home and nationalist opinion in the Commonwealth been shaken in some of its preconceptions. But there was little evidence of such a hard, uncompromising stand.

British apologists for Munich and especially members of Chamberlain's cabinet have in their memoirs attached importance to the influence of the dominions on British policy at that time.[30] Dominion pressures, Lord Templewood (Sir Samuel Hoare) recalled later, were a major consideration in the shaping of United Kingdom policy and he noted that had war come in September 1938 'we should have started with a broken Commonwealth front'. The critics of Munich, complained Lord Halifax, either 'did not know or greatly care that there was grave doubt whether the Commonwealth would be at one in supporting the United Kingdom in a policy of active intervention on behalf of Czechoslovakia in 1938 . . .'.[31] The first point, Lord Templewood's, was substantially true in the negative sense already indicated, namely of discouraging ideas of resolute resistance to Hitler's demands at the risk of war; the second, Lord Halifax's, erred if anything on the

side of understatement. There was more than doubt, there was
certainty that a united Commonwealth would not have entered a
war to preserve the integrity of Czechoslovakia. In general terms,
and well in advance of the Munich crisis, the more nationalist
dominions had made it clear that they would not consider a war to
uphold the territorial provisions of the Versailles Treaty in central
Europe justified and more particularly, at the 1937 Imperial
Conference, General Hertzog had indicated through his High
Commissioner and directly that he was not prepared to see South
Africa engaged in any war to preserve the territorial integrity of
Czechoslovakia. Emphasis was placed upon reports of Commonwealth concern lest Britain should accept commitments that might
involve the Empire in war by the British ambassador in Paris in
conversation with the French prime minister and foreign minister
on 20 July 1938, and account was also taken of dominion attitudes
in a memorandum expounding British policy which was handed to
the State Department in Washington on 7 September 1938 by the
British Chargé d'Affaires, who further commented that it was
'becoming clear that the dominions were isolationist and there
would be no sense in fighting a war which would break the British
Empire while trying to secure the safety of the United Kingdom'.[32]
This did not accurately reflect the position of the dominions but it
was correct as far as immediate prospects went. When it was
written, moreover, the British government were not aware of the
Hertzog-Smuts compact formally committing both leaders and
their principal lieutenants to a policy of non-belligerency for South
Africa in the event of war on the Sudeten issue.

Apart from discouragement of war on the Czech issue at the
official inter-governmental level, dominion official or unofficial
representatives sought to exercise and doubtless exercised at one
remove a seemingly significant but necessarily indeterminate
influence upon British public opinion. Two of the dominion high
commissioners, Vincent Massey of Canada and S. M. Bruce of
Australia, were in close touch with Geoffrey Dawson, the editor of
The Times, a paper which gave wide, but selective, coverage, to
dominion news and views. Dawson was also a member of the *Round
Table* and while the influence of the *Round Table* in Britain at this
time is not to be overestimated, nonetheless, supplied with material
by overseas groups, it reflected dominion opinion on foreign policy
more accurately and more fully than any other periodical, and both
editorially and regionally strongly supported appeasement. Yet it is
a long step from saying that, officially or unofficially, the dominions influenced or urged Britain to pursue a policy of appease-

ment, to stating that they were responsible for it. In order to demonstrate this it would need to be shown (as D. C. Watt who has explored this theme allows) that Neville Chamberlain at the formative stage of a policy which he made peculiarly his own was moved to adopt it in response to dominion pressures. No sufficient evidence has been adduced to show that this was so. The Commonwealth, however, was widely deemed a vital British interest and it is an illusion to suppose that it was so regarded only by appeasers. 'On the whole', wrote Amery to Smuts on 18 March 1938, 'I believe the policy of saying "Halt" to Germany now is ... the more likely to avert war. But I should greatly hesitate before committing myself to a policy disapproved of by the other Governments of the Empire.' In September appeasement ensured Commonwealth unity: resistance did not. Had the British Cabinet contemplated the latter course the prospect of consequent dominion disunity would inevitably have become a major factor; as it was it remained no more than a contingency.

On the larger issues of dominion policies in the Munich crisis it is worth noting that the range of options open to their governments was narrower than is often credited. Dominion governments were not asked as were the false prophets of Samaria by King Ahab, 'Shall I go against Ramoth Gilead to battle or shall I forebear?'[33] They were informed, they had opportunities of expressing their views but their opinion was not directly invited. Responsibility for policy rested with the British government and there it remains. The dominions could, as they did, press for concessions to be made by a third party, Czechoslovakia, that would avert war at that time and on that (Sudeten) issue, they could acquiesce in British policy or they could lend encouragement to it. They could not honourably or realistically urge Britain to take steps that might involve an unprepared country with a virtually undefended capital in a war in which most people supposed, with Stanley Baldwin, that the bomber would always get through. Conceding this limitation in realistic choice, the general verdict is that of the courses open to the dominions they took the wrong one. Here a *caveat* may be entered. What was 'wrong' in a European context was not necessarily 'wrong' in a Commonwealth context. But for that extra year, reflected Mackenzie King in 1943, 'there would have been divided counsels everywhere'. All the evidence suggests this was precisely true.

The policy of appeasement perished with Hitler's midnight march on Prague in March 1939. This time no nationalist or racial chords of sympathy were struck. It was not Germans who were being reunited with their own *volk*, but Czechs who were to be subjected to German rule. Nor could the occupation of Czechoslovakia be explained away in terms of rectification of the injustices of Versailles. For dominion as for British statesmen, the fruits of appeasement had now a bitter taste, and while not allowing that the policy had been initially misconceived, they were prepared for its abandonment. The initiative was British and the change of course in British policy was signalled dramatically by the unilateral Anglo–French guarantee given to Poland on 31 March 1939. Churchill wrote later that history might 'be scoured and ransacked to find a parallel to this sudden and complete reversal of five or six years' policy of easy-going placatory appeasement, and its transformation almost overnight into a readiness to accept an obviously imminent war on far worse conditions and on the greatest scale', while nearer the time, on 6 April 1939, Smuts recorded his astonishment in a letter. 'Chamberlain's Polish guarantee', he wrote, 'has simply made us gasp – from the Commonwealth point of view. I cannot see the dominions following Great Britain in this sort of imperial policy the dangers of which to the Commonwealth are obvious. We still remember Lloyd George's Chanak[34] escapade . . .' But his early reaction was soon qualified. The need that was felt by the British government to take new, near-desperate steps to halt aggression came also – and it is a remarkable fact – to be accepted by dominion governments, who had neither been consulted nor forewarned of the British break with appeasement – Menzies, now Prime Minister, commenting to the UK High Commissioner after the outbreak of war that the Australian Government had known nothing of the guarantee until it was decided to give it.[35] A new Commonwealth consensus on resistance – in which Hertzog, however, did not share – following close upon the old Commonwealth consensus on appeasement, may reasonably be thought to indicate a capacity, on the part of Commonwealth countries, to think and react alike. And in the last resort such consensus of British and dominion views on great and critical issues was the only basis, on which the Commonwealth could endure in those testing days.

While there was community in sentiment, there was no community in commitment. In September 1939 the dominions had no external military or political treaty obligations or understandings. None of them were parties to the Anglo–French guarantees to Rumania, Greece or Poland, nor to the Anglo–Polish Treaty. Their hands were free. In 1914, they went to war because the United Kingdom was at war. In 1939, the decision rested upon them individually. They had full freedom of choice. How they exercised that freedom gave new insight into the meaning of, and the deeper realities that lay behind the constitutional developments of the inter-war years.

The Federal Parliament was sitting in Canberra on 3 September 1939, but the prime minister, R. G. Menzies, without consulting it, declared in a broadcast, 'Britain is at war, therefore Australia is at war.' There was one king, one flag, one cause. The New Zealand response was similar without being identical, the New Zealand declaration of war being later submitted to and confirmed by Parliament. New Zealand's prime minister coined a sentence which came to symbolise the sentiments of an island people. 'Where Britain goes, we go,' said Savage, 'where she stands, we stand.' The New Zealand government thought in fact that Britain might have stood a little earlier, but there was no recrimination, only a phrase at the end of the message to London noting that the stand had been taken 'not a moment too soon'. In Canada it was otherwise. Mackenzie King had never departed from his conviction that Parliament should decide. And when the day came, Parliament decided. The British declaration was made on 3 September. The Canadian Parliament assembled on 7 September. The prime minister told the House of Commons that he wished to make it perfectly clear that Parliament and no other authority had to decide the question of peace or war. No one would be able to allege that Canada was being dragged into an imperialist war. Six days separated the United Kingdom and Canadian declarations and during the interval, since Canada was not listed as belligerent, supplies from the United States poured over the Canadian border. The test of King's policy came in the vote of 9 September. Fewer than five members opposed Canadian participation and so in accordance with the rules of procedure, Canada went to war without a division in the House. The attainment of so great a measure of unity, in support of participation in war in a culturally divided country bordering on a great republic committed to neutrality, must surely rank as one of the outstanding achievements of Commonwealth statesmanship.

There was no unity in South Africa. The cabinet divided on the issue of peace or war with the prime minister, General Hertzog, supported by five ministers reconmending the former, and the deputy prime minister, General Smuts, with the backing of seven of his colleagues advocating the latter. Perforce the issue was left for Parliament to decide. Hertzog moved a neutrality motion in the House of Assembly, Smuts an amendment to it, proposing participation without the dispatch of troops overseas. The course of debate was fluctuating, the outcome almost to the last uncertain. There were two speeches that were thought to have swayed opinion – in each case contrary to the speaker's intention. The first was General Hertzog's overstatement of a case, which rested essentially upon the interpretation of the concept of 'South Africa first', by the introduction of a provocative and essentially irrelevant *apologia* for Hitler. The second was overstatement on the other side by Heaton Nicholls,[36] an English-speaking member from Natal, who argued that the South African Parliament had no power of decision, since all South Africans owed allegiance to the king and the king being at war, his subjects *ipso facto* were at war. The impact of this second speech which, as its author himself candidly recalled, 'fell on the House like a bomb', and was the more damaging in as much as it came from an English-speaking source, was at least qualified by an immediately succeeding contribution from B. K. Long, another English-speaking member, who argued that there was no limit to South African freedom under the Statute of Westminster. When the speeches were ended, the tellers recorded eighty votes for General Smuts' amendment, sixty-five for General Hertzog's original motion. But the tension was not yet finally resolved. Hertzog advised the governor-general, Sir Patrick Duncan, to dissolve Parliament and to hold an early general election. The governor-general declined, on the ground of an election having been held as recently as May 1938 at which the issues in debate had been before the electorate, and also because of the risk of violence and of the known ability of Smuts to form an alternative government. This was the first occasion in Commonwealth history in which a governor-general had set out in a memorandum his reasons for refusing a dissolution to an outgoing prime minister. Cumulatively they were something short of convincing in constitutional terms, but politically the conclusion which they sustained was of the highest moment, if it be accepted that informed opinion, including that of J. H. Hofmeyr, was right that Hertzog would have won an election. The British High Commissioner, Sir William Clark, was among those who advised the governor-general in the privacy of a bedroom at a Club where both were staying and hence his remark, 'Well, I think I can say I made my contribution to the war effort.'[37] An administration was accordingly formed by Smuts which, reinforced in its electoral support in the 1943 wartime election, survived till 1948. But its constitution made clear not only that the Fusion experiment had ended but that with Hertzog's departure and his subsequent political eclipse the way had been opened for the electoral triumph in 1948 of the more extreme, or Purified Nationalists as they were known, under the leadership of Dr Malan.

The Balfour Report had confidently asserted that no common cause would suffer as a result of separate dominion control of foreign policies. In September 1939 its faith was justified. It is true that Eire, as the Irish Free State was now known, decided upon neutrality but by then Eire was on any reckoning a dominion with a difference and in the view of its own government not a dominion at all. For the rest the dominions by their own decisions had reached conclusions that had brought them into war by the side of Britain and France. They were belligerent from first to last and for one year it was not Britain, it was the Commonwealth, that stood alone. That year was perhaps not so much Britain's as the Commonwealth's finest hour.

The contribution of the Commonwealth to the victory of the United Nations is part of the history of the second world war, but some facts may be recalled to serve as a reminder of the place of war in Commonwealth experience. In 1939 Canada became the headquarters of the British Commonwealth Air Training plan by which the countries of the Commonwealth, including Britain, were enabled to train their airmen under favourable Canadian conditions and secure from enemy air attack. By early 1944 more than eighty-six thousand air crew cadets had been trained in this way. There was a smaller but similar scheme in Rhodesia and many other such examples of sharing military, naval and other facilities or resources to the advantage of a common cause. Nor was there at any time any weakening in Commonwealth purpose. In the dark days that followed the fall of France, messages were received from all dominion prime ministers endorsing Britain's decision to fight on and pledging their support in men and materials. There was, too, in that summer of destiny evidence of a growing co-operation between a belligerent Commonwealth and a non-belligerent United States with a United Kingdom–United States destroyers-bases deal and a Canadian–United States defence agreement signed at Ogdensburg. During the year when the Commonwealth stood alone, Canadian divisions manned the shores of Britain against invasion; Australian, New Zealand and Indian troops fought a second time to protect the middle eastern artery of imperial communications, while the South African forces played their part in the East African campaigns which freed Abyssinia from Fascist rule before joining the other Commonwealth forces in North Africa. The irruption of the Japanese into south-east Asia

and their threatened invasion of Australia led to the withdrawal of
the Australian forces from the middle east, first to protect their
own homeland and then, with the Japanese threat to it ended by the
United States naval victories at Midway and in the Coral Sea, to take
part in bitter fighting across the south-western Pacific. The
Australian demand for a voice in the higher direction of the Pacific
War was met, in part at least, with the creation of a Pacific War
Council in 1941, with headquarters first in London and then jointly
in London and Washington. Dominion participation in 'mutual
aid' agreements with the United States on the model of the original
United States–United Kingdom agreement drew them economically as well as militarily into the orbit of United States' influence
and power. Their often first-hand knowledge of the vast resources
the United States could deploy under pressure of war made its own
enduring impact. But inevitably most deeply graven upon the
minds and memories of Commonwealth peoples were their own
experiences of war from September 1939 in the west, till its final
ending in August 1945 in the east. Statistically the number and
casualties of Commonwealth forces were estimated as in the Table,
though for a generation it was not statistics but memories that
mattered.

Country	Strength	Killed	Missing	Wounded	Prisoners of War
United Kingdom[38]	5,896,000	264,443*	41,327	277,077	172,592
Canada	724,023	37,476	1,843	53,174	9,045
Australia	938,277†	23,265	6,030	39,803	26,363
New Zealand	205,000‡	10,033	2,129	19,314	8,453
South Africa	200,000‖	6,840	1,841	14,363	14,589
India	2,500,000	24,338	11,754	64,354	79,849
Colonies and dependencies	473,250	6,877	14,208	6,972	8,115

* There were additionally some 93,000 civilians killed
† Net full-time service figure, June 1945
‡ Includes women
‖ Approximate figure

The coming of war provoked questions of Commonwealth
political organisation. How far were the lessons of the first world
war relevant to the second? In particular, ought an imperial war
cabinet to be reconstituted? Survivors from the earlier period,
L. S. Amery among them, maintained that it should. There was debate, but it lacked something of the edge of reality. The changes of
the inter-war years both in politics and in technology accounted for

this. By 1939 there was a working basis for consultation among equals, of a kind that had not existed twenty years earlier. The dominions had high commissioners in London, Britain had high commissioners in dominion capitals, and the importance attached to the office in critical times was reflected in Winston Churchill's appointment of former cabinet ministers as United Kingdom high commissioners in Ottawa, Canberra and Pretoria in 1940. In London, meetings of the high commissioners, beginning informally during the period of sanctions against Italy and assuming more definite shape and greater importance in the Munich crisis, became a main factor in Commonwealth co-operation during the war years. The high commissioners often met more than once a day with the secretary of the state for dominion affairs and discussed with him the great and small questions that arose from the co-operation of their countries in a common cause. The meetings were informative and frequently the debate was vigorous, covering in 1939–40 topics such as the appropriate response to Hitler's peace offer after the Nazi conquest of Poland, the need for the formulation of allied peace aims and their substance, the Finnish winter war and Commonwealth attitudes to the Soviet Union, to the desirability and possibilities of military aid for the Finns, with the consequent need for securing passage of troops through Sweden, and then, in sudden succession, all the problems that followed upon the Nazi invasions of Norway, the Low Countries and the fall of France, including the possibility of a German invasion of neutral Eire.[39] The meetings provided dominion representatives with a forum for the expression of their views and for a statement of their interests. It was of great importance to them that the secretary of state for dominion affairs should be a member of the war cabinet, so that he might transmit their opinions or conclusions to his colleagues. This was the case for most, but not for the full period, of the war.

High commissioners' meetings were reinforced by visits of individual ministers to London during the war and of British ministers to dominion capitals. There was also correspondence and communications on a scale not hitherto approached. The use of cables and the long distance telephone – Lyons had used it and got Chamberlain out of bed during the Munich crisis – meant there need be little loss of time in securing decisions at critical moments. In general, with consultation and opportunities for consultation on this scale, the case for an imperial war cabinet was sensibly weakened. But the possibility of some co-ordinating cabinet or council continued to be canvassed.

The demand for an imperial cabinet or Conference in the early years of the second world war served one constructive purpose. It elicited exposition in public of the disadvantages of the older and the advantages of the newer system of Commonwealth relations, which the public till then had had little or no opportunity of weighing. The most substantial contribution to debate was made by Mackenzie King, in whose opinion an imperial cabinet was undesirable, unnecessary and in time of war 'an impossible thing'.[40] The ground for each of these objections merits consideration.

Why was an Imperial Conference or cabinet undesirable in time of war? It was undesirable, in the opinion of the Canadian prime minister, because it meant taking prime ministers and experts away from their own countries, where in time of crisis they were most needed. Speaking to the House of Commons in Ottawa in February 1941, Mackenzie King said:

> I think I have only to ask hon. members of this House of Commons if they were, at the moment, called upon to decide whether it would be better to have the prime minister of Canada attending at the present time a council in London or to have him here in this House of Commons in immediate association with his colleagues and in a position to confer with them, not only from day to day, and hour to hour, but from moment to moment; whether they would not consider, in a situation such as exists at this time, that it is better for him to be here at the head of the government, and at the head of the country which has elected him to office.[41]

And apart from the preferences – not lightly to be disregarded – of the Canadian or other dominion Parliaments, there was the even more difficult question of authority. If a Canadian prime minister or cabinet minister were present over a long period of time in London as a member of an enlarged war cabinet, then his slightest word would probably be regarded as the opinion of Canada. It would be equally difficult and awkward for him to refer or not to refer questions to his colleagues in Ottawa. If he made a practice of consulting them, he would appear to have little authority himself; if he failed to consult them, the result would be divided responsibility and uncertainty of jurisdiction, which could hardly fail to have unfortunate results. In sum, the proper place for a dominion prime minister was at home and Mackenzie King wasted no time on his first wartime visit to London in conveying his opinion to Churchill. When, on 22 August 1941, the British government gave a luncheon at the Savoy Hotel in honour of the prime minister of Canada and when the conversation had become general Mackenzie King turned to Churchill and said: 'I hope you and your ministers will not expect to have the prime ministers of the dominions leaving their own countries to any more extent than is necessary.'[42] For quite different reasons, this accorded well with Churchill's own views.

While such considerations made an imperial war cabinet undesirable, other factors made it (as the imperial war cabinet of 1917–8 had not been) unnecessary. Chief among them, in Mackenzie King's opinion, was the improvement of communications in the intervening years which enabled dominion governments to keep in touch with the government of the United Kingdom and one another by telegraph or telephone, by brief ministerial visits by air for particular purposes, through high commissioners posted in Commonwealth capitals and by a reasonably comprehensive exchange of written communications on matters of mutual interest or concern. As a result there was no need for one Commonwealth cabinet for there was in existence – to quote Mackenzie King again – 'the most perfect continuing conference of cabinets that any group of nations could possibly have'. 'You have already got war cabinets – five of them', he told Churchill, and in illustration of what was becoming for him a favourite theme, 'You have got a continuing conference between the lot, what more do you want?'

Churchill, to whom Mackenzie King's question was rhetorically addressed, but at whom it was not directed, wanted (contrary to the unfounded assumptions of some later commentators but as Mackenzie King already knew) no more. And the one survivor of the earlier imperial cabinet, Field Marshal Smuts, to King's 'immense satisfaction' telegraphed Churchill at this time saying,

> I was glad to see Mackenzie King's outspoken condemnation of agitation for imperial cabinet. It seems to me unwise, with vast dangers looming in Africa and Pacific, to collect all our prime ministers in London. Our Commonwealth system, by its decentralisation, is well situated for waging world war, and diffuse leadership in all parts is a blessing rather than handicap. I agree with him that our system of communications leaves little to be desired.[43]

Even though the Australians, exposed in the Pacific to dangers that threatened neither Canada nor South Africa, never came to share these views, the evidence now available makes it clear that under the extreme stress of world war predominant Commonwealth opinion was in favour of co-operation through a system of informal consultation. The debate continued, especially in 1944, but the outcome was hardly in doubt and in succeeding years the aim of most – possibly all – Commonwealth governments was that consultation should ensure the existence of something that might, without straining the ordinary use of language, be termed a continuing conference of cabinets.

Why did Mackenzie King, and Mackenzie King alone among his contemporaries, go further and speak of an Imperial War Conference or cabinet as 'impossible'? Though he did not mention it specifically, one dominant consideration was implicit in all his arguments. That consideration was power. The existence of any such central imperial body would mean that power and undivided responsibility for its exercise would, so far as Canada was concerned, no longer remain in Canada. That was why an imperial war cabinet was 'impossible'. Whether Mackenzie King gave the right answer or not, at least he asked the right question. Where would power reside? And he thought it 'impossible' that in respect of Canada it should reside in any significant measure outside Canada.

Successive Australian governments entertained very different views. They desired, if not an imperial war cabinet, dominion, and more especially, Australian representation in the British war cabinet. They felt that such representation was essential if proper attention was to be given to Australian interests and due attention paid to the problems of the Pacific. Churchill however was not forthcoming. To Arthur Fadden, who succeeded Menzies as prime minister on 29 August 1941, Churchill summarised his views in a telegram[44] that takes its place beside Mackenzie King's speech of February 1941 as an exposition of the principles at stake in all discussions on the constitution of an imperial war cabinet or Council. The tenor of Churchill's argument was that the cabinet which he had the honour to lead was responsible to parliament and held office because its members collectively enjoyed the support of a majority in the House of Commons. The presence of an Australian minister who was responsible to the legislature of the Commonwealth of Australia, as a member of that cabinet, would involve organic changes. While in practice a dominion prime minister was always invited to sit with the United Kingdom cabinet and to take full part in government deliberations during the period of his visit, that was because he was the head of the government of a sister dominion and might be presumed to be in a position to speak not only on instructions from home but with the authority of the dominion of whose government he was the head. But a dominion minister other than the prime minister would not be a principal at all but only an envoy. That deprived him of authority and made his possible contribution to the discussions of the war cabinet unequal to the disadvantage of the greater number which his presence implied. The prime ministers of Canada, South Africa and New Zealand, noted Churchill, had said that they did not desire such representation, and some of them had taken a very strongly adverse view on the ground that no one but the prime minister could speak for their government except on instructions. What might happen otherwise was that the liberty of action of dominion governments might be prejudiced by any decisions to which their minister in London became a party. From the point of view of the United Kingdom, the proposal was equally objectionable. The addition of four dominion representatives would involve the retirement from the war cabinet of an equal number of British ministers. That would destroy the basis of the coalition government, since Churchill was not prepared to increase its numbers so that they became too large for the efficient conduct of business.

Churchill suggested to Fadden, by way of compromise, the possibility of the appointment of a special envoy to discuss any particular aspect of the common war effort, but he pointed out that such an envoy would not and could not be a responsible partner in the daily work of government and, if he remained in London as a regular institution, there would be the risk of duplication of function between such an envoy and the Australian high commissioner in London. While such a risk could not be obviated, its existence should be frankly faced, especially in view of the fact that the whole system of the high commissioners, in daily contact with the secretary of state for dominion affairs, was working well.

The Australian government, with Churchill's suggestion of a special envoy before them, decided to proceed with the appointment of a ministerial representative to the British war cabinet. The choice fell on an elder statesman and former prime minister, Sir Earle Page, who was minister of commerce at the time of his appointment. Before he reached London, however, the Fadden government fell. Curtin's Labour government which replaced it invited Sir Earle Page to continue as Australia's envoy extraordinary to the war cabinet, but the authority which he could reasonably hope to command was undermined by the fact that he was now a member, not of a government, but of an opposition party. On his arrival in London, Sir Earle Page defined the nature of his mission in terms which suggested that it was partly representative and partly exploratory. His function, he said[45] was

> to establish personal cabinet liaison between the United Kingdom and Commonwealth governments. The primary purposes of [my] mission would be the presentation of Australia's point of view on certain immediate problems of war strategy and the arrangement of the best mechanics for maintaining a system of direct cabinet representation in London.

But the nature of Australian (or other dominion) representation in the British cabinet was a matter for the British prime minister, and Churchill gave no indication of being prepared to relinquish his authority in this respect. Sir Earle Page attended the meetings of the cabinet by invitation, when matters of interest to Australia were to be discussed, but not as of right. On this Churchill stood firm. It was not what the Australians, anxious chiefly lest preoccupation with the war in Europe should lead to a neglect of the Pacific, desired. But they had perforce to acquiesce. In 1942 a new situation developed as a result of the resignation of Sir Earle Page, who was despised by Bruce and who 'found himself in unfamiliar waters that were too deep for him',[46] and the appointment of Bruce to the post of Australian representative in the war cabinet over and above his existing office of high commissioner. The arrangement, irksome on political and also personal grounds to Churchill – Bruce allowed himself the luxury of forthright criticism of the higher direction of the war in a memorandum he sent to Churchill – came to an end in 1944.

In the meantime the Japanese attack on Pearl Harbour in December 1941 had realised all Australia's worst fears and left her for some desperately anxious months, bereft of aircraft and with her seasoned troops far away in the middle east, as Nazi propaganda pictured her to be, 'the orphan of the Pacific'. The reaction was sharp. While there were renewed demands for a fuller voice in London, Australia's Labour government recognised that it was from the United States that succour must come and in Washington that the critical strategic decisions would be taken. The prime minister expressed his view of the political and strategic reality of Australia's position in undiplomatic but telling phrases. 'We refuse', he wrote in a newspaper article,[47] 'to accept the dictum that the Pacific struggle must be treated as a subordinate segment of the general conflict.' What was needed was 'a concerted plan evoking the greatest strength at the democracies' disposal, determined upon hurling Japan back'. Australia, he continued,

> looks to America, free of any pangs as to our traditional links or kinship with the United Kingdom.
> We know the problems that the United Kingdom faces. We know the constant threat of invasion . . . But we know too that Australia can go, and Britain can still hold on.
> We are therefore determined that Australia shall not go . . .

Through the Pacific war council, Australia obtained a voice in the making of strategic decisions in the Pacific war, though not as influential a one as her government hoped for. But far more important for the future, Australia was drawn decisively into the United States strategic orbit. In more senses than one it was her hour of destiny.

When it was apparent that however hard and protracted the task might prove, both Germany an Japan would suffer total defeat, Commonwealth statesmen displayed renewed interest in methods of Commonwealth co-operation in the post-war world. In September 1943 the Australian prime minister, in a well-established Australian tradition and once again with Pacific problems foremost in mind, proposed the formation of a Commonwealth consultative council to be served by a Commonwealth secretariat. Both were intended to bring about a closer co-ordination of Commonwealth foreign and defence policies. In November 1943 Field Marshal Smuts in a speech to the Empire Parliamentary Association in London,[48] recognising that however great might be the moral prestige of the Commonwealth after the war it would necessarily emerge materially weakened, advocated a grouping of the Commonwealth countries with the like-minded democratic states of the western European seaboard so as to form in association a power equal in stature to the Soviet Union and the United States and capable of holding the balance between them. Finally in January 1944 Lord Halifax, then British ambassador in Washington, expounded in Toronto somewhat similar views. He spoke of the need for Commonwealth unity in foreign policy at least on major issues for, in his opinion, 'if we are to play our rightful part in the preservation of peace, we can only play it as a Commonwealth, united, vital, coherent'.[49] Interesting though these speculations were, more important was the response they elicited. Generally speaking it was unfavourable. Commonwealth governments did not desire formal unity in policy nor centralised machinery to bring it about. Not only did they believe that for them that would be 'a step along the road to yesterday', to quote from the comment of John Dafoe, the editor of the *Free Press*, but that in the international field it would not contribute to but might well lessen the prospect of lasting peace. It was not by the revival of a balance of power on a world scale but by the creation of an effective international organisation supported by all peace-loving states that peace could best be preserved. On this no one was more emphatic than Mackenzie King. On 31 January 1944 in the Canadian House of Commons he observed,[50] with reference to the supposed need to preserve a proper balance of power in the post-war world:

> Field Marshal Smuts thought that this might be achieved by a close association between the United Kingdom and 'the smaller democracies in western Europe' . . . Lord Halifax on the other hand declared: 'Not Great Britain only, but the British Commonwealth and Empire, must be the fourth Power in that group upon which, under Providence, the peace of the world will henceforth depend.'
>
> With what is implied in the argument employed by both these eminent public men I am unable to agree.
>
> It is indeed true beyond question that the peace of the world depends on preserving on the side of peace a large superiority of power, so that those who wish to disturb the peace can have no chance of success. But I must ask whether the best way of attaining this is to seek a balance of strength between three or four Great Powers. Should we not, indeed must we not, aim at attaining the necessary superiority of power by creating an effective international system inside which the co-operation of all peace-loving countries is freely sought and given?

King told the British High Commissioner, Malcolm MacDonald,[51] 'it looked to him like part of a deliberate design by the United Kingdom Government and some Dominion statesmen to revive an imperialism which left the Dominions something less than national sovereignty' and amounted furthermore 'to an attack on his personal position'. Remarkably, however, Halifax had left out of the reckoning the interpretation likely to be placed on his words.

The Meeting of Commonwealth prime ministers which assembled in London in the spring of 1944 by chance or intent gave scant consideration to Curtin's proposals and discountenanced any suggestion that new machinery for the co-ordination of Commonwealth policies was required. On the contrary, the faith of the

prime ministers in the existing independence in policy, coupled
with active, informal consultation was explicitly reaffirmed. The
praise which the Canadian prime minister bestowed in a speech to
both Houses of Parliament upon a system which made possible 'a
continuing conference of cabinets' was echoed by his Commonwealth colleagues, other than Curtin, who continued to feel that
while good as far as it went the system did not go far enough. But
whatever the differences, one thing was apparent. Within the
Commonwealth that faith in decentralisation which had inspired
General Botha more than thirty years earlier remained not merely
undimmed but actually strengthened by the experiences of the
second world war. In 1944 Commonwealth leaders met not in
Imperial Conference, but at a Prime Ministers' Meeting, the
distinguishing qualities of which were held to be a lack of formality
or of fixed agenda so as to allow for intimate exchanges of view
between prime ministers, uninhibited by the restraining presence
of official advisers. In the communiqué[52] issued after the second of
the Prime Ministers' Meetings, held in London in the spring of
1946, the talks were described as 'an informal exchange of views',
and were said to have, 'contributed greatly to the elucidation of
many problems' and to 'a mutual understanding of the issues
involved' while 'existing methods of consultation' were said to be
'peculiarly appropriate to the character of the British Commonwealth' and 'preferable to any rigid centralised machinery'. The
1944 Meeting, Lord Garner has observed,[53] 'marked the
apotheosis of Mackenzie King and all that he stood for ... This was
for him virtually the last round – and he won completely'. It may
also be thought to mark the apotheosis of the *British* Commonwealth. How well King's concept of Commonwealth would serve a
less compact, less homogeneous grouping in the future remained
to be seen.

4 India: the Tryst with a Divided Destiny

The outbreak of the second world war ushered in the last phase of British rule in India. The war's impact was twofold; it intensified the Indian demand for independence and progressively weakened the British will and capacity to withhold it. The resulting possibility, or probability, of a withdrawal of the British *Raj* sooner than had hitherto been anticipated on either side, in turn and by the natural working of the laws of politics, sharpened the struggle for the succession to power within India. Where formerly the Congress and the League had stood side by side, by March 1940 at the latest, when the Muslim League at their Lahore meeting formulated a demand for separate Muslim homelands and a separate Muslim state, they stood face to face. Where once there had been a possibility of association in independence now there was, in the idiom of a later period, confrontation.

The twin pressures of the struggles for national independence and for control of the levers of power after independence were exerted within a single context, the one at every stage reacting upon the other. That context was provided at the highest political level by the policies of the British government, themselves compounded of immediate military considerations and long-term constitutional aims. First the war and then, and largely in consequence of it, the consolidation of British opinion in favour of an early transfer of power, invested those policies retrospectively with a clarity of outline that historically they did not possess. Nonetheless the record of Britain's wartime and immediately post-war advances to Indian independence on the basis of responsible government and dominion status, summarily restated, provides a necessary background to any analysis of the interrelation between constitutional advance and domestic division.

The outbreak of war underlined not so much the measure of autonomy India had so far acquired as the extent of her dependence. The viceroy, Lord Linlithgow, declared war on behalf of

104

India without calling the leaders of the principal Indian parties, the Congress or the Muslim League, into a consultation. Constitutionally the viceroy's action was warranted by reason of the fact that the federal provisions of the Government of India Act 1935 had not come into effect. But constitutional rectitude was no compensation for so grave a lapse in political judgment. The Congress, in particular, was deeply resentful; and Pandit Nehru contrasted the position of the dominions, including Ireland, free to decide in their several parliaments whether or not to declare war upon Nazi Germany, with that of an India committed to war without even so much as a reference to its representative political figures.[1] From this inauspicious start there was to be no sustained recovery in Anglo–Indian, or more especially in Anglo–Congress relations for the duration of the war. In as much as British and Congress, and indeed British and Indian, opinion as a whole, far from being in conflict, coincided substantially in respect of the causes for which war was being waged, there was in this a certain irony.

There were differences in the attitudes of the League and the Congress to wartime co-operation, that of the League being essentially pragmatic while the Congress characteristically defined their position in conceptual terms. They professed sympathy for the Allied cause deriving from their love of liberty and the strong anti-Fascist, anti-Nazi sentiments embodied in the pre-war Congress resolutions, but maintained that despite these bonds, co-operation with Britain was precluded by India's continued dependence. India, unfree, could not fight for freedom. Such was the Congress assertion of principle. Was it reasonable to infer from it that a free India under Congress leadership would support the Allied cause in arms? The answer, and it was clearly one of potential importance in the shaping of British policy, remained debatable. In December 1939 the Congress governments in the provinces resigned rather than co-operate in a war effort directed by an alien authority. In itself and for the future this was a significant step. But it did not provide a conclusive answer about attitudes in quite different conditions. That could be founded only on less tangible and necessarily hypothetical evidence. The main body of the Congress, attentive to Jawaharlal Nehru's impassioned pre-war denunciation of militarist régimes both in Europe and Asia, would presumably have favoured the participation of a free India, provided it were unmistakably at her own choice and on her own terms, in the war on the side of the western allies. But there were also the disciples of Mahatma Gandhi, already regarded with veneration as the conscience of the Congress, who accepted without qualification his doctrines of non-violent resistance and believed them to have an absolute validity in the international, as in the domestic, field. In 1942 they were prepared with Gandhi to advocate such passive resistance to a Japanese invasion from the north-east but not active participation. That was a factor in the Indian political equation that could not be disregarded. There was another. The British government, even assuming that it had been able to reach a conclusion reassuring to itself about the co-operation of a Congress wartime government, could not consider the Indian problem in its Congress setting alone. There were also the League and the princes. In terms of Britain's survival – and no less was at stake between 1940 and 1942 – was there solid advantage in conceding freedom to India, even on the assumption of thereby enlisting the aid of the Congress in the prosecution of the war, if the consequences were to be the estrangement of loyal princely allies, the alienation of Muslims and the opening of a struggle for power within India between the Congress and the League? Even if the answer were in the affirmative, it was at best speculative and few governments are prepared to indulge in wartime speculation so risky as this. So it was that from 1939 onwards the British government were caught in a dilemma from which, despite some facile subsequent comment, there was no escape. It may well be that the chief responsibility for the existence of such a dilemma was their own, and that in wartime Britain was paying the price of the procrastinating policies of the later 1920s and early 1930s.

It is in terms of this diminishing freedom of manœuvre and of the impact of the successive major crises of the war that British attempts to end the constitutional deadlock in India are to be viewed. On 23 October 1939 the secretary of state, Lord Zetland, reminded the war cabinet that when Parliament had 'accepted dominion status as the goal, the feeling was that the journey was a long one, but the effect of the outbreak of the war has been to bring us hard up against the implication of dominion status for India . . .'[2] The nature of British war-time proposals underlined the correctness of this analysis. The first, following closely upon the fall of France, was the so-called 'August offer', 1940. It proposed the immediate enlargement of the viceroy's council so as to include a certain number of representatives of the Indian political parties, but little otherwise. Further essays in constitution-making were to be firmly relegated to after the end of the war, though it was conceded that when the time came, and in accord with dominion precedent, any new constitution should be drafted in India. But even in this context, there was a restatement in uncompromising terms of Britain's obligations to the princes and of British inability to contemplate the transfer of their responsibility for the peace and welfare of India to any system of government, the authority of which was directly denied 'by large and powerful elements in India's national life'.[3] The offer concluded with the hope that, as a result of Indian co-operation in the war, a new understanding would emerge paving the way to 'the attainment by India of that free and equal partnership in the British Commonwealth which remains the proclaimed and accepted goal of the imperial Crown and of the British Parliament'.

The 'August offer', its modest attractions for the most part prospective and conditional, was spurned by the Congress and rejected, albeit with some judicious qualification, by the League. There followed a period of constitutional quiescence. It came to an end with the Japanese entry into the war in December 1941, which was reported to have 'sharpened speculation' about internal political developments and the appeal on 1 January 1942 by a group of distinguished Indian Liberals led by Sir Tej Bahadur Sapru to the Prime Minister for some bold stroke of imaginative statesmanship to enlist India's wholehearted cooperation in the War. Churchill, L. S. Amery, now secretary of state, and the viceroy were at one in discountenancing any such initiative, Churchill and Linlithgow on grounds of wartime expediency, reinforced by a pronounced dislike of change in the governance of India; Amery additionally for the more particular reason that, to quote his submission to the war cabinet on 28 January 1942 – 'The political deadlock in India today is concerned, ostensibly, with the transfer of power from British to Indian hands. In reality it is mainly concerned with the far more difficult issue of what Indian hands, what Indian Government or Governments, are capable of taking over without bringing about general anarchy or even civil war.' But the tide of war and, more immediately, Attlee's appeal to Durham and Canadian precedent prevailed over even so powerful a triumvirate.[4] On 11 March the prime minister announced in the House of Commons that 'the crisis in the affairs of India arising out of the Japanese advance has made us wish to rally all the forces of Indian life to guard their land from the menace of the invader'. In consequence the war cabinet had decided to send out one of their number, the lord privy seal, Sir Stafford Cripps, to India armed with a declaration designed to give greater precision to earlier British statements, notably the 'August offer' 1940. The conclusions of the war cabinet, as set out in the declaration, were in terms of such precision, if not of principle, a decided advance upon anything hitherto formulated. At the heart of them was dominion status, with the constitution of the new Indian union to be drafted, as the Congress had consistently demanded, by an Indian Constituent Assembly in accord with dominion precedents. The new dominion was to be 'associated with the United Kingdom and the other dominions by a common allegiance to the Crown, but equal to them in every respect, in no way subordinate in any aspect of its domestic or external affairs'.[5] What was contemplated, as Sir Stafford Cripps made plain on arrival in India, was dominion status without reservation or qualification. At a press conference in New Delhi he was asked whether the new dominion would be free to secede. He replied in the affirmative. He was asked whether Canada was free to secede. He replied, 'Of course.' While these answers, when reported, gave George VI some cause for uneasy reflection,[6] they gave, in so far as they were credited, a measure of reassurance in Delhi. However, the offer of dominion status which Sir Stafford Cripps thus expounded, while unconditional, remained prospective. Once again constitution-making was deferred till victory had been won. This was a major disappointment to Indian nationalist sentiment. There was the certainty of delay and, for many, no corresponding assurance about victory. Gandhi was alleged to have spoken of a postdated cheque upon a failing bank, and even if the phrase was not of his own invention – it has been attributed to K. M. Panikkar – he entertained the sentiment. Nor were Congress feelings of frustration on the constitutional front counterbalanced by the prospect of some immediate transfer of substantial administrative responsibilities to Indian hands. At the crisis of the eastern war, the British government decided on the contrary that it must retain final control of the levers of power and direct control over defence in India. Accordingly much of what it was prepared to transfer to Indian hands was of marginal relevance to government at such a time. Moreover, while these were the chief, they were not the only causes of Congress reserve. The Cripps proposals introduced a new concept of non-accession, by which any province of British India which was not prepared to accept the constitution to be drafted after the war was to be enabled to retain its existing constitutional position unimpaired and outside the new Indian dominion. It was later added that the British government would be prepared to agree upon a new constitution giving the non-acceding provinces, collectively, if they so desired, the same status as the Indian union. The League had reason to welcome these concessions to its position, though it professed to feel that they did not go far enough. The formulation of the principle of non-accession enhanced Congress suspicions of British intentions. It could hardly have been otherwise. 'Express opening left for partition', Smuts warned Churchill, when he learned of these provisions, 'may be taken as a British invitation or incitement to partition.'[7] The final outcome was rejection of the Cripps offer, first by the Congress on the specific ground of inadequate Indian control over the defence of India but clearly also for more general reasons and then by the League. The failure to reach agreement was followed by Congress endorsement in August 1942 of a 'Quit India' resolution,[8] which resulted in rebellion, led to the imprisonment of the principal Congress leaders for the remainder of the war, and in the provinces principally affected left scars on the relationship between the British administration and the Congress that were never healed.

The Cripps mission did not achieve its immediate purposes but it succeeded in its other aims. One by which Churchill set the highest store was that of persuading allied and more especially United States public opinion of British good intentions; another was in effect to dispose of the Indian question for the duration. In India, and certainly no less in London, it also changed the context of discussions about Anglo–Indian relations. Churchill, who had sent Cripps, the radical, socialist friend of Nehru, depart on a highly problematic mission with mixed feelings, and who was enabled to endure its failure – if indeed he thought of it in such terms at all – with fortitude, remarked to the king shortly afterwards that 'his colleagues and both, or all three parties in Parliament were quite prepared to give up India to the Indians after the war. He felt they had already been talked into giving up India.'[9] More precisely, there could be no going back on the offer of a constituent assembly and dominion status. And it was on this basis that negotiations were resumed after the war, first in conference at Simla and then, following rather tardily, as many Indians were disposed to think in view of past professions, upon the accession of the Labour government to office in July 1945, by the sending of a cabinet mission consisting of Lord Pethick-Lawrence, the secretary of state for India, Sir Stafford Cripps, president of the Board of Trade, and A. V. Alexander, the first lord of the Admiralty, to India early in 1946. Yet there could no longer be serious doubt about the purposes of the British government. The first was to preserve the unity of India and the second to transfer power. These dual aims were, however, conflicting. Unity might conceivably be preserved were independence deferred; independence might be conceded forthwith but at the price of unity. That much was made plain by the Indian response to the cabinet mission and its Report.

The mission, unable to secure the agreement between Congress and League, formulated their own plan. It was published and is known as the Statement of 16 May. In it the mission examined but unequivocally rejected the possibility of partition and by so doing moved Vallabhbhai Patel to observe: 'Thank God, we have successfully avoided a catastrophe which threatened our country . . . for the first time, an authoritative pronouncement in clear terms has been made against the possibility of Pakistan in any shape or form'.[10] In its place the mission offered a package deal. It proposed that there should be a union of India, embracing both British India and the princely states, with responsibility for foreign affairs, defence and communications, thus meeting in minimal form the Congress demand for continuing unity. All other subjects and all residuary powers were to be vested in the provinces and the provinces, meeting in sections, were to be left free to form groups, two Muslim, one of them in the north-west, the other in the north-east and a third of the remaining Hindu majority provinces, with each group empowered to determine the provincial subjects to be dealt with in common.[11] The potential groupings, albeit far short of Pakistan since they would be within the Union, were none the less a principal attraction for the League, in as much as they opened the way to a consolidation of the League's position in the north-west and north-east. This was as far – and it was a considerable way – as the cabinet mission felt it possible to go towards satisfying minority sentiment while preserving a framework of federal unity. Were the constitutional balance thus struck to be acceptable to Congress and League the mission proposed that a constituent assembly representative of all parties be called and an interim government formed.

First reactions to the Statement were critical but not discouraging. It was accepted initially, though with reservations in respect of Pakistan, by the League and subject to special interpretation by the Congress, particularly with regard to the rôles of sections and groups about which the mission's Statement, while clear in intention, was insufficiently conclusive in wording to preclude acrimonious and protracted debate. It was the League's view that 'grouping' was in the first instance compulsory and the Congress interpretation that only the initial meeting of the Sections was predetermined, Sections accordingly being left free to form Groups or not as they wished.[12] The issue was of critical importance for, with meetings of Groups even at risk, what likelihood would there be of a Pakistan within the Union of India, such as some Leaguers thought might prove an alternative to a sovereign Pakistan outside it, which Jinnah demanded? These differences between Congress and League, never in fact to be resolved, were the principal cause of the League's withdrawal in July of its earlier acceptance of the mission's Statement, the long-term consequence of which was the League's non-participation in the work of the Constituent Assembly. Furthermore the viceroy's first attempts to obtain joint Congress–League participation in the interim government, which was intended by the cabinet mission to prepare for the transfer of responsibility to Indian hands, foundered in sharp dispute with Jinnah and only a predominantly Congress government was constituted.[13]

The last phase, from the autumn of 1946 to the summer of 1947, was marked by the reconstitution, through the addition of League members, of the interim government on 15 October; by the meeting in December 1946 of the long-promised, but now by reason of the League boycott, unrepresentative Constituent Assembly, by the announcement, on 20 February 1947, of the 'definite intention' of the British government 'to take the necessary steps to effect the transference of power into responsible Indian hands by a date not later than June 1948';[14] by the arrival in March 1947 of Lord Mountbatten as the last viceroy and one who had welcomed the fact 'that his task was to end one regime and to inaugurate a new one';[15] by the succeeding weeks of intense and dramatic discussion between the new viceroy and the Indian leaders,[16] in which he sought to ascertain their views on the great issues soon to be resolved*; by the resulting final acceptance, or acquiescence, silent on the part of Gandhi, by the leaders of the Congress and the League in the inevitability of partition; by the announcement of partition and of the transfer of power to two successor dominions by the viceroy at a press conference on 4 June, at which with unfailing assurance he answered nearly a hundred questions put to him by Indian and world correspondents;[17] by the passage through both Houses of Parliament at Westminster of the Indian Independence Act, introduced in the House of Commons by the prime minister, Clement Attlee, in a speech, which contained an apposite and moving quotation from Mountstuart

---

*The remarkably full records made at the time of what was said at the interviews between the viceroy and Gandhi, Nehru, Patel, Jinnah, Liaquat Ali Khan, Baldev Singh and others are reproduced in *The Transfer of Power*, vol. x, the more important taking place between 22 March and 9 April 1947.

Elphinstone and an allusion, deemed more felicitous then than later, to Campbell-Bannerman's parallel act of faith in restoring self-government to the defeated Boers[18]** which bore fruit both in 1914 and in 1939'; and finally, on the midnight hour of the 14–15 August 1947, by the coming into existence of the two new dominions of India and Pakistan, with Mohammed Ali Jinnah speaking in Karachi, the new capital of a new state, of 'the fulfilment of the destiny of the Muslim nation' and with Pandit Nehru in Delhi reflecting upon the long years ago when 'we made a tryst with destiny' and of how the time had come 'when we shall redeem our pledge'.[19]

It had proved, however, to be a tryst with a divided destiny. Muslim achievement of Pakistan represented at once the frustration of Congress hopes and a defeat for British interests. The first was self-evident and the second well put in a letter from Lord Wavell to the king, in which he spoke of 'the vital necessity, not only to the British Commonwealth but to the whole world, of a united, stable and friendly India'.[20] Why then did India not remain united? That remains one of the most vexing and difficult questions of modern Commonwealth history. To seek for an answer it is necessary to leave the chronological, constitutional road and to examine the conflicts of interests, hopes and fears which produced the situation, and the psychology from which partition derived.

The advantages and disadvantages of partition, as a solution of India's major community problems had not been carefully weighed or long considered by any of those principally concerned before it took effect, with the one exception of the British Chiefs of Staff, who were active in preparing contingency plans in the context of experience of the war that was ended and against the prospect of a divided Indian army. It is easy to be misled by words. But dialectical exchanges about controversial proposals do not necessarily, as in this case, in themselves indicate that those proposals are being advanced, criticised or rejected in terms of political or still more administrative actualities. Certainly it was the case that after the Lahore resolution[21] of the All-India Muslim League in March

---

** The *Manchester Guardian* in a leading article reproduced *in extenso* by special arrangement in The *Hindu* on 10 July remarked of the Prime Minister's speech: 'Mr Attlee was entitled to feel happy. He likened the present bill to the gift of self-government to the Boers, but he was too modest to say . . . that there is a fair prospect that he himself may hold the place in the history of India that . . . Campbell-Bannerman does in that of South Africa.' (As reproduced in Rangaswami Parthasarathy, *A Hundred Years of the Hindu. The Epic Story of Indian Nationalism* (Madras, 1978) p. 658.)

1940 – the so-called 'Pakistan Resolution' though the term Pakistan did not in fact appear in it – partition had its passionate protagonists, its outraged opponents and those, Nehru, Patel and at the very last, Mahatma Gandhi – he thought, however, it should take place, if it had to, *after* the British had left – who came to acquiesce with resignation in a prospect less distasteful to them than the thought of enforced minority inclusion in a unitary state. Yet the debate was not practical and purposeful; rather was it long-range and emotive. The language used on the one side was that of Muslim homelands and a Holy War to defend them; on the other, to employ the phrase Gandhi made his own, that of the vivisection of Mother India. There is only scattered evidence of consideration before 1947 on the part either of advocates or opponents as to what partition would mean in terms of administration, and still less, apart from generalities, in terms of frontiers, economics, social disruption, division of the armed forces and the administration, communications, distribution of assets or control of irrigation. So much indeed was understandable. The Muslim League was fighting to establish 'an impossible' aim; the Congress to defeat a stratagem which its leaders believed down to the 'Great Calcutta Killing' of August 1946 (and in some cases into 1947) to have been adopted in order to secure a strong negotiating position for the entrenchment of Muslim minority rights within an independent India. One consequence was, according to his own graphic account, that when on 3 June 1947, the day after Partition had been accepted in principle, Lord Mountbatten threw on the table copies of a memorandum on *The Administrative Consequences of Partition*, which his staff had prepared, 'the severe shock it gave to everyone present would have been amusing if it was not tragic'.[22]

It was not so much the complexity as the nature of relations in India on the eve of partition that made foresight difficult and discouraged realistic appraisal of future possibilities. The more important of those relations were without exception triangular. There were the three principal communities, the Hindus, the Muslims and the Sikhs, in descending order of magnitude; there were the three political groupings, the princes, the Muslim League and the Indian National Congress in ascending order of importance; and there were the three arbiters of national destiny, the British, the Congress and the League. In each triangle there was the predisposition – it is almost a law of politics – of the lesser to combine against the greatest. The League thus looked more kindly than the Congress on the pretensions of the princes; almost to the last, until in 1946 Jinnah became convinced that the viceroy, Lord

Wavell, was to be regarded as 'the latest exponent of geographical unity', the League was apt to be more understanding or at least less unreceptive of British proposals than the Congress. At one time indeed, before Gandhi took up their cause, the League seemed prepared to champion the outcastes, and in early 1947 there were intermittent negotiations with the Sikhs, on the basis of possible Sikh autonomy within an undivided Punjab. The British for their part showed a preoccupation with the outcastes and with minorities generally which was thought by the Congress to have been less than wholly altruistic. There was also the continuing Congress suspicion, only dispelled or partially dispelled in the period immediately before partition, of British, and not least a British ICS predisposition towards Muslims in two of the disputed provinces, the Punjab and the North-West Frontier. Behind allegations or assertions, deeply felt but difficult as they were for the most part to substantiate or refute, lay the inconsistencies, the dissembling, and the tactical devices inseparable from triangular political situations. Purpose and reality were difficult to disentangle from stratagem and manœuvre, even at times by those engaged in employing them. In the maze of tactics the sense of direction was apt to become clouded. The existence of so many variants seemingly discouraged cool appraisal of realities – not least in one respect on the part of the Government of India and the India Office in London.

Successive British governments and viceroys, it now seems evident beyond dispute, overestimated the power base and authority of the Indian princes. Even the Labour government was in part the victim of such miscalculation, and as for the viceroys, only the last – perhaps because he was himself of royal blood and German background, and thus mindful of what had happened to German princes after unification – proved in this respect to be without illusions. Over the years this British overestimate was a complicating factor on the Indian scene. Within a few months of the transfer of power the princes were shown to be, as Gandhi had earlier claimed, at any rate not much more than 'British Officers in Indian dress'. And if *some* among a number of estimable and public spirited rulers were not shown to have been 'sinks of iniquity', as Pandit Nehru had once alleged, that may have been partly because the political adviser to the princes, Sir Conrad Corfield, to the subsequent annoyance of Mountbatten and the anger of Nehru in May 1947 ordered his subordinates in the Political Department to extract from the files confidential reports reflecting unfavourably on the public or private behaviour of the princes – 'eccentricities' was the favoured term in respect of the latter – and burn what has been calculated to have been four tons of them.[23] But in that same year, 1947, there were those who conceived or cherished the hope that in an independent India, the greater at least of the states might have an autonomous existence. There were enquiries from princely officials about the nature of external association and, in Bombay businessmen discussed prospects of development in Hyderabad and Travancore on the assumption that as autonomous units within the Commonwealth – a possibility explicitly raised by the Dewan of Travancore – they might be the most stable and solvent parts of a new India. Eighteenth-century analogies were fashionable, and if they were too artificial to carry much conviction at least they were illustrative of a trend in British–Indian thinking – and one incidentally wholly in conflict with British interests in the creation of one or if need be, two strong, stable successor states after independence. Nor was the predisposition of the British, both at the official and the unofficial level, to exaggerate the potential rôle of the princes without its lasting importance. It was the princes, not as the Congress had urged,[24] the peoples of the states who by virtue of being empowered to sign or not to sign Instruments of Accession to either of the successor powers on the lapse of British paramountcy, who were placed in a position to determine the destiny of the states. That authority is alleged to have been given to them by the Labour government, partly to appease the Conservative opposition at Westminister. Whether this was so or not – and *prima facie* it would seem questionable, despite the close contact maintained notably between Sir Walter Monckton, advising the Nizam of Hyderabad and Conservative party leaders – the fact of princely decision made prediction about states and accession difficult in some cases, and virtually incalculable in Hyderabad and – even apparently to princely advisers – in Kashmir.[25] Assuredly there were obligations of honour, nostalgic notions of a 'gorgeous east' and a belief in the stability of autocratic rule, but in essence continuing British concern for the princes derived from long indulged preoccupations with the tactics of a triangular political situation, reinforced, be it added, by a sense of obligation on the part of the paramount power to those who had helped in peace and war to sustain it.

In the struggle for power on the highest plane, that is to say between the British, the Congress and the League, it was the British who were familiarly cast in the rôle of the third party. In the Congress view the British in India had followed for some forty years before partition a policy of divide and rule. 'It has been the traditional policy of Britain', complained Gandhi, after the Congress rejection of the 'August offer' of 1940,[26] 'to prevent parties from uniting. "Divide and rule" has been Britain's proud motto. It is the British statesmen who are responsible for the divisions in India's ranks and the divisions will continue so long as the British sword holds India under bondage.' This was the language of politics, not history. Thoughts of 'divide and rule', however, were not absent from the minds of twentieth-century British officials and statesmen. So much is clear from files dealing with the Liberal administration of the pre-first world war years and not necessarily only in relation to India. Nor was it absent in the 1930s and 1940s. Lord Zetland, who was secretary of state for India at the outbreak of the second world war, noted, without sharing, the satisfaction which evidence of communal division gave among 'diehards', Churchill not least among them – in February 1940 he commented at a meeting of the war cabinet that the communal feud between the Hindu and Muslim communities had been 'a bulwark of British rule'[27] – while a year earlier the viceroy, Lord Linlithgow, largely because of it, thought of dominion status for India as a still distant goal.

> No one [wrote the viceroy in January 1939[28]] can, of course, say what, in some remote period of time, or in the event of international convulsions of a particular character, may be the ultimate relations of India and Great Britain . . . but that there should be any general impression . . . that public opinion at home, or His Majesty's government, seriously contemplate evacuation in any measurable period of time, seems to me astonishing.

No doubt the Congress leaders sensed that such was the viceroy's mind. In general, the more the British government showed itself preoccupied with the position of minorities and with communal divisions, the more suspect it became to the Congress. If, as Gandhi argued, the communal problem was insoluble so long as the third party remained and if, as the British argued, they could not go until it was resolved, might that not mean they would stay forever? Or to pose the dilemma in a broader, impersonal context, how was the British view, that the resolution of the communal problem was a necessary precondition of their departure, to be reconciled with the Congress conviction that their departure was a necessary precondition of its resolution?

There was, however, an alternative analysis. It was suggested to the Round Table Conference in 1931 by a distinguished Indian

Liberal. For the 'divide and rule' of Congress he substituted 'we divide and you rule'. Pushed to its logical conclusion this meant, presumably, that the divisions at root were domestic. At the Round Table Conference logic was not pressed to such extremes. Princes and Muslims were at one in proclaiming that they had no wish to create 'Ulsters in India'. But was this really so? In respect of some of the princes (and their friends) that was, or came to be, precisely what they had in mind; in respect of the Muslims it posed the fundamental question: Were they a community, the second largest within India, or were they a separate nation? If they were the former, then the pattern of a self-protective policy might have been expected to be (as indeed it was at least down to 1940) limited cooperation with the British and the Congress in the working out of a federal structure in which the position of the Muslims, at least in Muslim majority provinces, was entrenched against a centre certain to be dominated, under any form of representative government, by representatives of the great Hindu majority in the country. But if the Muslims were not the second largest community in India but a separate nation, then any such policy of limited co-operation was precautionary and preliminary to a demand for a separate national recognition. In these matters words are not conclusive. But they are important, particularly when invested with the force which Jinnah gave them at the Lahore meeting of the League in March 1940. He castigated the British for their conception of government by parties functioning on a political plane as the best form of government for every country. He assailed *The Times* for having earlier concluded, after recognition of the differences not only of religion but also of law and culture between Hindus and Muslims, that in the course of time 'the superstitions will die out and India will be moulded into a single nation'. For Jinnah it was not a question of superstitions or of time but of fundamental beliefs and social conceptions.

Hindus and Muslims [he said] have two different religious philosophies, social customs, literatures. They neither inter-marry, nor even interdine. Indeed, they belong to two different civilisations . . . Their views of this life and the life hereafter are different . . . The Muslims are not a minority as the word is commonly understood . . . Muslims are a nation according to any definition of the term, and they must have their homelands, their territory and their state.[29]

If there is substance in Jinnah's contention then it would seem to follow logically that the British must be acquitted of any final responsibility for the partition of India; or in the language of contemporary dialectics, it did not much matter in this respect whether the third party stayed or went. Had the British succeeded in imposing unity then the consequence, again accepting the fundamentals of Jinnah's analysis, might well have been, as he threatened in 1947, the bloodiest civil war in the history of Asia. For the essence of his argument was that it was the unity of India that was artificial and imposed; the division natural. And by way of epilogue it is worth noting that one of the Congress High Command, the formidable Vallabhbhai Patel, infuriated by League intransigence and as a party boss influenced by Congress party provincial interests which came to be in favour of partition in the Punjab and Bengal (in default of autonomy with unity within the Indian orbit for the latter) argued with Maulana Azad, the leading Congress Muslim, in favour of overall partition by saying 'whether we liked it or not, there were two nations in India'.[30] If, on the other hand, Jinnah's analysis is to be questioned in its essentials, then the arguments for a more probing enquiry into the aims and purposes of British as well as Congress and League policies are conclusive. More immediately it is to be noted that while Jinnah staked his claim for Pakistan in March 1940, there was no certainty whether its dramatic presentation was a stratagem or a literal statement of his objective. Reports of some contemporary conversations he had in Lahore suggest that for all the vehemence of his language he may himself have remained undecided.[31]

Whatever the Lahore resolutions might portend for the future, they indicated at the time a shift in Muslim priorities. While the Congress continued to fight on one front against the British to secure independence, the Muslim League was engaged on two fronts against the British and against Congress; and after 1940 the second assumed even greater importance. Here was an open challenge to the claims of the Congress to represent Indian nationalist opinion. When the Congress governments in the provinces resigned in December 1939 after two and a half years of office – on the issue of non-co-operation in the war – Jinnah proclaimed Friday 22 December 1939 a Day of Deliverance from 'the tyranny, oppression and injustice' from which Muslim India had suffered under Congress rule. The proximate source of Muslim grievances is not in dispute. It lay in the fact that the Congress, after its massive victory in the 1937 provincial elections, had formed one-party governments in provinces in which the Muslim League had expected coalition governments in which they would be partners. This repudiation of the League derived fundamentally from the Congress conviction that it represented all India. There were only two forces in India, Nehru had claimed in the course of the election campaign, British imperialism and Indian nationalism, and when Jinnah had retorted there was a third party, the Muslims, Nehru had dismissed out of hand the notion of the Muslims of India as 'a nation apart'.[32] There was no need accordingly for political concessions to a minority grouping or, more particularly, for recognition of a ministerial rôle for the League, which anyway had fared poorly in the elections. Muslims there would certainly be in the provincial governments – but they would be Congress Muslims or League Muslims who had renounced the League and joined the Congress as a condition of office. This general presumption was reinforced, so both Jawaharlal Nehru and Rajendra Prasad have remarked in their recorded reflections,[33] by a conviction that the conventions of British cabinet government should prevail. If there were League members of the provincial governments in, for example, the United Provinces and Orissa, what then became of notions of collective responsibility? 'Congressmen', so Rajendra Prasad recalled,[34] 'thought it contrary to the spirit of parliamentary democracy to appoint any outsider in their ministry.' If Muslims were to serve then first claim, as party stalwarts were quick to emphasize, lay with those Muslims who were loyal members of the Congress and not with supporters of the League. Yet in retrospect, as written records suggest and personal conversations underline, most of the prominent Congress leaders remained preoccupied and even questioning as to the correctness of their 1937 conclusions. And at the time one of the Congress leaders, not surprisingly the perceptive and courageous Congress Muslim, Maulana A. K. Azad – who was to serve as president of the Congress throughout the war years – challenged and fought in vain to prevent or reverse these exclusivist decisions dictated largely by party loyalists in the provinces. What was at issue was a question of political judgment. On any reckoning the decision would seem in retrospect to have been ill-advised. Whether it was more is a matter of opinion. Sir Penderel Moon deems it to have been 'the *fons et origo malorum*' and argues that the Congress leaders 'were responsible, though quite unwittingly' for the critical change in Muslim sentiment from readiness to contemplate cooperation in an all-India federation to insistence upon separation. The Congress 'passionately desired to preserve the unity of India. They consistently acted so as to make its partition certain'.[35] But, it may reasonably be asked, did the partition of India derive from so comparatively trifling a cause? Were there not fundamental forces at work? An error or a series of errors in judgment is one thing, the source of a political event so momentous as partition ordinarily another. Or to put the issue in another way, was partition implicit in the Indian scene or not? If it were, tactics were of secondary importance and only if not, whether well- or ill-conceived, of first significance.

Before the concept of Pakistan could pass from the realm of stratagem to that of near reality, certain conditions had to be fulfilled. The first was that the imperial power should become increasingly sensitive to the claims advanced by the Muslim League. This in fact happened. It is attributed by V. P. Menon and others who have followed him[36] to Congress policies of non-co-operation and non-participation in provincial government during the war. It is an opinion to be accepted with considerable reserve in that non-cooperation during the war was almost certainly a condition of continuing Congress unity. Immoderate policies, furthermore, ensured the survival of moderate leadership during the war and its triumph thereafter. By reason of their adoption there were no significant, surviving enemies on the left; whereas war-time co-operation might well have divided and correspondingly weakened the Congress in the face of the League. But, if explanation must remain speculative, the step by step advance on the British side towards the meeting of Muslim League claims is hardly disputable, as a brief recapitulation in this context suffices to show. Where the British statement that accompanied the 'August offer' of 1940 remarked: 'it goes without saying that they [the United Kingdom government] could not contemplate transfer of their present responsibilities for the peace and welfare of India to any system of government whose authority is directly denied by large and powerful elements in India's national life',[37] the Cripps Mission acknowledged the right of any province 'not prepared to accept the new constitution to retain its present constitutional position' and further contemplated that should such non-acceding provinces 'so desire, His Majesty's Government will be prepared to agree upon a new constitution, giving them the same full status as the Indian Union'[38] while in turn the introduction of 'this novel principle of non-accession' was followed, after two conferences at Simla, by the purposely vague recommendations of the cabinet mission in 1946, outlining the three-tier constitutional structure with the union government vested with minimal central powers at the apex and, in an intermediate position, three groups of provinces, the one comprised of predominantly Hindu, the remaining two of predominantly Muslim provinces in the north-west and the north-east, dealing with all such subjects as the provinces comprising each group might desire to have dealt with in association, and, at the base, the provinces themselves dealing with all other subjects and possessing residuary sovereign rights.[39] Certainly this was not tantamount to Pakistan, for as has already been noted the cabinet mission had considered and deliberately rejected partition. The contemplated Union of India in itself testified to that. But the Council of the Muslim League was not mistaken in considering that in the mission's proposals there lay 'the basis and the foundation of Pakistan'.

The second condition preliminary to the achievement of Pakistan was the consolidation of Muslim opinion behind the League. Despite the difficulties inherent in the geographical distribution of the Muslim population and in the reluctance of more Muslims than may now be supposed to contemplate partition, this condition also was substantially fulfilled. To appreciate the extent to which this was so, it is necessary only to place side by side the results, in so far as the Muslim League was concerned, of the elections of 1937 and of 1946. Where at the earlier date, even in Muslim majority provinces the League, then an élitist grouping not a popular mass movement, which accounted for its not contesting all the Muslim seats, had made an indifferent showing, by the later date it was polling in most if not all cases close to its maximum natural strength. This was a remarkable achievement in terms both of leadership and of organisation. One element in it was the dramatisation of issues. This was a rewarding technique but one which exacted a sometimes terrible price. The League proclaimed its day of deliverance, its days of protest, and finally after the elections, on 16 August 1946, Direct Action Day, on which the black flags of the Muslim League fluttered over Muslim homes – and in Calcutta provided the occasion for what has gone down to history as the 'Great Calcutta Killing', nowhere described with more sickening realism than in the restrained pages of General Sir Francis Tuker's *While Memory Serves*.[40] Well may one ask whether Pakistan was attainable without communal violence on a scale unparalleled in all the years since the Mutiny.

There was a further condition of partition. The League had to be equated with the Congress or, as Jinnah preferred to phrase it, Pakistan and Hindustan. In numerical terms this meant the equation of minority with majority. It had happened elsewhere. It had happened in Ireland when the six counties of Northern

Ireland and the twenty-six counties of Southern Ireland were given equal representation in the Council of Ireland, that 'fleshless and bloodless skeleton' as Asquith termed it, proposed in the Government of Ireland Act 1920.[41] In arithmetical terms such parity could not be defended in either case. But as Jinnah argued the debate was not about numbers nor even about communities but about nations. Nations were equal irrespective of their size. He secured his aim at the Simla Conference in 1945, when League and Congress representation was equated, with a sharp protest by the League at the nomination by the Congress of a Muslim, Maulana Azad, as one of their representatives. It was 'a symbolic affront'. In the interim Government as re-formed in October 1946 a position of approximate equality was sustained. Jinnah was certainly the most formidable proponent of a two-nation theory yet to appear within the confines of the British Empire. Positively his demand was for unequivocal recognition of the separate nationality of Muslim India, which in Bengal at least was not self-evident; negatively it was for the reduction of the Congress claims to speak for all-India to a Congress right to speak for Hindustan. Nehru was written off as a Hindu imperialist; Gandhi as a man with whom it was impossible to negotiate because by vast self-deception he had convinced himself he was a spokesman of something more than Hinduism; Maulana Azad, that prototype of Congress Muslims, denounced as a renegade or even a quisling; the idea of a secular state ridiculed as part of a design of characteristic Hindu subtlety to fasten Hindu rule upon the whole of India. Again, however, there was implicit in Jinnah's demands a price even for their formulation. The League could challenge the claims of Congress to speak for all India most effectively only by becoming ever more firmly imprisoned within the rigid concept of a future communal state.

Finally there was one last condition of partition. To the Congress demand that the British should quit India, Muslims responded with the demand that they should divide and quit – and in that order. Here again the League were largely successful. It is true that the division for which they asked was not the division they received. The full demand was for an independent state of Pakistan comprising two areas, one in the north-west consisting of the Punjab, Sind, North-West Frontier, and British Baluchistan, the other the north-east consisting of Bengal and Assam. Accession to that demand would no doubt have created a viable state. But the demand rested upon community and as the cabinet mission concluded 'every argument that can be used in favour of Pakistan can equally, in our view, be used in favour of the exclusion of the non-Muslim areas from Pakistan'.[42]

Later Mountbatten was to drive home the argument, as when on 8 April 1947 he told Jinnah that the case he had made for the partition of India applied also to the partition of the Punjab and Bengal and 'that by sheer logic, if I accepted his arguments in the case of India as a whole I had also to apply them in the case of the two Provinces'. Jinnah protested at the prospect of 'moth-eaten' Pakistan. The viceroy agreed, but argued that the objections, the validity of which he accepted, were an argument against the partition of India itself.[43]

In the meantime, between Cabinet Mission and last viceroyalty there had been experience of government that was coalition in form but not in spirit. It was on 24 August 1946 that the first interim government, initially predominantly Congress in its composition, was appointed, with Lord Wavell presiding over its deliberations with a splendid, if unhelpful, soldierly reserve. In October, the Muslim League accepted the invitation to join and Congress had, thereupon, to decide on a reconstitution of the government, and in particular on the more important posts to be offered to the League. Under strong pressure from Sardar Vallabhbhai Patel, understandably anxious to retain control of the Home Department and with it of relations with the princes, and against the warnings of Maulana Azad, the principal portfolio they offered was that of minister for finance. When Chaudri Mohamad Ali heard the news in the department it is said he told Jinnah that it marked a great victory for the League. So in some respects it proved. The post was filled by Liaquat Ali Khan, and when Liaquat became the finance member (records Maulana Azad) he obtained the possession of the key to government. Every proposal of every department was subject to his scrutiny. 'Not a Chaprasi could be appointed in any department without the sanction of his department.'[44] What is more, Liaquat drafted a budget the onus of which fell, as it was intended to fall, heavily upon the wealthy supporters of the Congress. And while, to descend to trifling matters, it may be questioned whether tact mattered much at this late stage, it is still worth noting that the Congress ministers were not diplomatic in their handling of their new League colleagues. It was the practice of Congress ministers to foregather for tea before the sessions of the interim government. The invitation to the new League members to attend these gatherings came from Pandit Nehru's private secretary. They were offended.[45] They never attended. But then, of course, they might not have done so anyway. What alone was certain was that experience of such government served most of all to undermine notions of reconciliation through working in association.

With the statement of 20 February 1947 the British government regained the initiative. It was a classic example of policy making by draftsmanship. In the course of this laborious but clarifying business undertaken chiefly by the Cabinet's India and Burma Committee over which the Prime Minister presided, as draft by draft came under consideration, the bolder step – that of fixing a time-limit to British rule in India – came also to appear the wiser. The final decision was taken by the full Cabinet on 18 February. In the face of contrary advice from the viceroy, the Commander-in-Chief, experienced Governors and General Smuts, as well as the weight of India Office opinion, but assured of the unqualified backing, indeed insistence of the viceroy-designate, Lord Mountbatten, whose appointment was to be associated with the Statement, on the need for precision in respect of the time of going, the Prime Minister displayed qualities of leadership and firm conviction which earn him a notable place in Anglo-Indian and in Commonwealth history.

The statement[46] put an eighteen-month time limit, till June 1948, on British rule in India. For weeks it was subjected to the most careful and suspicious scrutiny in Delhi but it was found to be without trade of equivocation. The time limit enhanced the prospect of Pakistan but diminished the chances of its orderly creation and establishment. In April, Liaquat Ali Khan explained[47] that while the statement presupposed the coming into existence of Pakistan and was therefore to be welcomed, the time limit was too short. A capital had yet to be chosen: government and administration to be organised, the inheritance of British India to be divided. On 3 June the time limit was foreshortened by nearly a year, 15 August 1947 being fixed as the date of the transfer of power. The effect was to heighten the double impact made by the statement of 20 February. Pakistan was brought that much nearer; its early administration made that much more difficult.

The initiative regained by the British government was exploited by the last viceroy. His outstanding contribution, as seen from Delhi, was to impart a sense of urgency, clearly defined purpose, direction and above all momentum at a time when, with relaxing control, communal tensions might have merged into civil war – a possibility of which he twice warned the Cabinet – and led to partial disintegration. History was being made and Lord

Mountbatten brought drama to the making of it. Perhaps there was some element of illusion in the new understanding he established with the Congress leaders. Nehru, so Michael Edwardes has suggested, thought of Mountbatten as a 'straightforward English socialist', 'a sort of Philippe Egalité in naval uniform'.[48] What was important, however, was the personal rapport established with the Congress, though not with the League, leadership. Moreover, in smaller as in greater things Mountbatten sensed the time for change. He was always 'taking tea with treason', to use the diehard terminology of denunciation employed against Lord Irwin's reception of Gandhi in the early 1930s, and in the vice-chancellor's office at Delhi University Sir Maurice Gwyer, a former chief justice of India, derived wry amusement from studying the lists of those who now at long last were being entertained in the viceroy's house.

The first Mountbatten plan, with strange insensitivity initially code-named 'Plan Balkan', envisaging partition and involving the transfer of power in the first instance to individual provinces, was discussed in outline or 'run through' with, but not shown to the Indian leaders, sent to London, then revised in Cabinet and on a 'hunch' shown in its revised form by the viceroy to Pandit Nehru, who was staying with him at Simla, on the evening of 10 May. On reading it, Nehru, in the words of his own impassioned manuscript letter written in the course of a sleepless night, said the draft had produced 'a devastating effect' upon him. And why? Not because of a partition, in the inevitability of which the Congress leadership had already, however reluctantly, acquiesced, but rather because of the Congress nightmare of a multiple partition with a resulting picture in Nehru's words of 'fragmentation and conflict and disorder'. Clearly a plan which created such an impression had to be retracted. This was quickly done and an earlier plan, devised by V. P. Menon,[49] who was also at Simla, reintroduced. The outstanding features of this plan were a transfer of power by means of the granting of dominion status to two, or possibly three, should the parties in Bengal so agree, new dominions. By reason of the element of continuity, which dominion status allowed for, a much earlier transfer of power than would otherwise have been conceivable could now be effected. It was that which, above all, commended the plan, and dominion status, to the Congress. The League, welcoming the concession of Pakistan even if in truncated form, had already indicated their intention to seek commonwealth membership, while the Princes saw in it some link at one remove with the dissolving world of the British *Raj*. This satisfaction with dominion status extended to dominion governments and to the Churchill-led opposition in London, who conveyed assurances of helpful cooperation to the government and viceroy who had contrived it. Whatever else the transfer of power may or may not have been it was a Commonwealth occasion!

Two last questions remain. The first is, why did the Congress leaders at the last agree to partition? The answer, it may be suggested, was three-fold. They had ambitions for India and those ambitions could not be fulfilled without strong central government. So long as the majority of Muslims were within a united India, that meant that strong, central government was out of the question. The second, entertained by Vallabhbhai Patel but by no means universally shared by his colleagues, was the belief that Pakistan would not long endure. Patel was convinced, records Maulana Azad, who was not a friendly witness, that Pakistan was 'not viable' and would 'collapse in a short time'.[50] Nehru also, though less categoric, did not think it could last[51] and V. P. Menon writing to Patel from Simla on the momentous 10 May 1947 had reported that this view was entertained by the Viceroy, who argued against delay in the effecting of partition on the ground that 'truncated' Pakistan, if conceded now, was bound to come back later. 'I agreed with H. E.'s observations', commented Menon, 'because our slogan should now be "divide in order to unite".'[52] The third dominant consideration was time. The Congress leaders had struggled long for independence, they were now ageing men and they were not prepared to delay independence further. Here indeed was a root difference between Congress and the League and a source of strength to Jinnah. He was prepared to let independence wait upon division, while his opponents for the most part were not prepared to let it wait upon unity. Not all of them, however, were agreed on this count. To the last, Maulana Azad remained convinced that time was on the side of unity.[53] One, two, years' delay and the cabinet mission plan with its weak centre and its provincial groupings would prove acceptable. Patel was against him, so was Nehru and at the last Gandhi himself appeared resigned to partition. Azad, as a Congress Muslim, had his own reasons for insistence upon unity and his own grounds for misgivings about the consequences of partition. But if in this he was percipient, it may well be questioned whether he was realistic in his own recommendations.

The possible deferment of independence for one year or more in the supposed interests of unity invites certain questions. Were the resources of the Indian civil service and the British Army in India at this stage equal to the responsibilities such delay would undoubtedly involve? Were the British public at home prepared to sustain the effort that might be needed? If not, who was to govern India in the meantime? The Muslim League, Gandhi suggested, as a desperate but not an original device – Rajagopalachari had proposed it in 1940 also to avert partition. The Congress would not hear of it. Most of all, was Maulana Azad right in his presupposition that with time passions would cool? Was it not more likely that with procrastination they would in fact be further inflamed? Was it not more probable that far from diminishing the ambitions of princes, subtracting from the negatives of the League, qualifying the uncompromising attitudes of the Congress, all would be accentuated. And what of the Sikhs, who accepted partition in June 1947? One of their leaders, Master Tara Singh – that prophetic-looking figure, whose words belied the benignity of his flowing beard – in late February 1947, brandishing an unsheathed sword at a mass rally in the Punjab, is alleged to have cried, 'O Hindus and Sikhs! Be ready for self-destruction . . . I have sounded the bugle. Finish the Muslim League', and 'Death to Pakistan'.[54] It was a few years later that he enunciated his creed 'I believe in chaos.' All that was to be observed in early 1947 suggested that if the momentum of events were slowed down, the risks of chaos in central and northern India were unlikely to diminish. If there was mistiming about the settlement, it may well be that it was some ten years too late, rather than one or two years too soon. Tragedy, however, there was and no doubt within the same timetable some part of it might have been avoided. But what is apt to be overlooked and ought not to be is that once partition was to be the solution then the possibilities were not simply tragedy or no tragedy in the Punjab, but the further possibility of even greater tragedy than in fact occurred.

In the view of Britain and Pakistan there were two successor states to the British *Raj*; in the predominant Indian view there was rather a successor state, the Union of India as indicated in the Report of the Cabinet Mission – Nehru was insistent on this – and a seceding state. The distinction is more than one of semantics. If there were two successor states then each was equally entitled to division of resources and authority within the prescribed terms of reference. If however there was one successor state from which territories were carved to form a seceding state, then the presumption was that resources and authority descended to the successor state except in so far as they were specifically allocated to the seceding state. In British statute law the issue may be readily disposed of. Under the provisions of the Indian Independence Act 1947, described in its Preamble as 'An Act to make provision for the setting up in India of two independent dominions . . .', there were twò successor states. Article 1(1) read: 'As from the 15th day of August, nineteen hundred and forty seven, two independent dominions shall be set up in India, to be known respectively as India and Pakistan'[55] – phrasing to which the Congress leadership raised persistent objection. But could the issue be settled by reference to British statute law alone? The Congress thought not. It claimed that the Dominion of India should continue as the international personality of pre-partition India and V. P. Menon, after consulting the Legislative Department advised the viceroy that post-partition would remain identifiable with pre-partition India. 'It was our definite view', he wrote, 'that neither variation in the extent of a state's territory, nor change in its constitution, could affect the identity of the state.'[56] In respect of international status this opinion was accepted (or in the case of Pakistan acquiesced in after protest and with reservation), with the result that India after independence remained a member of the United Nations and all international organisations whereas Pakistan, as a new state, sought such membership *ab initio*.

Psychologically the question of succession or secession was not as simple as it appeared, either in British statutory enactment or in international practice. The respective designations of the two states were in themselves significant. They were called India and Pakistan, not Hindustan and Pakistan, as Jinnah and the Muslim League deemed logical and desired. The reason was clear. Behind the name India lay the claim consistently advanced and never discarded, not even at the moment of partition, by the Indian National Congress that it was representative not of a class nor of a community but of a nation and that that nation was India. When the All-India Congress Committee met in Delhi on 14 June 1947 to approve the 3 June plan for partition, the resolution accepting partition contained these words:

> Geography and the mountains and the seas fashioned India as she is, and no human agency can change that shape or come in the way of her final destiny . . . The picture of India we have learnt to cherish will remain in our minds and our hearts. The A.I.C.C. earnestly trusts that when the present passions have subsided, India's problems will be viewed in their proper perspective and the false doctrine of two nations in India will be discredited and discarded by all.[57]

Acharya Kripalani, the president of the Congress, issued a statement on the eve of independence, 14 August 1947, saying it was a day of sorrow and destruction for India. Kripalani was at once a disciple of Gandhi and a man of Sind. But he was also the president of the Congress. His emotional reaction to partition was widely shared. It precluded neither acquiescence in the existence of Pakistan nor peaceful co-existence with her. But it rested upon considerations and derived from assumptions about partition and its meaning which neither were, nor in the nature of things could be, shared on the other side of the border.

On the subcontinent at least, the partition of India has not passed into history. It touched too painfully on sensitive nerves for that. The area of friction was progressively reduced in subsequent years – the armed forces and civil service were divided, government property and resources distributed so far as they ever would be, even the Indus Waters' dispute resolved by treaty in 1960 with the assistance of the International Bank. But reduction in the area of dispute led to no corresponding diminution in its intensity. Kashmir remained and not only Kashmir. Behind Kashmir lay wellnigh irreconcilable interpretations of what had happened in 1947.

Could the partition of India have been averted? This is a question to which no answer commanding a consensus of historical opinion has emerged or is likely to emerge for a long time. But two points may be noted in respect of the immediate context of partition. The first is that the British Labour Party, forming its first majority government in 1945, had been committed since 1920 not merely to self-government but to self-determination for India (a phrase admittedly never precisely defined and usually qualified) – in the Resolutions passed at party conferences, by an expression of hope that India would choose to remain within the Commonwealth – and that its leader Clement Attlee, prime minister in the critical years 1945–7, had a personal interest in Indian affairs, deepened by the unhappy experiences of the Simon Commission of which he was a member and well exemplified in his critical commentaries on the Government of India Bill 1935, coupled with a personal concern that the Labour Party's commitment to self-determination should be honoured by his administration.[58] No British government, therefore, was likely to give Indian affairs a higher priority, nor to seek more carefully for a solution on a basis of unity that would at once redound to the credit of its statesmanship and to the promotion of British and Commonwealth interests. If they failed, was any British government at that late stage likely to succeed? And that leads on to the second point, already underlined, namely the diminishing freedom of action of governments, parties and leaders. Partition was the product of a triangular situation which narrowed the range of options and of necessity limited the freedom of manœuvre even of a purposeful administration or enlightened leaders. All were the prisoners of a pattern of politics which constantly pressed in upon their liberty of choice. 'There would have been no partition', remarked Nehru in March 1958, had Mountbatten come to India as Viceroy 'a year earlier'.[59] He would have 'hustled' the British government and the speed of the transfer would have averted it. But is such a view credible?

There was contemporary awareness, even if insufficient allowance was made, for the inevitable consequences of the overall political pattern. A few months before partition the problems of India were discussed by a prominent business supporter of the Congress. He spoke, as was common at that time, about the nearly insoluble problems of the triangular relationship and of the disruptive influence of the third party. But the theme was not developed quite along accustomed lines. There was it is true, denunciation of the third party, but somehow it did not seem to fit the third party. It was only after a while that it became clear that it was not the British who were being denounced; it was the Muslims. They, it appears, were to be regarded – and it was consistent with Congress claims to speak for all-India – as the third party in India. Could they be wished off the scene, eighty million of them, then all would be well in the new-found friendship of Britain and Congress India. Paradoxical as it may seem, this Congress spokesman was perhaps too well-grounded in British interpretations of the history of the subcontinent. He assumed, as the British are apt to assume, that the determining event in its modern history was the impact of expanding Europe.[60] But the partition of India suggested that this was not so. In the last resort it was not the British, it was the Mohammedan invaders of India, who possessed the more inflexible because more deeply grounded influence upon events. By early 1947 this was gradually coming to be realised and it helps to explain a remark by B. R. Ambedkar the leader of the Scheduled castes in the Constituent Assembly, that the war 'of which a good many people in this country seem to support the idea will not be a war on the British. It will be a war on the Muslims.'[61]

Finally there remains the question, academic in its ordinary presentation but fundamental to partition in India and elsewhere. What is a nation? How is it to be identified? Is there some criterion

by which it may be judged whether or not there were two nations*
in the subcontinent? Or is it the case that political science does not
deal in such absolutes and that only history by way of trial, error
and much suffering can supply the answer?

---

* Or more? In 1971–2 Pakistan itself was partitioned by the break away of East
from West Pakistan to form the new independent state of Bangladesh, proclaimed
on 26 March and formally established after internecine warfare on 16 December
1971. So one might broaden one's enquiry and ask were there two nations,
coincident respectively with West and East in Pakistan and three in the
sub-continent? Such a question would be the product not only of hindsight. Some,
not *a priori* unfriendly to the concept, notably Richard Casey, the Australian
Governor of Bengal, in the later war years, doubted the enduring quality of
Pakistan on grounds of the reality of the single nationhood of its geographically
divided peoples, even as it was emerging, while Lord Mountbatten on 28 May
1947 foresaw the possibility of East Bengal (now Bangladesh), seeking membership of the Commonwealth as a separate dominion – as happened in April 1972.[62]

Part Two

The Commonwealth
Since 1947

'I think the chief value of this declaration and of what preceded it was that it did bring a touch of healing in our relations with certain countries. We are in no way subordinate to them and they are in no way subordinate to us. We shall go our way and they will go their way. But our way, unless something happens, will be a friendly way; at any rate attempts will be made to understand one another. And the fact that we have begun this new type of association with a touch of healing will be good for us, good for them and, I think, good for the world.'

JAWAHARLAL NEHRU IN THE INDIAN CONSTITUENT ASSEMBLY, 16 MAY 1949, ON THE COMMONWEALTH PRIME MINISTERS' DECLARATION OF APRIL 1949 ON INDIA'S REPUBLICAN MEMBERSHIP

'The wind of change is blowing through this continent.'

THE RIGHT HON. HAROLD MACMILLAN IN AN ADDRESS TO BOTH HOUSES OF PARLIAMENT AT CAPE TOWN, 3 FEBRUARY 1960

'L'Angleterre en effet est insulaire, maritime, liée par ses échanges, ses marchés, son ravitaillement, aux pays les plus divers et souvent les plus lointains.'

PRESIDENT DE GAULLE EXPLAINING THE EXERCISE BY THE FRENCH GOVERNMENT OF ITS RIGHT OF VETO ON BRITAIN'S ENTRY INTO THE COMMON MARKET, 14 JANUARY 1963

'I do not think any Prime Minister has . . . asked the House in time of peace to take a positive decision of such importance . . .
    'The Commonwealth . . . is a unique association which we value. But the idea that it would become an effective economic or political, let alone military bloc has never materialised.'

EDWARD HEATH PROPOSING A MOTION FOR THE APPROVAL OF H.M.G'S DECISION IN PRINCIPLE TO JOIN THE EEC, ON 28 OCTOBER 1971

'It is tomorrow then, and not yesterday, which bears our destiny.'

ROBERT MUGABE ON INDEPENDENCE DAY, 17 APRIL 1980, ZIMBABWE

5 Constitutional Transformation, Irish Republican Secession, Indian Republican Accession and the Changing Position of the Crown

The wartime trend towards decentralisation continued with increasing momentum after the war. It was implicit in Commonwealth attitudes towards the new international organisation, and explicit in Commonwealth reconsideration of constitutional forms, more especially those of citizenship and Crown.

When the Commonwealth leaders met in London in April 1945, their most important task was the examination of the proposals prepared at the Dumbarton Oaks Conference for the Charter of the United Nations as supplemented, or modified, at Yalta. Smuts thought the resulting document too legalistic in tone, and submitted to his colleagues an eloquent declaration which, conflated with an earlier and more soberly phrased draft of Sir Charles Webster, formed in essence the preamble to the UN Charter. It was Smuts specifically who introduced the idea of 'fundamental human rights', later to be turned against both his own and his successors' racial policies in South Africa.[1] But essentially it was not phrases but substance that mattered to Commonwealth leaders. And substance divided them. In the subsequent debates on the provisions of the Charter at San Francisco, there was no semblance of a united Commonwealth approach. On the contrary, a feature of the San Francisco Conference was the conflict of opinion, on a number of important provisions, between the United Kingdom, as one of the Five Great Powers, and those of the dominions which were to be numbered among the foremost of the middle powers, with Australia – whose representative, Dr. H. V. Evatt, combined an expert's grasp of constitutional technicalities with formidable dialectical pugnacity – especially critical of the Great Power veto. Nor were there British Commonwealth delegations, either for the negotiating of peace treaties or for appending an overall Com-

135

monwealth signature to them. Each dominion signed in the alphabetical order, as one of the independent allied nations who had fought the war.

Developments in international relations had their counterpart in developments within the Commonwealth. The use of the term dominion was increasingly discouraged before being discarded; the Dominions Office was renamed the Commonwealth Relations Office; Commonwealth citizen was approved as an acceptable alternative to British subject; and, more important, the basis of citizenship was changed. The initiative in this last instance came from Canada.

In September 1945 the Canadian government advised the United Kingdom government that it found it desirable to introduce legislation laying down the conditions of Canadian citizenship. As defined in the succeeding Canadian Citizenship Act 1946, these conditions were at variance with the traditional concepts of the status of British subjects. It had hitherto been regarded (except in the Irish Free State) as a fundamental part of Empire and Commonwealth that there should be a common nationality and that the common law rule, by which all persons born within the king's dominions were British subjects, should remain unimpaired. It is true that while the status was common, the privileges that flowed from it were particular, each self-governing member of the Commonwealth deciding for itself its own electoral and immigration laws, and while such legislation ordinarily took the fact of common status into account, it was not determined by its existence – as dominion immigration laws abundantly testified. Only in the United Kingdom was the 'open door' in terms of entry, political rights and equal opportunity a reality in law for all British subjects, whatever their country of origin. By reason of limited practical validity and in other ways, the old concept, deriving from more spacious times, no longer appeared either realistic or acceptable overseas. The Canadian legislation, taking account of the objections to it, transformed the basis of citizenship, by defining the conditions of Canadian citizenship and then providing that all Canadian citizens were British subjects. The British Nationality Act 1948 adopted this new principle. It established a local citizenship, that of the 'United Kingdom and Colonies', from which the common status of British subject or Commonwealth citizen, a term introduced for the first time, derived. The other member-states of the Commonwealth for the most part enacted legislation on the same pattern, making local citizenship the fundamental status and determining the privileges of the common status of British Subject or Commonwealth Citizen generally on a reciprocal basis – with the United Kingdom, however, continuing its open door policy on immigration until the Immigration Act 1962.[2] Reflected in these changes was recognition of the fundamental status of 'the Nations', as against 'The Commonwealth' they comprised.

But the tide of opinion was not all one way: nor were dominion governments always to be found in the vanguard of change. In 1926 the suggested use of the term 'independent' to describe the status of the dominions troubled Britain and the majority of the dominions; in 1947 at Attlee's suggestion 'Independence' was introduced into the title of the Bill that was to give freedom to India – the Indian Independence Bill, 1947. There were rumblings of impending Churchillian and other Conservative protest, which it was thought would be unhelpful when reported in the sub-continent. By way of possible counter, Attlee had enquiries made of Dominion Prime Ministers as to whether he might indicate their concurrence in the proposed entitlement. His simple enquiry, as it might seem, received no simple answer. Smuts deemed use of the term 'independence' regrettable – it was 'an apple of discord and may open dangerous controversy', as well as being embarrassing in South Africa, – and suggested 'India Status Bill'; Mackenzie King told Sir A. Clutterbuck, the British High Commissioner, that he thought its use liable to cause misunderstanding, as being taken to denote independence of the Commonwealth and went on to recall how in 1926 'after much coming and going behind the scenes he and Hankey between them had succeeded in coaxing Hertzog out of it'; while for Australia Evatt taking cryptic note of the near coincidence of Attlee's enquiry to Independence Day, reserved his position as did Peter Fraser, uneasy about how his own opposition might react. Attlee withdrew his suggestion without altering course. On 5 July when the text of the bill was published the *Statesman* (Calcutta) commented: 'Above all, there is the masterstroke, the title, "the Indian Independence Act"'.[3]

More complex issues arose in respect of forms of membership. The Balfour Report had written of common allegiance to the Crown as a conventional characteristic, tantamount to a condition, of dominion status. The language of the Report, restated in the Preamble to the Statute of Westminster, and reinforced by recollections of Lloyd George's unqualified rejection of any possibility of negotiation about an associated Irish republic, was widely though not universally interpreted as exalting allegiance as the principal fact of Commonwealth life and as excluding the thought of republican membership as verging on treasonable heresy. These

assumptions, under question in Irish relations with the Commonwealth since the enactment of the External Relations Act in 1936,
were disturbed in the years 1948–9 by an Irish decision to end an
equivocal relationship, on the assumption of the incompatibility of
Irish republican and Commonwealth monarchical institutions, and
by a near-simultaneous Indian request to establish republican
membership, on a basis of formal recognition. Despite the overlap
in time and substance in Irish republican withdrawal and Indian
republican admission, the problems they presented were separately unravelled. This was not fortuitous; it was an aim of British
policy to keep the two issues distinct.

Commonwealth attitudes to Irish constitutional developments
were considered at the Imperial Conference 1937 on the basis of a
memorandum[4] prepared by the dominions secretary, Malcolm
MacDonald. In the abdication crisis of December 1936, it will be
recalled, the Irish government had enacted the External Relations
Act, which had empowered the Executive Council of the Irish Free
State to authorise the use of the king's signature on the letters of
credence to be presented to heads of foreign states by Irish
diplomatic representatives, and in the following year a new
constitution, republican in all but name, was submitted to the
people in a plebiscite and approved by them. The British government proposed tentatively to respond to these developments,
actual in the case of the External Relations Act and still prospective
when the Imperial Conference met in respect of the constitution,
by taking the general line that while not saying, of course, that the
legislation makes no fundamental difference in the position',
stating none the less that 'we would be prepared to treat it as not
making such a fundamental alteration'. They enquired whether
dominion governments would concur generally in such a view. The
response was in the affirmative. MacKenzie King had no doubt of
its wisdom; Hertzog, feeling that 'whatever the British government
does now as regards Ireland is, in my opinion, most important for
the future of the Commonwealth', thought the proposed course
'very wise' and indeed could see no reason why the Irish Free State,
even if it declared itself to be a republic, should cease to be a
member of the Commonwealth, so long as the king's title remained
unchanged and the king continued to be recognised as the symbol
of the Commonwealth; while on the Australian side there were
regrets from Prime Minister Lyons at Irish developments and
hopes from Stanley Bruce that 'we are not going to take this Irish
question too seriously' or make an issue of it. Neville Chamberlain
summed up the discussion by saying that the disadvantages of

taking any decision that would have the effect of pushing the Irish Free State out when she wished to remain in, were so obvious that they could only be justified 'if they were clearly necessary to save the Commonwealth from some worse fate. We do not propose to lay down any conditions, which, if the Irish Free State were to transgress, she would put herself out of the Commonwealth.' From that position the British and the dominion governments did not depart in succeeding years.

The nature of the Irish association with the Commonwealth remained ambivalent when the war ended. The British and dominion governments for their part continued to regard Eire – to follow common practice and use the designation given to the Irish Free State after 1937 – as a member, in accord with the view formulated in 1937 that the Irish Constitution of 1937, read in conjunction with the External Relations Act of the preceding year, might be regarded as if it had effected no fundamental alteration in Irish relations with the Commonwealth, as defined in the 1921 treaty. Since common allegiance was a conventional characteristic of dominion status, this view necessarily implied Irish allegiance in some degree. The Irish government had, however, repudiated allegiance and the Irish view, as expressed by de Valera on many occasions, was that Eire could not, for that reason, be a member, but that she was, after 1937, a state outside the Commonwealth, associated externally with it, not owing allegiance to the Crown, and a republic in fact even though not specifically so described in the constitution. Irish association, therefore, continued, despite divergent and conflicting interpretations of its nature, because of mutual self-interest and on a presumably unspoken official understanding. But while it was thus the policy of governments to let sleeping dogs lie, there were others who thought it their duty to stir them up. In the Dáil, Deputies Flanagan and Dillon enquired of the Taoiseach in season and out whether the state was a republic or not, a member of the Commonwealth or not, while at Westminster, also, Labour ministers were troubled by Unionist questions, as to whether Eire was a dominion and whether, as a dominion, she had been consulted, for example, about the changes in the Royal Style and Titles, consequential upon the independence of India and Pakistan, to which the under-secretary of state, Patrick Gordon Walker, replied that she had been, as a member of the Commonwealth – a government within the Commonwealth.[5] Could the subtle, but politically fragile, ambiguities of the External Relations Act continue to serve a useful purpose, in the face of such hostile probing? De Valera, contemplating by 1947 the use of the enabling powers of the Act in other ways, so as to transfer the required formalities from· the Crown to the president, by a legislative enactment, evidently entertained some misgivings. But before he had occasion to show his hand, the scene was changed by the general election of 1948 which brought about his fall from office and the formation of an inter-party administration under J. A. Costello. A more drastic solution at once became probable, the new Taoiseach having been a critic from the first of the External Relations Act and being in office with Labour and republican support, Sean MacBride, the leader of the new Republican party, being Minister for External Affairs. On a visit to London early in 1948, Costello noted without satisfaction that at an official occasion at No. 10 Downing Street, Attlee proposed the toast of 'The King' as appropriate for the country of his guests, thereby implying that on the British view Eire continued to owe allegiance to the Crown and remained a member of the British Commonwealth of Nations.[6]

The decision in principle to repeal the External Relations Act and to designate the state formally as a republic was reached unanimously, as Costello later revealed,[7] by the incoming inter-party government in the summer of 1948, but the actual announcement was made by Costello under pressure of newspaper enquiries,[8] following unauthorised disclosure of the earlier decision of principle, while on a visit to Canada. It was the timing and not the event that was a matter for much speculation – the precise significance to be attributed to supposedly provocative gestures by the governor-general of Canada, Field-Marshal Lord Alexander of Tunis, an Ulsterman, remaining uncertain. More important were the implications of the decision. There was no dispute, as in the 1930s, about a dominion's right of secession and, therefore, on the British view, of Eire's right to secede. But in the Irish case possible ambiguity remained; did the impending repeal of the External Relations Act and the parallel decision to describe the state formally as a republic imply of necessity secession from the Commonwealth? Costello was asked that question, reputedly by a representative of the Tass agency at a press conference in Ottawa. He replied in the affirmative and so disposed of what might otherwise have been deemed on open issue. It is not known if the reply was premeditated, nor if secession was the agreed purpose of the cabinet in approving earlier the repeal in principle of the External Relations Act.

The Republic of Ireland Bill was introduced in the Dáil on 24 November 1948. The preamble stated that it was an Act to repeal the External Relations Act, to declare that the description of the state should be the republic of Ireland and to enable the president to exercise executive power or any executive function in connection with the state's external relations. This precisely described its purpose. In introducing it, the Taoiseach said that the Bill when enacted would have consequences which would mark it as a measure ending an epoch.

> This bill will end [he said] and end forever, in a simple, clear and unequivocal way this country's long and tragic association with the institution of the British Crown and will make it manifest beyond equivocation or subtlety that the national and international status of this country is that of an independent republic.

The measure was not designed or conceived in any spirit of hostility to the British people or to the institution of the British Crown; on the contrary, one result of its enactment would be that Ireland's relationship with Britain would be 'put upon a better and firmer foundation than it ever has been before', and it would be 'unthinkable', Costello continued, for the Republic of Ireland to draw farther away from the nations of the Commonwealth with which 'we have had such long and, I think, such fruitful association in the past twenty-five or twenty-six years'.[9] However, that was what he was proposing the country should do.

There were two immediate practical questions to be resolved. Did Irish citizens become aliens in Britain and in the rest of the Commonwealth as a consequence of Irish secession? And did existing trade preferences come to an end? With regard to the first the key was to be found in the British Nationality Act 1948, which in effect had made British and Irish citizenship reciprocal. Citizens of Eire, under the provisions of the British Act, were no longer to be British subjects though when in Britain they would be treated as if they were. After the announcement of Irish secession the question narrowed down to whether the provisions of an Act passed in one set of circumstances would continue to apply in another. The answer by agreement of the British and Irish governments was in the affirmative and on the basis of continued reciprocity. It was arrived at on both sides in the light of their own state interests and was generally, though not universally, welcomed – George Bernard Shaw, for his part and after living in England for nearly half a century, remarking 'I shall always be a foreigner here whether I have to register as an alien or not, because I am one of the few people here who thinks objectively.' These citizenship arrangements constituted in effect the foundation of a 'special relationship' and were in accord with Costello's concept of a continuing, but henceforward informal, Irish association with the Commonwealth.

In respect of trade it was suggested that after secession there was risk that the existence of preferential duties between Britain and Ireland would be challenged as conflicting with the most favoured nation clause in commercial treaties with foreign countries and with the General Agreement on Tariffs and Trade negotiated at Geneva in 1947. On this point however the Irish government were always and (it emerged) rightly confident. They argued that the very close and long-standing trading relations between the two countries warranted exceptional treatment and more particularly they pointed to the fact that the schedule to the Geneva Agreement listed Commonwealth countries by name and individually without any general heading implying that the preferences exchanged were conditional upon Commonwealth membership. Furthermore, in 1950 Ireland concluded a Treaty of Friendship, Commerce and Navigation with the United States, ensuring thereby among other things that the continuance of the existing trade preferences would not be questioned in Washington. Accordingly in terms of trade there was also acceptance of the idea of a 'special relationship' – which proved in immediately succeeding years of advantage to both countries but more especially to Britain's industrial exports.

What was the response to Irish secession in the wider Commonwealth setting? With the possible exception of the Canadian prime minister, Commonwealth ministers had no advance information of it. On this point the Lord Chancellor, Lord Jowitt, who made no complaint, was explicit, and to conservative critics who maintained that Labour ministers had not done enough to persuade the Irish government to hold its hand he replied that they were not given the opportunity and furthermore that he felt that if any of them had spoken to the Irish 'with the eloquence of Demosthenes and at greater length even than Mr Gladstone, I am convinced that he would have failed – as I failed'.[10] To that extent Irish secession was deliberately settled apart from the Commonwealth. Yet despite the lack of prior consultation and the absence of Irish delegates from the meeting of Commonwealth prime ministers in October 1948 because of partition, or more precisely because of the Irish wish to be given advance assurances, which were not forthcoming, that the subject might be raised, the Commonwealth did play, presumably for the last time, a rôle – it may be thought not an unhelpful one – in Irish affairs.

That Commonwealth rôle had two aspects. The first was

negative. The British government considered the possibilities of a sharper reaction, *inter alia* in respect of citizenship and trade, to Irish secession than in fact they expressed – or so it would seem reasonable to infer from the lord chancellor's defence against Conservative critics of the arrangements made. Britain, he argued, should consider where her own interests lay and he made it clear that he was not prepared, out of resentment, to sponsor measures that were going to hurt Britain more than they hurt Ireland. But he then went on to explain that if the British government had taken a different line from the one they decided to take, 'we should have acted in the teeth of the advice of the representatives of Canada, Australia and New Zealand...'[11] Lawyers choose their words carefully. What lay behind these observations? At the time of the Commonwealth prime ministers' meeting in October there were separate discussions, first at Chequers and then at Paris, between representatives of the Irish government and representatives of the British, Canadian, Australian and New Zealand governments. It was at these discussions that there emerged – and Costello subsequently confirmed that the reasonable inference to be drawn from the lord chancellor's remarks was correct – something like a united 'old dominion' view to the effect that Irish secession should not be allowed to impair relations between Ireland and the other countries of the Commonwealth, and that in so far as this was possible the way should be left open for her return – Australia's Labour prime minister, Ben Chifley, later making this point with some emphasis.[12] When Peter Fraser, New Zealand's prime minister, was asked what difference secession would make in New Zealand's attitude to Ireland, he replied, 'What difference could there be? There has been friendliness always', and in the New Zealand Republic of Ireland Act[13] it was expressly stated that New Zealand law should have operation in relation to the Republic of Ireland 'as it would have had if the Republic of Ireland had remained part of His Majesty's dominions'. In statutory terms friendliness could go no further than that!

But after Easter Day 1949, when the republic was proclaimed, Ireland was no longer, on any interpretation, part of His Majesty's dominions. This brought an end to constitutional ambiguity – 'the pirouetting on the point of a pin', said Costello, 'was over' – by the severance of all formal ties. That made a psychological difference. Professor J. D. B. Miller of the Australian National University has noted that

the 1948 arrangements put paid to the whole score, with

goodwill on all sides. Except for some mild scuffling between Mr Menzies's government in Australia and the Irish government about how the Australian ambassador to Eire should be designated, later relations between Eire and the old dominions have little to offer the historian.[14]

More formally, Irish representatives no longer attended prime ministers' meetings. It would be interesting to speculate about the views they might have advanced in the successive crises through which the Commonwealth passed after 1949 – African membership, the Suez affair, the Common Market, South Africa's secession, Southern Rhodesia. Two things are certain. One is that a distinctive voice, that of a European nationalism, was lost – and it may well be that the Commonwealth, especially on two of the issues mentioned – South Africa and the Common Market – was the poorer for it. The other is that thirty years later Ireland, constitutionally, would have been with the great majority, republics rather than monarchies having become the norm within the Commonwealth. It remains one of the ironies of history that Ireland seceded in the year that India as a republic became a member. How does one explain the apparent paradox? The answer is not to be found in simple constitutional contrasts but in the differences in the historic and the contemporary realities they represented. After 1916, the republic in Ireland symbolised the cause of independence whereas in India what mattered was the freedom movement, with the republic incidental to it. This enabled the Indian government, as Pandit Nehru reminded the Indian Parliament at the time, to take note of Irish external association precedents which, as he explained, had shown Indians that it was possible to reconcile republicanism with Commonwealth membership but also to be flexible in respect of the monarch as symbolic head of the Commonwealth. To that extent others followed the path Ireland had pioneered, while Ireland herself elected to travel other roads. Yet history was powerfully reinforced in each case by more immediate considerations. At the moment of decision the Republic of India acceded to and the Republic of Ireland seceded from the Commonwealth because of their respective governments' interpretation of their respective state interests.

In the Irish case, those interests were interpreted increasingly in European terms. In those terms, Irish relations with Britain remained fundamental but her relations with the Commonwealth, despite ties of kinship with the old dominions which accounted in large measure for their 'friendliness', appeared an artificially

imposed superstructure. The counterpart to Irish secession from
the Commonwealth was accordingly her rapprochement with
Europe through Irish association with the European Recovery
Programme and her foundation membership of the Council of
Europe in the 1940s, her negotiation in the 1960s of the Anglo-
Irish Free Trade Agreement, the Irish application, without reservation or qualification, to subscribe to the Treaty of Rome and
her subsequent membership of the EEC, approved in a referendum in 1972 by 84 per cent of the electorate. In the broadest sense
all these developments may be taken to reflect a shift of Irish
interest from countries overseas, where many Irish emigrants had
settled, to the geographical area of which Ireland was a part. Not
for the first time might this be represented, with certain trans-
Atlantic qualifications, as a triumph of geography over recent
history.

India was the counterpart to Ireland. If Indian attachment to
republicanism was less deeply embedded in the national consciousness, the pull of its continental environment in the years after
the war was the more pronounced. 'Strong winds are blowing all
over Asia', declared Pandit Nehru at the opening of the Inter-
Asian Conference at New Delhi in March 1947[15] and there were
many who attended this gathering of the leaders of a resurgent
continent who believed that the ending of western imperialism
should also bring to an end all formal relations with the western
powers. 'Asia for the Asians' was the watchword and in that time of
high emotion allied to sanguine expectation, the development of
friendly associations within a continent, so long kept apart under
the rule of various Western empires, was deemed to have a first or
even an exclusive claim. The creation of an Asian bloc was a
possibility that was accordingly widely canvassed and hopes were
expressed that south-east and south Asia might become a neut-
ralised region. Yet however attractive such proposals might seem at
first sight closer analysis brought to light rivalries within Asia, as
well as other factors, which cast doubt upon their practicability,
apart altogether from their wisdom. Did not the maritime interests
of the countries of the area in effect preclude a policy of
contracting out, or of isolation from world affairs? Was it prudent,
moreover, in the longer-term to dissociate Asian countries, with
their large and under-nourished populations, even politically from
the technologically advanced west? 'The service of India means the
service of the millions who suffer',[16] declared Pandit Nehru as the
day of Indian independence dawned. But was that service to be
discharged without all the aid that the west might be persuaded to

give? Whatever the ultimate answers, considerations such as these, and especially about some future association with the west, had their influence on Asian thinking and had perforce to be weighed by Asian leaders.

There were also, however, other countervailing factors. Two of the chief aims of Indian and of Pakistani foreign policy were proclaimed to be national freedom for colonial peoples and the ending of racial discrimination. In themselves these aims implied antagonism to European imperialisms. And freely though a distinction was drawn between Britain's liberal policies, as applied in India, Burma and Ceylon and epitomised in Attlee's assertion that the Commonwealth desired to have no unwilling members, and the Asian policies pursued at that time by the 'reactionary imperialisms' of the Netherlands and France, it was also noted that Britain retained the greatest of the colonial empires and that its vast possessions in Africa seemed for the most part far from the goal of self-government. Furthermore it was observed, to quote from a memorandum on the Commonwealth issue drafted by eminent and independent Indians,[17] that 'in the Union of South Africa and in some of the African British colonies, racial prejudice dominates legislation and administration in regard to Indians'; and it was argued 'that we should have no link with the British Commonwealth whose policy is marred by such glaring disregard of our just rights'. Certainly the fact that South Africa, a member of the Commonwealth, enforced racial discrimination as a matter of political principle by itself, seemed to many leading Congressmen in 1947 sufficient reason why India should secede once the transitional advantages of membership had been reaped. Moreover, apart from South Africa, the older dominions were largely British and almost wholly European in origin and outlook, while Indians were never more mindful than on the morrow of independence of the fact that they were citizens of a mother country with memories and traditions that went back to prehistoric times and with a cultural influence that had at one time or another spread over much of Asia. 'At the dawn of history,' to quote from Pandit Nehru's speech of 14 August 1947 once more,[18] 'India started on her unending quest, and trackless centuries are filled with her striving and the grandeur of her success and her failures.' Could a country trailing clouds of ancient tragedies and glories find a satisfying sense of fulfilment in the membership of a Commonwealth formally united by the symbolism of another people, race and culture? Dominion status as a practical expedient, by which a threatened deadlock over the tranfer of power in 1947 might be most expeditiously resolved, was one thing; as an enduring element in the Indian political scene, it was another.

The problem of India's relations with the Commonwealth required both study and reflection on the part of India's leaders; for in their hands lay the freedom to decide. To the majority of politically minded Indians the Constituent Assembly resolution of 22 January 1947, which had declared that India would become a sovereign, independent republic, seemed to dispose of it. Even though republican sentiment in India did not possess the doctrinaire, uncompromising character of Irish republicanism after the Easter Rising of 1916, Indian leaders and their followers felt that republicanism was the only form of government appropriate to their circumstances. Monarchical institutions were associated with the British and, before them, the Mughal emperors. A republic was, moreover, the only form of government which made clear beyond question that India was an independent nation. It could be, and was argued, that dominion status too conferred full autonomy, but these arguments carried at most partial conviction. Recurring, and at times somewhat acidulous, pre-war discussions about the right of a dominion to secede or to remain neutral in a war in which the United Kingdom was engaged, had sown doubts about this which were not easy to remove. There was, however, one immediate factor which may well have been decisive. Pakistan was committed to Commonwealth membership; on that Jinnah had been explicit all along. If India seceded, did not that, in view especially of the post-partition disputes on division of assets, evacuee property, river waters and above all Kashmir, mean the likelihood of an anti-Indian Commonwealth with continuance of military assistance to Pakistan? On 16 April 1948 Tej Bahadur Sapru, the veteran moderate who had twice been President of the National Liberal Federation, wrote to M. S. Aney, the governor of Bihar:

There is going to be a resolution before the All-India Congress Committee asking for complete severance of all connection with England. I have no objection to India declaring herself a republic but I think it would be very unwise at least at this juncture to pass a resolution of this character. Pakistan is following a different policy. It is receiving much more support from England than Hindustan and is likely to get more support, if the Indian union completely severs its connection with England. Can you not exercise your influence and persuade your friends in the Congress not to sever connection of every kind with England?[19]

On 19 April 1948, Sapru wrote further, this time in the same terms both to Chakravarti Rajagopalachari, who in June of that year was to succeed Lord Mountbatten and serve as the last governor-general of India, and to the governor of Bombay on this theme as follows:

> I always thought that the republican form of government about which eloquent speeches were made in the Constituent Assembly was by no means inconsistent with alliance with England. If you cut off connection altogether with England and Pakistan continues to be like a dominion and if trouble arises in future between Hindustan and Pakistan, why should you blame the British if they openly render military help to Pakistan? The relations between the two dominions of Hindustan and Pakistan are by no means very pleasant at present. They may easily become worse ... I am, therefore, writing to you frankly that whatever form of government may be established you must not go out of the British Commonwealth of Nations at least for some time to come.

His letter was shown by the governor of Bombay to Jawaharlal Nehru, who declared himself to be in full agreement with its views, while Rajagopalachari noted that what Sapru had said 'about republican forms being not inconsistent with Commonwealth relations is quite true and now fairly well recognised'. Here the Irish precedent was important. 'I entirely agree with you,' wrote a correspondent to Sapru, 'that if the state of Ireland continues as a member of the British Commonwealth, in spite of its being a republic, there is absolutely no reason why India should walk out of it immediately, because it is going to be a republic.'[20]

The question of continued Commonwealth membership concerned two of the smaller Asian countries as well as India and Pakistan. Burma, which had been separated from India in the Government of India Act 1935, had experienced the full rigours of war and of enemy occupation between 1941 and 1945. But Japanese propaganda on the theme of 'Asia for the Asiatics' had made an impact little qualified by the harshness of their military rule, and with the return of peace-time conditions younger men impatient of the old order, with Aung San (who struck Lord Wavell as an unattractive personality, of strong character but questionable wisdom), outstanding among them, came to power. They demanded independence and they were met more than half-way by the British government, which declared that it had no wish to stand in the way of Burma's freedom, nor to limit in any way

Burma's freedom of choice thereafter in leaving or remaining within the Commonwealth. In January 1947 a Burmese delegation led by Aung San came to London to make arrangements for the transfer of power. Examination of the possibility of the association of a Burmese republic with the Commonwealth on the Irish model was discouraged as being at once impractical and undesirable in view of impending and larger decisions still to be taken in respect of Indian independence and membership. The positive outcome of the discussions with the United Kingdom government was an agreement for the Commonwealth issue to be left in continuing suspense, for a constituent assembly in Burma (for which elections were in fact held in April that year) to be called, and for the process of the transfer of power to be completed within a year.

The elections resulted in an overwhelming victory of the Anti-Fascist People's Freedom League, the party of Aung San. On 9 June soundings by Aung San, who personally was so inclined, about the possibility of Burma becoming a dominion or state within the Commonwealth by way of interim device to ease the transfer of power and with little or no prospect of its continuance were firmly, though surprisingly in view of the nature of parallel discussions with Indian leaders, discountenanced by Prime Minister and Cabinet Committee on the ground that adoption as a short term expedient would bring dominion status into contempt.[21] With the Burmese thus discouraged a door, which was at most ajar, was firmly closed, an outcome much regretted *inter alia* by Earl Mountbatten of Burma. On 16 June Aung San moved a resolution in the Assembly declaring that the constitution should be that of 'an Independent, Sovereign Republic to be known as the Union of Burma'. It was to be outside the Commonwealth. Aung San's assassination, with eight others in the executive council a month later, did not modify the attitude of the Constituent Assembly towards Commonwealth membership, and when the draft constitution was approved in September all that remained to complete the process of separation was the enactment of the necessary legislation by the United Kingdom Parliament.[22] Was this not a step that India, in two stages if not one, was bound to take? The Burmese leaders at least entertained no doubt when they acted, that it was. They were mistaken.

The secession of Burma was counterbalanced by the progress of another Asian country, Ceylon, towards dominion status. Since 1931 the island had enjoyed representative though not responsible cabinet government. During the war its strategic importance was great and its people, influenced by the rising tide of nationalism in

Asia, were accordingly well placed to press for self-government. The response in London, at first somewhat hesitant, became more forthcoming by 1945 and the United Kingdom government then declared its willingness to co-operate with the Ceylonese in establishing it. They were much influenced in their policy by the argument of the colonial secretary, Arthur Creech-Jones, that what was being conceded to Indian nationalism after Congress policies of non-cooperation in the war could not properly be withheld from the Ceylonese after their co-operation. Under the Soulbury Constitution of 1946, which was based largely on the recommendations of a commission of which Lord Soulbury had been chairman, the island attained self-government in all matters of internal administration. In June 1947 the colonial secretary stated in the House of Commons that the United Kingdom government was preparing to negotiate with the government of Ceylon for the amendment of the constitution so as to give to Ceylon full self-government in external as well as in internal affairs. In November 1947 the Ceylon Independence Bill was introduced in Parliament and it came into force on 4 February 1948. It was supplemented by agreements on defence and external affairs which were signed on 11 November 1947. The first was short-lived, being terminated in 1956 at the request of the Ceylon government, while under the second the government of Ceylon undertook to adopt and follow the resolutions of past imperial conferences and to observe the accepted principles and practice of Commonwealth consultation. For its part the United Kingdom government undertook to support Ceylon's application for membership of the United Nations, which was not in fact secured, owing to Russian objections, till 1956.[23]

Ceylon's advance from colonial to dominion status was 'the first occasion in our history', as Lord Addison, the lord privy seal and a former dominions secretary, remarked, in introducing the second reading of the Ceylon Independence Bill in the House of Lords on 4 December 1947,[24] 'upon which a colony, developing this system of self-government of its own accord, has deliberately sought to become a dominion state in our Commonwealth ... but we hope and expect it will not be the last'. Encouraging however though the implications of Ceylonese membership might be thought to be in London, as evidence of the potential appeal of Commonwealth to non-European peoples it was on the decision of India and Pakistan that the prospect of a Commonwealth in Asia ultimately depended. Would they follow the precedent set by Burma or the example of Ceylon?

The Meeting of Commonwealth prime ministers in London in October 1948 was notable in the history of the Commonwealth because it was the first time at which the three new dominions of Asia were represented at such a gathering. But if the presence of their prime ministers was the outward sign of a new phase in Commonwealth relations, a phase in which non-British and non-European peoples were to take part as equals in Commonwealth deliberations, the form of their membership or relationship was not discussed in full session at all. On the contrary, the Meeting concerned itself with questions of defence, security and economic development, and though the consequence of the Irish repeal of the external relations had to be considered coincidentally, a prior understanding that constitutional questions affecting the Asian dominions should be left on one side was adhered to. The purpose of these characteristically Attleean tactics was to enable the prime ministers of the Asian dominions to gain some first-hand experience of how the Commonwealth worked before formulating their conclusions about their countries' future relationship with it.

But while the topic was not raised at the Conference table it had been and continued to be under public and official consideration. In papers laid before the India and Burma Committee of the Cabinet after the Indian commitment to a republican form of government in the Objectives Resolution approved by the Constituent Assembly in January 1947 and before the transfer of power in August, analysis was made of the desirability or otherwise in terms of British and/or Commonwealth interests of republican India's membership of the Commonwealth. On both counts there were divided opinions, strong reservations being entertained on the British side in respect not only of republicanism but also, particularly by the Colonial Office, of India's future policies, neutrality or non-alignment in general, anti-colonialism in particular. Furthermore there was a widespread presumption that India would not wish for membership, which the Congress had traditionally regarded as less than independence. But it was not, and could hardly have been more than a presumption, once the Congress had accepted dominion status, even if on a provisional basis, as a means for hastening the transfer of power.

There was precedent in all but name for republican association with the Commonwealth deemed[25] by Britain and the dominions as more or less tantamount to membership. It was not, as may be seen from the deprecating comments on almost every minute on the topic, well regarded in Whitehall: but it was a fact the implications of which were well known to the Indian leaders. In moving the

Objectives Resolution Nehru, while declaiming: 'India is bound to be sovereign; it is bound to be independent: India is bound to be a Republic', took occasion to remind the Assembly that 'even in the British Commonwealth of Nations today, Eire is a Republic and yet in many ways it is a member – so it is a conceivable thing'.[26] To the Labour government and more especially to the prime minister and the last viceroy it was also 'a conceivable', indeed, in the case of the viceroy, an altogether desirable thing. In June 1947 a Cabinet Committee on Commonwealth Relations under the chairmanship of the prime minister met to consider the possibility of finding a formula to 'enable the greatest number of independent units to adhere to the Commonwealth without excessive uniformity in their internal constitutions'. The attention of the Committee was concentrated first on the devising of some form of relationship with the Crown, but thereafter, other possibilities, less restrictive, including the setting up of a 'Commonwealth' of 'British and Associated States' were examined. The last did not commend itself to Sir Charles Dixon, the constitutional adviser to the Commonwealth Relations Office, on the ground that associate states while possessing the same status, save in respect of allegiance, as the member-states would none the less be deemed in some way to be inferior and he concluded therefore, that if India would not accept membership on the basis of the Balfour Report she should follow Burma out of the Commonwealth.[27]

In March 1948, with the Commonwealth Conference still pending, Attlee took a direct personal initiative enquiring privately of Nehru[28] whether India might not remain in the Commonwealth, accepting common allegiance to the Crown, commending the latter with the reflection that republicanism was basically an importation from the West. Mountbatten followed this up with the suggestion that 'republic' be replaced in the Indian Constitution by either 'commonwealth' or 'state'. The assumptions behind these, as behind later British proposals, were first that the Constituent Assembly's Resolution in favour of a republic was open to modification or reversal and secondly that a republican relationship with the Commonwealth was in itself not impossible clearly in view of Irish precedents but undesirable. Nehru formulated proposals of his own to the effect that India would be a republic, a member of the Commonwealth and he further envisaged possible provision for common Commonwealth citizenship, the last a proposition to which he remained wedded, practical details being left to be worked out by experts. From Britain and the dominions, other than South Africa, the response came in the form of concern for Indian membership coupled with continuing representations to India to give weight to the sentiment of allegiance to the Crown. In respect of the latter, Nehru in a letter to Krishna Menon, recognised there was a basic difference in approach 'between the United Kingdom people and our people. The very point the United Kingdom wishes to emphasise for legal or sentimental reasons is objected to here . . . Our people want to make it perfectly clear that they are making a new start and that, as the Constitution will itself declare, sovereignty resides in the people and in no one else in any shape or form'.[29] He was and continued to be disconcerted by British suggestions about Privy Council appeals, designs for a flag and a royal fount of honour, some, as it seemed to him, irrelevant and others trivial. Even Attlee, under dominion pressure and presumably a desire to conciliate the opposition at home, allowed himself, as did Gordon Walker at the Commonwealth Relations Office, to sponsor notions which could have been acceptable to Congress India only on the assumption that there was not a final Indian commitment to a republican constitution.

In the light of Congress resolutions on full independence since 1929, the most striking element in the post-independence situation was India's readiness to contemplate a Commonwealth relationship on more than the temporary basis for which the Working Committee had pressed in 1947 so as to make possible an early transfer of power. That her prime minister, and in his hands lay decisive responsibility in this matter, was so inclined is to be attributed to some personal factors, notably the influence of the Mountbattens, the element of continuity in defence Commonwealth Membership would allow, relations with Russia, its attitude at that time being distant and unpredictable, misgivings about the activities of the Communist party, especially in Bengal, all reinforcing a feeling that it would be prudent not to over-estimate India's strength and stability so soon after the wounds of partition, and to preserve links with the Western World, through a Commonwealth relationship which would be on a basis of equality by contrast with that of client state in the case of the United States – 'an overdependent bilateral relationship' as Professor Gopal[30] aptly terms it – while in a regional context there were also misgivings about the wisdom of the course Burma had taken, alluded to by M. Masani in a letter to Patel[31] as 'the rather sad example' of a state 'which chose the other alternative'. And there existed above all the risk that if India seceded and Pakistan remained, the Commonwealth would be under pressure to take up an anti-Indian stance.

But interests of state, which seem to point one way, had to be weighed against the psychology of national revolution. Before proceeding Nehru deemed it desirable to win for himself some freedom for manoeuvre in negotiation, otherwise he might feel himself or be felt to be constrained within a limiting interpretation of the terms of the Objectives Resolution. Such degree of freedom was obtained through approval of a judiciously worded resolution at the Congress meeting on 18 December 1948 at Jaipur. The Resolution read:

> in view of the attainment of complete independence and the establishment of a Republic of India which will symbolise that independence and give to India a status among the nations of the world that is her rightful due, her present association with the United Kingdom and the Commonwealth of Nations will necessarily have to change. India, however, desires to maintain all such links with other countries as do not come in the way of her freedom of action and independence, and the Congress would welcome her free association with independent nations of the Commonwealth for their common welfare and the promotion of world peace.

The Jaipur Resolution however, in reflecting a more accommodating attitude to Commonwealth membership, also implicitly but with finality indicated that it was a republican India that contemplated continued association with the Commonwealth. The only question, therefore, was could the two be reconciled? The problem was similar in principle to that posed by the Irish in 1921 though in practice there was a distinction, in as much as India was already a dominion as Ireland had not been. It was accordingly an existing partner that intended to adopt a republican constitution and expressed a wish to continue thereafter as a full member of the Commonwealth. Undoubtedly this in itself strengthened the Indian bargaining position and eased the situation for other members. In that respect interim dominion status devised for purposes of early transfer had paid off, as the viceroy surmised, on the longer term. But even so the Indian desire to reconcile republicanism with full membership could be met only by a modification of one of the conventional characteristics of membership, namely allegiance to the Crown, as set out in the Balfour Report and restated in the Preamble to the Statute of Westminster.

On 12 November 1948, Nehru formally conveyed his request that a republican India be enabled to stay in the Commonwealth. There were consultations with dominion governments and after a meeting of the High Commissioners of Canada, Australia and New Zealand with the prime minister on 11 December it was conveyed to Nehru that there would have to be some link with the Crown, the common citizenship he had in mind not being enough.[32]

In January 1949 Gordon Walker[33] repeated in a memorandum to Attlee a suggestion he had made the preceding July to Mountbatten to the effect that India's membership as a republic should be accepted with all members including India acknowledging the King as Head of the Commonwealth. In the same month the Committee on Commonwealth Relations produced a memorandum which was read, as well it might be, with deep interest by the king. His private secretary, Sir Alan Lascelles, summarised the point for decision in these terms:

> ...we are at a fork in the road. If we follow one arm, we tell India that, unless she agrees to pay allegiance to the Crown, she must go. She will then go – with the consequence which anybody can foresee.
>
> If we follow the other arm, we agree to the principle of 'inner and outer' membership of the Commonwealth: we admit that the Balfour declaration must be revised; that the 'common allegiance to the Crown' is no longer the *sine qua non* of membership; that it is possible for membership, with all its political and economic privileges, to be enjoyed by states that do not recognise the Crown – in other words, by republics...[34]

Phrased in these terms republican membership no doubt seemed alarming. But Lascelles also reminded the king of a warning of Mackenzie King's to the effect that any attempt to find a 'link' between republican India and the Crown would 'inevitably tend to make the position and functions of the sovereign the subject of violent political discussion, not only in India itself but all over the world'. On 17 February 1949, after considering 'Ten Points' and 'Eight Points' memoranda from the Indian prime minister, Attlee himself submitted a paper to the king in which he allowed that he had always found it difficult to discover any satisfactory nexus for the Commonwealth other than allegiance to the Crown and in consequence to see 'how a republic can be included'. He was at the same time impressed with India's desire to remain a member and with the strong expressions of view, especially from Australia and New Zealand, that she should be enabled to do so. Moreover, were India's request to be rejected, the likelihood was that she would become the leader of an anti-European Asiatic movement whereas if she remained 'there is a great possibility of building up in south-east Asia something analogous to Western Union'. As for the constitutional issue, the prime minister thought it an open question whether the admission of a republic would lead to the spread of republicanism or whether insistence on allegiance, as an essential nexus, might not lead to the secession of other Commonwealth states. Only a Commonwealth Conference, he concluded, could decide and it was impossible to forecast 'what conclusion will be reached by the Conference members'. But a few days later the prime minister had himself decided that the political advantages of Indian membership were so great as to justify adapting the Commonwealth to include a republican state, owing no allegiance to the Crown. The cabinet agreed with this conclusion on 3 March.[35]

The Commonwealth Conference meeting was duly arranged for April 1949. For the first time, Lord Garner tells us[36], the British government resorted to the device (later followed but with less success, in respect of British application for membership of the EEC) of despatching emissaries to Commonwealth governments so as to ensure the fullest possible consultation and consideration beforehand. This was evidently advantageous though there appeared still to be more than a hint of ambivalence in attitudes, reflecting a desire to retain both India and allegiance. It was implicit in the Canadian Prime Minister, Louis St Laurent's message to Nehru indicating the difficulty he found in visualising 'the continued existence of the Commonwealth relationship without some link with the Crown', while conveying to him, as also to other Commonwealth prime ministers, the strong hope that even as a republic India could be kept in the Commonwealth.[37] In fact agreement was reached in the short period of six days.

At the outset of the meeting Nehru was appreciative especially of support from the South African Prime Minister, Dr Malan, and the statement he made on the need for a reassessment of the forms of the Commonwealth relationship. The idea of a dual declaration on the one part reaffirming the traditional allegiance of the old dominions and on the other the basis of the new Indian relationship was discarded as underlining differences and it was a question therefore, given the consensus on aim – India's continuing republican membership – of devising an appropriate formula. The phrase Head of the Commonwealth was viewed with reservations by Pearson, on the ground that it was open to misinterpretation, with dislike by Nehru and positively objected to by Malan on the ground that it might be deemed to imply a super-state apex.

Misgivings were lessened, though not in the case of Malan (who was to insist on a supplementary statement to dispel any notion of super-state), with the suggestion which Pearson claimed as at least in part his own[38] but which Gordon Walker[39] attributed to Zafrullah Khan, that after the King's having been described as the symbol of the free association of the Member Nations the words 'as such' be placed before 'Head of the Commonwealth', and Nehru, in the interests of cooperation and influenced by what Malan had placed on record, was willing to acquiesce. For his own part he secured the substitution of 'liberty' for 'security' in the declaration of Commonwealth aims and made a telling case for the change.[40]

When agreement had been reached, Nehru cabled Patel (23 April 1949) 'United Kingdom, Canada and in particular Malan showed clear and sympathetic understanding of our position', to which in reply Patel sent what must have been the reassuring comment: ' "Headship" in no sense derogatory to our republic(an) sovereign status.'[41] The text of the communiqué issued at the conclusion of the Meeting read as follows:

> During the past week the prime ministers of the United Kingdom, Australia, New Zealand, South Africa, India, Pakistan and Ceylon, and the Canadian secretary of state for external affairs have met in London to exchange views upon the important constitutional issues arising from India's decision to adopt a republican form of constitution and her desire to continue her membership of the Commonwealth.
>
> The discussions have been concerned with the effects of such a development upon the existing structure of the Commonwealth and the constitutional relations between its members. They have been conducted in an atmosphere of goodwill and mutual understanding, and have had as their historical background the traditional capacity of the Commonwealth to strengthen its unity of purpose, while adapting its organisation and procedures to changing circumstances.
>
> After full discussion the representatives of the governments of all the Commonwealth countries have agreed that the conclusions reached should be placed on record in the following declaration:
>
>> The Governments of the United Kingdom, Canada, Australia, New Zealand, South Africa, India, Pakistan, and Ceylon, whose countries are united as members of the British Commonwealth of Nations and owe a common allegiance to the Crown, which is also the symbol of their free association, have

considered the impending constitutional changes in India.
The Government of India have informed the other governments of the Commonwealth of the intention of the Indian
people that under the new constitution which is about to be
adopted India shall become a sovereign independent republic.
The Government of India have, however, declared and
affirmed India's desire to continue her full membership of the
Commonwealth of Nations and her acceptance of The King as
the symbol of the free association of its independent member
nations, and as such the Head of the Commonwealth.
The governments of the other countries of the Commonwealth, the basis of whose membership of the Commonwealth
is not hereby changed, accept and recognise India's continuing
membership in accordance with the terms of this declaration.
Accordingly the United Kingdom, Canada, Australia, New
Zealand, South Africa, India, Pakistan and Ceylon hereby
declare that they remain united as free and equal members of
the Commonwealth of nations, freely cooperating in the
pursuit of peace, liberty and progress.
These constitutional questions have been the sole subject of
discussion at the full meetings of prime ministers.

The settlement reached, it will be noted, was specific, not
general, in application. There was no decision that a republic as
such could be a full member of the Commonwealth. The Conference simply recorded that when India, under her new constitution,
became a sovereign, independent republic, in accordance with her
own wishes she would remain a full member of the Commonwealth
and would acknowledge the king as a symbol of the free association
of its independent member-nations, and, as such, the head of the
Commonwealth. The Indian republic, therefore, owed no allegiance to the Crown and the king had no place in its government.
It was in this respect that the settlement involved a break with the
doctrine enshrined in the Preamble to the Statute of Westminster
in which the members of the Commonwealth were declared to be
'united by a common allegiance to the Crown'. Republicanism, in
the past synonymous with secession, was now accepted as compatible with full membership. It has been maintained that this
compatibility extended only to the case of India and that one
exception did not constitute a category and did not modify the
general conditions of Commonwealth membership. This was
clearly untenable from the outset. In 1955 and 1956 it was,
however, agreed that Pakistan and Ceylon should continue their

membership on the same basis and thereafter the majority of
Commonwealth states opted to follow the same course.

The Indian constitutional settlement was important not because
of its metaphysical refinements but because it went far to reconcile
constitutional forms with political realities. In the dominions, and
particularly in the older dominions which were predominantly
British in extraction, loyalty to the Crown had been a strong
unifying force. For them all the constitutional position remained
unchanged. But the different traditions, the very different history,
of India required that she should have another symbolism, which
with the agreement of all her partners, was accepted in April 1949
as compatible with membership of the Commonwealth.

In Delhi, the Constituent Assembly endorsed the settlement
reached in London with only one dissentient voice. This did not
fairly reflect the balance of opinion within India, for the settlement
was criticised by Socialists as well as by Communists both then and
later when India's first general election was held in 1951–2. Yet the
general satisfaction with the solution reached was unmistakable.
Pandit Nehru's carefully balanced language did something to
explain it.

'We join the Commonwealth [he told the Constituent Assembly]
obviously because we think it is beneficial to us and to certain
causes in the world that we wish to advance. The other countries
of the Commonwealth want us to remain, because they think it is
beneficial to them . . . In the world today where there are so many
disruptive forces at work, where we are often at the verge of war,
I think it is not a safe thing to encourage the breaking up of any
association that one has . . . it is better to keep a co-operative
association going which may do good in this world rather than
break it'. He allowed that he was 'a bad bargainer', that he was not
used 'to the ways of the market place' and that he had thought it,
in London, 'far more precious to come to a decision in friendship
and goodwill than to gain a word here or there at the cost of ill
will'.[42]

There were mutual and substantial interests in making a
settlement, on the British side of trade, investment and security,
and on the Indian of stability, aid and as a counterpoise to Pakistan.
But given the existence of those interests, there was also, and
additionally, magnanimity on the Indian side, to which the prime
ministers of the Commonwealth responded with imaginative
understanding. It was to the two men on whom the main

responsibility rested – Jawaharlal Nehru and Clement Attlee – that the chief credit for the settlement belonged though Attlee on this occasion displayed less incisiveness than on the statement of 20 February or on the Indian Independence Act. There followed in the early 1950s, despite differences in the attitudes of newer and older members to world politics, some brief and, retrospectively, golden years of hope in a multi-racial Commonwealth and in its potential contribution to human understanding.

The 1949 settlement modified the position of the Crown in the Commonwealth. The period of potentially self-destructive rigidity on this issue was ended, though it may still be questioned, in the light of Burmese and Irish secession and the critical debate on Indian republican membership, whether there had been lack of foresight in not considering earlier the bearing of the central position accorded to the Crown in the Statute of Westminster Commonwealth, upon prospective post-war problems and not least those related to possible non-European Commonwealth membership. In any event after 1949 the Crown could no longer be spoken of in Baldwin's phrase as the 'only link'. There was no longer common allegiance, as a condition of membership, but only, so to speak, as an option. The result of free constitutional choice was a variety of constitutional relationships, reflected in 1953 in the variety of titles, with which Queen Elizabeth II was invested at her coronation. It was the newest, 'Head of the Commonwealth', that alone was common to all. In time, for the majority of Commonwealth states, it became the only formal acknowledgement of the position of the Crown. This was chiefly because a direct relationship, in terms of allegiance, appeared inappropriate to independent states with non-British populations, but also because the monarchical system on the British model presupposed an executive responsible to Parliament. Since, in subsequent years, the practice continued in Africa and elsewhere of transferring power at the outset, as in India, to a successor authority, monarchical in form, independence was apt to be followed after the lapse of a year or more by the declaration of a republic remaining, with the explicit consent of Commonwealth prime ministers, within the framework of Commonwealth. This provided a second occasion for national celebrations, but was hardly conducive to the enhancement of the dignity of the Crown in the Commonwealth.

One African example may suffice to illustrate the process and to suggest some of the factors that lay behind it. In March 1961 the Tanganyika government reaffirmed its intention to apply for membership, and this was subsequently agreed by existing members of the Commonwealth. Tanganyika's membership at the outset was monarchical in form. On reconsideration it was decided however that the country should become a republic one year after independence, namely on 9 December 1962. The reasons were set out in a White Paper, understood to have been drafted by Julius Nyerere, the leader of the dominant National party. It read:

On 9th December 1961 we became – suddenly – a monarchy. By deciding to remain within the Commonwealth, without making immediate provision for introducing a republican form of government at independence, we automatically followed the precedent set by the other non-republican countries of the Commonwealth. The Queen, who is Head of the Commonwealth and Sovereign of its several member countries, became our Sovereign . . .

This direct association of Tanganyika and the British monarchy was something quite new; for, until the 9th December, their association was only indirect. When the British government assumed responsibility for the administration of Tanganyika at the end of the first world war it was not as a colony or a protectorate but by virtue of a mandate conferred on Britain by the League of Nations. So long as the mandate and Trusteeship system continued, Tanganyika was not part of Her Majesty's dominions, and the relationship between the people of Tanganyika and the Crown was an indirect relationship depending on the position of the Monarch as Head of State in the country charged with the duty of administering the territory. For Tanganyika, therefore, the British monarchy has always been a foreign institution.[43]

Independence, the White Paper proceeded, had increased the sense of alienation. Tanganyika therefore should have an indigenous, republican form of government. This was consistent with membership of the Commonwealth and that, according to the prime minister, Kawawa, was a link 'it is very important to maintain'. Why? Because 'whether we like it or not, we have something in common and we understand each other'. And also because the Commonwealth helped better understanding in the world. 'If we dissolve a means of understanding, I think, we are doing a disservice to the world.'[44] The Indian precedent, therefore, was followed in republican membership of the Commonwealth. But as distinct from India there was in Tanganyika more in the change than the discarding of an alien and the adoption of an indigenous symbolism of nationhood. The substance as well as the form of government was at issue. That also was made clear in the White Paper.

> Broadly speaking [it read] there are two types of republic. There are republics where the Head of State occupies the same constitutional position as that occupied by a Constitutional Monarch: his position is largely a ceremonial and formal one. This is the 'Westminster Model'. Except in very unusual circumstances he acts only on the advice of the prime minister, or the cabinet, who are the real government. This division between formal authority and real authority can be understood in countries where it has come about as a result of historical changes . . . Such a division, however, is entirely foreign to our tradition. The honour and respect accorded to a Chief, or a King, or, under a republic, to a President, are forces indistinguishable from the power that he wields.
>
> The other type of republic is that in which the President of the Republic is both Head of State and Head of the Government. He is called an Executive President. This is the type the Government is proposing.

The preference for the American presidential, as distinct from the Westminster parliamentary, model might therefore, as in the case of Tanganyika, have a bearing upon the relationship to be established with the Crown and on the form of Commonwealth membership. But essentially this was a secondary factor. It was as a symbol of indisputable indigenous national sovereignty that a republican constitution appealed to African and to Asian peoples.

6 The Climax of Commonwealth and a Time of Disenchantment

The final stages in the transformation of the British Empire into a Commonwealth of Nations was the product partly of conviction, partly of experience and perhaps, most of all, of circumstances. Britain and the dominions stood side by side in both world wars from their outbreak to their victorious close. Their overall participation in them was longer than that of any other country on either side.[1] The dominions had entered the second world war by their own free choice. For a year, in the (not quite exact) Churchillian phrase, they had 'stood alone' and they had made their contributions in every theatre of war from the Mediterranean and western Europe to south-east Asia and the Pacific. To the peoples of Britain and the dominions it seemed as if their experiment in free and equal association had been memorably vindicated. But it was far otherwise with the Colonial Empire. It emerged from the second world war, despite the evidence of a greater sense of social responsibility on the part of the metropolitan power, implicit in the Colonial Development and Welfare Acts (notably that imaginatively enacted in the summer of 1940), with its image tarnished and itself discredited. This was due immediately to the collapse of south-east Asia before the Japanese, and most of all to the fall of Singapore, one of the great humiliations of British arms in modern times. In beleaguered, wartime Britain the disintegration of western colonialism in Asia was interpreted, not in terms of mistaken strategy, inadequate military preparation, insufficient allocation of military and desperately needed air resources, but rather viewed against a backdrop of easy living, gin drinking, demoralised colonialists drawn from the novels of Somerset Maugham or of the ridiculous pomposities of Noel Coward's 'Mad dogs and Englishmen'. On the longer view, it may be accepted, as A. J. P. Taylor remarks at the end of his *English History 1914–1945*, that in the war 'traditional values lost much of their force. Other values took their place. Imperial greatness was on the way out; the

163

welfare state was on the way in.'[2] But it was 'Empire' in its limited sense that was out. It was the diminished reputation of the dependent Empire and the enhanced reputation of the free dominions that combined at one and the same time to destroy an old faith in Empire and to produce a new faith in Commonwealth.

To a widely shared conviction and wartime experience were to be added the circumstances of the post-war world. That world was dominated by two great Powers, both of which were anti-colonial. The psychology and concepts behind Russian and American anti-colonialism were very different. But what mattered after 1945 was their common antipathy to colonial rule. This at once encouraged the anti-colonialism of subject peoples, and diminished the capacity and possibly also the will of the western metropolitan powers, Britain included, to resist what had the appearance of the march of history. But here again, at least in the United States, a distinction was increasingly drawn between the British Commonwealth and the British Empire. After all, the northern neighbour of the United States was the oldest of the dominions and a founder member with Britain of the Commonwealth of Nations. No sensible American (admittedly not all Americans qualified on this topic) any longer supposed that Canada, which had played so notable a part in the war and which under Mackenzie King's leadership had firmly yet judiciously underlined its autonomy, was a political dependency of Britain. In the Soviet Union, note was taken of the phenomenon of Commonwealth as something distinct from a relic of empire, while in 1954 China's Foreign Minister, Chou En-lai alluded to its beneficial influence.[3] But most significant was the fact that one of the world's leading anti-colonial powers, India, was also of its own choice, a leading member of the Commonwealth. In the abstract, therefore, the external circumstances deriving from the new balance of world power tended to encourage the advance of Commonwealth, in much the same measure as they pressed for the dissolution of empire. What remained to be tested was the opinion of hitherto subject peoples. That they were anti-imperialist was no longer seriously doubted. But were they prepared themselves to distinguish between Empire and Commonwealth and to contemplate membership of a society of states, which had grown historically out of empire, or would memories of conquest or sense of past exploitation, reinforced by the tide of Asian and African nationalism, carry them to an independence beyond its confines?

Burma pointed that way, but India's Commonwealth membership, reinforced by that of Pakistan and Ceylon, provided the critically important formulation of another answer from the most prestigious of sources. The image of Commonwealth was thereby embellished in the eyes both of Asian, African and other colonial nationalist leaders and also in those of hitherto unenthusiastic or, more usually, sceptical left-wing progressives in Britain and the old dominions. The age of Smuts and King was ending and in their place there was emerging Jawaharlal Nehru as a representative figure with views that were compulsively attractive to an unusually wide conspectus of opinion in an emerging multi-racial society of nations. But more than personal appeal, or new-found enthusiasm for multi-racial association, was required to ensure effective existence or even survival. The enlarged Commonwealth, Eurasian in its membership for the decade 1947–57, had first to demonstrate its capacity to hold together, despite the conflicting pulls and pressures of an external world upon its membership, even as its member states were seeking to come to terms with the realities of their own relationship. Time was what was needed most to ease national sensitivities and to work out an acceptable pattern of association founded on equality and recognising interdependence. And of time in the post-war world, there was short measure.

The Commonwealth was in no sense self-sufficing; its member-states being able neither to disregard nor to defer their own post-war problems pending the emergence of a Commonwealth consensus upon them. Britain and Canada had to determine their relations with Europe and the emerging Atlantic Community; Australia and New Zealand to decide, in the light of their wartime experiences, upon the future of their relationship with the United States; Asian members had to formulate for the first time regional and international policies, acceptable to the nationalist anti-colonialist sentiments of their peoples, and at the same time consistent with their national political and more especially economic interests. The pursuit of such varied and at times conflicting purposes within the framework of Commonwealth was evidence of the flexibility of its decentralised system of co-operation through consultation. By this much store was set by governments and their officials. What was apt to be overlooked, however, in the earlier years of this new Commonwealth experiment, was the fact that there was bound to be a limit in practice, even if it were not susceptible of theoretic definition, to such flexibility, beyond which meaningful Commonwealth existence ceased for its member-states. In international and racial policies that frontier between reality and nothingness was approached in the post-war decades in which, paradoxically as it may seem, the Commonwealth idea acquired content and substance in respect of social, economic and educational cooperation, such as it had not hitherto possessed.

In the immediate post-war years Commonwealth thinking was dominated by problems of regional security, international alliances and the Cold War. As early as 1943 Smuts had outlined ideas of how the Commonwealth, through association with the free peoples of the western European seaboard, might contribute to European and world stability.[4] In the form in which he presented them, these ideas were not realised. Smuts foreshadowed an association of like-minded western European and Commonwealth states which would together form a third great Power, balancing between the Soviet Union in the east and the United States in the west, whereas the grouping that eventually emerged was regional, thereby automatically excluding the overseas members of the Commonwealth from membership of it and diminishing its potential in the scales of power. Yet in the early and largely defensive stages in the evolution of western European union, overseas Commonwealth members were, as they were bound to be in the light of recent history, concerned with its purposes and composition, and most of all with Britain's rôle in it.

The strategic commitments into which the United Kingdom entered in western Europe after the war, notably the Five Power Brussels Pact of March 1948, were generally welcome to the governments of the old dominions on grounds of a common interest in the military security of the treaty area. In an established tradition, the treaty itself was not subscribed to by any of the dominions, but there were indications of a significant departure from pre-war precedents in Canadian readiness to participate as a member in the work of the permanent military committee set up in London under the terms of the treaty. It was indeed on the political, not on the military or still less the economic side, that there were signs of dominion misgivings about the possible and progressive absorption of the United Kingdom in a purely European grouping. In Australia and New Zealand especially, it was felt, even at this early date, that the closer Britain drew to Europe, the further it must necessarily draw away from the Commonwealth, with the consequence that it would not have a sufficient margin of resources to sustain its position in the world overseas, and particularly east of Suez. It was to allay these misgivings that Attlee emphasised in May 1948 that, in respect of every development in western Europe the United Kingdom government had kept in the closest touch with the other Commonwealth countries . . . and we take very full account of their views . . . I was disturbed with the suggestion . . . that we might somehow get closer to Europe than to our Commonwealth. The Commonwealth nations are our closest friends. While I want to get as close as we can with the other nations, we have to bear in mind that we are not solely a European Power but a member of a great Commonwealth and Empire . . .[5]

For the Commonwealth overseas these were reassuring words and at the meeting of Commonwealth foreign ministers in Colombo in 1950 it was formally accepted that 'there need be no inconsistency between the policy followed by the UK government in relation to western Europe and the maintenance of the traditional links between the UK and the rest of the Commonwealth . . .'[6] But there was a price to be paid. At a time of new economic departures as reflected in the constitution of the World Bank, the negotiations of the Geneva Agreement on Trade and Tariffs and the shaping of the Common Market, Britain generally, and especially in the case of the last, tended to remain semi-detached. By so doing she deprived herself of opportunities of influencing developments in the formative stage from within so that they might be in conformity with her existing ties with the Commonwealth overseas. With regard to Western Europe observers sensed a parting of the ways when, with the coming into existence in 1953 of the first Western European institution, the European Coal and Steel Community stemming from the Schuman Plan (1950), there was British association, but – by deliberate decision at an early stage by the Attlee, and at a later stage by the Churchill, administration – no British commitment to this experiment in supranationalism.

Outside Europe, large and divisive questions were posed by the extension of military alliances. For Canada, Anglo–American accord on the broad issues of foreign policy had long been recognised as a principal objective of policy. It received formal fulfilment in the North Atlantic Treaty 1949, to which the United States, Britain and Canada were all signatories. The treaty marked the opening of a new phase in Canadian and, as it was to prove, in Commonwealth foreign policies. The active Canadian rôle in the negotiation of the treaty and the subsequent Canadian signature of it indicated a dramatic departure from the Canadian, and indeed general dominion reluctance to assume specific commitments, which had been so pronounced a feature of their policies in the inter-war years. Two things, in the Canadian case, prompted this radical break with the past. The first, already mentioned, was the joint Anglo–American sponsorship. The second was experience. 'We must', said Louis St Laurent, the secretary of state for external affairs in 1948, 'at all costs avoid the fatal repetition of the history of the pre-war years when the nazi aggressor picked off its victims one by one. Such a process does not end at the Atlantic.'[7]

It did not end at the Pacific either. Australia and New Zealand, with a lively recollection of how United States naval power had ended the threat of Japanese invasion, with decisive victories at Midway and in the Coral Sea, followed the Canadian precedent in 1951 by signing a Pacific Security Agreement with the United States. It was the first treaty signed by the two Pacific dominions with a foreign country, and since Britain, to Churchill's chagrin, was not a party to it, the treaty signified in effect the future military dependence of those two Commonwealth members upon the United States, in the same way as the North Atlantic Treaty had indicated the dependence of Canada and of Britain itself on American power. For Australians, and more especially for New Zealanders, far out at the end of the line, it represented a triumph of strategic realism over deep, sentimental attachment. It led on directly to Australian and New Zealand association with United States policies in the Far East and south-east Asia, and in 1967 reached a temporary culmination in Australian participation at divisional strength in the war in Vietnam at the side of the United States, while Britain and the other members of the Commonwealth apart from New Zealand remained non-belligerent and for the most part critically aloof.

In 1954 the growing network of regional alliances was more controversially extended to south-east Asia, with the creation of the South-East Asian Treaty Organisation under the terms of the Manila Pact. This treaty underlined not Commonwealth unity but Commonwealth disunity. Britain, Australia and New Zealand were signatories; so also was Pakistan, but India and Ceylon were not. Nehru was angered by it and by the Baghdad Pact which followed a year later and of which Pakistan was also a member, the more so since India was not consulted.[8] His principal cause of complaint was that major decisions about Asia were being taken without the agreement of the principal Asian states in the area concerned. 'Asian problems, Asian security and Asian peace', he complained in September 1954, 'are not only discussed but actions are taken and treaties are made in regard to them chiefly by non-Asian countries.' 'Our Hon. Members may remember the old days . . .' he told the Lok Sabha a little later, when Great Powers had spheres of influence in Asia and elsewhere – of course, the countries of Asia were too weak to do anything. The quarrel was between the Big Powers and they, therefore, sometimes, came to an agreement about dividing the countries in spheres of influence. It seems to me, this particular Manila Treaty is looking dangerously in this direction of spheres of influence to be exercised by powerful countries . . .[9]

Apart from the fact that Pakistan was a signatory to the treaty, the critical Indian reaction was to be attributed to two principal reasons. The chief aim of Indian foreign policy was to preserve south and south-east Asia as an area of no war, and it was thought that military alliances extending to the area would prejudice the prospect of its fulfilment. The other, which often received emotional expression during the Korean war, was a suspicion that the western world, of which the United States was conceived of as a part, was almost as insensitive to the sufferings as they had been to the subjection of ancient Asian peoples. The response, therefore, to the treaty alignments of the older Commonwealth countries, reinforced in 1954 by Pakistan, was renewed insistence in Delhi upon the virtues of the policy of non-alignment, to which India had subscribed since independence and which was held, not without reason, to have contributed significantly to the ending of the war in Korea. Some aspects of that policy, as well as the attitude behind it, were given formal expression in the Preamble to the 1954 Indo–Chinese Treaty on Tibet where the *PANCH SHILA* or *FIVE PRINCIPLES* summed up in familiar phrases – mutual co-existence, co-operation and non-interference in the domestic affairs of friendly countries – were enunciated. Thereafter non-alignment assumed the character of a dogma in the conduct of Indian foreign policy, receiving widespread acclaim among the uncommitted nations, not least among African countries that were soon to become independent. It was not however to be confused with neutrality – India, as Nehru put it, was too considerable a power to withdraw from its world responsibilities. On the contrary it would discharge them, but on the basis of its own judgement and without prior commitment. Such essays in the exercise of independent judgement were to be the occasion of much resentment by the Great Powers in the Cold War years.

Alignment and non-alignment dividing the older from the newer members of the Commonwealth – Pakistan always excepted – imposed strain upon Commonwealth co-operation and the system of consultation, which was its foundation. Where the member states could not agree on major issues of international policy, were they still prepared to consult and confer about them? The answer would seem to have been broadly in the affirmative down to 1954, a year which, with the SEATO Pact and an agreement on American military aid to Pakistan, deeply resented in India, marked a parting of the ways. Before that date on some issues, for example the recognition of the Chinese People's Republic and the ending of the war in Korea, consultation was close, continuous and productive, even where there was no consensus as in the case of recognition, of positive action on the part of some governments. There was also a succession of ministerial and prime ministerial meetings; and the attendance at them, with almost unfailing regularity, of men carrying great domestic and, in some instances world responsibilities, was an impressive tribute to the vitality and vigour of the refashioned Commonwealth. Yet satisfaction was less apt than in earlier years to be untempered by judgment. The conference of cabinets continued; it was the principal means whereby an experiment in co-operation between nations, of a kind to which history afforded no exact parallel, was not unsuccessfully attempted; it brought and kept together, as perhaps nothing else could have done, men of influence from all continents. Yet, despite these achievements, praise for the system became more muted, faith in it more qualified as the years went by. Where there was no agreement on defence policies, there could be little fruitful discussion on defence. Was this also to be true of the wide range of issues dominating world politics in the Cold War Years?

In 1947 Ceylon, it will be recalled, in a formal document,[10] agreed generally to observe the principles and practice of Commonwealth consultation in regard to external affairs. In no later instance was this formula repeated. It belonged to earlier, less questioning, years. In the speech from the throne at the opening of Parliament at Westminster in 1955 the Queen stated: 'My government will maintain and strengthen consultation within the Commonwealth for the fulfilment of our common aims and purposes'.[11] That was not repeated in comprehensive form either. It proved the prologue to the failure of the British government to consult or inform its Commonwealth partners in advance about the joint Anglo–French intervention at Suez the following year, consequent upon President Nasser's nationalisation of the Suez Canal. Of their neglect in this respect the first thing that needs to be said is implicit in the words of Greville's famous judgment on Sir Robert Peel's sudden and surprising conversion to Catholic emancipation: 'I do not see how he can be acquitted of insincerity save at the expense of his sagacity and foresight.'

The second thing to be remarked is that for a Commonwealth accustomed to thinking of consultation, or when time did not allow of it of the prompt communication of information about immediate intentions, as the foundation of its informal system of inter-state co-operation, the deliberate failure to consult by the senior partner marked a departure from principle and a breach in practice which signalised lack of confidence on the part of the British government in its power to persuade its Commonwealth partners even to acquiesce in the enterprise on which it was resolved to embark, and added to the sense of outrage with which many of them first received news of it. Of course consultation or no consultation, there would have been open and undisguised conflict of opinion within the Commonwealth, but with consultation something of the dangerous edge of acrimony might well have been blunted. It is true that even as things were the tone of most of the correspondents, disposed to disapprove of the Anglo-French action at Suez in the Canadian press, more critical generally than that of any other in the old dominions, was said to be one of pain and sorrow rather than anger, 'almost tearful', as the correspondent of *The Economist* observed 'like finding a beloved uncle arrested for rape'.[12] But in initial Asian reactions, surprise and regret little softened the sharpness of judgment. The prime minister of India 'after fairly considerable experience in foreign affairs' could not think 'of a grosser case of naked aggression' and felt that in the middle of the twentieth century 'we are going back to the predatory method of the eighteenth and nineteenth centuries'.[13] The government of India dispatched a formal protest to London; Rajagopalachari, that most respected of elder statesmen, recommended that India should leave the Commonwealth;[14] while to Lester Pearson, the Canadian secretary of state for external affairs, as to many others less well informed, it seemed in the first days of the fighting as if the Commonwealth had been brought to 'the verge of dissolution'.[15] Nor did feeling all run one way. It is difficult for governments, as for individuals, to accept rebuke without resentment, even when its expression is deemed sincere and the scales of judgment evenly balanced. When in late October Soviet tanks moved into Budapest to suppress a popular revolt, Nehru allowed censure and action to wait upon fuller information which he sought in Moscow. By contrast with the Indian condemnation of Suez, such hesitancy seemed, even to those predisposed to concur in it, somewhat partial and Sir Anthony Eden retrospectively laid emphasis upon this apparent defect. 'The Indian reaction', he wrote,[16] 'was remarkable. Mr Nehru declared in a speech that whereas in Egypt "every single thing that had happened was as clear as daylight", he could not follow "the very confusing situation" in Hungary.' The Indian prime minister's studied restraint in judgment upon the Soviet action in Hungary, which might be regarded as a part of the price of the Suez diversion, in fact supplied retaliatory ammunition for its protagonists. A campaign of recrimination, with the Rhodesian crisis a decade later as the only near parallel in Commonwealth history, was opened; how and when would it close?

If the British advance to Suez was precipitate, the retreat was masterly. It was eased by the re-emergence of a near-consensus of Commonwealth views. 'Britain's action, I personally say – and I will say it if I am the only one left to say it – was brave and correct.'[17] So the Australian prime minister, Robert Menzies expressed himself as early as 12 November 1956 – and his choice of words betrayed his isolation. Apart from Sir Anthony Eden, soon to withdraw from public life, Menzies was left alone among leading Commonwealth statesmen to say it. For the rest, whether initially supporters or critics, two broad considerations prompted restraint and calmer reappraisal. On the one hand, the prospect of possible dissolution enhanced appreciation of the value of the Commonwealth, and on the other there was recognition that the Suez adventure was not only out of character with the pattern of recent British policy overseas but out of line with the realities of her power position. In conjunction the two encouraged Commonwealth policies outwardly restoring the *status quo ante*, but inwardly marking a readjustment in intra-Commonwealth relations. For the Commonwealth overseas Britain remained the principal and predominant partner, but with a leadership less likely than hitherto to secure backing, or at the least acquiescence, in doubtful or disputed issues; while in Britain itself, and especially within the ranks of the ruling Conservative party, the traditional assumption that the Commonwealth was an asset for the first time came in for questioning that was often uncongenial but none the less persistent. There was a link in psychological terms between the traumatic experiences of 1956 and the manner of the British application for membership of the Common Market six years later, even if the latter was dictated chiefly by economic considerations.

One lesson of Suez was not to be overlooked. In Commonwealth relations, as in other matters, it is not conventional procedures but substance and purpose that matter. At the time over-much weight was paid to the one and too little to the others. The Commonwealth Relations Office made a practice of publishing the number of telegrams sent to their missions in other Commonwealth countries – twenty thousand it may be or thirty thousand, or even thirty-five thousand – in a year.[18] From the context in which these figures appeared it seemed that the public was expected to infer from them that the increase denoted a growing intimacy – to use a phrase regrettably embedded in the Commonwealth vocabulary – in relations between Commonwealth governments. But it could also have meant – and this in retrospect appears the more likely – differences that were getting harder to resolve, coupled no doubt with a fashionable depreciation in Commonwealth cable currency.

The Suez crisis in its Commonwealth context was the reflection rather than the cause of changing concepts of Commonwealth. Sir Winston Churchill, presiding in 1955 over the last Prime Ministers' Meeting he was to attend, had spoken of it in terms of 'a fraternal association'.[19] This was a description that came readily to the lips of those who had worked together closely over the years, as representatives of a comparatively small group of sovereign states, all governed in accord with the principles of the British parliamentary system. It was perhaps peculiarly appropriate in the brief years of exclusively Eur-Asian membership, when mother-daughter analogies were outdated[20] and there existed a fresh and lively sense of an experiment in equal relations between peoples and governments of different races. A decade later the use of 'fraternal association' would have seemed forced and an Australian commentator, Professor J. D. B. Miller, came nearer to reflecting the spirit of that later time when he wrote of the Commonwealth as 'a concert of convenience'[21] with the pull of sentiment, notably in the United Kingdom itself, much diminished and survival conditional, therefore, upon calculations of national advantage on the part of all the member-states. This was made self-evident, even in traditionalist circles where the time-lag between reality and reputation was most pronounced, with the expansion of Commonwealth into Africa. But it was antecedent to African, or indeed to Asian membership and may be thought implicit in the notion of free association.

The political transformation of the continent of Africa dominated Commonwealth, and indeed world affairs in the decade 1957–67. That an African revolution should succeed to the greater Asian revolution was not in itself surprising. This is not to suggest that independence in British Africa came as a byproduct of the ending of colonialism in Asia, though unquestionably the Indian struggle for independence eased the way for independence in

Africa without protracted struggle in many cases and without struggle at all in some. Even in the age of late Victorian imperialism, British expansion in Africa was largely determined by British preoccupation with the stability and security of the Indian Empire[22] and the premise, therefore, that policy in Africa should be conditional upon developments in South Asia was well grounded in British thinking. What requires explanation is not, therefore, the fact of change so much as the pace of it and the outcome in terms of Commonwealth membership.

Ghana became the first African member of the Commonwealth, on achieving independence in 1957, evidently not discouraged by the Suez crisis of the preceding year. Nigeria followed after a three year interlude in 1960 and then in quickening succession came Sierra Leone and Tanganyika in 1961, Uganda in 1962, Kenya, and Zanzibar (later to form with Tanganyika the Union of Tanzania) in 1963, Nyasaland (renamed Malawi) and Northern Rhodesia (renamed Zambia) in 1964 the Gambia in 1965 and two of the high commission territories in southern Africa, Basutoland as Lesotho and Bechuanaland as Botswana, in 1966, with Swaziland following in 1968. The transformation seems the more remarkable when stated in broader terms. On 1 January 1957 the British Colonial Empire in Africa remained at its fullest extent: on 31 December 1967 nothing remained of it in fact, and in name only Swaziland shortly to become independent, and sanction-beleaguered, rebel-administered Southern Rhodesia. Or, in more positive Commonwealth terms, where on 1 January 1957 there had been no African member-state, by the close of 1967 there were no less than twelve,[23] all of whom had freely opted for membership and none of whom by that time, even under the strains of the Rhodesian question, had renounced membership.

Why was the process not more protracted? Two reasons may be offered. One, the more obvious, was the nationalism of many of these African states, varying in intensity and still in most instances awaiting systematic historical analysis, strongly reinforced by the pressures of anti-colonial powers at the United Nations and anti-colonial opinion in the world at large. Here the report of the UN Committee on Trusteeship in 1959 had been one landmark: the passing of a resolution in the General Assembly of the UN by 97 votes to none for the speedy ending of colonialism another. What was less evident, but no less real in the later phase, was the resolve first of a British Conservative government more sensitive than was publicly allowed to the movement of international opinion, and then of its Labour successor, to end British colonial responsibilities,

not only in Africa, but in the West Indies, where Jamaica, and
Trinidad and Tobago became independent states in 1962 with
Barbados and mainland Guyana following in 1966; in south-east
Asia, with Malaysian independence dating from 1957 and that of
secessionist Singapore from 1965; in the Mediterranean, with
independence for Cyprus after a four year state of emergency in
1960 and for Malta in 1967; and elsewhere, ultimately even in
islands such as Mauritius, scattered around the oceans, irrespective
of whether or not there was any strong indigenous pressure for
that sovereign status.

The trend of British thinking was first publicly indicated in an
address by the British prime minister in Cape Town in 1960
towards the conclusion of a tour of Commonwealth and British
Colonial Africa. On 3 February that year Harold Macmillan,
speaking 'very frankly' told a joint session of the South African
Houses of Parliament that:

> what governments and Parliaments in the United Kingdom *have*
> done since the last war in according independence to India,
> Pakistan, Ceylon, Malaya and Ghana and what they *will* do for
> Nigeria and other countries now nearing independence – all
> this, though we must and do take full responsibility for it, we do
> in the belief that it is the only way to establish the future of
> the Commonwealth and of the free world on sound found-
> ations.
>
> All this, of course, is of deep and close concern to you. For
> nothing we do in this small world can be done in a corner and
> remain hidden. What *we* do today in West, Central and East
> Africa becomes known to everyone in the Union whatever his
> language, colour or traditions . . .
>
> . . . in our own areas of responsibility we must each do what we
> think right. What we British think right derives from a long
> experience both of failure and success in the management of
> these affairs. We have tried to learn and apply the lessons of
> both . . . This experience of ours explains why it has been our
> aim, in the countries for which we have borne responsibility, not
> only to raise material standards of life, but to create a society
> which respects the rights of individuals – a society in which men
> are given the opportunity to grow to their full stature, and that
> must in our view include the opportunity of an increasing share
> in political power and responsibility; a society finally in which
> individual merit, and individual merit alone, is the criterion, for
> a man's advancement, whether political or economic.

The impact of the British prime minister's unexpectedly explicit challenge was heightened by the use of phrases earlier in the speech which became the current coin of African commentaries. The most striking of all the impressions he had formed on his African travels was, he said, 'of the strength of this African national consciousness. In different places it may take different forms. But it is happening everywhere. The wind of change is blowing through this continent.'[24] It was true. It was also true, and almost as important, that there was a change of wind in Downing Street. This was something on which Macmillan understandably preferred not to dwell. But British settlers in Kenya and the Rhodesias were soon to feel the breath of anti-colonialism from London, as well as from indigenous Africa, in what one of them later termed *So Rough a Wind*.[25]

Conservatives are well placed under the British party system to carry through radical measures, as Parnell well understood, when he sought first a Conservative alliance to carry Home Rule for Ireland in 1885. It was accordingly without serious domestic opposition that a Conservative government was able to wind up British colonial responsibilities in Africa, south-east Asia, the West Indies and elsewhere at a pace, which had not been contemplated by the leading colonial experts in Britain, which surprised the majority and shocked a minority of their own supporters, and incidentally outdistanced not a few of their critics. The government's principal concern had become how to grant independence to its remaining colonial possessions, whether in Africa or elsewhere, in the shortest possible time.[26] In Tanganyika power was transferred some years before the date first demanded by the principal nationalist party or that recommended by a visiting U.N. Mission. At the Malta Independence Conference held in London in July, 1963 the secretary of state for the colonies, Duncan Sandys, found it necessary to reassure Maltese delegates by saying 'We in Britain have no desire to hustle Malta into independence . . .', while at the British Guiana Conference later in the year he spoke with every sign of mounting irritation about the need to settle domestic differences so as not to delay the plans of Her Majesty's government for an early transfer of power.[27] For the Tacitean 'divide and rule' of Empire, there was thus substituted an injunction more appropriate to Commonwealth – 'unite and abdicate'. The secretary of state for the colonies in the Labour government, formed in October 1964, Anthony Greenwood, declared that his main purpose at the Colonial Office was 'to do himself out of a job' and by 1966 he had succeeded. The Colonial Office was no more.

The virtual completion of the policy of transforming an Empire into a Commonwealth accounted for a new assurance, even an occasional asperity, in British reactions at the United Nations to anti-colonial critics. In a debate on colonialism in the United Nations General Assembly on 1 October 1963, the British foreign secretary, the Earl of Home, after alluding 'to the vicious attack on us' by Indonesia, following the establishment of the Federation of Malaysia and the rupture in diplomatic relations between Somalia and the United Kingdom because of the disputed Kenya frontier, went on to say that these events 'seem to us to be strange byproducts of the grant of independence which is urged upon us as a policy by every Asian and African country'. For Britain the only issue was not *whether* any country should become independent, but only *when*.

> The only check on the transfer of power from the United Kingdom to the government of the country concerned is that we want to be sure that, when independence is granted, the country will be able to make both ends meet economically and that it was accepting a constitution, from the day of independence, which will work for the well-being of every section of society . . .

He hoped Britain could

> go along with the majority of the United Nations in these colonial matters since it accepted the principles of unqualified self-determination, majority rule and safeguards for minorities.[28]

Lord Home's contribution to the United Nations deserves attention for three reasons. There is always a time-lag in reputation and the conviction that a western imperial power was deliberately divesting itself of the remnants of empire was too unexpected to strike quick roots. The anti-colonialists continued to campaign, slow to understand that the campaign in respect of Britain was concluded. The second reason why Lord Home's speech merits attention flows from the first. In the years following Indian independence it was widely maintained, not least in the United States, that a Commonwealth divided between colonialists and anti-colonialists could not endure. This view, which *inter alia* discounted the strength of anti-colonial, pro-Commonwealth sentiment within Britain, and especially within the then dominant Labour party, was evidently without substance. All were anti-colonialists, as all were socialists in Harcourt's day. This meant there were some strange figures in the ranks, looking for their chance to break away, but the solid mass of opinion kept them more or less in formation. Nor was there reason to doubt that in bringing about this new measure of agreement on a potentially divisive issue, the influence of Asian membership of the Commonwealth over a period of years was pronounced. In that sense, as Professor Rajan maintained,[29] it proved to be a Commonwealth new in character that came into existence in 1947.

Finally Lord Home's assertion that the issue for Britain was not *whether* but *when* any country should become independent, may serve as a touchstone by which to review British policy at this time. Certainly it had not been universally true, even a few years earlier. On 28 July 1954, the minister of state for colonial affairs, Mr Hopkinson, told the House of Commons that Her Majesty's government had decided that the time had come to take 'a fresh initiative' in the development of self-governing institutions for Cyprus, but it emerged under questioning that this development was not intended to lead to self-government. On the contrary, in the words of the minister, 'there are certain territories in the Commonwealth which, owing to their particular circumstances, can never expect to be fully independent'.[30] As Louis Napoleon once observed: '*en politique on ne doit jamais dire "jamais"*' and neglect of the maxim on this occasion exacted a harsh price in British involvement in years of island strife. Elsewhere there was no parallel to such a policy of negation, nor indeed to a situation of such complexity and elsewhere, with the qualified exceptions of Ghana and Kenya, no organised national revolt against British colonial rule took place.

In the earlier years of African, as of Asian decolonisation, there was a disposition to transfer power by stages – internal self-government with certain powers reserved, full domestic self-government, the chief minister becoming prime minister with a cabinet responsible to an elected Assembly, consideration of administrative needs and internal security, enquiry into the position of minorities – the Willink Commission report on Nigeria, despite the civil war *dénouement* of later years, being the classic document of the period in this field – [31] the holding of a constitutional conference preparatory to agreement on a constitution and the inclusion in it of any necessary entrenchment, as in the Nigerian Constitution of 1960[32] or that of Trinidad and Tobago in 1962, of fundamental freedoms or human and minority rights, then independence embodied in an Independence Act of the British Parliament, with all the governments of the Commonwealth being invited to concur in Commonwealth membership. Time was allowed for each advance to be tested and for misgivings, notably on the part of minorities, to be expressed and this was coupled with mistrust of a timetable defining and committing the British government in advance. Subsequently this phased transfer of power, with either implied or stated conditions for each further advance, gave way to transfer with time as the first priority. Symptomatic of it, noted one contemporary observer,[33] was 'an increasing readiness to see the preparations for independence as a paper exercise of Lancaster House conferences, a challenge to chairmanship rather than a duty to find a constitutional framework genuinely acceptabe to the people of the country concerned and relevant to their needs and conditions'. And some confirmation of this may be seen in the perceptible decline in the substance and quality of British ministerial speeches introducing independence bills in the House of Commons. What had once been a venture in statesmanship, essayed with deliberation, was now reduced to little more than the application of a formula. While this reflected chiefly the change, if not in outlook at least in temper on the part of the metropolitan power, it was also, it is proper to add, in part also the product of growing experience. In the twenty-five years after the second world war, the Commonwealth collectively probably produced the largest number of written constitutions ever composed in so short a period. The many devices of federalism, the varying balances between executive and legislature, the machinery of judicial control, were all there to be copied or exploited as occasion demanded. One thing that was lacking – and it was soon to be in some demand – was a blue-print to serve as the prototype for the creation of a one party state.

In the process of decolonisation the British government encouraged the creation of federations in the West Indies, Malaysia and in Central Africa, but none of them in fact survived intact. In the case of the West Indies the causes of failure lay on the one hand in the strength of regional loyalties, which stood in the way of comprehensive membership – British Honduras, observed the federal prime minister, Sir Grantley Adams, 'having no more intention of joining the federation than I have of going aloft in a Sputnik!' – and strengthened psychological resistance even to the idea of federation, and on the other, in economic inequalities, which rendered impossible the negotiation of a generally acceptable apportionment of fiscal burdens. The Federation of Malaysia, it is true, survived, but with the secession of the Chinese-dominated port of Singapore. Both remained within the area of Commonwealth, and especially of Anglo–Australian–New Zealand defence interests, with Malaysia receiving significant support in her confrontation with Indonesia and the base at Singapore being made available, while use for it remained, by the government of Singapore to Britain, as a strategic centre east of Suez. It was, however, significant that it was increasingly the Australians who wished to maintain and the British, under economic pressure, who desired to diminish to vanishing point, Britain's historic east of Suez rôle. The third of the federations – that of the Rhodesias and Nyasaland – posed fundamental issues and in so doing confronted Britain and the Commonwealth with its last major problem of decolonisation.

Given the will, the liquidation of colonialism, in the sense of imperial rule over other peoples, presented issues which were in character partly technical and partly political, that is to say, it had to be decided in each case to whom power should be transferred and how it should be transferred. Both could ordinarily be decided by the imperial power with a certain impartiality and detachment. But the liquidation of imperial rule in territories where there were colonists in the Greco–Roman sense, while posing the same technical problems was apt to raise the political question in a form so acute as to be virtually different in kind. Popular emotions, notably in the territory concerned but also in the metropolitan country, were likely to be stirred and to sway the judgment and the actions of governments. Ireland between 1886 and 1921 had provided a classic example of this. In South, Central and East Africa British colonists had settled, with the encouragement of their fellow-countrymen in most instances, and had become in varying degrees privileged, influential or ruling minorities, differing in cultural background and above all in race from the indigenous majorities. Usually, but not invariably, well intentioned spokesmen encouraged thoughts of partnership, but while this commended itself warmly to liberal opinion, the principal protagonists, mindful of the impending withdrawal of imperial government, were more preoccupied with the retention, or the succession to power. In high degree the former was the concern of the white settlers in Southern Rhodesia.

That so small a community became the dominant preoccupation of the Commonwealth for more than a decade and a matter of concern to the world derived as much from historical setting as from contemporary circumstance. That setting embraced far more than the colony itself: it was that of British power in Southern Africa. The royal charter given to the British South Africa Company in 1889 was conceived of as the means by which Cecil Rhodes, whose company it was, might be given the necessary authority to realise his dream of establishing British influence north of the

Transvaal republic and of tapping the mineral resources the
hinterland was believed to, but did not possess. The territory was
company, not colonial office, administered until 1923 and thereafter a British colony with full self-government, except for some
reserve powers exercisable by the British government. It was
deemed a white man's country though it was understood by the
more perceptive, Milner among them, that it would never be closely
settled. None the less in London it was thought of down to the
mid-twentieth century as a significant factor in the South African
power equation, either by way of external counterbalance to
Afrikanerdom or of internal counterpoise, through union of
Southern Rhodesia with South Africa, to Afrikaner predominance
within South Africa. After the first world war the second was the
favoured alternative in London, but the settlers by plebiscite
rejected it and in so doing upset British calculations. On this
Dr Chanock has commented that the crucial question seems to be
not why the settlers made such a decision but why they were allowed
to make it. And the answers he offers are first that on all reckoning
the white Rhodesian community was a small but important part of
the white South African political community and, second and more
particular that if the settlers were coerced into Union, their
resentment would be likely to counterbalance the purpose of such
coercion. 'There could be, after all', he concludes, 'no point in a
Trojan horse filled with disaffected Greeks.' After the second
world war, and with the Nationalist victory in the 1948 elections in
South Africa, settler spokesmen in search of recognition of
Rhodesia as a Commonwealth member-state once again deployed
the argument of Afrikaner counterbalance, this time the counterbalance being thought of was an autonomous Rhodesia external to
South Africa but serving as a check upon expansionist policies it
might entertain. Superficially at least settler views were met with
the bringing into being of a long considered but, at the last,
somewhat hastily improvised Central African Federation.

The federation came into being in 1953. It comprised Southern
Rhodesia, which exercised responsible self-government, dominated by a European settler minority, on a restricted but not a rigid
colour franchise; Northern Rhodesia, with a white community on
the copper-belt but with an administration controlled by the
Colonial Office in London; and Nyasaland, also under Colonial
Office jurisdiction, without white settlement, poor in resources, but
with an African population educationally comparatively advanced
through the work of Mission schools. Theoretically, at least, the
federation was conceived in terms of ultimate partnership between

European minority and African majority and to this end its constitution contained built-in safeguards for the Africans.

The attractions of federation in terms of administration, communications and development of resources were not in serious dispute. It possessed economic advantages for all its component parts, but most of all for Nyasaland, the poorest of the three. But politics were in conflict with economics, and politics in these circumstances and at this juncture in time, were bound to prevail. The Federation of the Rhodesias and Nyasaland was not so much misconceived as conceived out of time and place. It belonged to an age when there was if not acceptance then acquiescence by Africans in European control. That age was passing at the very time the federation was brought into existence. To politically self-conscious Africans in all three territories, federation consequently appeared to be essentially a device for extending the period of colonialism and of economic exploitation to the profit of the European settlers. They protested. In 1959 the Report of a Commission of Enquiry under the chairmanship of Mr Justice Devlin into disorders in Nyasaland, noted the resolve of the African majority that federation should be liquidated and enquired why it was so strongly entertained. The answer was as follows: 'Federation means the domination of Southern Rhodesia: the domination of Southern Rhodesia means the domination of the settler: the domination of the settler means the perpetuation of racial inferiority . . .'[34] A year later the commission appointed to review the working of the Constitution of Rhodesia and Nyasaland under Lord Monckton's chairmanship elaborated the same point. They reported:

> It is inevitable and natural that the prospect of independence, seven years ago unthinkably remote, should now appear to many Africans to be a right from which they should be no longer debarred: and racial feeling, far from having merged into a sense of multi-racial nationhood, has grown sharper and stronger. It now appears to many Africans that only the presence of the European community politically entrenched behind the federal constitution stands between them and the form of freedom already granted to their fellow Africans in most other parts of the continent.[35]

The British government decided to dismantle the federation. The process was painful – how painful may best be judged by reading the account of the federal prime minister, Sir Roy Welensky[36] – there were allegations of misleading assurances given by British

ministers and even of broken pledges, and a mistrust between the
British settlers in Rhodesia and the British government was sown
which later developed into open antagonism. Yet as early as 1954,
at a Commonwealth Conference in Lahore, a British spokesman
had remarked, to the dismay ironically enough of British Conservative delegates, that if at any time Britain was compelled to choose
between the white settlers, practising racial discrimination in Africa
and 'Gold Coast democracy' she would be bound in her own
self-interest and in the interests of Commonwealth unity, to come
down on the African side.[37] That is precisely what happened in
Central Africa nine years later. With anti-colonialism, anti-
racialism in the ascendant in the Commonwealth as well as at the
United Nations, what had been seen in London as an asset now
appeared as a liability and with a rapidity that outdistanced settler
comprehension, earlier regard for settler interests gave way to
hostility towards them. But 'as coming to grips with settler power
had not been on the British Agenda, because settler power had
been seen as a plus factor in Southern African politics' there was,
once both internal and external counterpoise policies had collapsed, so Dr Chanock tellingly remarks, 'no British policy for
Southern Rhodesia itself because there had never been one'. This
explains the lack of direction in Whitehall when on 31
December 1963, the federation was dissolved. In Nyasaland and
Northern Rhodesia, as already in Kenya, the privileges and the
power of the colonists were ended: African majority rule established. But in Southern Rhodesia there was no such assurance
about the next step. The colonists, whose privileged minority
position the British government now deemed politically expend-
able and the African majority desired to see politically expended,
were more numerous and prepared to be recalcitrant. For Britain
without a clear aim and for a multi-racial Commonwealth, their
resistance to the winds of change was for fifteen long years to
present issues, touching on sensitive racial chords.

One result of the African, following upon the Asian, transfers of
power was the elevation of race equality, or multiracialism, to a
basic principle, shared by the Commonwealth community of states.
In an earlier period allegiance to the Crown had been made, and
after 1949 the practice of responsible parliamentary government
was generally considered to be a condition of membership. But by
the mid 1960s not only did the number of republican exceed the
number of monarchical member-states, but furthermore about
one-third of the members no longer practised parliamentary
government on the Westminster model and it was accepted,

though not in some instances without misgiving, that this also was a matter of domestic concern. But in respect of the ordering of race relations such a plea was conclusively rejected. South Africa provided, as had been long foreshadowed, the test case, for as the Commonwealth was moving towards equality and multi-racialism, the government of the Union was enforcing within South Africa its theory of racial separation. First known as apartheid and then in the face of world-wide criticism, reformulated with more sophistication as differential development, it was little distinguishable in its earlier application from racial discrimination, though it had as its professed goal, towards which some advances were made in the creation of so-called Bantustans by the end of the seventies, the separation of African and European into racially homogeneous states within a South African Commonwealth. The test, as it happened, came in such a way as to associate newer and now dominant racial with older constitutional issues.

The background was provided by developments in South Africa. In 1960 the Pan-African Congress planned a number of demonstrations to protest against the pass laws, and on 21 March many thousands of Africans marched on the police station at Sharpeville, near Vereeniging. Their leaders maintained that they had gathered to make a peaceful protest; the police, discounting this, opened fire with rifles and automatic weapons and sixty-seven Africans were killed and about 180 injured. The massacre, with pictures of it circulated round the world, caused a wave of horror. A week later on 31 March some thirty thousand non-Europeans marched on Cape Town, and were halted not far short of the centre of the city. While the racial question in South Africa thus apparently neared a violent climax, the Nationalist government decided the time had come at last for the declaration of a republic. The question was submitted, as had been consistently promised, to a referendum (in which voting was restricted to Europeans) and approved. A republican constitution, substituting a state president for the governor-general, was given a first reading in January 1961 and later enacted by the South African Parliament.

When the prime ministers of the Commonwealth met in London on 8–17 March 1961, they had, like the rest of the world, every reason to 'remember Sharpeville', and they had before them an application from the Government of the Union for South Africa's continued membership of the Commonwealth as a republic. Commonwealth precedent in respect of India, Pakistan, Ceylon and Ghana suggested that such a request couched in conventional form would be acceded to if constitutional considerations alone were at issue. But while the desirability of distinguishing the constitutional from broader political considerations was recognised by most of the Commonwealth prime ministers,[38] John Diefenbaker of Canada being, however, a notable exception, South Africa's application was made the occasion, as public opinion in many Commonwealth countries demanded, of a general debate upon South Africa's racial policies. This debate, as the brief communiqué issued on 15 March recorded,[39] took place with the consent of the South African prime minister, Dr Verwoerd. There followed an open attack upon South Africa led not, as might have been expected, by an African or an Asian leader, but by the Canadian prime minister who, according to Menzies (who was not a friendly critic), 'came armed with a resolution of his parliament and presented his views with immense emotion', not even 'some side-queries to him about the Red Indians and Eskimos in Canada' deflecting him from his course.[40] The Canadian initiative, significant in itself of the Commonwealth-wide revulsion against South Africa's racial laws – Menzies disapproved of the policies, while not approving of Commonwealth debate upon them – contributed to the Commonwealth consensus that emerged.

Subsequent accounts given by prime ministers to their individual parliaments revealed something of the fluctuating course of the prime ministers' discussions and dramatic conclusion.[41] At the heart of it lay the simple fact that Dr Verwoerd was prepared to make neither apology nor concession. Apartheid, in his view, was not a matter of convenience or expediency: it was an expression of the right view of race relations and as such had to be defended with the uncompromising zeal of a religious conviction. With 'brutal honesty' he replied, when asked, that he would refuse to meet any of his coloured colleagues socially in his own country.[42] There would be no change in practice or direction and his Commonwealth colleagues, thus faced with the prospect of acquiescence and the threatened price of division among them, or of pressing home their criticisms, adopted the latter course. Dr Verwoerd thereupon foreshortened debate by announcing the withdrawal of South Africa's application, thereby fixing 31 May, the fifty-first anniversary of the Act of Union, and the date already determined for the inauguration of the republic, as the date when South Africa's membership of the Commonwealth would lapse.

Dr Verwoerd subsequently stated that he took this step with 'great regret'. South Africa's request had been made in the expectation that it would have been willingly granted, 'as was done also on behalf of South Africa in the previous cases of India, Pakistan, Ceylon, Ghana . . . in spite of our great differences with them', but he had been amazed at, and shocked by, the spirit of hostility and even vindictiveness shown towards his country. This had made it clear that South Africa's continued membership would no longer be welcomed. He believed it marked 'the beginning of the disintegration of the Commonwealth'. The comments of his fellow prime ministers, other than Sir Robert Menzies, who confessed himself because of Commonwealth debate upon the management by a member-state of its own affairs, 'deeply troubled' by what had happened, were regretful, but also in varying degree indicated their relief at South Africa's departure. The president of Pakistan thought that as a result the Commonwealth would emerge as a stronger organisation; Diefenbaker that South Africa's withdrawal was unavoidable because discrimination in respect of race or colour could not continue if the Commonwealth was to be 'a force for good'; Mrs Bandaranaike of Ceylon saw in it 'a dramatic vindication of the equality and human dignity for which the Commonwealth stands'; Nehru though he wondered (and it would seem not without cause) whether the decision would in any way benefit non-Europeans in the Union, had little doubt the effect 'will be to strengthen the Commonwealth', and Macmillan, for whom the outcome represented the frustration of initial aims – he had pleaded in advance and 'with great eloquence'[43] at the meeting for a continuance of South African membership – spoke more simply of regrets that circumstances had made the breach inevitable. Implicit in all that was said was the conviction that a turning-point in Commonwealth history had been passed and hope predominated over anxiety as to what it might portend. It was widely noted that this was the first occasion on which the views of a United Kingdom government had not prevailed in a matter of major importance in Commonwealth internal policy. Virtually unnoted was the fact that the issue was decided by the prime ministers themselves in a tense atmosphere in London, apparently without continuing consultation with their own cabinets and after a protracted debate, the course of which was seemingly not uninfluenced by an inspired article by Dr Julius Nyerere, then prime minister of Tanganyika and later, president of Tanzania, published in the *Observer*, of Sunday 21 March. In it, Nyerere gave notice that Tanganyika, which was not to become independent till 9 December that year, could not 'join any "association of friends" which includes a state deliberately and ruthlessly pursuing a racialist policy'.[44] The strength of Pan–African sentiment was beginning to make itself felt in Commonwealth councils, with the president of Ghana, Dr Nkrumah, its most formidable protagonist.

The South African government by its decision to withdraw from the Commonwealth indicated a resolve not to be blown off course by the winds of change, but to withstand them. They had confidence in their ability to do so and on the short term assessed more justly than the majority of their critics the actual as distinct from the apparent balance of power in Africa. The Europeans in South Africa were long established, their society rested upon resources of wealth and economic experience without parallel in the continent and capable, as was to be strikingly evidenced in the years of economic growth that followed secession, of development at a rate that placed the republic among the world's leaders. But none of these things applied to the whites of Southern Rhodesia, numbering less than two hundred thousand in a population of nearly four million Africans.

When in 1963 the Federation of the Rhodesias and Nyasaland was dismantled, Northern Rhodesia as Zambia, and Nyasaland as Malawi, became independent member-states of the Commonwealth. Southern Rhodesia did not. For nearly twenty years the prime ministers of Southern Rhodesia and of the Federation had successively attended Prime Ministers' Meetings by courtesy, though not as of right. But it had been widely assumed, certainly in Britain and Rhodesia, that in one capacity or another the right would follow with an independence that, as a matter of policy, would not precede but shortly succeed upon the acquisition of independent member-status by an African state. That status was attained by Ghana in 1957; Nigeria and East and Central African states followed, but far from there being signs of early Rhodesian advancement, there were indications that independence and Commonwealth membership were to be made conditional upon assurances of majority African rule in some foreseeable future. The settlers, their experience of the dismantling of federation fresh in their minds, decided if need be to go down fighting rather than concede by stages, as seemed otherwise inevitable, their position of predominance. As it became increasingly apparent that they could not secure independence on their terms by constitutional means, they threatened to seize it unconstitutionally and by unilateral declaration of the independence of Rhodesia. 'There should be no delusions in Rhodesia', they were warned by Britain's Labour prime minister, Harold Wilson, 'about the ability and determination of the British government to deal with the utmost firmness with any act of rebellion; or about the effects of the mass of international condemnation to which Rhodesia would expose herself.' But the white Rhodesians, led by Ian Smith, were not to be deflected. On 11 November 1965 they declared independence unilaterally, the first settler revolt against British imperial authority since the American War of Independence. UDI was interpreted in Africa as a challenge to the new Africanism, a test of British and Commonwealth good faith, and an expression of settler intention to disregard fundamental African rights. It was greeted with loud protests from the leaders of Commonwealth Africa, with the imposition of limited trade sanctions by Britain and other Commonwealth states, but not by force. Britain, which was entitled in international law and might have been able to apply it in practice, was not prepared to do so; while the African states, who had not themselves the military resources, sought passionately and provocatively to pressurise Britain into using it. One result was that the Commonwealth in Africa came near to foundering on the suspicions and antagonisms aroused by the Rhodesian settler régime's existence and still more its survival. Another was that for the first time, the Commonwealth collectively sought and secured an active rôle in a matter which in principle lay between the British government in London and a colony in Africa under its jurisdiction and within its sphere of responsibility. How that rôle was played affords an insight into politico-psychological stresses and organisational changes within the newly-enlarged Commonwealth at this time.

At the Commonwealth prime ministers' Meeting 1961 the British government, as has already been remarked, for the first time failed to achieve a major aim. From the British point of view this was not, however, the only or on the longer term, the most unsatisfactory feature. There were indications, not only among the newer members, of diminishing readiness, or even regard, for Britain's leadership. Both were pronounced at the meeting held the following year, at which the going, from a British point of view, has been described as 'sometimes rather rough' in consequence not of African but of Canadian, Australian and Indian representations on Britain's Common Market application. Then in 1964, when UDI was known to be in near prospect, the British prime minister found himself assailed by the leaders of the African states on the Rhodesian issue which occupied the time of the Conference to the exclusion of almost every other topic. Publicity, propaganda, pressure no longer concealed behind conference doors, but openly exerted with advance texts of speeches, all were there and all in full measure applied. The climax was still ahead in 1966, but two

successive British governments – those of Douglas Home and
Harold Wilson – with their colleagues and advisers were dismayed
and affronted. 'By 1964', writes Lord Garner, 'British officials were
being placed in an intolerable position at these meetings.'[45]

It was at this juncture, but not seemingly the direct consequence
of these changes in the style and character of Commonwealth
Meetings, that the possibility of establishing a Commonwealth
Secretariat for making the arrangements and providing the
administrative support for Commonwealth Meetings was revived
and formally proposed by Dr Nkrumah. It was thought of in the
first instance as being in the interests of the newer members, or
some among them, but it had the further advantage of relieving
British officials of responsibilities difficult and self-evidently dis-
agreeable to discharge, once meetings were large and British policies principally under fire at them. The proposal for a Secretariat,
therefore, had British support for the first time, the interests of
the government as formulated by the Commonwealth Relations
Office, being to ensure that the British were relieved of an
invidious task and that a competent organisation took over the
servicing of Commonwealth Meetings. So Deakin had won his
point – nearly sixty years after he had urged it upon Elgin. But the
Australian government, in 1965, approached the question with a
caution exceeded only by the Indian, concerned as it was to exclude
all risk of interference. The Canadian government in this superficially strange, but altogether explicable reversal of rôles not only
advanced 'the most emphatic case' for a Secretariat but, later, in
Arnold Smith supplied the first of a succession of Secretaries-
General, who by their own enterprise, in conjunction with force of
mainly African circumstances, ensured the centrality of the
Secretariat organisation (which was formally established on approval by the Commonwealth Prime Ministers' Meeting 1965 of a
Memorandum drawn up by officials) to the Commonwealth.
Without its timely coming into existence it is in question whether
the African Commonwealth would have survived the traumas of
the Rhodesian crisis.

There was substantial consistency in the approach of successive
British governments on the conditions on which independence
might be conceded to Southern Rhodesia. They were formulated
first by the Conservative administration as five principles, which
were restated by the succeeding Labour government on 21
September 1965, and then extended in January 1966, with the
addition of a sixth. These principles were as follows: 1. The
principle and intention of unimpeded progress to majority rule,

already enshrined in the territory's 1961 constitution, would have to be maintained and guaranteed. There would also have to be 2. guarantees, against retrogressive amendment of the constitution; 3. immediate improvement in the political status of the African population; 4. progress towards the ending of racial discrimination. 5. The British government would need to be satisfied that any basis proposed for independence would be acceptable to the people of Rhodesia as a whole. 6. It would be necessary to ensure that, regardless of race, there was no oppression of majority by minority or of minority by majority.

These principles envisaged no immediate transfer of control from Europeans to Africans, which indeed was apt to be deemed unrealistic in London in view of Rhodesian African divisions and the untested quality of African leadership in the colony at the time, but they sought, with earlier South African experience much in mind, to ensure that power would be progressively transferred beyond possibility of retraction over a period of years. It was, however, precisely this prospect of steady erosion of their position, which the settlers, or the great majority of them, had sought to avert by their unilateral declaration of independence. Would economic restrictions suffice to persuade them to retrace their steps, return in effect to the *status quo ante*, accept the six principles, and so open the way to African majority rule within a reasonable period of years? The British government, in a position to use force only at the price of dividing opinion at home, and risking confrontation with South Africa, professed their confidence in an affirmative answer.

On 10 December 1965, the British prime minister told the House of Commons that the economic measures Britain had undertaken to bring Rhodesia at the earliest possible moment back to constitutional government were harsh and would cause hardship, but the government considered that 'quick and effective measures will involve less suffering than a long drawn out agony'. The prime minister's confidence, however, was not shared by the majority of African states, clamorous for war against Rhodesia, regardless of any risk of South African involvement.

It was in an attempt to remove growing African mistrust of Britain's resolution and even of her good faith, and so to preserve the threatened unity of the Commonwealth that two meetings of Commonwealth heads of government – a designation embracing both presidents and prime ministers – were held in 1966, one in Lagos in January, at the invitation of Sir Abubakar Tafawa Balewa, the prime minister of the Federation of Nigeria, the other in

London in September. The Lagos meeting was notable, as the first held outside Britain and also as the first to be organised by the Commonwealth secretariat, the existence of which facilitated the organisation of conferences in capitals other than London. One consequence was that it was not the British prime minister, as heretofore, but the prime minister of the host-country, the Federation of Nigeria who presided. This was of some moment since the Lagos Conference had been called on Nigerian initiative to discuss a single topic – Rhodesia. Two member-states, Ghana and Tanzania, which had already broken off relations with Britain on the Rhodesian issue, were not represented, while Australia sent an observer indicating, so Sir Robert Menzies explained, the concern of his government lest other Commonwealth countries should interfere in what was properly a British responsibility, and by pressing for the use of force in Rhodesia should strain the structure of the Commonwealth. The final communiqué in fact reaffirmed that the authority and responsibility for guiding Rhodesia to independence rested with Britain. But it also acknowledged that the problem was one of wider concern to Africa and the Commonwealth leaders expressed their sense of the danger to all multi-racial communities, particularly in East and Central Africa, and to the future of the multi-racial Commonwealth itself, if the situation in Rhodesia were to continue. But while all were agreed that the rebellion should be brought to an end, some expressed their forthright concern that the steps taken so far had not ended it. The use of military force was discussed and it was accepted that it could not be excluded. On the other hand, the British prime minister stated that on the expert advice available to him[46] the cumulative effects of the economic and financial sanctions might well bring the rebellion to an end within a matter of weeks rather than months. The forecast was received with general, and as it was to prove, justified scepticism. The Conference decided accordingly and by way of reinsurance to appoint two continuing committees, composed of representatives of all Commonwealth countries, and assisted by the Commonwealth secretariat to meet with the secretary general in London, one of them to review regularly the effect of sanctions and the other to co-ordinate a special Commonwealth programme of assistance in training Rhodesian Africans for future responsibilities. The heads of government left it open to the sanctions committee to recommend the reconvening of their Conference when it was judged to be necessary, and in any event decided they would meet again in July if the rebellion had not been ended before then.[47] The Commonwealth over whose destinies

Britain had once presided, was in effect to act as a watch dog upon Britain. This was accepted but not relished in Whitehall.

The Rhodesian rebellion was not in fact ended in July, nor yet in September when, somewhat behind their self-appointed timetable, the prime ministers met again in London. Between the two Conferences there were informal talks between British officials and members of the Rhodesian administration. They were talks on the British side directed to finding out whether a basis for negotiation existed: they were, as the phrase went, talks about talks and without commitment. They served, however, despite British protestations, to heighten African suspicions of British intentions. As the talks continued intermittently, with rumoured breakdown followed by resumption, these suspicions continued the more to flourish. They dominated the September Conference.

The September Meeting was attended by the heads of government of Australia, Britain, Canada, Cyprus, Gambia, Guyana, Malawi, Malaysia, Malta, New Zealand, Sierra Leone, Singapore and Uganda; by the acting prime minister of Jamaica and by ministerial and governmental representatives of Ghana, Trinidad and Tobago, India, Pakistan, Zambia, Ceylon and Nigeria. Tanzania alone did not send a delegation. Nine of the eleven days' Meeting were devoted to Rhodesia. Most of the heads of government expressed their firm opinion that force was the only sure means of bringing down the illegal régime in Rhodesia. The British government, nearly but not altogether isolated, stood firm in its objections to force as a means of imposing a constitutional settlement. There was also very strong pressure upon the prime minister that Britain should make a categorical declaration to the effect that independence would not be granted before majority rule, on the basis of universal adult suffrage. Here the prime minister conceded much without conceding all. He agreed that any settlement must be, and be seen to be, acceptable to the people of Rhodesia as a whole and that this implied that there would be no independence before majority rule, unless the people of Rhodesia as a whole were shown to be in favour of it. There was less optimism than in January about the impact of sanctions. The illegal régime was, therefore, to be presented with an ultimatum by the British government. It was to the effect that, unless the initial and indispensable steps were taken to end the rebellion and to vest executive authority in the governor before the end of the year, the British government would in the first place withdraw all previous proposals for a constitutional settlement and in particular would not thereafter be prepared to submit to Parliament any settlement

which involved independence before majority rule, and in the
second place they would be prepared to join in sponsoring in the
Security Council a resolution, providing for selective mandatory
economic sanctions against Rhodesia.[48]

The time limit, reinforced with the threat of international action,
implied an intensification of the struggle and a prospective
widening of the area of it. But its acceptance neither stilled doubts
nor silenced criticism in the African Commonwealth. The Zambian
foreign minister, who left before the Meeting was over, commented that Zambia had got nothing at the Conference – President
Kaunda had been the principal and consistent protagonist of the
use of force by the British to end the Rhodesian rebellion – but the
vice-president of Kenya was more temperate, remarking that while
the African, Asian and Caribbean delegations had not achieved all
they had hoped for, the very dangerous situation of independence
before majority rule had been avoided. As for Harold Wilson,
under the extremes of Commonwealth pressures, in a situation
which allowed him little freedom of manoeuvre, given the
Portuguese and South African gaps in the sanctions ring, he felt
that

> We are getting a little tired of carrying the can internationally for
> a régime that has no regard for international opinions. We have
> had to pay a very heavy price for carrying that can in the last ten
> days. We have faced very serious dangers of the break-up of the
> Commonwealth, because of the actions of a small group of
> men.

The ultimatum, with its end of year time limit encouraged
further talks between the British government and the Smith
régime with the governor, an isolated figure, with his telephone
wires cut in his residence in Salisbury, continuing to serve as an
intermediary and an insistent advocate of negotiations. In
November there was a visit by the commonwealth secretary to
Rhodesia, and on 1 December, the prime minister having 'reason to
think we were within hailing distance of a solution', gave the
dramatic news to the House of Commons that he was flying out that
evening for a 'sea-summit' with Ian Smith off Gibraltar on board
HMS *Tiger*. The talks lasted two days. A working document[49] for a
constitutional settlement within the framework of the six principles
was drafted and the Rhodesian leader given the opportunity of
discussion with his colleagues in Salisbury before accepting or
rejecting it as a whole. They rejected it professedly on the ground

that the procedure outlined for a return to legality was objectionable, and that, in view of its nature, the Rhodesian government, so Ian Smith maintained, 'would be extremely foolish were they to abandon the substance of their present constitution for the shadow of a mythical constitution yet to be evolved'.[50] Rejection was followed forthwith by British application to the United Nations for the imposition of selective mandatory sanctions, which were extended under Commonwealth African pressure to include oil, and by a declaration that all previous offers made by the British government were invalidated and that in consequence there would be no independence before majority rule [NIBMAR].

A mandatory embargo on all trade with Rhodesia followed in May 1968, but the rigour of language was not matched by a like rigour in action. Settlement by negotiation without sacrifice of principle remained, however, the British purpose, irrespective of party. In pursuit of it, Harold Wilson essayed without success further seaborne talks, this time on HMS *Fearless* in October 1968, though on the return of the Conservatives to office Lord Home as Foreign and Commonwealth Secretary seemingly made more progress signing proposals for a settlement after talks in Salisbury. The proposals in their turn, however, foundered when tested on the fifth principle that of 'acceptability to the people of Rhodesia as a whole'. But still the commitment to negotiation on the British side remained, exploratory talks by various emissaries were continued until in March 1976 fresh proposals, *inter alia* prescribing elections within two years and no independence before majority rule as preconditions to negotiations on an independence constitution, coupled with United States intervention and a worsening security situation as seen from Salisbury, opened new possibilities with a faint stirring of seemingly long lost hopes of an honourable British disentanglement from the last and most unwelcomingly tenacious of her African territorial responsibilities. But the psychological impact of the experience of those years had made its mark.

In no previous phase in the process of decolonisation had Commonwealth participation in the shaping of British policy been so pronounced, nor British freedom of manœuvre become so narrowly constricted, nor the limits of British authority been so painfully and so publicly demonstrated over a long period of time. For the short term, the political price of Commonwealth in Africa was seen to be high. Disillusion spread and it was deepened by African disorder. The Lagos Conference was followed within a matter of days by an army revolt in Nigeria, hitherto the most stable as well as the most populous of Commonwealth states in Africa, in which the premiers of the Northern and Western Regions were murdered and the prime minister of the federation, who had presided over the conference with quiet distinction, kidnapped and subsequently found dead. In less than a month President Nkrumah, while on a state visit to Peking, was ejected from power, also by an army revolt in neighbouring Ghana. These things played their part in hardening an existing and already pronounced predisposition on the part of parties and people in Britain to look in hope not to Africa, nor to other parts of the Commonwealth overseas but nearer home – to Europe.

It was not long after South Africa's withdrawal from the Commonwealth that positive steps towards effecting a change in the direction of British policy were taken. On 13 June 1961, Harold Macmillan announced that three senior ministers were to visit Commonwealth capitals to consult with Commonwealth governments about Britain's relations with the European Economic Community. The announcement was rightly interpreted as indicating a major shift in British policy. The three emissaries, however, and for that reason, proved more successful in eliciting misgivings about the effects, political as well as economic, for the Commonwealth overseas of Britain's membership of the EEC, than in persuading overseas Commonwealth governments of its desirability. While the economic and political strengthening of western Europe was recognised to be a general Commonwealth interest and while it was explicitly conceded in communiqués[51] issued after the talks that Britain's membership of the EEC was a matter for decision by the British government, Australian ministers, to take a not unrepresentative example and to quote the communiqué issued on 11 July, expressed their concern at 'the weakening effect they believed this development would have on the Commonwealth relationship' and while they 'did not feel entitled to object to the opening of negotiations by the British government', they made it clear that 'the absence of objection should in the circumstances not be taken as implying approval'. When the question was considered collectively by Commonwealth ministers attending the meeting of the Commonwealth Economic Consultative Council at Accra, 12–14 September that year, such strong language was used by the Canadian delegates as to suggest that the Canadian government considered that Britain had to make a choice between the Commonwealth and the EEC. The official communiqué[52] itself spoke of 'the grave apprehension and concern' of all overseas Commonwealth representatives regarding 'the possible results of the initiative taken by the United Kingdom'.

The Accra communiqué represented a position more extreme than was in evidence in subsequent negotiations or at the Commonwealth Prime Ministers' Meeting in September 1962. The difficulties of Britain's economic position and the lack of any convincing Commonwealth alternative to membership of the EEC were becoming increasingly apparent. In the crucial export field, United Kingdom exports to the Commonwealth between 1955 and 1963 remained nearly static, her exports to the United States and the EEC more than doubled.[53] It is true that exports to Commonwealth countries in 1962 remained greater in value than those to the United States and the EEC put together, and more immediately relevant, that exports to the Commonwealth that year amounted to £1,032 million as against £720 million to the Six. Commonwealth trade, in other words, remained immensely valuable, accounting for about one-third of Britain's total trade. But it was also either stagnant or in slow decline, holding out, so it seemed to most economists, little possibility of growth. Yet there remained many in the Commonwealth overseas, even where so much was conceded, especially in the old dominions, who accepted the truth of some things that were said by General de Gaulle on 14 January 1963,[54] when he used his country's right of veto to terminate negotiations on Britain's entry into Europe. They were disposed to agree that Britain was in fact insular, maritime, bound by its history, its political, financial and trading systems to many and distant countries. While they had become generally reconciled to the thought of Britain's membership of the Common Market, with hardly negotiated safeguards and with reservations of their special interests, her complete absorption in the European community, which the General professed to consider then and later a necessary condition of membership, was something which other member-states of the Commonwealth were apt to view with dismay. Resentment, therefore, at the brusqueness and the lateness – after months of thought and bargaining in which all Commonwealth governments had been in some measure involved – of the president's pronouncement was not wholly dissociated from a sense of temporary relief. There was now time to make new dispositions. The course of British policy had been checked, but its direction was not changed. Where Macmillan left off, Wilson resumed four years later. By then debate within the Commonwealth, aside from some outspoken Australian protests, was over, new dispositions where possible were made or being made – in 1967 Australian trade with Japan for the first time exceeded her trade with Britain – and the consequences for Commonwealth were awaited with resignation.

When on 22 January 1972 the British prime minister, Edward Heath, signed the Treaty of Accession in Brussels, that assumption proved correct. This time there was no de Gaulle to exercise once more a twice used veto, and despite continuing concern for New Zealand lamb and West Indian sugar, there was no semblance of collective Commonwealth protest such as had occurred a decade earlier. The continuing debate was *within* Britain, no longer within the Commonwealth – though this did not preclude Common-wealth interests being deployed in domestic dialectics. And even in these, there was little serious suggestion that the Commonwealth collectively offered, or desired to offer, Britain an alternative to EEC.

On 28 October 1971 when Britain was about to make her final application to join the Common Market, Edward Heath told the House of Commons that the idea that the Commonwealth might become 'an effective economic and political let alone military bloc had never been realised' and that none of its members con-templated that it should. On the contrary, it was generally accepted that trade with the Commonwealth overseas, unlike that with the Common Market, held out no prospect of dynamic growth. But while the White Paper which had set out the reasons for Britain's renewed application for membership dwelt upon the contrast, it was at pains to refute the allegation that EEC membership would mean that Britain would become increasingly 'inward-looking'. Yet the probability remains that such reassurances may stand less well the test of time than Professor J. D. B. Miller's verdict that 'the importance of the EEC lay in Britain's turning away from the open sea towards the narrow seas'.[55] Were this indeed to be so, de Gaulle's critical appraisal of British interests, as transcribed at the beginning of Part two of this volume, would lose its validity and in so doing remove the fundamental objection de Gaulle had ad-vanced to Britain's Common Market membership. But by the eighties another possibility, envisaged by neither, forced itself into consideration, namely that Britain disappointed in her high expectations in terms of politico-economic groupings might turn away from the open and the narrow seas alike.

The doors of Western Europe were opened: the problems of Central Africa remained. To outward appearance, the risks inherent in them had been enhanced. What had begun as a local issue, albeit one with wider implications, had become an interna-tional question, bringing, or accentuating, Great Power rivalries in the area. Yet, paradoxical as it was in many ways, negotiation continued to follow upon negotiation, as in turn each series was terminated with indications of finality. In the end this commitment to negotiation yielded a positive result. But if the question is posed why, the answer even among all the uncertainties of recent history, is hardly open to dispute. It was because of the use of force – force in the form of guerillas within Rhodesia and from across the borders, notably of Mozambique – added to that of international pressures, by which is to be understood not only Commonwealth and United Nations sanctions, but also the admonition of a South African government not wishing to see the Republic involved in racial struggle in an exposed, and for them disadvantageous situation. Such was a condition of 'peaceful' transfer. In no other combination of circumstances, it may be safely presumed, would the white minority under Ian Smith's leadership have conceded the return to a colonial status by way of necessary preliminary to a transfer of power to a government founded upon majority African rule.

The sequence of events that led to the curious, and in some ways rather moving climax to the decolonisation process was itself the product of a strange conflation of circumstances. External pressures political and military (in the form of guerilla action) produced in the first instance not a settlement from without but from within. In November 1977, Ian Smith, faced by new Anglo–American proposals involving the surrender of power by his régime, containing the outline of an independence constitution and a plan for the administration of the territory under a British Resident Commissioner for a transitional period while free elections were held, as well as being under pressure from many quarters, including South Africa nearer home, himself announced by way of distracting device the acceptance of the principle of majority rule. Following this in March 1978, he reached agreement with three internally based, but apart from Bishop Muzorewa, little known African leaders, on independence under majority rule by the end of the year. On 21 March he ceased to be prime minister becoming a member of a transitional government headed by an Executive Council comprising himself and the three African leaders with an 18-member Ministerial Council in which one African and one European held responsibility over each portfolio until the introduction of a new constitution providing for majority rule. Outside Rhodesia, these arrangements made no favourable impression, being condemned by the OAU and the Front line Presidents, while from the Patriotic Front they elicited Nkomo's bleak comment 'we are not going to allow it'.

Elections under the new constitution were, however, held in April 1979 and on 1 June 1979, Bishop Muzorewa took office as Prime Minister, his party, the United African National Council having won a majority of the 72 seats reserved for Africans in the Assembly. The gain was an election on the basis of one man one vote for Africans and Europeans (28 seats) in their respective constituencies and the emergence of a black majority: the liability inbuilt powers vested in the European community under the Constitution and widespread and evidently well-founded doubts as to the authenticity of the results of an election declared null and void in advance by the United Nations. The incoming British Conservative Prime Minister, Mrs Thatcher, withheld recognition and in late May initiated a further round of talks with a view to a return to legality, it being the view of the British government that no satisfactory outcome was possible without the participation of the Patriotic Front and the 'Front Line' States.

At this juncture the Commonwealth in the person of its Head and in the form of its traditional Conference moved into the Central African scene. The Queen arrived in Lusaka on 27 July 1979 after visits to Tanzania, Malawi and Botswana, to be in attendance for the first time at such a Conference in a republican member-State. The Conference met on 1 August with discussion on the Rhodesian issue deliberately deferred until the third day. A group of six, comprising Presidents Kaunda and Nyerere, Mrs Thatcher, Mr Manley, Mr Fraser and Major-General Adefobe (representing Nigeria) together with the Commonwealth Secretary General, Mr Ramphal, were appointed to draft an agreement for submission to the full Conference. They did so. It was approved. After making due allowance for the major contribution of the five 'Front Line' Presidents, three Commonwealth, those of Zambia, Tanzania, Botswana and two from outside, those of Angola and Mozambique, and the exchanges that preceded the conference, it may still be thought that rarely has the Commonwealth in its bringing together of differing views been seen to better advantage.

The principal recommendation of the Lusaka Conference was the calling of a Constitutional Conference at Lancaster House. It met on 10 September 1979 and agreed upon a *Summary of the Independence Constitution* which was duly enacted by Order in Council on 6 December 1979. With it went agreement, hardly obtained, upon arrangements for the pre-independence period and for a cease fire.[56]

The forms were important – the Conference, as the British

Foreign Secretary, Lord Carrington noted, was different from all other meetings on Rhodesia since 1965. It was 'a constitutional Conference, the purpose of which is to decide the proper basis for the granting of legal independence to the people of Rhodesia. Many conferences like this have been held in this very building.' They had indeed. But here again it had its distinctive qualities. The leaders of the Patriotic Front, Mr Mugabe and Mr Nkomo, pointed them out. 'The Conference is not only unique .... because it must achieve peace as well as a future constitution: it is unique because this is the first time that two decolonising forces have to co-operate in this task. The Patriotic Front representing the people of Zimbabwe are here as the effective decolonising factor, while Britain is here asserting her diminished legal authority.'[57] The cooperation of the two decolonising forces, as identified by the leaders of the Patriotic Front, was in the first instance made possible and in the second sustained, by the firm commitment to majority rule entered into by Mrs Thatcher and subscribed to by the representatives of other member-States. The conditions for establishing such rule were laid down at Lusaka and translated into practical terms at Lancaster House.

The terms included by way of legal and symbolic return to the due process of decolonisation, the appointment of a Governor – Lord Soames – to preside over an interim administration together with representatives of the UK and some other Commonwealth forces to supervise a cease-fire and observers to monitor the election.

'There is something of an irony', Lord Soames later reflected[58], 'in the fact that, in the end, Britain could only terminate her constitutional connection with Rhodesia by taking on a rôle – and attendant risks – that was more extensive and demanding than any which she had played at any previous stage in Rhodesia's history. In Rhodesia the drama of colonial history was played in reverse – metropolitan power having been very limited at the beginning, but with total responsibility being assumed at the end. Indeed one cannot help feeling that this end was somehow connected with that beginning by the obscure workings of nemesis: that the half-heartedness of the commitment accepted by the British Government at Cecil Rhodes's instance in 1889 was the first step down the road which led to a British Cabinet Minister going out to Salisbury almost a hundred years later, equipped with the full panoply of executive and legislative powers to return to the people whence they had come.'

To the surprise of the well-informed, most things went according to plan and Robert Mugabe following upon a decisive electoral victory* took office as the first prime minister of the Republic of Zimbabwe. As was remarked to the author on that day in the Department of External Affairs, New Delhi, 19 April 1980 joined 15 August 1947 on the Commonwealth Calendar. And how fitting also it was that the Order in Council which set in train the events that led to independence should have been dated 6 December – thus linking the last major act of British decolonisation in a non-British setting with the first, the Anglo–Irish Treaty signed on 6 December 1921.

There remained, however, remnants of Empire in the form of strategic outposts, Gibraltar chief among them, and scattered island territories too small to be self-governing, too British in the origin or outlook of their peoples to be readily associated with neighbouring territories which, as the Falkland Islands crisis of 1982 dramatically testified, might yet impose on Britain obligations carried over from another age and which she was no longer well-equipped to meet.

---

* It was this that prompted the observation, 'It is difficult to recall a more inaccurately predicted election result than this.' M. Gregory, Zimbabwe, '1980 Politicisation through armed struggle and electoral mobilisation', *Journal of Commonwealth and Comparative Politics*, vol. XI, March 1981. For the impressions of an official observer, sensitive to the hazards involved and of the miracles needed for a successful outcome, see Ronald Robinson, 'Cliff-hanging from Rhodesia to Zimbabwe', *Balliol College, Annual Record*, 1980.

7 Men of Commonwealth: Smuts, Mackenzie King and Nehru

History and circumstance permitted, even it may be predicated the emergence of Commonwealth in some form. But they did not determine, still less predetermine, the pattern of it. That is to be traced to the influence of individuals and, in some measure, the collective will of peoples. The latter, at all times hard to assess, is in this case chiefly to be inferred from response to challenge, and in less exacting days from participation or at the least acquiescence in the activities necessary to meaningful Commonwealth existence. The former, the place of personality, at times seemingly defined with deceptive ease in records which appear to offer convincing and on occasion even conclusive interpretations in personal terms of the developments they describe, affords with certain cautionary reservations more fruitful ground for reflection. The emergence or existence of a Commonwealth of Nations gave to many men in official or unofficial capacities opportunities for influencing or seeking to influence a segment of international relations which otherwise they would not have enjoyed. Chamberlain and Milner; Botha and Campbell-Bannerman; Laurier and Deakin, Borden and Hughes; Balfour, Hertzog and O'Higgins; Montagu, Amery, Irwin, Mountbatten; Mackenzie King, Curtin, Fraser, Menzies, Attlee; Liaqat Ali Khan, Louis St. Laurent, Macmillan, the Bandaranaikes, Abubakar Tafawa Balewa, Julius Nyerere, Lester Pearson, Jomo Kenyatta, Pierre Trudeau among statesmen with many more besides; and Jebb, Lionel Curtis, Geoffrey Dawson and the Round Tablers, J. W. Dafoe and Canadian liberal-radicals, K. M. Panikkar, among exponents or prophets, and, if little known to a wider public, by no means least many distinguished administrators – all left a mark on the politics, the concept or the working of this association of nations and, outside their own countries, are remembered chiefly or largely for their impact upon it. There are others, cast in a larger mould, whose influence is to be thought of in a more spacious context, J. A. Hobson among writers,

Smuts, Churchill, Gandhi, Nehru, Jinnah, de Valera, Nkrumah and Mrs Gandhi, among national leaders, but whose impress upon the Commonwealth was, in some instances at least, no less pronounced than that of those to whom its development in whole or in part was a principal preoccupation.

It would no doubt be possible to write the history of the Commonwealth in biographical terms, and in many respects it would be illuminating. But historically the attempt would be almost as misconceived, though no doubt a good deal more entertaining, as the constitutional straitjacket into which the story was for so long forced to fit. It would be misconceived because it would rest upon a false equation of man and circumstances. It was the latter, in the first instance brought into play by British expansion and settlement overseas, which made possible and conditioned the experiment of Commonwealth. What remained, and it was much, for individuals was to impart where they could present meaning and a sense of future purpose to political, cultural and human connections, which they had as a result inherited. The system was important but so also were the men who worked or developed it. What sort of men were they? What were their dominant interests and purposes? Francis Bacon concluded his essay upon the Greatness of Kingdoms with the reflection that while 'no man can, by care-taking (as the Scripture saith) add a cubit to his stature, in this little model of a man's body; . . . in the great frame of kingdoms and common-wealth, it is in the power of princes, or estates, to add amplitude and greatness to their kingdoms'. The age of princes is past, but even in a century of scientific discovery, technological revolution and the common man, individuals in positions of power or symbolic significance may still enhance or diminish the reputations of states or societies and either enrich or impoverish that historical tradition which, by illuminating the way a country or community has come, may serve to cast light on some parts of the road ahead.

GENERAL J. C. SMUTS: HE WAS DEFEATED.

In May, 1902, when the Boers debated the issue of peace or war at Vereeniging, Smuts maintained that peace must be made. His presentation of the case was factual and formidable, though the suppressed emotion comes through in the climax. 'Brothers, we resolved to stand to the bitter end; let us admit like men that the end has come for us – has come in a more bitter form than we had ever thought possible'.[1] He was thirty-one. He was defeated. His biographer has termed it 'strange defeat'.[2] It provides, however, a clue to an understanding of the strangest of all Commonwealth careers.

His biographer, Professor Hancock, has shown Smuts on both sides of the hill. In Smuts' lifetime, the far – the Boer – side remained unfamiliar to the great body of Smuts' English and Commonwealth admirers. But to Smuts it was home. It was there, brilliant and intense, that he went to school, taking no part in the games of 'the puerile element', and with no reason to pay any special regard to that slow, persistent plodder, D. F. Malan, three years his junior. Stellenbosch and then Cambridge followed with firsts and prizes all the way. But at Cambridge they did not compensate for being away from home. In his first year he was 'utterly desolate'. Yet Cambridge and England left their mark. 'An anglicised Afrikaner is as disgusting a creature as an anglicised Scotchman', his benefactor and early mentor, Professor Marais, felt reason to warn him.[3] The events of succeeding years might seem to have made the warning superfluous.

Misplaced faith in Rhodes, shattered by the Raid, was followed by Smuts' migration to the Transvaal, where he became Kruger's state attorney and the leading personality in the republic after the president. He negotiated with Milner who thought him high-minded, recognised his outstanding ability, but doubted his staying power and political insight. For his part, Smuts, though tempted to dismiss Milner with 'the academic nobodies who fancy themselves great imperial statesmen', finally realised that Milner was resolved to confront the republic with total capitulation or total war. The second was chosen. Smuts campaigned. He found that 'military life agrees wonderfully with me'.[4] It equipped him, moreover, at the outset of the century, for what was to be the dominant international factor of his lifetime – preparation for war and war. But in 1902, after the exhilaration of commando raids there came the end, not merely in the form of defeat but defeat in a war which Smuts believed to have been unjustly forced upon his people. 'Perhaps it is the fate of our little race', he reflected to his wife in the first letter which she received from him for over a year, a year in which their son died, 'to be sacrificed on the altar of the world's ideals; perhaps we are destined to be a martyr race.'[5]

Defeat, and especially defeat in such circumstances, usually prompts either despair or an uphill climb by paths that are often devious. It is the vanquished, not the victors, who have need to be 'slim'. 'Mr Smuts', wrote a Colonial Office official of him, at the time of his visit to London early in 1906, 'is a Boer and a lawyer. His

memorandum ... exhibits all the cunning of his race and calling.'[6]
There was some truth in this. Smuts was concerned not with means
but with the long uphill climb from defeat. The most notable step
on it was his famous meeting on the evening of Wednesday, 7th
February 1906, with Campbell-Bannerman. That meeting was 'the
creative encounter'[7] of his political life. With advancing years,
Smuts' recollection of it became more vivid and he came to attribute
to it a significance greater than it could in reality sustain. But his
instinct was sound. A man who has been defeated is apt to be a good
judge of the political magnanimity that opens the way to recovery
from defeat. There followed the day, 4 March 1907, on which
Smuts was sworn in as a member of His Majesty's Government in
the Transvaal. He wrote of it to Merriman:

One is apt to look upon an event such as this as a matter of
course ... but after all, viewed from a larger standpoint, it is
really most remarkable. My mind went back to Vereeniging –
separated from the present by only six brief years – and the
determination to win finally which buoyed me up even there in that
darkest hour of our history.[8]

And one step still further on in the upward climb, at the National
Convention 1909, Patrick Duncan noted how

the fertile mind of Smuts busies itself in producing compromises
on ... contentious issues. He does not care much what he gives
away as regards constitutional principles or power, and still less
as regards material interests so long as he thinks the thing will go
through in a form not too tightly tied up for him to pull it about
afterwards as a member of a strong government with a docile
Parliament ...'[9]

Smuts was sanguine enough to believe that the contagion of
magnanimity would spread. But in one respect he himself had
ensured that it should not. The original draft of the relevant
provisions of the Treaty of Vereeniging stated that the franchise
would not be given to natives until after the introduction of
self-government. It was Smuts, so Professor Hancock revealed,
who re-wrote the article completely so that it read: 'The question of
granting the franchise to natives will not be decided until after the
introduction of self-government.'[10] For the clear implication that
the natives at a later date would enjoy the franchise, there was

thereby substituted a franchise at the discretion of those who had stated their unqualified objection to granting it. Here is, according to the point of view, a classic example of Smuts's skill as a draftsman or of his 'slimness'. Of course the final responsibility for accepting the amended draft rested with the British government. But Smuts got what he and his people wanted. In 1902, it can reasonably be argued, it was his duty, the more bounden upon him because he was a Transvaaler only by adoption, to salvage what he could from defeat. But the views he expressed in the formative period of union indicate that there was for him a frontier beyond which the contagion of magnanimity did not spread. The natives, he continued to think, were better out of politics and he helped through his subsequent long years of power to keep them in the position in which he had found them.

What mattered to Smuts was the reconciliation of Boer and Briton and the Union which symbolised its achievement. In the pursuit of the first, he moved far and fast – too far and too fast for the majority of his fellow Afrikaners. Even as early as the Convention, Patrick Duncan remarked upon the feeling that Botha and Smuts

> are losing the true national spirit, and have been contaminated by the Anglicising influence of the Transvaal. Botha's liking for bridge seriously disturbed some of them, especially since he was found playing one Sunday evening. It is one of those small things which strike the imagination of the staid Boer as a sign of a falling away from . . . the ideals of the people.[11]

In the deeper sense Smuts never 'fell away'. But at times he did become dangerously insensitive to some of the innermost aspirations of his own people. He neglected language, he was unwise, if even more unlucky, in his reaction to the 1914 rebellion and, preoccupied with Commonwealth and world affairs in London, he so lost touch with the source of his own being as to regret that he had not stood in 1918 as a candidate for the British House of Commons. Was the price of increasing absorption in the idea and the possibilities of Commonwealth to be detachment from his own Afrikaner people? That was a suspicion, and far more than a suspicion, on the part of many, who found no satisfaction in the spectacle of a Boer general finding fulfilment as a 'handy-man of Empire'.

The price of detachment, however, was something to be paid in the future. In the London of the concluding war years it may well have been a positive advantage. Smuts had a range of experience and of gifts to which few of his contemporaries could aspire. Professional soldiers, it is true, were apt to be critical of his strategy, professional philosophers to discourage his philosophising,[12] while politicians felt that in dealing with problems of intermediate range Smuts's judgment was not altogether reliable. Yet when so much has been said, his qualities, supported by an almost terrifying industry, remained. No one can read the concluding chapters of the first volume of Professor Hancock's biography, telling of Smuts's contribution to the creation of the Royal Air Force, to the transformation of Empire, to planning for a future international order and to thinking about war and peace, without enlarging his understanding of the history of those years, without sensing in Smuts the quality, albeit fallible, of greatness and without recognising how much even one man of vision and political stature might do to give meaning to the new idea of Commonwealth.

Behind the Commonwealth and international statesman, there remained the man conditioned by his experiences. During the Boer war Smuts knew enough to know that there was an England other than the country of Rhodes, Chamberlain and late nineteenth century imperialists. Even if it is hard to believe that intimations of John Bright played quite so large a part as Professor Hancock suggests, there was the importunate, impossible, meddlesome 'messenger sent from Heaven' when 'our race seemed doomed to extermination', Emily Hobhouse, who had first brought home to the British public and to Campbell-Bannerman the evils of the War Office concentration camps in the South African war. With her, with Quakers, anti-imperialists and pacifists who worked and pleaded for South Africa in her hour of need – Smuts's association was lasting. Years later when he was a member of the war cabinet, his biographer tells us how Smuts spent his weekends, not with Lloyd George at Churt, nor with other political colleagues, but more congenially with those who mistrusted empire and detested war. Emily Hobhouse, seeing his name in big print in *The Times*, 'that mighty organ that emulates Divinity for it putteth down one and setteth up another', hoped that something of the old 'Oom Jannie' remained; enough to enjoy association with the 'pacifist and anti-imperialist I am prouder than ever to be'. It did. Friendships dating from the days of defeat were still cherished. Away from the citadels of power which so strongly attracted him, Smuts relaxed with those who scorned them. This may be held up as an example of 'slimness'; it might equally well be regarded as a healthy antidote to the corruption of power.

When Smuts's intellect and his emotion were harnessed, as they were in peacemaking, then the man in his full stature appeared. General Botha who in the eyes of Smuts and of many others bore with Campbell-Bannerman the stamp of magnanimity, wrote on his agenda papers after he had signed the Treaty of Versailles on 28 June 1919, 'Today I recall 31 May 1902 (Vereenigning).' For a year or more that thought had been constantly in Smuts's mind. In 1900–2 Milner had striven for total victory and unconditional surrender; in 1917–8 Smuts argued for limited objectives, early peace and above all magnanimity in victory. The spirit of magnanimity did not, however, pervade Versailles. His pleas rejected, Smuts resolved, in turmoil of heart and mind, not to sign the treaty. Yet in the end, a man without illusions, one sinner, as he said, with the rest, he signed.[13] It was loyalty to South Africa and to Louis Botha, whose faithful friend he was in calm and storm, that decided him; it may be at the expense of those larger claims of suffering humanity which he at least had the vision to comprehend. But rarely indeed, can a political decision have been more hardly reached. Smuts's whole attitude to peacemaking was ambivalent and it was his experience that made it so. He sat with the victors at Versailles but his heart was more often with the vanquished. He too, had been defeated.

For Smuts it was not only '*The Sanguine Years*' of the first volume of Professor Hancock's biography that had drawn to a close by 1919; it was also that his range of freedom was henceforward to be restricted. With Botha dead, Smuts became, and remained for the rest of his days, in office or out of it, imprisoned within the South African political system. From shipboard in July 1919, he wrote of feeling like Ulysses coming home at last and of wondering 'what will Ulysses do in his little Ithaca?'[14] Given Smuts's immediate past it was understandable speculation; given his national background it was no less understandable that his South African critics should denounce his known indulgence in such reflections. Either way not much harm would have been done had his Ithaca been little. But it was not, either in the obvious geographical sense, or – far more important – in deeper political reality. On the contrary it comprehended most of the problems that trouble the twentieth century and some of them in their most acute form. The returning Ulysses, superbly endowed by intellect and breadth of experience, lacked one of the qualities required to deal with them – the predisposition to give them, consistently and over the years, the priority they demanded.

On 3 September 1919 he wrote to Mrs Smuts of the 'colossal

responsibility' that would begin for him with the swearing-in of his first Cabinet that afternoon. It was shortly followed by a letter to Margaret Gillett saying more revealingly: 'I am now prime minister but my heart is not in the thing . . . Botha's loss to this country is quite irreparable.' This was followed in turn by one from Botha's widow saying that Botha thought of Smuts as 'the greatest man in our country, the coming man of the age'. This much proved to be true. Smuts's responsibility was 'colossal', his heart was not always 'in the thing' – the problems of the great world far away from South Africa and, at a deeper level, botany, philosophy, and other intellectual interests all attracted or distracted him, reflecting 'the striving for mastery [between] the creative and the instrumental' so evenly balanced in him, as one correspondent shrewdly wrote.[15] In terms of human leadership, Botha's loss was irreparable, as Smuts was the first to acknowledge – and there was something direct and very moving in the tribute he paid at the unveiling of the statue of his old leader in Pretoria in 1946,[16] while beyond question Smuts was, and remained, a coming man of the age in the sense that in most, but not all, of the great issues of his time he took, despite dreadful discouragement, the constructive forward view.

The great exception was colour. In his earlier years Smuts had understood the gravity of the long-term implications of the native question and had reflected that beside the ultimate realities of relations between black and white differences between Boer and Briton would appear superficial and prove transient. But throughout his political life, and never more conclusively than in the Fusion ministry of the 1930s he subordinated the first to the second. Anglo-Afrikaner co-operation remained, as at Union, his first priority. This may have been mistaken but it was a deliberate choice consistently adhered to. 'South Africa', he wrote in intensity of feeling on 6 September 1939, 'has a divided soul, but if we are faithful to the vision of forty years ago that soul will be one yet. Time is a causal factor and there has not yet been enough time.' The soul once more so deeply divided by war was a European soul. It was that division which he sought to heal and his attitude to the native question was conditioned by that overriding purpose. 'Let them develop', remained his philosophy of race relations – if it may be so described – and only in his last years of office, did he come to sense that they were developing far and fast.

For these failures in insight and comprehension in respect of colour Smuts has been forgiven neither by white racial supremacists nor by liberal humanitarians nor yet by the leaders of a new Africa. 'It has always seemed to me a pity', wrote Chief Luthuli,[17] 'that a man as gifted as Smuts should have gone into eclipse, not because of adherence to any principle, but because of obtuseness. Yet, since he did not at home ever stand on principle, perhaps that was just.'

Smuts' reputation as a statesman was served indifferently by his frequent commentaries on world affairs. His experiences at Versailles conditioned his thinking and accounted for many of his insights as well as his fallibility as a guide in the inter-war years. It had not been a magnanimous peace; in his view it should have been. The difference accounted for much; but not quite so much as Smuts supposed between 1935 and 1938. As a result the pronouncements on European affairs which he felt called upon to make and which he made without being shown the secret information from London which was sent to General Hertzog as a dominion prime minister, were apt to reflect surprisingly many of the misconceptions of the times. He was later to be memorably mistaken as when in 1943, outlining a possible future Western European–Commonwealth association, he spoke of France as having gone as a Great Power and continued, 'We may talk about her as a Great Power, but talking will not help her much. We are dealing with one of the greatest and most far-reaching catastrophes in history, the like of which I have not read of . . . France has gone and will be gone in our day, and perhaps for many a day.'[18] These were words neither overlooked nor forgotten in later-day Paris!

But if like others Smuts made his misjudgements, he was not lacking in firm conviction. His faith internationally rested first in the League to which he remained loyal long after it had ceased to be loyal to itself, and second in the Commonwealth, which by his thinking (he was out of office in 1926) he had done so much to fashion. Of these two pillars, the Commonwealth weathered better the tensions of the time. But Smuts, who had protested at the 'Carthaginian' peace in 1919, was clear before Munich about what, in Commonwealth terms, was needed and what was possible – 'a resolute policy of appeasement and reconstruction of the peace by Great Britain'[19] and no commitments in central or eastern Europe – 'the Dominions . . . will fight for Great Britain if attacked: they will not fight in the battles of central or south-eastern Europe. I even have my doubts whether they will fight again for France or Belgium. They are now out of that business under the Locarno Treaty . . .'[20] He was writing to Amery and his assessment of dominion attitudes was correct.

It was the prospect of attack on Britain that was crucial – as in any case was implicit in the 1938 Hertzong–Smuts compact on South

African neutrality in the event of war. Chamberlain's Polish guarantee of March 1939 'has simply made us gasp', partly on politico–strategic grounds, but still more because of its possible impact on the unity of the Commonwealth, the overseas members of which from 1926 had been expressly and consistently averse to commitments in Eastern Europe. Yet Smuts's attitude to Munich and his reactions to the Polish guarantee serve in longer perspective not to demonstrate his fallibility – though in some measure it was there – but the heroic stature of the man who, having travelled so far along one road because – on this he insisted time and time again – of the abandonment of the League (which he never ceased to regard as the great error of the 1930s), recognised that it was his responsibility in 1939 to bring South Africa, against the domestic odds, into the war against a world-menacing tyranny, and see that war through to a successful conclusion.

Smuts responded heroically to the challenge of a second German war. Largely by force of his own personality and conviction he brought South Africa in on the allied side in September 1939. Few will be disposed to quarrel with his biographer's assessment of the significance of his action at that time or of the consequences which flowed from it. From 1939 to 1943, notes Professor Hancock, Smuts' achievement was immense.

> If Hitler's image was not to be stamped upon this planet his country was geopolitically necessary and he was politically necessary. The Cape of Good Hope lived up to its name and assumed once again its historic primacy in oceanic strategy. Without the Cape route, the Commonwealth could hardly have survived the war; without the Commonwealth, the Russians and Americans could hardly have won it. But the victory in Africa changed all that. Henceforward the Mediterranean was open again and the Cape route, although still useful, was no longer indispensable.
>
> It was the irony of fate that Smuts and his country should find themselves so much diminished by victories they had done so much to win.[21]

There was a deeper irony in store. If South Africa dissociated herself from her friends in the British Commonwealth, Smuts had argued in September 1939, the day would come when she would find herself isolated in a dangerous world. She did not dissociate herself but the day none the less came when she found herself isolated. But by then Smuts's world was in ruins.

Not only in Africa, but throughout the Commonwealth, that sequel, coupled with recollections of Smuts' own passivity in matters of racial policy, shadowed his later reputation, as he himself was reminded most of all away from home, '... the going is very bad here', he wrote from New York in November 1946. 'Violent opposition both on the Indian and South West Africa questions. Colour queers my poor pitch everywhere. I ... can look at it all philosophically. But South Africans cannot understand. Colour bars are to them part of the divine order of things.' There it all was, the present understood, the future foreseen and Smuts trapped in old age between forward-looking international opinion which had long been his source of hope for the world, and domestic opinion which alone could provide him with authority. It was the stuff of personal tragedy and he felt it to be so. Yet however large race relations may loom in the mind of a succeeding generation they should not be allowed to obscure foresight or achievements in other fields, at least as immediate in their importance and as challenging in their nature, in earlier times. Union itself, a memorable part in two world wars, an unrivalled perception of the principles that determined the transformation of Empire into Commonwealth – these were things in their own day of counter-balancing weight. In the perspective of history, after all, it was not colour but war, peace and their consequences that dominated the years of Smuts' political maturity from 1897 down to 1945 and what the times immediately demanded Smuts supremely gave. It may be that he owed more than is commonly allowed to others, before and during the first world war to Botha, a man of wiser counsel though not of comparable intellectual attainments and during the second world war to J. H. Hofmeyr, the 'boy prodigy' of earlier years, who assumed responsibility for three or more departments of state as well as serving as deputy prime minister while Smuts played his part on a wider stage and with whom Smuts' relationship remained strangely tentative and by no means uniformly to his credit.[22] Yet the crowds that acclaimed Smuts in Johannesburg on triumphal tour when the second world war had finally ended with the surrender of Japan were not mistaken in their tremendous tribute to one who at decisive moments throughout a long life had shown supreme gifts of leadership.

Down the years, at least until 1945, Smuts's faith in the Commonwealth was not diminished but enhanced. For him it was the continuing basis of Anglo-Afrikaner reconciliation at home and the chief hope of peace abroad. 'I am a firm believer', he wrote in January 1940, 'in the Commonwealth, not only for its own sake and that of South Africa, but as the first tentative beginnings of great things for the future of the World.' The source of that faith, embellished though it was by philosophy, may be traced to his experience. And in that experience there were two decisive events – defeat and reconciliation. The second had reality because of the first, and it was the man who had been defeated who sensed more truly than any of his contemporaries the meaning with which the phrase, 'Commonwealth of Nations' might be invested and the beckoning vision which it might offer of equal brotherhood of those who had ruled with those who had been ruled. De Valera recalled many years later, that if any man could have convinced him of the advantages of dominion status for Ireland, it was Smuts, who on a secret visit to Dublin on 5 July 1921, under the improbable pseudonym of Mr Smith, expounded its characteristics with a force and logic beside which Lloyd George's later explanations appeared shallow and counterfeit.[23] Smuts, the man who in his younger days had written of 'a century of wrong', who deemed that he had himself experienced its climax, late in life spoke in clipped part-foreign accent to the people who had perpetrated the 'wrong', as partners in friendly and equal association with his own in a Commonwealth of Nations, which he thought of even in the darkest days of the second world war as the proudest political monument of time. Whether inspired or mistaken, it was a judgment few men were better qualified by their own experiences to make.

W. L. MACKENZIE KING: PRIME MINISTERS' PRIME MINISTER.

As Edmund Spenser is traditionally spoken of as the poets' poet and Gustave Flaubert often thought of as the writer's writer, so Mackenzie King may be thought of as the prime ministers' prime minister. In each instance the appeal is less to the public than to the professional – be he poet, writer, or politician. What is common is a mastery of technique of a kind likely to be appreciated in all its refinements, only by those who practise the self-same art. William Lyon Mackenzie King was not a man of profound intellect, he possessed power without popularity, he abhorred the spectacular, he had an intriguing but not a commanding personality, and there would be little reason for him to be remembered were it not for his mastery of the techniques of politics.

Memoirs and biographies, especially of nineteenth-century

English statesmen, were Mackenzie King's favourite reading. No doubt he perused them, as he did most things, more for the possible political profit than for the pleasure to be derived therefrom, but whatever the motive the fact renders the more fitting the biographical monument on a more than Victorian scale (even if somewhat lacking in the reticences then conventional) now completed in seven volumes (including four based on the diary entries of his later years) and by several hands to preserve the memory of his doings.[24] The subtitle of the second volume of the biography, 'The Lonely Heights', has an overall appropriateness – so long as it does not elicit misplaced sympathy for the subject of it. King was single-minded in his resolve to reach and stay on the heights, and he liked being alone. Even when his closest friends left his country home at Kingsmere after the briefest of sojourns, his diary usually recorded his satisfaction at being alone once more, free to walk the fields with his dog at his side. Whether he was solitary because he was single-minded or single-minded because he was solitary may remain a matter for speculation. But that he was single-minded in the pursuit and the exercise of power is not to be doubted. This indeed was the abiding source of strength for one who lacked, as he was himself well aware, many of the superficial gifts of leadership.

Mackenzie King's attention to detail – that hallmark of the professional in all human activities – became proverbial. He always wished to have things, and above all, words, exactly right. He delivered few speeches without complaining afterwards that there had not been enough time for their preparation. He was almost boyishly pleased when a speech went well and there were no limits to his satisfaction when words of his succeeded in discomforting his Tory opponents. Late in life, with the example of Roosevelt and Churchill before him, he was encouraged to speak more often impromptu, and the later pages of *The Record* contain many expressions of regret that he had not done so more frequently in earlier years. Yet if in this he had missed opportunities he had also avoided risks. In the long run his care in the choice of words repaid him well. Those anxious and exacting days of preparation, for his secretaries as well as for himself, represented not wasted time but time spent in the consolidation of his political position. He also derived from them a heightened awareness of the meaning of words and the implication of phrases, and he was from time to time able to use this with devastating effect against careless or ill-considered assertions by political opponents. It also enabled him at Imperial or Commonwealth Meetings to seize upon small but significant points of drafting, the implications of which might otherwise have been overlooked. Such unremitting attention to detail was not only part of the man but an important factor in his political survival.

'At least, from 1938, when I began to observe him closely', recalls J. W. Pickersgill,[25] 'he [King] was not a thinker, and I have found no evidence in his writings that he ever was.' Mackenzie King, remarks his biographer, Dr Neatby, 'was no crusader, eager to ride a white charger to oblivion'. Both were certainly true. But despite deficiencies as a thinker and dislike of crusading, Mackenzie King had a cause. That cause, to which he sacrificed both friends and principles when he deemed occasion demanded it, was not an ignoble one. It was the unity of Canada. No other leader, and no party other than the Liberal, the only truly national party as he thought of it, was really equipped to serve that cause. But a condition of such service both for himself and the Liberal party was the consistent maintenance of a moderate, central, national position on all issues. In all the difficult situations which politics present, so King argued, 'there must be a point somewhere at which a proper balancing can be effected'. With fixity of purpose, he sought for it. The very phrase – a proper balancing – epitomised the temper of his approach to politics. And this appreciation of the importance of balance made him correspondingly mistrustful of extremes. 'The extreme man', he once observed to a friend, 'is always more or less dangerous, but nowhere more so than in politics. In a country like ours it is particularly true that the art of government is largely one of seeking to reconcile rather than to exaggerate differences – to come as near as may be possible to the happy mean.' This was because the difficulty, as King observed on another occasion, 'of maintaining unity in Canada is very great indeed'.[26]

Mackenzie King approached imperial-commonwealth relations from the standpoint of his abiding preoccupation with national unity significantly reinforced by a temperamental mistrust of imperialists and their manifold machinations. Where Empire would certainly divide, Commonwealth would equally certainly help to unite Canada. He wished, therefore, to dispose of the remnants of centralised Empire and to substitute for them only such links as were consistent with decentralised Commonwealth. But while he saw his goal with something of the deceptive clarity of the single-minded, the successive British administrations with which King had to deal, appeared to him to be confused about Commonwealth goals and in the 1920s double-minded in many of their ways. The chilling indignation with which he damped Lloyd George's imperial impetuosity at Chanak is a matter of history, while as for Ramsay MacDonald, King's only doubt (and one evidently shared by his biographer) was whether Britain's first Labour prime minister was stupid, or untrustworthy, or both. Mackenzie King accordingly, with 'wary vigilance and stubborn insistence at every turn' persisted in his attempts to bring enlightenment about the nature of dominion status and to defeat the stratagems of the outdated and recalcitrant in Downing Street. 'Bourbons', his biographer calls them, and comments with appreciation on how 'amazingly patient' the Canadian prime minister was in trying to get them to understand, amid the intricacies of conference representation and treaty-making, the essentials of dominion autonomy. But Ramsay MacDonald, it is clear, remained either uncomprehending or resolute in his refusal to comprehend. 'On the basic concept of future Empire relations', concludes Dr Neatby bluntly of these years, 'Mackenzie King was right and Downing Street was wrong.'[27] If by this is meant that Mackenzie King had correctly diagnosed the forces at work and foreseen the outcome for Commonwealth relations in, so to speak, the middle distance, the judgment seems warranted.

In terms of political and personal drama, the refinements of Commonwealth were overshadowed in King's early years of office by the controversies and confrontations of domestic politics carrying overtones of Empire. Of none was this more true than of the tangled, triangular relationship of King, Meighen, Byng, which bore so closely upon Canadian attitudes at the 1926 Imperial Conference. While Dr Neatby does not share King's own belief that the constitutional issue decided the general election of 1926, called, it will be remembered, when the governor-general conceded to Meighen the dissolution he had refused to King – considering rather that it was the fervour of King's convictions that won him votes[28] – he is clear that because this opinion came to be generally accepted, electoral victory also gained for King an enviable reputation for political infallibility. That reputation, by reason of the imperial issues involved, extended beyond Canada. It was not altogether unmerited. In the fluctuations of fortune, which make the King-Byng incident at once remarkable and memorable, King, it is true, had luck – but also a reliability of judgment and a grasp of essentials to which Meighen, a rival whose debating qualities he feared, could not pretend. But equally it was not an episode calculated to win esteem for King, for all the political expertise he displayed. Indeed the strongest feeling may be one of sympathy for

Lord Byng, the soldier, who was misled at the outset by notions of fair play altogether alien to politics; who showed more foresight than is often allowed; who perhaps unwisely but not unpardonably excused himself from studying the constitutional works of Berriedale Keith and Kenneth Pickthorn, which Mackenzie King had thoughtfully brought along to Government House, on the ground 'that the situation was different to anything that had arisen at any time' and who, despite a telegram of birthday greetings from Mackenzie King during the election campaign (the dispatch of which was duly recorded in King's diary with expressions of self-congratulation upon his observation of the constitutional proprieties even at a time of tension) did not respond, as King later had occasion to note without gratification, with a card for Christmas 1926. No doubt the time had come when the soldier felt, 'enough is enough'.

Mackenzie King came to the Imperial Conference 1926 with his decisive constitutional victory already won. He was by reason of this the better placed to adopt the mediatory rôle that was most congenial to him. He was moreover in a middle position in as much as he thought Australian–New Zealand predisposition to assume imperialist postures needed to be discountenanced and South African (if not Irish) nationalism to be restrained. Vincent Massey wrote of King as having made 'the greatest contribution towards conciliation' at the Conference and recalls Amery's speaking of him as 'the great constructive figure among the dominion statesmen' there. But all that emerges conclusively is that Mackenzie King, well grounded in the implications of the root principle of equality as the touchstone of future Commonwealth relations, was unusually well placed to help to find a balance. There is no formula, least of all the published one, to bear his name. He was happy, remarks J. W. Pickersgill, 'to leave the definition to others and he was not blind to the political advantage at home of defending a British rather than a Canadian formula'.[29] If, further, it be accepted that, as his biographer suggests, Mackenzie King was the only prime minister who believed that the Commonwealth had been strengthened by the Conference,[30] that is illustrative first of a more positive faith in the idea than is customarily attributed to him and secondly of his belief that Canadian national unity would be strengthened by Canada's free and equal association within the reconstituted Commonwealth.

The pinnacle of Mackenzie King's political good fortune was attained when he was defeated in the general election 1930, and in consequence out of office during the years of the Great Depression.

But King was not out of office in the later 1930s and his support for the policy of appeasement (already related) remains, less fortunately for him, a part of Commonwealth history. Unlike others, he never saw reason to repent of it. And there was his visit to Hitler in 1937 at which the German chancellor impressed him as a man of deep sincerity and a genuine patriot, who despite some observations of expansionist purport about eastern Europe, was not contemplating war against France or Britain. It is clear, and it remains surprising, that Mackenzie King was not so much deceived – there is no evidence that Hitler was planning a war against the west in 1937 – as duped.[31] But it is not clear that this had significant political consequences – essentially it was the situation in Canada, not the situation in Europe that determined his approach.

The Czech crisis a year later threatened to bring Mackenzie King face to face with the domestic prospect he dreaded most. He hoped, as we have seen, that the Czechs would make, or be persuaded to make concessions sufficient to avert war, but, so he told two of his principal colleagues on 31 August, if war came he could 'not consider being neutral in this situation for a moment'. The price of participation – namely that 'the Liberal party – and the country – would be more deeply divided than in 1917' less because of war than because of conscription which French Canada feared more than war, appalled him. According to his biographer the prospect was so shattering that 'for the first time in his life he lost hope'.[32] A year later not only had the country become psychologically conditioned to thoughts of war but the balance of forces had changed – for the worse. The Nazi–Soviet pact was announced on 22 August. 'Curiously enough', commented King, 'I felt instantly a sense of relief.' Quebec's natural antagonist among the Great Powers was now on the other side: King would have his wartime problems but they might well prove manageable.

Mackenzie King was superficially as ill-equipped for survival as a wartime prime minister as Asquith or Neville Chamberlain. But, unlike them, he survived. How he did so may be studied in *The Mackenzie King Record*[33] based on extracts from the diary which he had kept since boyhood. It is an illuminating if not always an inspiring story. In war as in peace Mackenzie King's conception of leadership was not, it need hardly be said, in the romantic Churchillian tradition. Far from it. 'I really believe', he wrote on 26 September 1940, 'my greatest service is in many unwise steps I prevent'.[34] A leader, he explained later to the leader of the Progressive Conservative party, could guide 'so long as he kept to the right lines. I did not think it was a mark of leadership to try to make the people do what one wanted them to do...'[35] He regarded himself essentially as the representative of the people of Canada. His power derived from them and he believed that 'the people had a true instinct in most matters of government when left alone'. They were not swayed, as especially favoured individuals were apt to be, by personal interest but rather 'by a sense of what best served the common good'. When in August 1941 Beaverbrook asked him in London how he gauged public opinion so accurately, Mackenzie King replied that he did the thing he thought was right and held to 'a responsible self-government and the supremacy of Parliament in everything'. The people, he continued, understood common sense; they believed 'in one's integrity to one's word'. He attributed his success to these things; above all to the fact that he had been close to the people as a source of government.

Mackenzie King was at once affronted and dismayed by criticism of his wartime leadership. He was disposed to regard it, and for most of the period not wholly without cause, as criticism of a professional in the art of government by amateurs. He was also, in the manner of English Conservatives, in times of crisis apt to conclude that such criticism was in essence 'factious'. It was something that he, like Laurier before him, was called upon to suffer – in political extremity he was deplorably disposed to make allusion to the Garden of Gethsemane – and rarely indeed did he attribute creditable motives to those who assailed him. Under stress of war also the Gladstonian overtones in many of his utterances became more pronounced. He had the same sense of Providence guiding his actions and (as critics of both would allege) the same capacity for deceiving himself and others with high-sounding moral platitudes. King felt proud that he had declared in Parliament that the Bible was the foundation of his beliefs, and he always hoped 'that the day might come when, in the Canadian Parliament, I might stand for the kind of thing that Gladstone stood for in the public life of England in the matter of political action being based on religious convictions and the latter known and boldly stated'. There is no reason to doubt these convictions were deeply held. Paul Martin, later one of King's ministers, has recalled how one night in Geneva when they came to the monument to Calvin, Mackenzie King took his hat off, saying to Martin, a Catholic, 'Oh, of course, you wouldn't understand'.[36] These were things which, while sustaining him in the responsibilities of wartime office neither blunted the resolution with which he acted nor the ruthlessness of his actions when he deemed that the interests of his party or his country – and he did not always distinguish very carefully between the two – demanded it. In 1940, in an election which he had timed with his customary sureness of political instinct, he noted of his own final national broadcast that he was 'particularly happy about its references to the tone of public life', and after the sweeping Liberal victory he felt that his own name and that of Lapointe would be linked together in the history of the country as 'a not uncertain example to those who may follow us in the administration of its public affairs'.[37]

While Mackenzie King's emphasis on precept and example was wholly Gladstonian, his dislike of crusading was not. There is no Midlothian campaign by which he will be remembered; he weighed the consequences too nicely ever to champion uncertain, far away causes. But this should not obscure the fact that Mackenzie King, despite his unGladstonian repudiation of the spectacular in word or deed, had at the very fibre of his being a Gladstonian feel for 'the politics of virtuous passion'.[38] The 'virtuous passion' which he felt was not for massacred Bulgarians and against the unspeakable Turk; it was for Canada and against imperialism. If there was no campaign it was because the imperialists, unlike the Turks, gave no occasion for one. But no one could doubt that the smouldering fires of self-righteous passion were there. As late as 1944, Lord Halifax, by talking in his innocence in Toronto of a post-war common foreign policy fanned them into flame.

Mackenzie King's instinctive fear of imperialist machinations was, if anything, heightened under stress of war. Asquith once remarked of John Bright: 'There is the only man in public life who has risen to eminence without being corrupted by London society.' King to the last accepted the implication of that comment. Society was corrupting, London society peculiarly so, and worst of all by subtle influences likely to wean Canadians from the loyalty they owed to Canada first and all the time. 'It required a lot of courage, if I say it myself, to hold firmly to the line I felt would be right, and not be influenced by . . . hospitality.'[39] So he wrote one evening in London during the Commonwealth Prime Ministers' Meeting in the Spring of 1944 when his prestige in Canada and in the Commonwealth was at its zenith.

The more I think [he wrote a few days later][40] of the high pressure methods that have been used, the more indignant I feel. It makes me tremble to think of what Canada might be let in for if a different type of person were in office. Where would we have been had Bennett been in office at this time? What annoys me is the social devices and other attentions paid with a view to getting some things done, to influence one's mind even against one's better judgment. I think I have gone through this battle without wavering.

His fears were not groundless but it is astonishing that they should be so vividly entertained at this time. While Churchill certainly sought to influence what he should say in his Address to Parliament,[41] his friendship with Churchill was firmly established and his views on the future of the Commonwealth had been accepted. Smuts, who had fought against the British, Nehru, who had suffered long years of imprisonment under the *Raj*, appeared untroubled by such inhibitions, why Mackenzie King? History, more particularly family history, is usually offered by way of explanation for them. Certainly memories of his rebel maternal grandfather were remarkably easily stirred to life. Was this because he felt that his anti-imperialist credentials might otherwise hardly suffice?

Mackenzie King's dislike of centralised empire was matched by his increased attachment, even occasional enthusiasm for the idea of Commonwealth. Both were derivative. At the heart lay Canada. It was his country's interests and her place in the society of states that moved him. 'My first duty is to Canada.' That was something he rarely forgot. He had hard words for those who were seemingly prepared to sacrifice Canada to the interests of crown or empire or of North American solidarity . 'My view', he wrote in 1941, 'is that the only real position for Canada to take is that of a nation wholly on her own vis-à-vis both Britain and the United States.' Only by taking such a line would Canada secure recognition of her national identity.[42] It was because Commonwealth membership with full equality of status furthered this aim that he valued Commonwealth membership. He referred in December 1942 to

> the efforts that would be made by the Americans to control developments in our country after the war, and to bring Canada out of the orbit of the British Commonwealth of Nations into their own orbit. I am strongly opposed to anything of the kind. I want to see Canada continue to develop as a nation to be, in time, as our country certainly will, the greatest of nations of the British Commonwealth.[43]

Mackenzie King's conception of Canadian interests, coupled with his belief in parliamentary government determined – one might say predetermined – his attitude towards Commonwealth wartime developments. There is an account in *The Record* of how Mackenzie King first came to fashion the telling phrase 'a continuing conference of cabinets' and of how much thought generally he devoted to the question of reconciling full parliamentary responsibility with some effective means of Commonwealth co-operation. He appears to have at least partially convinced Menzies of the impracticability of an imperial war cabinet in 1941, and the enunciation of his objections to its reconstitution and his reaffirmation of faith in existing methods of consultation on his first wartime visit to London elicited a personal message of warm-hearted agreement from General Smuts.[44] In Commonwealth affairs he remained concerned with the meaning of words. In 1944, he asked first Cranborne and later Churchill the meaning of the then fashionable phrase 'Empire and Commonwealth', and he got very different answers! He was careful to ensure that not the singular 'policy' but the plural 'policies' should appear in communiqués. He elaborated on the distinction between a prime ministers' meeting and an Imperial Conference to Churchill and other members of the war cabinet, who (perhaps not altogether surprisingly) found some difficulty in grasping all the niceties of the distinction by which King set such store. With characteristic attention to detail and by a constant reiteration of the main lines of his thought Mackenzie King exercised the decisive influence on the Commonwealth of the later war and early post-war years. This is an impressive tribute to the cumulative effect of his carefully assembled arguments in an international context when one recalls that Churchill, Smuts and Curtin were among those with whom he had to deal.

Mackenzie King's Commonwealth contribution reflected, however, the weakness as well as the strength of his professional approach. His industry, his power of political penetration, his appreciation of Canada's long-term Commonwealth interests – all were there. But good judgment cannot dispense with the need for popular appeal. Mackenzie King thought in terms of government, but if the refashioned Commonwealth was to play the part that he hoped then it would have to appeal also to peoples. Here his distaste for the spectacular stood in the way of comprehension. He failed to understand, as Churchill and Roosevelt both understood so well, the need for a dramatic element in democratic leadership, especially in wartime. A message was received from Churchill through the British high commissioner, Malcom MacDonald, on 6 August 1941, expressing the hope that Mackenzie King would approve of Churchill's Atlantic Meeting with President Roosevelt. But Mackenzie King did not approve. He wrote in his diary that evening:

I feel that it is taking a gambler's risk, with large stakes, appalling losses, even to that of an Empire, should some disaster overtake the gamble. To me, it is the apotheosis of the craze for publicity and show. At the bottom, it is a matter of vanity. There is no need for any meeting of the kind. Everything essential can be done even better by cable communications, supplemented by conferences between officials themselves. Neither the prime minister of Britain nor the president of the United States should leave their respective countries at this time.[45]

He was wrong. It was a meeting that gave hope to beleaguered Britain and encouragement to defeated but not subdued European peoples. With better reason, but on the same grounds, he dismissed all idea of an early wartime Imperial Conference. The unobtrusive, businesslike behind-the-scenes approach he judged right for others irrespective of occasion he practised himself. With quiet persistence he pressed for recognition of Canada's part in the war but he refrained, even when he felt that the occasion might demand it, from all dramatic protest. Within two weeks of the American entry into the war, he told a cabinet meeting in Ottawa of the problems that were likely to arise. He pointed out that

it might be necessary for Canada to realise Churchill's difficulties in not showing preference as between dominions. Also in making allowances for a certain aggressiveness on the part of America and her probable effort at a monopoly of control. Also a certain forgetfulness on the part of Britain and the United States combined of Canada's part in the struggle.[46]

This showed astonishing foresight. Here, in these few sentences, are the dominant themes of Professor Trotter and C. C. Lingard's volume covering the years 1941–4 in the *Canada in World Affairs* series.[47] As the editor (J. W. Pickersgill) of *The Record*, pointed out, Mackenzie King was to complain of all the things that he had foreseen before the war was over. Vehement public protest on some well-chosen issue might well have been more effective than the series of pained reproaches privately communicated now to Whitehall and now to Washington. But it was not in character. Nor was it in accord with the chief aim of his wartime policy, the bringing together of Britain and the United States in a great alliance of the English-speaking peoples. Part of the price he paid was popular underestimate of his very considerable achievement and part popular misconception of his aims.

Mackenzie King found a continuing and human satisfaction in reflections on the changes which time had brought in Empire and Commonwealth, and he was apt to moralise about them. When the governor-general, the Earl of Athlone with his wife, Princess Alice, stayed in the farmhouse at Kingsmere for the period of the first wartime Conference in Quebec, King reflected:

> Little could my grandfather have seen when he was in prison and in exile, or my father and mother when they were making their sacrifices for the children's education, that some day one of their name would be entertaining the president of the United States and the prime minister of Britain at the Citadel of Quebec (where my father's father's remains lie) at a time of world war, and that, in the same week, the granddaughter of Queen Victoria would be finding her moment of rest and quiet and peace in the home of one of their own.[48]

However the moment there was a suggestion that the governor-general might be given a more prominent place than Canada's prime minister on this international occasion, the realist came brusquely into his own again.

With the progressive publication of three biographical volumes on the period up to 1939 and the four volumes of *The Record*, covering the years 1939–48, Mackenzie King became a more knowable Canadian. He was, like the superstitious John Aubrey some three centuries earlier, 'a little inclinable to credit strange relations'. He indulged in North American neo-Gothic fantasies by assembling ruins at Kingsmere. Much importance is likely to continue to be attributed to his eccentricities since the New World expects greater conformity among its public figures than the Old. But it is not as a perplexing personality but as a professional in the art of politics that Mackenzie King will be remembered and written about in Canada and in the Commonwealth. He was a wholetime and a calculating politician. Perhaps he was something more. He may even, in time, come to be accepted as one of those rare beings – a statesman masquerading as a politician. In years when Canadian unity was not threatened his qualities of judgment and restraint came to be discounted or disparaged by Canadian historians. A historian from a country that has been partitioned is unlikely to be critical of unity 'bought by the method of evasion',[49] rather to be over appreciative of it. But whatever the changes in reputation that time has brought and may yet bring to Mackenzie King, the carefully recorded reflections and actions of a prime minister's prime minister will surely continue to be read and pondered by all whose eyes are drawn by interest or ambition to Parliament Hill in Ottawa. And so long as there remains a Commonwealth of Nations, predominantly parliamentary in their form of government, recollections of this prickly, prudent, unspectacular and solitary man will remain to guide, to counsel and to warn.

JAWAHARLAL NEHRU: THE SPOKESMAN OF LIBERAL-INTERNATIONALISM.

'He could hardly at this time be described as a politician at all. He was a revolutionary. Whenever there appeared some tenuous hope of settlement, he was always at hand to urge extreme courses, and his efforts were reinforced by a beautiful appearance and a glowing eloquence.' ... 'He was at this time an agitator who thrived on tumultuous meetings where motions subversive of British rule were passed amid wild excitement. He was one of the foremost agents of the new "propaganda of war" which, indifferent to truth, organised hatred with ice-cold logic.'[50] The period was the later 1920s; the man Jawaharlal Nehru, most gifted son of a distinguished father; the writer, Lord Birkenhead in his biography of Lord Halifax, who as Lord Irwin had served as viceroy, looking forward with well-intentioned, liberal-imperial gaze to a dominion status for India which would concede autonomy within the British Empire, but not the complete independence which the younger Nehru demanded. Other, and first-hand, judgements from the *Raj* were more temperate but not dissimilar. In the tense aftermath of the Cripps Mission, Lord Linlithgow remarked that 'Nehru may be a considerable orator and in many ways he has the qualities of a leader. But he is torn at all times by an internal conflict of ideals and he is too lacking in consistency ever to be the sort of basis on which one could build with confidence', while Wavell who worked closely with Nehru, especially in the Interim Government, said he 'could not help liking him. He is sincere, intelligent and personally courageous... But he is unbalanced...' Or again a year later, 'cultured, intelligent, highly strung, usually likeable but quite unstable...'[51] The last viceroy with whom Nehru formed a friendship which was of historic moment, while altogether more appreciative of his gifts, also had occasion to observe his moods and emotional over and above physical tensions which drove him to near exhaustion. But even with the passage of time, *Swaraj*, Indian membership of the Commonwealth and Nehru's standing in the world, Englishmen of conservative temper found it hard to efface earlier impressions of the handsome young Indian with his English schooling and his imperial friends[52], who left his affluent home in Allahabad to challenge the British Raj with weapons forged in the armoury of English liberal thought and sharpened with an edge of Marxist dialectic. To Smuts, who had fought against the British, all might be forgiven and more than forgiven, but against Nehru, who had suffered long years of imprisonment, even when an elder statesman of the Commonwealth, much was remembered. Both were intellectuals, both graduates of Cambridge, the one in Law, the other in Natural Sciences, both were at once nationalist and internationalist, both were leaders, as Mackenzie King so emphatically was not, of charismatic appeal. But where Smuts – and herein perhaps from the point of view of continuing British sensitivities lay the crucial difference – was a traditionalist in social as in racial policies, Nehru was at once a national and a social revolutionary, deeply influenced by Marxism though certainly in later life highly critical of its rigid conceptual framework and hostile to its dialectical certitudes. Moreover, he came to power with little experience of administration and possibly no great aptitude for it – hence his reliance to a degree not yet clear upon Mountbatten in his first turbulent post-partition months of office – and this was reflected in things he did and how he did them. Where Smuts devoted his gifts to immediate and definable purposes – the winning of war, the refashioning of Commonwealth, the drafting of a constitution for a new world order – Nehru, in pursuit of aims that might appear equally commendable, advocated means and employed arguments which were in many cases not only revolutionary in much of the thought that lay behind them but abstract in their conception or presentation. Non-alignment, the Panch Shila or Five Principles, areas of 'non-war', coupled with pained rebuke and admonition to those who sought security in alliances and built up strength against possible aggression – all these were attitudes or policies or, and perhaps most of all, language which many in Britain found it hard to stomach. In the past it had been the British who had lectured others on the folly of their ways – they found it in consequence doubly difficult to bear with equanimity the admonitions of another couched in intellectual-moral terms. They noted inconsistencies, or detected them where none existed. They were apt to associate and to confuse Nehru's with Gandhi's views on non-violence, and having done so, to point an accusing finger at Nehru's policy in Kashmir or Indian absorption of Goa by the use or threat of force. Nehru's immediate and unqualified condemnation of the Suez adventure, coupled with delayed and qualified denunciation of Russia's rigorous suppression of the contemporary Hungarian revolt – in itself an error of judgment, indicating a political imbalance deriving from over-sensitivity to the type of imperialism against which he had struggled and insufficient sensitivity to manifestations of one with which he was unfamiliar – rankled, in many minds besides that of Sir Anthony Eden. On many occasions Pandit Nehru gave hostages to political fortune by his practice of relating international affairs to first principles and expressing his opinion on how they ought to be conducted. To conservative pragmatists the first was an irrelevance and the second, when actions of theirs had fallen short of the prescribed standard, hard to forgive.

Many of the things that made Jawaharlal Nehru suspect to the right served to enhance his standing with liberal-internationalists of the left. Over Smuts there hung the shadow of native policy (or lack of one), and while liberals and nationalists alike welcomed Smuts' insistence upon a Commonwealth decentralised to the limit, he remained for them an enigmatic figure, enlightened in his concepts of a world order, but the protagonist of a white sub-imperialism in Africa; too preoccupied with preserving intact the domestic jurisdiction of national states to be the authentic herald of a new international society concerned to uphold and to advance human rights; over-much occupied with power politics to give sufficient attention to the claims of the weak or the downtrodden. In Nehru they found their ideal. Eloquent and sensitive, he possessed at once personal magnetism and the gift of effortless leadership. His credentials as an opponent not only of imperialism – he had spent almost nine years in jail* – but in the 1930s of Nazism, Fascism and Japanese militarism, were impeccable. On his European travels he had scorned the advances of Mussolini, sensed the deeper significance of the civil war in Spain, looked down with critical regard from the Gallery of the House of Commons upon Neville Chamberlain speaking in the dramatic debate which preceded his flight to Munich and felt that there was a man in whose countenance there seemed to be 'no nobility', who

---

* The exact period, as recorded in the display at the Nehru Memorial Museum, was 3262 days, i.e. nine years less twenty-three days. Nehru's first period of imprisonment was in the Lucknow District Jail from 6 December 1921 to 3 March 1922: his last and longest (following upon the 'Quit India' resolution) from 9 August 1942 to 15 June 1945 at Ahmadnagar Fort. There were three periods, with short interludes between them, each of two years in the early thirties.

looked 'too much like a business man', who was very evidently 'not a man of destiny but a man of the earth, earthy'.[53] He had warned his contemporaries, in the language of a Churchillian internationalist, of the awful consequences of the rise of militarism in Europe and Asia, and he recalled, when on trial for sedition at Gorakhpur in 1940, that there were few Englishmen who had denounced Fascism or Nazism with the same consistency and outspokenness as he had done. Having seen 'with pain and anguish how country after country was betrayed in the name of this appeasement and how the lamps of liberty were being put out', had he not the more reason for resentment that 'the hundreds of millions of India' should be thrust in 1939 'without any reference to them or their representatives into a mighty war' fought 'in the name of freedom and self-determination'?[54] When eight years later the hour came for him, as prime minister of an independent India, to tread the stage of history he showed his ability, as was noted at the time, to rise to great responsibilities. 'He has developed', wrote Rajagopalachari to Sapru in April 1948, 'in a most remarkable way . . . You must have seen this about Jawaharlalji with natural pleasure and gratification.'[55] In that same year Mackenzie King in London discussed with him India's future relations with the Commonwealth, King indicating his belief that emphasis should be placed upon the 'Community of Free Nations' and what was common to the Community 'rather than having emphasis upon the Crown'. He was greatly impressed and found that Nehru 'reminded him a little of Sir Wilfrid Laurier in his fine sensitive way of speaking . . .'[56] a high tribute indeed from such a source. While Nehru always lacked capacity for sustained and purposeful administration, few could match his sense of style or occasion. From the midnight hour on 14–15 August 1947, when the Congress kept 'its tryst with destiny', to that memorably moving broadcast six months later on 30 January 1948 which told India and the world of Gandhi's assassination – 'the light is gone out of our lives, and there is darkness everywhere' for 'our beloved leader, Bapu, as we called him, the Father of the Nation, is no more'; from crowded demonstrations in the capitals of Asia, from Prime Ministers' Meetings in London, at which his attendance was unfailing, to the dramatic symbolism of Delhi's Republic Day celebrations on 26 January each year, to the receptions of potentates and presidents, prime ministers and revolutionary leaders from all over the world, at dusk in the Red Fort where, presiding over the ceremony, immaculate in Gandhi cap and white achkan, with a red carnation in his buttonhole, he rarely failed to leave upon his hearers the impress of his personality and his pervasive sense of the movement of history.

Jawaharlal Nehru was a prolific writer, with autobiographical reflections, deepened in the seclusion of his prison years, in almost every work. The breadth of his appeal lay in his ability to reflect the aspirations of his time, as much as of his own people and to speak in their own terms, both to the villagers of India in their millions and to the new political élites of the cities. He was enabled to do so because he spoke quietly and directly, a microphone always with him, in a personal way – as though he were among close friends, obviously happy to communicate his thoughts to them – and also because, as has been truly said, both as a man and in his style of speaking he 'transcended sophistication with a certain natural simplicity'.[57] Secularist and humanist, Nehru was the spokesman of a liberal reformist approach at once to the divisions of community and caste at home, and to questions of peace and war abroad. He never wavered in his faith in the parliamentary process in India and, deploring the long-range abusive, propagandist dialectic of the Great Powers in the Cold War, urged quiet discussion in conference even of the most intractable issues. There was a transcendent quality in his appeal to the intellectuals, to the sometimes self-consciously enlightened, to younger generations finding neither psychological satisfaction nor congenial refuge in the alliances of the cold war years and who, weighed down by the menace of nuclear annihilation, responded wholeheartedly to Nehru's concern to harness the twentieth-century technological revolution to the service of the over-populated and under-nourished areas of the former colonial world. The new, more sanguine, more meaningful, more idealistic and, be it added, simpler approach to the complexities of international relations which they looked for, they found, as nowhere else, in the utterances of India's prime minister. The aristocratic, westernised high-caste Kashmiri Brahmin thus became the mouthpiece of the new, classless societies of the mid-twentieth century. He hated war, and denounced the armaments and alliances which threatened to bring it nearer to Asia. He was the proven enemy of imperialism; he was the angry champion of the underprivileged, and he was outraged by the pretensions of racialists whether in Asia or in Africa. When the Mau Mau rebellion erupted in Kenya in 1953 he regretted the violence but he came round to the opinion that the African had no alternative to violence.[58] 'I am not', he said, 'interested at present in petty reforms for the Africans, that is a matter for them to decide. I am interested in standing by people who are in great trouble and who have to face tremendous oppression . . . I should condemn of course every species of violence and give no quarter to it. But I shall stand by the African nevertheless. That is the only way I can serve them and bring them round to what I consider the right path.' If Jawaharlal Nehru loomed so large in the world and the Commonwealth of the 1950s that was because, while moving on a world stage, he continued to express with insight and foresight so many of the feelings and aspirations of his time.

While Nehru's appeal was world-wide, his heart came to beat with the continent and the people to whom he belonged. There was, it is true, an earlier time when with his westernised education he felt that he had 'become a queer mixture of the east and west, out of place everywhere, at home nowhere . . . I am a stranger and alien in the west. I cannot be of it. But in my own country also, sometimes, I have an exile's feeling.'59 But in maturity, and under Gandhi's influence, his roots struck deep in his native land. Constantly, as prime minister of India, he returned to the theme of the awakening of Asia and of India after a long sleep; of the attention after long neglect the west must pay to Asian interests and Asian opinions; of the 'torment in the spirit of Asia', 'the tremendous ferment of change' in a continent whose growth had been arrested for some two centuries.60 While there was much that dismayed or distressed him in this stormy resurrection of a continent, he did not doubt that with national freedom and the ending of the 'dire poverty' of so many of her people, Asia would become 'a powerful factor for stability and peace'. 'The philosophy of Asia', he said, 'has been and is the philosophy of peace'. 'India', he said at another time, 'may be new to world politics and her military strength insignificant in comparison with that of the giants of our epoch. But India is old in thought and experience and has travelled through trackless centuries in the adventure of life. Throughout her long history she had stood for peace and every prayer that an Indian raises, ends with an invocation to peace.'61 The sceptics remained unconvinced, but for a time at least a Gandhian image was partially superimposed not merely upon a nation, but a continent. It was tarnished by Indian intransigence in Kashmir and Indian action in Goa, and destroyed by the Chinese attacks upon the Indian frontier. In each case Nehru's reputation was damaged, and these events must now be commented on.

The Maharajah of Kashmir acceded to India. The circumstances were debatable, but the Indian title rested upon the legality and the finality of that accession. Nehru, the liberal, offered a plebiscite.

There was no obligation upon him to do so. Nehru, the Kashmiri and nationalist, found a succession of reasons, some convincing, others unconvincing, for ensuring that, in circumstances that had admittedly changed, the offer was not given effect. For his own reputation it would have been better had he rested his case throughout upon the signature by the Maharajah of an Instrument of Accession in the form approved by the Indian Independence Act 1947. But Nehru desired, over and above the sanction of law, the approval of the people of Kashmir. This, in a sense satisfying to world opinion, he did not secure. Likewise Nehru desired to gain possession of Goa by persuasion; in the end, confronted with Portuguese intransigence and under political pressure at home, he was persuaded to sanction force. To the nationalist in him the acquisition of Goa represented the fulfilment of the national movement for independence and, in this instance again despite many hesitations, Nehru's nationalism proved stronger than his sense of an internationalism that conceived of change only by peaceful means. On his own nationalist argument, little weighed by critics in the west, his error may well have been in delaying so long. In the late 1940s the take-over by a newly independent India of the small Portuguese enclaves in the subcontinent might well have been accepted by the world at large as a further and inevitable step in the liquidation of western colonialism in Asia. But once decision was deferred to a point in time when the national movement had lost its initial momentum, and an air of stability had been recreated, the liquidation even of so minor an outpost of European colonialism by forceful means was received in the west not with resigned acquiescence but with a storm of protest. There remained the liberal image of a pacific Asia, to be brutally shattered by the Chinese invasions across the Indian border in October-November 1962. Many had forewarned Nehru, not least Acharya Kripalani in the Lok Sabha,[62] but cherishing illusions of Sino–Indian friendship he had not taken their words to heart. He had, *per contra* allowed himself to be beguiled by Chou En-lai at the Bandung Conference in 1954 and twice persuaded by K. M. Panikkar, speaking with the authority of Indian Ambassador in Peking, to let generalities about imperialistically determined frontiers go by, when his own instinct was to question and, if need be, to challenge them, while opportunity was favourable. Disaster came, writes Professor Gopal, 'not because of Nehru's unrealistic assessment of China's strength or his failure to attach importance to the frontier issue but because he allowed his own views and those of his senior advisers, to be set aside by an ambassador who rationalised a shirking of unpleasantness' – something which helps to explain but not to exonerate Nehru's inaction. The bitter disillusionment that in 1962 drew from him the confession 'we were getting out of touch with reality in the modern world'[63] must have been heightened by the recollection of lost opportunity. Therein was reflected the tragedy of more than a man, or even a country. It was a hope of the new independent Asia that had been undermined.

Nehru reinterpreted the idea of Commonwealth to fit his own philosophy of international relations. The Commonwealth was an association of governments and peoples brought together by history which – and this to him was of first importance – gave to India, as to other Asian members of it, equal standing with members of European origin and afforded to Asian governments opportunities, not otherwise open to them in quite the same way, of influencing world politics, particularly in respect of Asia. The Commonwealth was a means, more generally, of associating in fruitful partnership the technological achievements of the west and the age-old wisdom of the east. It was a bridge between peoples and continents. It must be made, at the deepest level, multi-racial. It was, also, something of an example to the world of Gandhian principles applied to relations between states in circumstances that might ordinarily be expected to lead to estrangement or lasting hostility. Mahatma Gandhi, remarked Nehru, 'taught us a technique of action that was peaceful: yet it was effective and yielded results that led us not only to freedom but to friendship with those with whom we were, till yesterday, in conflict'.[64] And later, addressing the Canadian Parliament, Nehru returned to the same theme.

I am convinced [he said] that this development [India's republican membership] in the history of the Commonwealth, without parallel elsewhere or at any other time, is a significant step towards peace and co-operation in the world.

Of even greater significance is the manner of its achievement. Only a few years ago, Indian nationalism was in conflict with British imperialism and that conflict brought in its train ill-will, suspicion and bitterness, although because of the teaching of our great leader Mahatma Gandhi, there was far less ill-will than in any other nationalist struggle against foreign domination. Who would have thought then that suspicion and bitterness would largely fade away so rapidly, giving place to friendly cooperation between free and equal nations? That is an achievement for which all those who are concerned with it can take legitimate credit. It is an outstanding example of the peaceful solution of difficult problems and a solution that is a real one because it does not create other problems. The rest of the world might well pay heed to this example.[65]

Pandit Nehru was apt to dwell more positively on the nature of the initial achievement of Indian membership in freedom and equality than on subsequent practice. This was partly because he wished to define beyond doubt or dispute the limits of Commonwealth action or cooperation. 'Presumably', he said in 1950, 'some people imagine that our association with the Commonwealth imposes some kind of restricting or limiting factor upon our activities ... That impression is completely unfounded ... We may carry out any policy we like regardless of whether we are in the Commonwealth or not.'[66] He underlined, against Pakistan, the principle of non-intervention in domestic affairs, and India's objection to any Commonwealth tribunal or any Commonwealth mediatory responsibilities in intra-Commonwealth disputes. And against the aligned members of the older Commonwealth (and Pakistan after 1954) he emphasised India's non-participation in common war or defence policies. 'We have never discussed', he stated categorically to the Lok Sabha in June 1952, 'defence policies in the Commonwealth, either jointly or separately.' He was equally explicit about India's political and constitutional independence. 'The Republic of India', he said, 'has nothing to do with England constitutionally or legally.' Indeed the attraction of the Commonwealth was its freedom from the notions of obligation or commitment. 'Our association with the Commonwealth is remarkable in that it does not bind us down in any way whatsoever ...'[67]

Was Indian membership then to be thought of only in terms of negation? The answer to that in part is that it was often expressed in terms of negation not to concede advantage to its critics. But on essentials Nehru did not retreat from his initial constructive approach. He, more than any other man, had brought India into the Commonwealth and he stood by his action. He believed he had good reasons for so doing. They were not, however, reasons that by their very nature allowed of public exposition. 'We do hardly anything', he said in December 1950, 'without consulting the countries of the Commonwealth.' He believed such consultations to be useful in themselves and valuable for the opportunities they presented. To those who wanted India to leave because of South African racial policies Nehru replied in 1952 that in principle this was one of the reasons why he thought India should remain. And why? Because by remaining 'we have better chances of being able to influence the larger policies of the Commonwealth than we otherwise would. Being in the Commonwealth means a meeting once or twice a year and occasional consultations and conferences. Surely, that is not too great a price to pay for the advantages we get.' He never doubted in those early years that those advantages were substantial, not least among them being that as India was open to other influences so also there was 'the possibility that we may also greatly influence others in the right direction'.[68] That right direction was greater world understanding of Indian and Asian problems, of the strength of anti-colonialist, anti-racialist sentiment and the concern of mankind for peace. And the measure to which the Commonwealth was moved along it is recorded in many of its collective conclusions and sometimes in phrases or sentiments in official communiqués which bear unmistakably the impress of Nehru's thoughts and use of language. If the sense of developing partnership never recaptured its earlier part-emotional appeal after the Suez crisis of 1956, when Nehru, however, firmly resisted demands for secession even from the conservative Rajagopalachari on the ground first that India had been in no way inhibited in word or action by membership, and second that any severance of the relationship should be the outcome of cool consideration not angry reaction to a particular crisis,[69] it had not wholly departed. 'I wish I could paint to the House', said Harold Macmillan on his return from a Commonwealth tour in 1958, 'a picture of the thousands of people gathered in Shah Jehan's great courtyard in the Red Fort. Here there was something more than the traditional courtesy of the Indian people. I felt both then and in the meetings I had with the Indian prime minister . . . and his colleagues, a real sense of partnership in the truest sense of the word.'[70] If, on the Indian side, it was Gandhi who had laid the foundations of partnership, it was Jawaharlal Nehru who had built upon them. Even if it should prove that his service was chiefly to his own generation, it remains an honourable one, reflecting largeness of mind.

Nehru will be remembered for failures of judgment no less than for his insights into the minds of men – in pre-partition days his share of responsibility for the rejection of proffered Muslim League co-operation in Indian Provincial governments in 1937, for the opportunities given to the Muslim League to strengthen its position during the war, for the Congress failure to sense the reality of the Muslim threat to partition India until it was imminent, remains to be precisely assessed but was certainly considerable. After 1947 as prime minister of an independent state Nehru is open to the charge of mistaking the enunciation of highsounding principles for foreign policy, of disregarding the likely price of non-alignment in terms of isolation, of blindness to the threat of Chinese aggression in the 1950s, of alternating resolution and irresolution in Kashmir. The indictment is formidable, yet in essence it is so because Nehru was a natural leader with ideas, themselves inconstant, at times irreconcilable, often pursued with insufficient regard for the realities of India's power or his own position, but for all that often stimulating, original, and uplifting in their purposes and beneficial in their consequences. One of those ideas was India's membership of a multi-national, multi-racial Commonwealth. It was in his lifetime amazingly fruitful. But for him, India almost certainly would not have become the first republican member-state of the Commonwealth, and but for Indian membership almost certainly nationalists elsewhere in Asia and, still more, in Africa would not in their turn have opted also for membership. In the consequent addition of anti-imperialist Asian and African states to a Commonwealth which had grown out of an Empire, by procedures that became so conventional as to cease to cause remark, an idea achieved its most spectacular triumph. Not Smuts, not Mackenzie King but Nehru was the principal architect of that achievement. Nor was he only chief among the creators of the new multi-racial Commonwealth; he was in 1956, as his biographer writes, 'also in its first major crisis, its saviour'.[71] In the short term nothing can detract from the greatness of his contribution; on the longer run its endurance will depend upon the reality of those virtues – the touch of healing, the equal association of races, the readiness and the capacity of the richer Commonwealth states to assist the poorer – which in his more sanguine moments Nehru believed the new Commonwealth might come to possess.

Part Three

Retrospect 1838–1981

The Historical Experience

'Here I sit and govern it with my pen: I write and it is done: and by a clerk of the council I govern Scotland now, which others could not do by the sword.'[1] Such may be thought the British ideal of imperial government – trouble-free; economical, with a clerk of the council sufficing as the agent of imperial authority; and pacific. But while King James I of England and VI of Scotland could boast in these words of having achieved it in his northern kingdom, no nineteenth-century British statesman, plagued by the 'small wars of empire' and their expense, could even aspire to so happy a state. By then the Empire was too large, too variously composed and too expensive to allow of the direct, economical exercise of authority or of a reasonable prospect of general peace. On the contrary by Victorian times its administration had come to be popularly, and not unreasonably, associated with troubles, expense and wars. That association meant that the argument of Empire was rarely stilled. But by 1870 one outcome of the argument at least was clear. It was, as Lord John Russell contended in the sentences reprinted on the title page of this book, that there could be no going back. *'Tu regere imperio populos, Romane, memento.'** The British Empire was the nineteenth-century heir to the Roman; it had its colonies of settlement and conquered peoples of other races under its sway and while it had, as the Roman Empire had not had, the rivalry of European Empires with which to contend, it out-distanced them all in extent and, so most nineteenth-century Englishmen would have claimed (or more probably simply assumed) in the enlightenment of its imperial administration. And the prospect before that

---

* Virgil *Aeneid* vi, 851. Because of the varied implications of *imperium* the passage is not easy to translate. A. G. Lee, who has helped me with it, suggests 'Roman, remember to rule the nations with might and right.' Cecil Day Lewis' translation reads: 'But, Romans, never forget that government is your medium.' And Jackson Knight's: 'But you, Roman, must remember that you have to guide the nations by your authority.' Some elements of all three would seem to have been implicit in Russell's thought.

Empire, as sketched for example in Sir John Seeley's by no means uncritically expansionist lectures in 1881, was of still further territorial acquisitions and an apogee of greatness yet to be attained. Well might the later nineteenth century be retrospectively regarded, and not only in India, as the Augustan age of the British Empire.

Unlike Scotland under King James that Empire was not to be governed by a pen. In the last resort it was, one category excepted, governed if not by the sword then in knowledge of the existence of the sword. That exception, at time subject to some qualification, was provided by the colonies of British settlement overseas. They were not held by force; they were tied to Britain by kinship. She was their mother country; they were her children. Surely, it might be thought, that they at least, even more than the Scotland of King James, might be governed by the pen. But it proved otherwise. They were far away, their peoples were at once of independent mind and accustomed to a share in government, and the dispatches through which authority was perforce expressed still, as in Burke's day, might take months to come and go across the oceans. Overmuch reliance upon the imperial pen, indeed, was more likely than anything else to necessitate recourse to the imperial sword. For that reason, considerations of self-interest combined with good sense prompted the transfer of responsibility for the domestic government of these colonies of settlement to their own peoples. That was the step that marked the foundation of Commonwealth. It was not taken with any such end in view. It was taken to avoid further, unnecessary dissension and in a way that was consistent with the Victorians' sense of responsibility, economy – defence, it is always to be remembered, was expensive and the Gladstonian dictum that self-government begets self-defence always relevant – and their belief in the aptitude of British people, wherever they might be, to govern themselves.

The first and critical step in the colonial self-government that led to Commonwealth was taken in British North America. It was followed, sometimes on the initiative, as with Cape Colony, of the imperial authority, but more usually under pressure from the colonists, with the result that, at the end of the century, it was generally accepted, and specifically by the colonial secretary, Joseph Chamberlain, that in respect of the ordering of their domestic affairs, the will of the colonists in all ordinary circumstances should prevail. 'The mother of Parliaments', to quote again the assertion made by R. B. Haldane in the debate on the Commonwealth of Australia Bill, 'does not coerce her children.'[2]

By then it was true. But it invited a question. Who were her
children? Were they to be thought of literally as being only those of
British descent? The Irish member who interrupted Haldane to
say, 'We do not accept that statement', presumably did not
interpret the phrase so narrowly. Nor did the leaders of the
defeated Boer republics brought by force within the confines of
Empire, nor yet the moderates of the Indian National Congress,
who in the earlier years of the century proclaimed self-government
on the colonial-dominion model to be the goal of their political
endeavours, consider that there should be a frontier fixed by
kinship to non-coercion or to constitutional autonomy.

The breaking down of that frontier and with it successively of the
barriers of culture and race was an important part of the
cumulative experience of Commonwealth. It had happened in
respect of culture with the French in Canada, but then they had
obtained self-government within the reassuring confines of a
majority English-speaking confederation. The more significant
breakthrough occurred two generations later when the Boers in
South Africa, destined to comprise the majority European community in the Union, had self-government restored to them. The
Irish Free State followed, after attempted coercion which left scars
that did not heal, but the barrier in respect of race was not broken
until India obtained her independence eighty years after the
making of the first dominion. This was an event of critical
importance in Commonwealth history.

Until 1947 the emphasis within the self-governing Commonwealth had been upon the status of the dominions and their
equality in all respects with Britain, not upon extending the
frontiers of national freedom to non-British dependencies. In the
later nineteenth and earlier twentieth century Canada outside
Quebec, Australia and New Zealand, and English-speaking South
Africa had shown themselves predisposed to lend moral or as need
arose material support to British imperial rule or expansion. In
1889 Canada and Australia had sent troops to fight in the Sudan;
Canadian, Australian and New Zealand contingents had fought in
the South African war, the Australians being criticised by Irish
nationalist members during the passage of the Commonwealth of
Australia bill for being a people prepared to assist in the suppression of the liberties of others while engaged in securing their own;
and collectively the dominions had shown themselves to be
concerned to ensure and perpetuate their own regional predominance. Australia and New Zealand were intent before 1914 in
establishing an Anglo–Saxon hegemony in the Pacific, and in

keeping the foreigner out, and in 1919 Australia's prime minister flatly rejected notions of race equality for Japanese or other migrants, while in South Africa Briton and Boer were at one chiefly in their resolve to consolidate minority European rule, over an African majority. The peace treaties in 1919, transferring responsibility for former German colonies in the Pacific and in south-west Africa to Australia and New Zealand in the first instance and to South Africa in the second, albeit under trust, on balance probably strengthened for a brief period the 'imperial' element in the old dominion tradition.

An anti-imperialist bias at national level was introduced into the Commonwealth in 1921 with the addition of the Irish Free State to the number of the dominions. In its conceptual origin, however, Irish anti-imperialism derived from European rather than extra-European sources, and partly for that reason, but also because of Irish preoccupation with their own national struggle, did not extend to a theoretic assertion of the right of non-European colonial peoples to be freed from imperial rule. But with the accession of India and Pakistan in 1947 the position was transformed. The voice of non-European anti-colonialism was henceforward to be heard in the innermost councils of the Commonwealth, both persistently and powerfully. It was that, rather than events in Africa itself, important as the 1949 Gold Coast riots and the Mau Mau rebellion in Kenya unquestionably were, which predisposed British and other Commonwealth statesmen to rethink their attitudes to the dependent Empire. It was not chance but rather the product of a developing experience that within three decades of Indian independence, the Mother of Parliaments had not merely ceased (with the unwished-for exception of Rhodesia) to coerce or seek to coerce any of the territories formerly under her jurisdiction, but had abandoned or was in process of abandoning even her power of coercion. There was, apart from some few small scattered outposts or islands, nothing left of the Empire on which the sun never set and no more occasion for the witticism that it did not do so, because even God Almighty could not trust it in the dark.

The ending of Empire broadly viewed and including southern Asia as well as the colonial Empire is apt increasingly to be interpreted in terms of resistance of subject peoples and changing patterns of world power. Both were very important elements in it, but they were not all-sufficient. Had they been so, there would have been in 1980 no succeeding Commonwealth in existence at the will of some forty independent states. There was a further factor – it was the British imperial response to such pressures. It was individual and it was conditioned by ideas and by history. 'No western peoples', Professor Plamenatz has remarked,[3] 'have cared more for freedom than the British and the French, or have done so much to elucidate it and to elaborate the rules and institutions needed to establish it. They have also created the largest empires in Asia and Africa.' That regard for liberty continuing side by side with Empire was one factor, as the lessons drawn from history were another, in determining the British reaction. It was the past that suggested, first in a limited and mainly British colonial context, that in the face of quasi-nationalist or nationalist demands for autonomy, there was a possibility other than counter-resistance or abdication. That possibility was association, ultimately to be interpreted in terms of equality. Once the idea of forceful subjection was abandoned – and this happened at different times in relation to different peoples and places – such association offered, in place of the bleak prospect of abdication, with a final severance of all ties, the possibility of a new and, after the first world war, of a tried relationship, on the basis of co-operation, progressively between equals. The extent to which there was an element of illusion on the British side about what was taking place, remains debatable. But even conceding that there was apt to be an over-sanguine interpretation of what the Commonwealth that superseded Empire would mean in terms of continuing British influence, that fictional ingredient served only to reinforce fact in easing psychologically, and in a way that would otherwise have been inconceivable, the concluding stages of British decolonisation.

In Corneille's *Cinna*, from which the second extract on the title page is taken, Maxime, a republican conspirator, seeks to persuade the Emperor Augustus to abdicate and so become famous among later generations, less for having conquered than for having despised and abdicated Empire. Cinna made reply to Maxime:

> On ne renonce point aux grandeurs légitimes;
> On garde sans remords ce qu'on acquiert sans crimes;
> Et plus le bien qu'on quitte est noble, grand, exquis,
> Plus qui l'ose quitter le juge mal acquis.

Not surprisingly it was the arguments of Cinna, not those of Maxime, to which Augustus Caesar paid heed; for whatever may be the glory with posterity, neither emperors nor empires are easily persuaded to abandon their dominion, be it well or ill acquired. It is true that in Britain between the wars, and more especially during and after the second world war, there was evidence of a predisposition – revulsion is possibly too strong a word – against Empire which more widely, though probably less justly than at any time hitherto, had come to be associated with the class structure, with exploitation overseas which underpinned the foundations of capitalist society at home, and with war. But while reconsideration of Empire in consequence appeared to much left-wing opinion as a fitting and necessary counterpart to the coming of the welfare state and of peace, renunciation was bound to cause deep division in a country with so long a tradition of imperial greatness, and heart-searching even among professed anti-imperialists. It did both in the early post-war phase, but thereafter it came to be accepted by stages as a national policy. Two things in particular helped to bring this about – positively, the prospect of Commonwealth membership which softened the sharp edge of finality, and negatively, earlier Commonwealth experience which warned of the hazards of attempted repression. Without either prospect to encourage or experience to warn, there might have been, despite the anti-colonialist tide of opinion at home, in the British case also, as Bacon presumed there would always be, the wars associated with 'the shivering' of great empires.

There remained a price to be paid. While the existence and experience of Commonwealth made easier the ending of Empire, the earlier existence of Empire, coupled with its increasingly rapid foreclose, made the more difficult the life of Commonwealth. There was little time for readjustment; ideas did not keep pace with actualities; the imperial past bore in oppressively upon the Commonwealth present; attitudes appropriate to Empire were carried over into Commonwealth and what had been associated with the former survived to trouble the latter.

The psychological carry-over from Empire to Commonwealth, inevitable under any circumstances, was the more pronounced because of British concentration on one element in the evolutionary process. That process, of its nature, comprises both continuity and change, but the British emphasis was consistently upon the first. It is true that no one in the revolutionary situation in Ireland in 1921 and the near-revolutionary prospect in India in 1947 could doubt that a momentous change was taking place, with the respective transfers of power to indigenous successor authorities. But subsequent transfers of power in south-east Asia, Africa, the West Indies and elsewhere, in accordance with precedents and procedures that were becoming increasingly familiar, and leading without sign of serious debate in almost every case to Common-

wealth membership, made a delayed rather than an immediate
impact upon British opinion. It was some time before possessive
imperial attitudes, expressed for example in references to 'our
Commonwealth', disappeared. Britain forgot, complained
Mrs Pandit after seven years as Indian high commissioner in
London, 'that you cannot run a Commonwealth as you run an
Empire'.[4] In a sense the actual process of transformation encouraged Britain to do so. True, in the territories that had themselves
passed from a state of imperial dependency to sovereign independence there was no possibility of such forgetfulness. No one in
Dar-es-Salaam after 9 December 1961 could doubt that political
authority resided with Julius Nyerere and the dominant party of
which he was the leader, or in Nairobi after 12 December 1963 that
it rested with Jomo Kenyatta (destined in old age to assume the
mantle of the elder statesman of Commonwealth Africa), or listen
to the prime minister of Malta, Dr Borg Olivier, welcome Queen
Elizabeth II in the presence of Commonwealth high commissioners
and diplomatic representatives of some twenty nations, in
November 1967, in the sixteenth-century Palace which had been
for more than two centuries the residence of the Grand Masters of
the Knights Hospitallers, as Queen of Malta and as such a 'visible
sign' of the Island's nationhood and of its three year old independence,[5] without having borne in upon him the reality of change.
But in Britain itself and in the world outside nothing so diminished
regard for the Commonwealth's rôle in assisting such change as the
ease with which it was in most instances effected and the air of
continuity with which it was deliberately invested.

In one instance only was that continuity broken. In the case of
Cyprus there was an interval in time between the ending of British
rule and the accession of the Island Republic, under the presidency
of its autocephalous archbishop, to the Commonwealth, by and
with the consent of Greek and Turkish representatives – in the
former case for a trial period – and also of the Communists on the
unusual ground that in the conditions created by a 'long period of
colonial servitude' there remained no immediate alternative to
Commonwealth membership.[6] This Cypriot break between imperial ending and Commonwealth beginning, not only held the
balance evenly between change and continuity but underlined that
the element of continuity was at the will of the representatives of an
independent people. In the post–1945 era this was so in every case,
but nowhere else was it expressly indicated *after* a transfer of power
had been effected.

The evolutionary process of the transformation of Empire into

Commonwealth had a further, overall consequence. It meant that there was no dividing line between Empire and Commonwealth but instead a protracted process of transition during which the two existed side by side, together appearing (as Palmerston forthrightly complained of the 'semi-Byzantine design' first proposed by Sir Giles Gilbert Scott for the block of buildings in Whitehall in which for a period both the Dominions and Colonial Offices were to be housed) as 'neither one thing nor t'other – a regular mongrel affair',[7] neither Empire nor Commonwealth. But while Palmerston could decree, despite 'the terrible state of mental perturbation' caused to the architect, that the building should be in the Italianate style, the processes of peaceful political transition, whatever the price that time exacts, were not to be thus peremptorily foreshortened. Indeed in respect of individual territories in the later phases, the period may well have been less rather than more than that demanded by local circumstances. But even if and when this was so, it did not diminish the problem for a Commonwealth, entangled with a still continuing Empire, and suffering in popular comprehension and often esteem from the association.

The continuing association of Commonwealth with Empire was the product of time and unfolding circumstances and not of an overall conception. Empire meant the government of men by a superior authority, Commonwealth interpreted, notably by Lionel Curtis, in idealistic terms as the government of men by themselves, at the least rested minimally upon the foundation of government of peoples by themselves. On any reckoning, and with whatever qualifications, Empire and Commonwealth represented incompatible and antithetical concepts comprehended for half a century or more within one polity.

The government of men by themselves, that was the ideal and in many instances the distinguishing characteristic of Commonwealth throughout the greater part of its history, was expressed institutionally in the adoption and where necessary the adaptation of the British system of parliamentary government to conditions overseas. This meant, whatever the variations or qualifications, that there was brought into being a common pattern of politics and administration, which in its turn provided a community of experience which was a strong, perhaps the strongest, bond of Commonwealth.

The Westminster model, transplanted to other environments and to other societies, was apt, especially in the eye of a critical foreign beholder, to be chiefly remarkable for the air of artificiality or even incongruity with which its proceedings were invested. The open-

ing and closing of the session', wrote André Siegfried of what he
had seen of them in Ottawa,

> are carried out just as they are in London, with an antiquated
> ceremony somewhat out of keeping with the simplicity of this
> colonial milieu, but to which Canadians of all races and classes
> are tenaciously attached. As to the debates, they partake of that
> curious mixture of discipline and *laisser-aller* which characterises
> all English gatherings from which the women are excluded.
> Members wear their hats while seated, the lounging attitudes are
> allowed – are even considered to be a sign of elegant noncha-
> lance. Members refer to each other not by their own names, but
> by that of the constituency represented. This often produces a
> quaintly exotic effect in the French Canadian language, such as
> the following exordium: 'Monsieur l'orateur, l'honorable
> membre pour Québec a dit...'. Approbation is signified by
> sonorous guttural cries of 'Hear, Hear!' The whole impression is
> thoroughly British.

But M. Siegfried further observed, and he was well qualified to do
so, that the French Canadians were very proud of being affiliated in
some way to the venerable *Mater Parliamentorum*.[8] The ambition to
become associated and that pride in affiliation with Westminster
was widely shared by non-British as well as by British peoples. As
late as 1954 the common practice of parliamentary self-
government and a common faith in democracy were recognised, at
a Commonwealth Conference,[9] to be the foundation of the
Commonwealth relationship, even if not in themselves sufficient to
preserve it. Historically that remains of importance.

Initial overseas attachment to parliamentary government was
not of itself surprising. Peoples of British descent had inherited it;
peoples of non-British extraction had learned in dependence to
desire it. Few notions are more erroneous or more persistent than
that Britain thrust parliamentary institutions upon reluctant dependencies. This was no more true of Africa in the 1930s than it
had been of southern Asia in earlier decades. In 1937 the British
approach to government in African colonial territories, conveniently summarised in a memorandum circulated for the information of dominion delegations to the Imperial Conference,
indicated that almost the precise opposite was the case.[10] Reliance,
the memorandum stated, was placed not upon the development of
parliamentary institutions in African dependent territories but
upon indirect rule through native institutions. The aim was to

make 'the native a good African' and that aim 'cannot be achieved if we destroy all the institutions all the traditions and all the habits of the people, superimposing upon them what we consider to be better administrative methods and better principles but destroying everything that can make the administration really in touch with the thoughts and customs of the people'. For this reason alone direct rule was not possible since it meant 'the imposition of British ideas through the intermediary of a bureaucracy of half-educated native clerks' whereas the policy of indirect rule by contrast aimed to establish a delegated machinery of government 'by maintaining and supporting native rule and native institutions'. For this reason the Colonial Office thought that it was most important to check 'the disintegrating influences which are impairing the authority of the chiefs over their peoples, as, if that authority is undermined and completely disappears, the only foundation on which it is possible to build has been destroyed'. They looked forward indeed to the days of literate and progressive chiefs just at a time when the urban African élites were beginning to see the future in terms of political parties and popular representation. It was accordingly not the Colonial Office but the indigenous leaders of African (and other) dependencies that came to demand responsible government on the Westminster model, the principal qualification being the reservations of minorities, by no means least of European minorities, about the consequences for them of the majority rule ultimately implicit in the British system. It was the British who changed their approach and responded at last to these overseas demands.

Nowhere was the true position more succinctly set out than in some paragraphs of the 1945 Soulbury Report on Constitutional Reform in Ceylon. They read:[11]

> The constitution we recommend for Ceylon reproduces in large measure the form of the British constitution, its usages and conventions, and may on that account invite the criticism so often and so legitimately levelled against attempts to frame a government for an eastern people on the pattern of western democracy.
>
> We are well aware the self-government of the British parliamentary type, carried on by means of a technique which it has taken centuries to develop, may not be suitable or practicable for another country, and that where the history, traditions and culture of that country are foreign to those of Great Britain, the prospect of transplanting British institutions with success may appear remote. But it does not follow that the invention of modifications or variations of the British form of government to

meet different conditions elsewhere will be any more successful. It is easier to propound new constitutional devices and fresh constructive solutions than to foresee the difficulties and disadvantages which they may develop. At all events, in recommending for Ceylon a constitution on the British pattern, we are recommending a method of government we know something about, a method which is the result of very long experience, which has been tested by trial and error and which works, and, on the whole, works well.

But be that as it may, the majority – the politically conscious majority of the people of Ceylon – favour a constitution on British lines. Such a constitution is their own desire and is not being imposed upon them. It is true that, if in our opinion it were manifestly unsuitable for Ceylon, our duty, notwithstanding the demands of the Ceylonese, would be so to report. We could not recommend a constitution of the British type and then, when its failure had become apparent, merely retort – 'Vous l'avez voulu, Georges Dandin.'

But we think Ceylon is well qualified for a constitution on the British model . . .

No man's knowledge, observed John Locke, goes beyond his experience; or to quote a medieval but equally relevant maxim *Nemo dat quod non habet* – no one gives what he has not got. Both conditioned the British response. They had experience of parliamentary government and their political knowledge in any deeper sense did not go beyond that experience. Parliamentary government was the one thing they could at least hope to give. But equally, and this was the other side of the transfer of power equation, the one thing the British had got, was what dependent peoples at the outset wanted. Even where, as in Pakistan, Ghana, Nigeria or elsewhere, that form of government was soon to be superseded or suspended, its initial adoption was important, if only in easing first the transition from dependence to Commonwealth and then the early phase of the new Commonwealth relationship. And remarkable to the point of paradox was the fact that the politics of race in South Africa and Southern Rhodesia, while in themselves, and especially in Rhodesia for some two decades, a cause of estrangement, helped to deepen the sense of Commonwealth commitment to a traditional, liberal, representative, responsible parliamentary solution, even on the part of those states that had themselves discarded parliamentarianism.

The parliamentary system of government predetermined the

Commonwealth system of co-operation through consultation, from the time of the first Colonial Conference in 1887, through Imperial Conferences to Meetings of Prime Ministers and Heads of State. It presumed that ultimate authority would reside in cabinets responsible to individual parliaments or, when circumstances required as increasingly they did, with a head of state and his advisers. In the two world wars, which played so great a part in earlier Commonwealth experience, there was no significant departure from parliamentary practices and the imperial war cabinet of the first world war and the continuing conference of cabinets that developed in the second both demonstrated anew and, in time of peril, the attachment of the older Commonwealth to the parliamentary system. That attachment, that pattern of co-operation, was carried over into the period of Asian and of early African membership. Deriving from parliamentary government, it was the second conditioning element in the Commonwealth experience. It also possessed its characteristic virtues and limitations.

The system of co-operation meant that at all levels the Commonwealth operated until the creation of a Commonwealth secretariat in 1965, not through a formal administrative organisation but by means of discussion and consultation as seemed natural to parliamentarians. If indeed discussion be deemed, as A. D. Lindsay argued in *The Essentials of Democracy* that it should be, the great essential of democracy, then the Commonwealth was democratic in its consultative processes. But discussion, with decisions left to be taken by individual governments in the light of that discussion, was not easily communicated or publicised to a wider audience. To the prudent reticences of governments was added thereby a problem of communication inherent in the system. 'Take the pen, Matucewic', said Talleyrand to the Russian Pole, who drafted the reports of many European congresses after 1815, 'You who know all the neutral words.'[12] Commonwealth conferences were, indeed, well served by officials who knew 'all the neutral words'. But even had this not been so the process of association through discussion, by its very nature, was bound to be lacking in dramatic quality or popular appeal. It was sensible, it was liberal, it was democratic and it was dull.

The near-attainment of one set of Commonwealth purposes in the independence and free association of all former subject peoples presented problems pressing upon the frontiers of earlier Commonwealth experience. Between 1940 and 1980 the total sovereign membership of the Commonwealth increased from six to forty-one. Even had all else remained equal, it was clearly more difficult, much more difficult, to maintain co-operation by traditional means of Imperial Conference or continuing conference of cabinets among forty-one than among six. To the problem of arithmetic was added the problem of interest, or more precisely, of range of interest. The Commonwealth at the outbreak of the second world war was dominated by the United Kingdom. Canada, the senior dominion, was diplomatically represented at that time in three foreign capitals; in 1981 in one hundred and seventeen. In the Commonwealth in earlier times there was only one state with the inclination and the resources to pursue interests which were world-wide, namely the United Kingdom. In the latter day Commonwealth, apart from the United Kingdom, there was India chief among the non-aligned nations and also seven or eight states with interests, actively pursued, which if not world-wide at least were more than regional or continental. By contrast, however, there were at this later period other states whose interests were narrowly restricted. Their resources, political, economic and administrative were strained even to support their recently acquired independent statehood. Inevitably as both numbers and range of interest increased, the system, and more especially the character, of Commonwealth meetings, which were its focal point, perceptibly changed.

To outward seeming a gathering of some forty prime ministers and heads of state, was an impressive, as it was apt to be a lively occasion. But it did not allow of the easy exchange of view or of the confidences by which such store was set in earlier days. On the contrary, with the larger audience there developed a tendency towards the statement and re-statement of national interests or policies at the expense of discussion, and by no means always with regard for the realities of power or of the resources available for any particular course of action. As a result the Commonwealth by enlargement of membership was brought face to face for the first time with difficulties, earlier encountered by the United Nations, the League of Nations and nineteenth-century European congresses, of seeking to relate the representation of states, unequal in size and resources, to the facts of political and economic life. At the European congresses of the post-Napoleonic period it was the practice for representatives of lesser as well as of greater powers to be present, and for all alike to attend the sessions of general interest, but it was the prerogative of the greater alone to attend all sessions. Such a precedent, though considered in modified form, did not commend itself to the Commonwealth, one, and in itself sufficient, reason being that among the lesser were also without exception to be found the newer member-states, the representatives of which were disposed in consequence to react sharply to any suggestion that distinctions in terms of political stature unfavourable, as it would appear, to their independent status, might be drawn. On more general grounds, moreover, it could be and was argued that any such distinction, even if required at international conferences by the exigencies of power politics, was alien to the concept of a fraternal, Commonwealth, relationship. On all these grounds the Commonwealth perforce had to adapt itself to its new numbers, with members resorting to informal arrangements for limited consultation when they deemed that circumstances so demanded.

The increase in Commonwealth membership coincided roughly in time with, but was not solely responsible for, a perceptible shift in dominant Commonwealth preoccupations in the decades that followed Suez. Negatively the cleavages in Commonwealth opinion on many of the larger issues of international politics discouraged thoughts of seeking to use it for diplomatic or defence purposes, while positively there was pressure for the pursuit of new ends. Liberalism and its expanding frontiers were of the past; development, economic growth and welfare conceived to be of the future. Any contribution which the Commonwealth could make to their advancement was understood to be of necessity limited and partial. Its members collectively might initiate or supplement; they could not ordinarily assume a full responsibility. It was realistic accordingly to think not in terms of Commonwealth solutions but, more modestly, in terms of Commonwealth contributions. So much, indeed, was predicated by the unfavourable ratio within the Commonwealth, as between developed and underdeveloped countries and their respective populations. Yet within the limits thus imposed by Commonwealth resources in relation to Commonwealth needs, and with awareness of them, there was a significant shift in Commonwealth interests represented by a concerted endeavour to further agreed economic and social purposes. Among these were the organisation of intra-Commonwealth aid for welfare and development: co-operative ventures in technical and university education, following upon the Report of a Conference held in Oxford in 1959: collaboration between professional organisations and interchange of many kinds; and collective endeavours to contribute to the raising of living standards, first under the aegis of the Colombo Plan, the first and constructive decade of whose working was completed in 1960[13] in south and south-east Asia and later by adaptations of it in Africa. It was these

new purposes and the possibility of their further advancement that
had been responsible for the creation, at African instigation, of the
Commonwealth secretariat in 1965, intended as it was to stimulate
an increase in the flow of aid for development and welfare, by
providing a necessary means for the co-ordination and direction of
planning and by encouraging governments to give effect to
policies, the application of which might have been collectively
approved at Commonwealth Prime Ministers' Meetings, but which
required subsequent individual state action for their implementa-
tion. No machinery, however, could be more than marginally
useful. What mattered was the availability of resources and the will
of the governments who controlled them to give priority to
expenditure for such purposes.

In the later nineteenth and early twentieth centuries when the
Empire was at its zenith, imperial historians have familiarised us
with the paradox of British imperialists living on the frontiers of
fear, their expansionist moves essentially defensive, and only their
courage obscuring 'the depth of their underlying pessimism'.[14] To
what extent these things were the product of a peculiarly British
imperial situation as distinct from manifestations of the inbuilt
neuroses of the territorially well endowed, fearful lest they be
bereft of possessions, might be further debated – Titian's famous
portrait of the Emperor Charles V and photographs of present day
rulers in the Kremlin suggest something of a common
phenomenon – but here it suffices to point to the contrast in
attitudes as between Commonwealth and Imperial statesmen. The
leaders of the Commonwealth after the First World War did not
speak as men of little hope on the defensive:[15] on the contrary, as
the opening pages of Professor Hancock's classic *Survey*[16] abundantly testify, they proclaimed their participation in a great
enterprise in international cooperation, from which the world at
large, if it would, might learn much. Again there was a time of hope
with the launching of the experiment in multi-racial membership
in 1947 from which, it was thought, the world might learn even
more. Commonwealth statesmen at that time delighted to extol
this great experiment in cooperation between peoples and nations
from every continent; to speak of the Commonwealth as a bridge
between east and west; between developed and underdeveloped
societies; between European, Asian and African; to emphasise its
unique character and to think of it as a model of what the whole
world might one day become. And even in later and less sanguine
years, was there not some continuing cause for gratification and for
hope in the fact that the governments of so many peoples should

have sought or retained Commonwealth membership? From India with a population of more than 600 million to Lesotho with a population of one and a quarter million, from thinly settled New Zealand where, as Pacific rollers broke on the wooded coastline by Kaikoura it could be felt that there was the end of the world, as surely as ever it was by the 'sad sea-sounding wastes of Lyonesse'[17] to West Indian islands, too widely scattered to compose one polity, too close historically to feel altogether apart, countries and peoples had decided to share in the bond of Commonwealth. That bond was described by a Maltese delegate to the Commonwealth Parliamentary Conference at Kampala 1967, as a symbol of community in independence and he added that coming there 'as a member of Parliament of a free and sovereign nation of the Commonwealth' was 'an object of pride in the judgment of history'.[18]

The phrase was apt. The pride in the judgment of history lay in the working out of a pattern which had widened the frontiers of national, if by no means always of personal, freedom. That was what many Commonwealth leaders had themselves experienced and about which they had reason, in many instances, to feel emotionally. They rarely doubted, even when as in many parts of Africa independence was followed by turmoil, by military *coups d'état* or even, as in Nigeria, by civil war, that expanding the frontiers of freedom had been and must continue to be the concern of Commonwealth. It had been first conceived in terms of a liberal-nationalist philosophy of politics and government; it was developed and interpreted within that framework of ideas and even when their power of attraction was in decline the Commonwealth remained, by reason of experience reinforced by the nature of the relationships it had established, in essence so bound to them that it was hard to conceive of a future in other terms.

By the middle 1960s there came, however, diminishing confidence in that future in most parts of the Commonwealth. The shift in emphasis from international politics to co-operative endeavour in policies of development and welfare while it served to give to the Commonwealth a more contemporary and a more human appeal also underlined Commonwealth insufficiencies in economic resources. In the past there had been reliance in all fields upon Britain, and in fact the presumption of British power and preeminence in the Commonwealth outlived the reality. But after the retreat from the Suez adventure in 1956, initial rebuff in Europe, defiance by Rhodesian rebels whose walls did not fall even at the third blast on the sanctions trumpet, unexpansive trade, a

succession of balance of payments crises (and the largely consequential withdrawal of a British military presence east of Suez) the
decline in Britain's position, both in the Commonwealth and in the
world was progressively, even cruelly, driven home. Neither
militarily, economically nor even perhaps politically could she any
longer provide, as in earlier years, the solid, material basis of
Commonwealth or retain, in consequence, her earlier predominant influence in the shaping of policies. What then was to be her
attitude towards it?

In the later nineteenth century Sir John Seeley, reflecting upon
past British expansion and contemplating Britain's 'prodigious'
future greatness, had remarked that some countries such as
Holland and Sweden 'might pardonably regard their history as in a
manner being wound up', its one practical lesson for them being
one 'of resignation'. Had that lesson its ironic relevance for a
latter-day Britain? If so, there was reluctance to accept it, in its
bleak finality. Debate about Britain's rôle continued, the range of
choice admittedly much contracted, but with some overtones from
more spacious days still to be heard. 'The issue is not a mean one',
Disraeli had told his Crystal Palace audience in 1872. 'It is whether
you will be content to be a comfortable England, modelled and
moulded upon continental policies, or whether you will be a great
country, an imperial country . . .' And Gladstone, it will be remembered, had retorted that Empire was not the source of British
power, which derived not from far flung possessions but from the
people and the wealth of 'these islands'. A century later the issue
was still thought to be 'not a mean one'. But it was widely concluded
that a sufficient foundation for a future, conceived in a spirit of
hope rather than resignation, lay either in Britain itself, externally
associated perhaps with other European or Atlantic powers or
alternatively in unreserved British participation in a wider European, or conceivably North Atlantic, community. On either view
there was no place for the Commonwealth that had superseded
Disraelian empire. And for that reason it was asked with increasing
insistence, how far were British interests still served by membership
of a scattered community of states, in which Britain's pre-eminence
was no longer tacitly acknowledged? *'Il a voulu que la France soit à la
tête de l' Europe'*, remarked Paul Reynaud in criticism of General de
Gaulle, *'et il n' a pas voulu l' Europe.'* That also had been the
underlying British attitude to Commonwealth, her governments
desiring leadership, but lacking consistency of purpose in willing a
Commonwealth. With leadership to be earned, not conceded, what
attitude was to be taken? Even the posing of such questions,

whatever might be the answers to them, indicated that for Britain the age of faith in Commonwealth had drawn to its close.

Sir Robert Menzies, who was prime minister of Australia 1939–41, and continuously from 1952–66, had a vision of Empire and Commonwealth, which belonged to the days when it was British in name, in loyalties, largely in composition and in its united purposes. To him it meant, as he once recalled,

> King George and Queen Mary coming to their Jubilee in Westminster Hall... at Chequers Winston Churchill, courage and confidence radiating from him ... Australian boys in tired but triumphant groups at Tobruk and Benghazi ... at Canberra, at Wellington, at Ottawa, at Pretoria, the men of Parliament meeting as those who met at Westminster seven hundred years ago; at Melbourne the lawyers practising the Common Law first forged at Westminster ... [and also] Hammond at Sydney and Bradman at Lords and McCabe at Trent Bridge, with the ghosts of Grace and Trumble looking on ...'[19]

In succeeding years for most people, it was likely to mean something rather less, cricket certainly, but also a protracted last essay in decolonisation in Zimbabwe–Rhodesia, with the ghosts of Rhodes and Lobengula looking on and Britain's turning aside to a chequered and contentious association with Europe. In 1964 a Conservative critic in *The Times* – and it was on the formerly imperialist right wing of the British political spectrum that expressions of disillusion were sharpest – had written of the Commonwealth in the mid-sixties as 'a gigantic farce',[20] while three years later *'Le Figaro'*,[21] with satisfaction, dismissed it as *'naguère qu'une chimère'* on the morrow of Britain's second application to join the Common Market and – a last irony – former imperialists, 'praisers of gone times' because now they had 'none of their own', cherished it as the offspring of Empire. But if it had been, or was being, reduced to all or any of these things – and that seemed less rather than more likely as new balance and purpose was attained in the seventies – it also retained its own unquestioned place in the longer perspective of time. There it was to be viewed as the product and the embodiment of an experience, familiarly charted by famous constitutional landmarks, yet to be thought of not in the constricting context of constitutional documentation nor of 'what one clerk said to another' but in terms of a historical process which had affected the lives of millions, and which had culminated in the national freedom and the association in partnership – at the least during critical years of transition – of the majority of the peoples whose destinies were formerly determined by the greatest of European empires. It may be that in the accomplishment of this end, the Commonwealth lost its *raison d'être*; or alternatively that it still had other causes to advance. But the interpretation of the past is neither to be subjected to 'the tyranny of the contemporary'[22] nor yet to be influenced by uncertain speculation on the future. It is an end sufficient in itself.

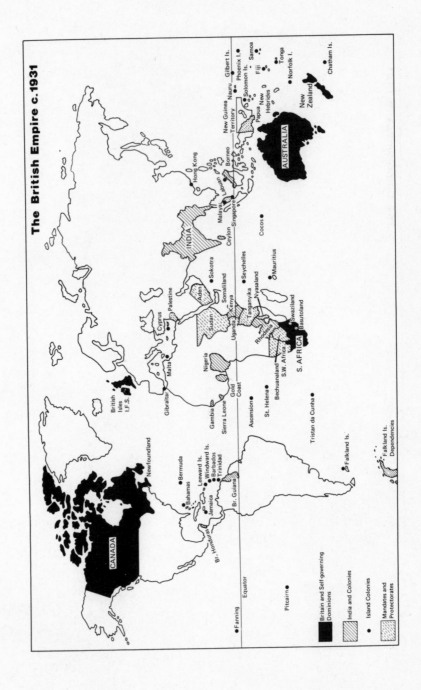

The British Empire c.1931

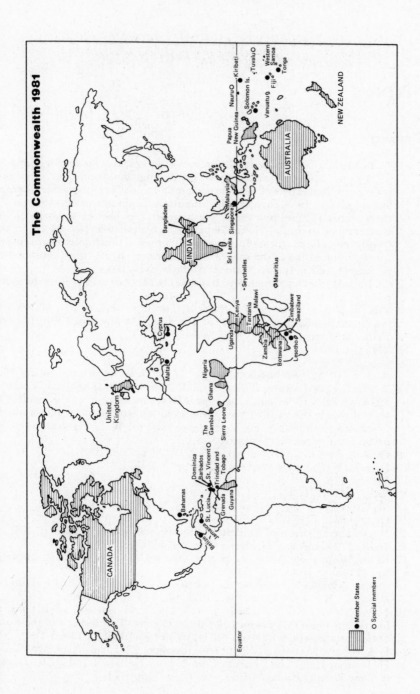

The Commonwealth 1981

Notes

CHAPTER 1

1 A. B. Keith, *The Constitution, Administration and Laws of the Empire*, London, 1924, pp. 21–34, examines the continuing limitations on dominion sovereignty in this period. See also the same author's *The Dominions as Sovereign States*, London, 1938, chapter I, for an historical appraisal of developments in their status. There is a brief but cogent unpublished analysis in the Government of India, Home Department Special File No. 94/29 on the Constitutional Growth and International Position of the Dominions, prepared for the information of the viceroy in 1929, which has also been consulted by permission of the Indian National Archives, New Delhi.
2 Cf. India Home Department 94/29 and Keith, *The Dominions as Sovereign States*, p. 16.
3 Vincent Massey, *What's Past is Prologue*, Toronto, 1963, p. 109. Massey was appointed first Canadian minister at Washington by Mackenzie King in 1926.
4 Keith, *The Dominions as Sovereign States*, p. 8.
5 *Ibid.*, pp. 15–16.
6 Cab., 23 E–6.
7 A. B. Keith, *Speeches and Documents on the British Dominions*, pp. 46 and 86.
8 R. MacGregor Dawson, *William Lyon Mackenzie King 1874–1923*, London, 1958, pp. 404–16, contains the most informative account of the incident as seen through the eyes of the prime minister who made it important in Commonwealth history. For a general account see W. K. Hancock, *Survey of British Commonwealth Affairs*, vol. 1, pp. 251–2.
9 Canada, *Parl. Deb.* (Commons), 1 Feb. 1923, vol. 1, p. 33.
10 Dawson, *William Lyon Mackenzie King*, pp. 432–5.
11 *Ibid.*, p. 425.
12 *Ibid.*, p. 423.
13 *Ibid.*, p. 438.
14 Quoted *ibid.*, p. 420.
15 Marchioness Curzon of Kedleston, *Reminiscences*, London, 1955, p. 181.
16 Dawson, *William Lyon Mackenzie King*, pp. 467–8.
17 Keith, *Speeches and Documents*, p. 318; Dawson, *William Lyon Mackenzie King*, pp. 477–80.
18 Philip G. Wigley, *Canada and the transition to Commonwealth: British Canadian Relations 1917–1926* Cambridge, 1977, pp. 2–4 and 279–81.
19 Massey, *What's Past is Prologue*, p. 135, and F. H. Soward, *Some Aspects of Canadian Foreign Policy in the Last Quarter Century*, Transactions of the Royal Society of Canada, 4th series, vol. iv, section iii (1966), p. 139.
20 L. S. Amery, *My Political Life* (2 vols), London, 1955, vol. 2, pp. 335–6.
21 H. Duncan Hall, 'The Genesis of the Balfour Declaration of 1926', *Journal of Commonwealth Political Studies*, vol. 1, no 3, pp. 171–8.

22 See Hansard, *Parl. Deb.* (Commons), vol. 188, coll. 520–1 for Chamberlain's speech quoted above, and for discussions at the Imperial Conference see CAB. 32/56 E (I.R.–26). For a fuller consideration of Dominion and more particularly Canadian attitudes, see Wigley, op. cit., pp. 240–55.

23 O. Pirow, *J. B. M. Hertzog*, Cape Town, 1957, p. 105.

24 Harold Nicolson, *King George V*, London, 1952, pp. 476–7.

25 L. J. R. 95 P.C.C. 114. Reprinted in Frederick Madden, *Imperial Constitutional Documents, 1765–1952*, Oxford, 1953, pp. 47–54.

26 On the Irish position see especially CAB. 32/56 E(I.R.–26) 3, and for comment on it E(I.R.–26) 31B, and also M. McInerney, 'Mr John A. Costello Remembers' in *The Irish Times*, 4 September 1967. For Canada see H. Blair Neatby, *William Lyon Mackenzie King, 1924–1932*, Toronto, 1963, p. 182, and CAB. 32/56 E(I.R.–26) 6th meeting.

27 Neatby, *Mackenzie King*, p. 183.

28 CAB. 32/56 E(I.R.–26). See also C. M. van den Heever, *General J. B. M. Hertzog*, Johannesburg, 1946, pp. 213–17.

29 T. de V. White, *Kevin O'Higgins*, London, 1948, p. 221.

30 CAB. 32/56 E(I.R.–26) 3 reproduced the Irish memorandum on existing anomalies; CAB. 32/47, E115 that on Privy Council appeals.

31 The drafts are reproduced in CAB. 32/56. For comments see de V. White, *Kevin O'Higgins*, p. 222.

32 Imperial Conference 1926; summary of Proceedings, Cmd. 2768, contains the Report of the Committee. It is reprinted in Keith, *Speeches and Documents*, pp. 161–70. See also Amery, *My Political Life*, vol. 2, pp. 379–98.

33 Blanche E. C. Dugdale, *Arthur James Balfour* (2 vols), London, 1936, vol. 2, pp. 281–2, and personal information.

34 This is very questionable. The belief that Britain retained control is implicit for example in the published German Foreign Office Documents on the origins of the second world war.

35 See Nicholas Mansergh, *Survey of British Commonwealth Affairs: Problems of External Policy 1931–1939*, London, 1952, pp. 73–9, 429–32, for some assessment of this.

36 Hancock, *Survey*, vol. 1, p. 263.

37 K. C. Wheare, *The Statute of Westminster and Dominion Status* (4th ed.), London, 1949, pp. 28–9.

38 There is a detailed analysis of Irish Free State aims together with an exposition of the tactics of their delegations in D. W. Harkness, *The Restless Dominion*, London, 1969, pp. 80–249.

39 Cmd. 3479.

40 Cmd. 3717 and 3718.

41 See Nicolson, *King George V*, pp. 483–4.

42 Cmd. 3717.

43 Nicolson, *King George V*, pp. 477–82.

44 Cmd. 3479, sec. 60; reprinted in Keith, *Speeches and Documents*, p. 189.

45 22 Geo. 5, c. 4.

46 The text of the statute and source material on dominion reactions to it are to be found in Nicholas Mansergh, *Documents and Speeches on British Commonwealth Affairs, 1931–1952* (2 vols), London, 1953, vol. 1, secs. 1 and 2 and pp. 53–6, 90–1.

47 Reprinted *ibid.*, pp. 4–6.

48 *C.f.* D. W. Harkness, 'Patrick McGilligan: Man of Commonwealth', in Hillmer

and Wigley (editors), *The First British Commonwealth*, London, 1980, pp. 117–135.

49 The statement of 22 March 1932, here summarised and the subsequent exchanges referred to below were reprinted in a British White Paper, Cmd. 4056 and an Irish White Paper, P. No. 650. See also Hancock, *Survey*, vol. 1, chapter 6.

50 The judgment, *Moore and Others versus the Attorney General for the Irish Free State* is reproduced in Mansergh, *Documents and Speeches*, vol. 1, pp. 305–14.

51 Lord Beaverbrook, when he learned of the procedure adopted, commented to the king, 'Sir, you have put your head on the execution block. All that Baldwin has to do now is to swing the axe.' *A King's Story. The Memoirs of H.R.H. the Duke of Windsor*, London, 1951, pp. 346–7.

52 The relevant legislation and speeches on the abdication are reprinted in Mansergh, *Documents and Speeches*, vol. 1, sec. 5.

53 Wheare, *The Statute of Westminster*, pp. 288–9. See generally chapter 11.

54 Ian M. Drummond, *British Economic Policy and the Empire 1919–1939*, London, 1972, *passim* – see generally pp. 43–114.

55 Quoted *ibid.*, p. 53.

56 *Ibid.*, p. 67.

57 *Ibid.*, p. 68 for an instructive account of the state of paralysis to which the government was reduced.

58 Hancock, *Survey*, vol. 2, part 1, p. 233. Chapter 1 contains the classic analysis of intra-Commonwealth trade in these years.

59 J. B. Brebner, *North Atlantic Triangle*, New Haven, 1945, p. 309.

60 Hancock, *Survey*, vol. 2, part I, pp. 245–51.

61 Drummond, op. cit., p. 114.

CHAPTER 2

1 And not only on the lips of South African politicians. In the debate in 1906 on self-government for the Transvaal, the under secretary of state for the colonies, Winston Churchill, the leader of the opposition, A. J. Balfour, and a young Labour member, J. Ramsay MacDonald, used it in this sense. The 'native question' was the phrase applied to relations between the peoples of European and African race. See Hansard, *Parl. Deb* (Commons), 4th series 1906, vol. 162, coll. 776–804.

2 See his speech of March 1954 at the opening of the Fifth (unofficial) Commonwealth Relations Conference at Lahore as reprinted in N. Mansergh, *The Multi-Racial Commonwealth*, London, 1955, p. 144.

3 J. A. Hobson, *Imperialism: A Study* (3rd ed.), London, 1938, p. 51.

4 S. Gopal, *British Policy in India 1858–1905*, Cambridge, 1965, p. 261.

5 Hansard, *Parl. Deb.* (Commons), Third series, vol. cccxlii (1890), col. 93.

6 See Government of India Reforms Office File 142/30–R, where extracts from the dispatches are reprinted in a paper on 'The Interpretation of the term Responsible Government' prepared by W. H. Lewis, dated 12 June 1930.

7 Hansard, *Parl. Deb.* (Lords), 4th series, vol. 198, col. 1985. See also John, Viscount Morley, *Recollections* (2 vols), London, 1917, vol. 2, pp. 172–3.

8 *Report of the Indian Statutory Commission*, Cmd. 3569 (1930), *vol. 2, Recommendations*, pp. 6–7.

9 *Cf.* Mansergh and Moon (eds), *India. The Transfer of Power 1942–47*, London, H.M.S.O. 1970– , vol. v, no. 256, vol. VII, no. 123 and Vol. x, no. 382.

10 Government of India Act 1858, 21 and 22 Vict., c. 106.
11 The Indian Councils Act 1861, 24 and 25 Vict., c. 67, reprinted C. H. Philips, *The Evolution of India and Pakistan 1858–1947: Select Documents*, London, 1962, pp. 35–8.
12 *Cf.* R. B. McDowell, *The Irish Administration*, London, 1964, p. 61, and chapter 2 generally.
13 Philips, *The Evolution of India and Pakistan*, p. 3.
14 Parl. Papers, vol. 56, no. 102, col. 1515, reprinted in Philips, *The Evolution of India and Pakistan*, p. 13.
15 The dispatches are reprinted in Philips, *The Evolution of India and Pakistan*, pp. 19–23.
16 Quoted in Gopal, *British Policy in India*, p. 249.
17 Philip Woodruff, *The Men Who Ruled India* (2 vols), London, 1954, vol. 1, *The Founders*; vol. 2, *The Guardians*.
18 H. A. L. Fisher, *James Bryce* (2 vols), London, 1927, vol. 1, pp. 259–60. The letter was to his mother and dated 20 November 1888.
19 Curzon to Hamilton, 4 June 1903. Quoted in Philips, *The Evolution of India and Pakistan*, p. 73.
20 K. M. Panikkar, *Asia and Western Dominance*, London, 1953, p. 16.
21 Gopal, *British Policy in India*, pp. 224–5.
22 Reprinted in Government of India Home Department Special No. 94/29.
23 Mansergh and Lumby (eds), *India. The Transfer of Power 1942–47*, vol. II, no. 662.
24 R. C. Dutt, letter to Gokhale, 24 May 1906, quoted in B. R. Nanda, *Gokhale. The Indian Moderates and the British Raj*, OUP, Delhi, 1977.
25 See Gopal, op. cit., pp. 176–8 and 182–4.
26 Indian Round Table Conference (Second Session) (7 Sept. – 1 Dec. 1931), Cmd. 3997 (1932), pp. 389–90.
27 Earl of Ronaldshay, *The Life of Lord Curzon* (3 vols), London, 1928, vol. 2, pp. 320–1.
28 *Cf.* Gopal, *British Policy in India*, p. 298.
29 Ronaldshay, *The Life of Lord Curzon*, vol. 2, p. 151.
30 Report on Indian Constitutional Reforms (1918), Cd. 9109, para. 6.
31 Government of India Home Department 94/29.
32 *Ibid.*
33 Reprinted in Sir M. Gwyer and A. Appadorai, *Speeches and Documents on the Indian Constitution 1921–47* (2 vols), Bombay, 1957, vol. 1, p. 220.
34 *Cf. ibid.*, pp. 221–2.
35 S. Gopal, *Jawaharlal Nehru* (2 vols), vol. 1, London, 1975, p. 129.
36 The Earl of Halifax, *Fulness of Days*, London, 1957, pp. 114–23.
37 Government of India File No. 29/37 – G (D) 1937 Lewis to Laithwaite and extract from a private letter of 21 June 1937 from the secretary of state to the viceroy.
38 Gopal, op. cit., vol. 1, p. 222.
39 On the second point see R. J. Moore, *The Crisis of Indian Unity 1917–1940*, Oxford, 1974, p. 316.
40 Govt of India, Home Department 9/M.A./39 letter of Ewart to Thorne 17 February 1939 in which the Muslim League outlook on elections is described as 'typically unbusinesslike and opportunist'.
41 Personal conversation with the secretariat of the Indian National Congress, 1958.

CHAPTER 3

1 Quoted A. B. Keith, *Speeches and Documents on the British Dominions 1918–1931*, Oxford, 1932, p. 275.
2 *Ibid.*
3 James Eayrs, *In Defence of Canada: Appeasement and Rearmament*, Toronto, 1965, pp. 16–27, provides a lively and authoritative account of the 'Riddell incident'.
4 G. P. de T. Glazebrook, *A History of Canadian External Relations*, Toronto, 1950, p. 411.
5 Quoted in Eayrs, *In Defence of Canada*, p. 26.
6 Canada, *Parl. Deb. (Commons), 1936, vol. 1*, p. 98. See also N. Mansergh, *Survey of British Commonwealth Affairs 1931–1939*, London, 1952, pp. 116–7. For general background see Frank Hardie, *The Abyssinian Crisis*, London, 1974.
7 R. G. Neale, editor, *Documents on Australian Foreign Policy 1937–49*, Canberra, 1975– , see passim vols. 1–3.
8 Mansergh, op. cit., p. 232, and generally. Also Gwendolen Carter, *The British Commonwealth and International Security*, Toronto, 1947, p. 243.
9 D. Carlton, The Dominions and British Policy in the Abyssinian Crisis, *The Journal of Imperial and Commonwealth History*, vol. 1, no. 1.
10 Lord Halifax, *Fulness of Days*, London, 1957, p. 197.
11 Quoted in J. Garner, *The Commonwealth Office*, London, 1978, p. 83.
12 *Daily Telegraph*, 23 March 1936. See also Mansergh, *Survey of British Commonwealth Affairs*, p. 234.
13 H. B. Neatby, *William Lyon Mackenzie King, 1932–1939*, vol. III, Toronto, 1976, p. 174.
14 Neale, op, cit. vol. 1, no. 40.
15 *Ibid.*
16 CAB. 32/130 (1937) records the discussions on foreign policy. For the published report see Imperial Conference 1937. *Summary of Proceedings*. Cmd. 5482.
17 Neatby, op cit., vol. III, pp. 214–15.
18 J. Shepherd, *Australia's Interests and Policies in the Far East*, New York, 1940, p. 73.
19 Mackenzie King's account of his conversation is reprinted in Eayrs, *In Defence of Canada*, pp. 226–31, document 3.
20 See also p. 218 below.
21 Reprinted in F. H. Soward *et al*, *Canada in World Affairs: The Pre-War Years*, Toronto, 1941, pp. 270–1.
22 C. M. van den Heever, *Hertzog*, Johannesburg, 1946, p. 271.
23 J. van der Poel (ed.), *Selections from the Smuts Papers*, vols V–VII, Cambridge, 1973, vol. VI, no. 440.
24 Neatby, op. cit., vol. III, p. 287.
25 Neale, op. cit., vol. 1, no. 209.
26 *Ibid.*, vol. 1, no. 237.
27 *Ibid.*, nos. 242, 245 and 253.
28 Vincent Massey, *What's Past is Prologue*, Toronto, 1963, pp. 259–62.
29 Quoted in Alan Watt, *The Evolution of Australian Foreign Policy 1938–1965*, Cambridge, 1967, p. 4.
30 D. C. Watt, *Personalities and Policies*, London, 1965, essay 8, on the Commonwealth and the Munich crisis, provides an interesting reappraisal. On

Canadian policies at Munich see Eayrs *In Defence of Canada*, pp. 67–72.
31 For Lord Templewood, see 'The Lesson of Munich' in *The Listener*, 9 December 1948 and for Lord Halifax, see Halifax, *Fulness of Days*, pp. 197–8.
32 E. L. Woodward and Rohan Butler (eds), *Documents on British Foreign Policy, 1919–1939* (10 vols), 3rd Series, London, 1949–61, vol. 1, p. 602 and vol. 2, p. 252; and Watt, *Personalities and Policies*, p. 169.
33 N. Mansergh, *Survey of British Commonwealth Affairs 1931–1939*, London, 1952, p. 432 and see generally Chap. XI. The views there expressed continue to represent a judgment which fuller evidence would seem to confirm.
34 W. S. Churchill, *The Second World War* (6 vols), London, 1950, vol. 1, p. 271; and W. K. Hancock, *Smuts* (2 vols), Cambridge, 1962 and 1968, vol. 2, p. 311.
35 Neale, op. cit., vol. II, no. 218.
36 G. Heaton Nicholls in *South Africa in My Time*, London, 1961, has a movingly candid account of the episode, pp. 339–44.
37 The remark was made to Sir Douglas Busk, who told me of it.
38 *Cmd. 6832* (1946), gives United Kingdom figures.
39 Viscount Bruce of Melbourne kept a record of the proceedings at these meetings throughout the war years and through his courtesy the author has had an opportunity of reading them. The range and liveliness of the discussions that took place was not widely appreciated because of their private and informal character.
40 J. W. Pickersgill, *The Mackenzie King Record* (2 vols), vol. I, Toronto, 1960, p. 241.
41 Canada, *Parl. Deb.* (Commons), 17 February 1941, reprinted N. Mansergh, *Documents and Speeches on British Commonwealth Affairs, 1931–52* (2 vols), London, 1954, vol. I, pp. 530–1.
42 Pickersgill, *The Mackenzie King Record*, p. 241.
43 *Ibid.*, p. 247.
44 See his telegram to Sir Arthur Fadden August 1941 in Churchill, *The Second World War*, vol. 3, pp. 758–60, reprinted in Mansergh, *Documents and Speeches on British Commonwealth Affairs, 1931–1952*, vol. 1, pp. 540–2.
45 *The Times*, 8 September 1941, quoted in N. Mansergh, *Survey of British Commonwealth Affairs, Problems of Wartime Cooperation and Post-War Change 1939–1952*, London, 1958, p. 114.
46 Garner, op. cit., pp. 211–12 and generally pp. 207–12.
47 *The Melbourne Herald*, 28 December 1941, reprinted in Mansergh, *Documents and Speeches on British Commonwealth Affairs 1931–1952*, vol. 1, pp. 549–50.
48 Reprinted in Mansergh, *ibid.*, pp. 568–75.
49 Ibid., pp. 575–9.
50 Canada, *Parl. Deb.* (Commons), 1944, vol. 1, pp. 41–2; reprinted in Mansergh, *Documents and Speeches on British Commonwealth Affairs, 1931–1952*, vol. 1, pp. 583–4.
51 Quoted in Garner, op. cit., p. 264.
52 Mansergh, op. cit., pp. 595–6.
53 Garner, op. cit., pp. 266–7.

CHAPTER 4

1 Jawaharlal Nehru, *The Unity of India*, London, 1948, p. 307.
2 Quoted by K. Veerathappa, *Britain and the Indian Problem (September 1939–May*

1940) in *International Studies* (Bombay), vol. 7, no. 4, p. 546. Also see article generally, pp. 537–67.

3 N. Mansergh, *Documents and Speeches on British Commonwealth Affairs, 1931–1952* (2 vols), London, 1954, vol.2, pp. 612–14.

4 See Mansergh and Lumby (eds), *India. The Transfer of Power 1942–47*, London, 1970– , vol. 1. nos. 1, 2, 43 and 60 and above vol. 1, p. 27.

5 Hansard, *Parl. Deb.* (Commons), vol. 378, coll. 1069–70, reprinted in Mansergh, *Documents and Speeches on British Commonwealth Affairs, 1931–1952*, vol. 2, pp. 614–15; see also pp. 616–17 and, for Indian reactions, pp. 617–25.

6 J. W. Wheeler-Bennett, *King George VI, His Life and Reign,* London, 1958, p. 697.

7 Mansergh and Lumby, op. cit., vol. 1, no. 244.

8 Reprinted in Mansergh, *Documents and Speeches, 1931–1952*, vol. 2, pp. 633–5.

9 Wheeler-Bennett, *King George VI*, p. 703.

10 Letter to K. M. Munshi, 17 May 1946, G. M. Nandurkar (ed.) *Sardar's Letters Mostly Unknown*, vol. 4, 1945–6, Ahmedabad, 1977, p. 195.

11 Cmd. 6821. Reprinted in N. Mansergh, *Documents and Speeches, 1931–1952*, vol. 2, pp. 644–52.

12 Mansergh and Moon, op. cit., see note by Sir Stafford Cripps, vol. VII, no. 593.

13 *Ibid.,* vol. VII, nos. 531, 591–2, 603, 615, 627.

14 Cmd. 7047. Reprinted Mansergh, op. cit., pp. 659–61.

15 Wheeler-Bennett, *King George VI*, p. 711.

16 Alan Campbell-Johnson, *Mission with Mountbatten*, London, 1951, pp. 38–114.

17 *Ibid.,* pp. 108–10, and for record see Earl Mountbatten of Burma, *Time Only to Look Forward,* London, 1949, pp. 26–47.

18 10 & 11 Geo. 6, Ch. 30, reprinted in Mansergh, *Documents and Speeches, 1931–1952*, vol. 2, pp. 669–85.

19 *Ibid.,* pp. 700–2.

20 Wheeler-Bennett, *King George VI*, p. 702.

21 Reprinted in Cmd. 6196, *India and the War*, and in Sir Maurice Gwyer and A. Appadorai, *Speeches and Documents on the Indian Constitution 1921–47* (2 vols), Bombay, 1957, vol. 2, pp. 443–4, and Mansergh, *Documents and Speeches, 1931–1952*, vol. 2, pp. 608–9.

22 Mansergh and Moon, op. cit., vol. XI, no. 39.

23 Leonard Mosley, *The Last Days of the British Raj*, London, 1961, pp. 162–5 tells the story and on p. 163 assesses the weight of the material destroyed. In the Preface he states that he put questions to Sir Conrad Corfield amongst others without their being responsible for what he subsequently wrote. The incident is also recorded in Michael Edwardes, *The Last Years of British India*, London, 1963, pp. 186–9.

24 E.g. The Resolution of the Congress at the Ramgarh Session, 20 March 1940: 'The Congress cannot admit the right of the rulers of Indian states . . . to come in the way of Indian freedom. Sovereignty in India must rest with the people, whether in the states or the provinces. . . .' Cmd. 6196 and reprinted in Mansergh, *Documents and Speeches*, vol. 2, pp. 606–8.

25 *Cf.* Wilfrid Russell, *Indian Summer*, Bombay, 1951, pp. 102–5.

26 D. G. Tendulkar, *Mahatma: Life of Mohandas Karamchand Gandhi* (8 vols), Bombay, 1951–4, vol. 6, p. 11.

27 Marquess of Zetland, *'Essayez': the Memoirs of Lawrence, Second Marquess of Zetland*, London, 1956, p. 292 and CAB 65/5 30 (40) 4, 2 February, 1940.

28 *Ibid.,* p. 265.

Notes 265

29 Reprinted in Gwyer and Appadorai, *Speeches and Documents*, vol. 2, pp. 440–2, and in Mansergh, *Documents and Speeches, 1931–1952*, vol. 2, pp. 609–12.
30 Maulana A. K. Azad, *India Wins Freedom*, Calcutta, 1959, p. 185.
31 Personal information.
32 S. Gopal, *Jawaharlal Nehru, A Biography*, London, 1975, vol. 1, pp. 223–4.
33 Jawaharlal Nehru, *The Discovery of India*, Calcutta, 1946, pp. 320–2, and Rajendra Prasad, *Autobiography*, Bombay, 1957, pp. 444–8, and personal conversations with both.
34 Prasad, *Autobiography*, p. 446.
35 Azad, *India Wins Freedom*, pp. 160–2, and Penderel Moon, *Divide and Quit*, London, 1961, p. 14.
36 V. P. Menon, *The Transfer of Power in India*, Bombay, 1957, p. 97, and cf. also Percival Spear, *India*, Michigan, 1961, pp. 404–5, on the Congress rejection of the Cripps offer 1942.
37 *Statement of 8 August 1940*. Reprinted in Mansergh, *Documents and Speeches, 1931–1952*, vol. 2, pp. 612–4, and see above pp. 106–7.
38 Cmd. 6350. Reprinted *ibid.*, vol. 2, pp. 616–17.
39 Cmd. 6821. Reprinted *ibid.*, vol. 2, pp. 644–52.
40 Sir Francis Tuker, *While Memory Serves*, London, 1950, chapter 12, 'The Great Calcutta Killing'. For the Governor's comprehensive report see Mansergh and Moon, op. cit., vol. VIII, no. 197.
41 Hansard, *Parl. Deb.* (Commons), vol. 127, col. 1112.
42 Cmd. 6821.
43 Mansergh and Moon, op. cit, vol. X, no. 101.
44 Azad, *India Wins Freedom*, p. 167.
45 *Ibid.*, p. 168. But Pandit Nehru mentioned to the author on 6 April 1954 and therefore long before Azad's work was published that at the morning session of the cabinet the Muslim league members had been invited to tea and had declined.
46 Cmd. 7047, reprinted in Mansergh, *Documents and Speeches, 1931–1952*, vol. 2, pp. 659–61 and Mansergh and Moon, op. cit., vol. IX, nos. 438 and 421.
47 To the author.
48 Michael Edwardes, *The Last Years of British India*, p. 95.
49 Menon, *The Transfer of Power in India*, pp. 358–65. See also Campbell-Johnson, *Mission with Mountbatten*, pp. 62, 88–90.
50 Azad, *India Wins Freedom*, p. 207.
51 Michael Brecher, *Nehru, A Political Biography*, London, 1959, pp. 376–7. Nehru, he notes, did not believe Pakistan was a viable state and took the view that 'sooner or later the areas which had seceded would be compelled by force of circumstances to return to the fold'.
52 *Sardar Patel's Correspondence* (Ahmedabad, 1971–4), vol. 4, p. 113.
53 Azad, op. cit., pp. 206–27.
54 Quoted in Brecher, *Nehru*, p. 338; Moon, *Divide and Quit*, p. 77. See also Ian Stephens, *Pakistan*, London, 1963, pp. 131–6, 143 and 182 *et seq.*, where there is an understanding account of the Sikh predicament and the Sikh reaction to it.
55 Indian Independence Act, 1947 (10 & 11 Geo. 6 Ch. 30).
56 Menon, *The Transfer of Power in India*, p. 404. See generally, pp. 404–7.
57 Quoted *ibid.*, p. 384.
58 Georges Fischer in *Le Parti Travailliste et la Décolonization de l'Inde*, Paris, 1966,

has written a detailed analysis of the Indian policies of the Labour Party: on self-determination see especially pp. 123–33; C. R. Attlee, a terse account of the policy of the Labour government in *As It Happened*, London, 1954, pp. 179–86, and some further comments are recorded by Lord Francis-Williams in *A Prime Minister Remembers*, London, 1961, pp. 202–19.

59 To the author in Delhi on 4 March 1958.
60 Personal conversation in Bombay, April 1947.
61 Legislative Assembly Debates (1947), vol. I, p. 101.
62 *Cf.* Mansergh and Moon, op. cit., vol. V, no. 151, 91, 96, 174 and vol. X, no. 553.

CHAPTER 5

1 W. K. Hancock, *Smuts* (2 vols), Cambridge, 1967, vol. 2, pp. 431–3.
2 The text of the legislation on nationality and citizenship in all parts of the Commonwealth is grouped with comment upon its purposes in N. Mansergh, *Documents and Speeches on British Commonwealth Affairs, 1921–1952* (2 vols), London, 1954, vol. 2, section xix and the Commonwealth Immigrants Act, 1962 (10 and 11 Eliz. 2, c. 21) is reprinted in N. Mansergh, *Documents and Speeches on Commonwealth Affairs, 1952–62*, London, 1963, pp. 741–7.
3 Mansergh and Moon (eds), *India, The Transfer of Power*, 1942–47, London 1970– , vol. XI, nos. 445, 481, 488, 492, 494, 531, 543 and 555.
4 Cab 32/130. E. 37 No. 12.
5 E.g. *Dáil Deb.* 29 November 1944, vol. 95, coll. 1024–5; *ibid.*, 19 June 1946, vol. 101, coll. 2181–2; *ibid.*, 24 June 1947, vol. 107, col. 87 and Hansard, *Parl. Deb.* (Commons), 22 April 1948, vol. 449, col. 1975.
6 Michael McInerney, 'Mr John A. Costello Remembers', in *The Irish Times*, 8 September 1967.
7 *Ibid.*
8 Prompted by a front page article in the *Sunday Independent*, 5 September 1948, carrying the heading '*External Relations Act to Go*' and alluding to the views of Ministers and to the author's article on 'The Implications of Eire's Relations with the British Commonwealth' in *International Affairs*, January 1948.
9 The Republic of Ireland Act 1948 (No. 22 of 1948), and Mr Costello's speech, *Dáil Deb.*, vol. 113, call. 347–87, introducing the bill are reprinted in Mansergh, *Documents and Speeches, 1931–1952*, vol. 2, pp. 802–9.
10 Hansard, *Parl. Deb.* (Lords), 15 December 1948, vol 159, coll. 1051–93; reprinted in Mansergh, *Documents and Speeches, 1931–1952*, vol. 2, pp. 811–21.
11 *Ibid.*
12 McInerney, 'Mr John A. Costello Remembers', and Australia, *House of Representatives Deb.*, 26 November 1948, vol. 200, pp. 3583–4; reprinted in Mansergh, *Documents and Speeches, 1931–1952*, vol. 2, pp. 809–11.
13 New Zealand. Republic of Ireland Act (No. 13 of 1950); reprinted in Mansergh, *Documents and Speeches, 1931–1952*, vol. 2, p. 837.
14 J. D. B. Miller, *Britain and the Old Dominions*, London, 1966, p. 147.
15 A Report of the proceedings of the conference was published under the title *Asian Relations*, Delhi, 1948. The author was one of the United Kingdom observers at the conference.

16 India, Constituent Assembly Deb., vol. 5, pp. 4–5, reprinted in Mansergh, *Documents and Speeches, 1931–1952*, vol. 2, p. 701.
17 Sapru Correspondence. Government of India, National Library, Calcutta, P. 381. Enclosed with letter from Sir Jagdish Prasad.
18 *Indian Constituent Assembly Deb.*, vol. 5, pp. 4–5.
19 Sapru Correspondence A–68.
20 *Ibid.*, R.42, R.43, S.253 and S.361, letter dated 24 April 1948 from S.Sinha.
21 Mansergh and Moon (eds), *India, The Transfer of Power 1942–47*, London, 1970–, vol. XI, no. 121 for the minutes and conclusions of the India and Burma Committee of the Cabinet.
22 H. Tinker, *The Union of Burma* (4th ed.), London, 1967, pp. 22–7. The relevant documents are reprinted in Mansergh, *Documents and Speeches, 1931–1952*, vol. 2, pp. 760–93.
23 The papers relating to the independence of Ceylon are reprinted *ibid.*, section xii.
24 Hansard, *Parl. Deb.* (Lords), vol. 152, col. 1205.
25 'The Implications of Eire's Relationship with the British Commonwealth of Nations' were considered in a lecture by the author in November 1947 in which *inter alia* attention was drawn to Mr de Valera's formulation of the phrase, 'Head of the Britannic Commonwealth' as appropriate acknowledgement of the Crown by an associated republican state. *International Affairs*, January 1948.
26 India Constituent Assembly Deb., vol. 1, no. 5, pp. 57–61, reprinted in Mansergh, *Documents and Speeches*, 1931–1952, vol. 2., pp. 652–8.
27 Joe Garner, *The Commonwealth Office 1925–68*, London, 1978, p. 318.
28 S. Gopal, *Jawaharlal Nehru. A Biography*, London, 1979, vol. 2, p. 47.
29 Ibid., pp. 49–50.
30 Ibid., p. 46 and generally pp. 46–55.
31 *Sardar Patel's Correspondence*, Ahmedabad, 1971–4, vol. 6, p. 432.
32 *Mike. The Memoirs of the Rt. Hon. L. B. Pearson*, Toronto, 1973, vol. 2, p. 98.
33 P. Gordon Walker, *The Commonwealth*, London, 1962, p. 183.
34 J. W. Wheeler-Bennett, *King George VI*, London, 1958, p. 722.
35 *Ibid.*, pp. 723–6.
36 Garner, op. cit., pp. 318–19.
37 Pearson, op. cit., vol. 2, p. 99.
38 *Ibid.*, p. 104.
39 Gordon Walker, op. cit., p. 184.
40 Gopal, op. cit., vol. 2, p. 53.
41 Patel, op. cit., vol. 8, p. 12.
42 Reprinted in Mansergh, *Documents and Speeches, 1931–1952*, vol. 2, pp. 847–57. See section XV generally for dominion comment and reactions.
43 Reprinted in Mansergh, *Documents and Speeches on Commonwealth Affairs, 1952–1962*, London, 1963, pp. 304–6.
44 *Ibid.*

CHAPTER 6

1 The point is made in A. J. P. Taylor, *English History 1914–1945*, Oxford, 1965, p. 600 note 1.
2 *Ibid.*, p. 600.

3 S. Gopal, *Jawaharlal Nehru*, vol. II, Delhi, 1979, p. 195.
4 See above pp. 292–3.
5 *Parl. Deb.* (Commons), vol. 450, coll. 1315–9, reprinted in N. Mansergh, *Documents and Speeches on British Commonwealth Affairs, 1931–1952*, London, 1953, vol. 2, pp. 1131–3.
6 Mansergh *ibid.*, p. 1138.
7 Canada, *Parl. Deb.* (Commons), 1948, vol. 4, pp. 3441–50; reprinted in Mansergh, *ibid.*, pp. 1128–9.
8 Gopal, op. cit., vol. II, p. 251.
9 *Lok Sabha Deb.*, 1954, pt. 2, vol. vii, coll. 3675–85, reprinted in N. Mansergh, *Documents and Speeches on Commonwealth Affairs, 1952–1962*, London, 1963, p. 463, and see *The Times of India*, 10 September 1954, for report of Speech to Delhi Press Association.
10 Cmd. 7257. See above p. 332.
11 *Parl. Deb.* (Commons), 19 June 1955, vol. 542, col. 42.
12 Quoted in James Eayrs. *Canada in World Affairs, October 1955 to June 1957*, Toronto, 1959, pp. 187–8, from *The Economist*, 10 November 1956.
13 Quoted in James Eayrs, *The Commonwealth and Suez: A Documentary Survey*, London, 1964, p. 194. This work provides a lively connecting commentary linking the documentary records.
14 In a statement issued in Madras on 4 November 1956, and reprinted in Mansergh, *Documents and Speeches, 1952–1962*, p. 521, and in Eayrs, *The Commonwealth and Suez*, p. 256.
15 Canada, *Parl. Deb.* (Commons), 27 November 1956, 4th (spec) sess. pp. 52–5, reprinted in Mansergh, *Documents and Speeches, 1952–1962*, p. 515. See also *The Memoirs of the Rt. Hon. Lester Pearson*, vol. 2, Toronto, 1973, pp. 244–74.
16 *Full Circle: The Memoirs of the Right Hon. Sir Anthony Eden*, Cambridge, Mass. 1960, p. 610. See Gopal, op. cit., vol. II, pp. 277–99.
17 Quoted in Eayrs, *The Commonwealth and Suez*, p. 168. For an account of Menzies' own role in the Suez crisis see Sir Robert Menzies, *Afternoon Light: Some Memoirs of Men and Events*, London, 1967, chapter 8.
18 Duncan Sandys, *The Modern Commonwealth*, London, H.M.S.O., 1962, pp. 9–10.
19 *The Annual Register, 1955*, p. 74.
20 *Report of the Committee on Representational Services Overseas appointed by the Prime Minister under the Chairmanship of Lord Plowden, 1962–3*, Cmnd 2276 (1964) observed that 'before the war the relationship of Britain to other Commonwealth countries was still largely a maternal one in the sense that British ambassadors in foreign countries normally looked after the interests of the dominions as well', pp. 3–7.
21 J. D. B. Miller, *The Commonwealth in the World*, London, 1958, p. 275.
22 This is a principal theme of R. E. Robinson's and J. Gallagher's *Africa and the Victorians*, London, 1961.
23 One former colonial territory, British Somaliland, on independence became part of the larger independent state of Somalia, which united British with Italian Somaliland in the Somali Republic, a state outside the Commonwealth.
24 Mansergh, *Documents and Speeches, 1952–1962*, p. 347. Professor Rajan drew the author's attention to the fact that Mr Macmillan used the self-same phrase – 'wind of change' – in Accra at the outset of his tour of Africa but it had attracted no particular attention.
25 The title Sir Michael Blundell chose for his autobiography (London, 1964).

26 S. C. Easton, *The Twilight of European Colonialism*, New York, 1960, p. 519 and generally.
27 Held in London in July and November 1963 respectively. See Cmnd 2121, Annex A and Cmnd 2203, Annex A.
28 *Commonwealth Survey* (London), 22 October 1963, vol. 9, no. 22, pp. 885–8.
29 M. S. Rajan, *The Post-War Transformation of the Commonwealth*, Delhi, 1963.
30 *Parl. Deb.* (Commons), vol. 531, coll. 504–5. Reprinted in Mansergh, *Documents and Speeches, 1952–1962*, pp. 213–18.
31 *Nigeria, Report of the Commission appointed to inquire into the fears of minorities and the means of allaying them*, Cmnd 505. See Mansergh *ibid.*, pp. 57–66.
32 Nigeria (Constitution) Order in Council S.I. No. 1652, 1960.
33 W. P. Kirkman, *Unscrambling an Empire*, London, 1966, p. 13. For the text of the reports of Colonial Constitutional Conferences, draft constitutions and speeches on Independence Bills in the House of Commons, see Mansergh, *Documents and Speeches, 1952–1962*, pp. 35–290.
34 *Report of the Nyasaland (Devlin) Commission of Enquiry 1959*, Cmnd 814. See Mansergh, *ibid.*, pp. 133–40.
35 *The Advisory (Monckton) Commission on the Review of the Constitution of Rhodesia and Nyasaland*, 1960, Cmnd 1148. See Mansergh, *ibid.*, pp. 141–52.
36 Sir Roy Welensky, *Welensky's 4000 Days. The Life and Death of the Federation of Rhodesia and Nyasaland*, London, 1964. See especially, chapters 11–14.
37 *The Multi-Racial Commonwealth, Proceedings of the Fifth Unofficial Commonwealth Relations Conference, Held at Lahore, Pakistan, 17–27 March 1954. A Report* by N. Mansergh, London, 1955, p. 114 and M. Chanock, *Unconsummated Union, Britain, Rhodesia and South Africa 1900–45*, Manchester, 1977, pp. 262–4. See generally, pp. 249–64.
38 Sir Robert Menzies thought the departure from 'sound procedure' fatal, *Afternoon Light*, p. 213.
39 *Cf. The Annual Register 1961*, pp. 63–4 for a contemporary record written by the author on which this account is based. See also the South African articles in *The Annual Register* 1961 and also 1960.
40 Menzies, *Afternoon Light*, p. 213.
41 The speeches are reprinted in Mansergh, *Speeches and Documents, 1952–1962*, pp. 365–400.
42 J. Garner, *The Commonwealth Office*, London, 1978, p. 349.
43 *Ibid.*
44 Reprinted in part, Mansergh, op. cit., p. 370, note I.
45 Garner, op. cit., p. 351. See pp. 349–54. Lord Garner was Permanent Under Secretary, the Commonwealth Relations/Commonwealth Office 1962–1968. He led the British delegation of officials to consider the nature and terms of reference of the new body in January 1965.
46 See Harold Wilson, *The Labour Government 1964–70*, London, 1971, pp. 193–6 for the British Prime Minister's account.
47 For Final Communiqué, see Cmnd. 2890. Earlier *Documents relating to the negotiations between the United Kingdom and Southern Rhodesian Governments*, November 1963–November 1965 are in Cmnd. 2807.
48 For Final Communique, see Cmnd. 3115.
49 Cmnd. 3171.
50 Prime Minister's Department, Salisbury CSR 49–1966.
51 Cmnd. 1449 and reprinted in Mansergh, *Documents and Speeches, 1952–1962*, pp. 634–45.

52 Mansergh, *ibid.*, pp. 650–1.
53 *The Commonwealth and the Sterling Area* Statistical Abstract no. 84, 1963 provides the essential figures. For as convincing an argument as could be made for Commonwealth trade expansion and its importance to Britain, see the Editorial in *The Round Table*, July 1967, entitled *Saving Commonwealth Trade.* For the statistical trend see B. R. Mitchell with Phyllis Deane, *Abstract of British Historical Statistics*, Cambridge, 1962
54 *Ibid.*, p. 667. For an official record, see Commonwealth Relations Office List 1964, London HMSO.
55 Cmnd. 4715, July 1971, and J. D. B. Miller, *Survey of Commonwealth Affairs, Problems of Expansion and Attrition 1953–1969*, London, 1974, chapter 13, where there is a critical analysis of the impact of Britain's Common Market application upon her relations with the Commonwealth overseas.
56 Cmnd. 7802.
57 *Ibid.*, p. 10.
58 Lord Soames, 'From Rhodesia to Zimbabwe', *International Affairs*, 1980, vol. 56, no. 3, p. 405.

CHAPTER 7

1 See above vol. 1, pp. 95–7.
2 W. K. Hancock, *Smuts* (2 vols), vol. 1, *The Sanguine Years, 1870–1919*, Cambridge, 1962, chapter 10.
3 *Ibid.*, p. 37.
4 W. K. Hancock and J. van der Poel, *Selections from the Smuts papers* (4 vols), Cambridge, 1966, vol. 1, part 3 include Smuts's correspondence during the Anglo-Boer War and his unfinished and heretofore unpublished Memoirs of it. For the quotation see his letter to his wife dated 2 June 1901 from Standerton, pp. 392–4.
5 *Ibid.*
6 *African*, 837a. The writer was Frederick Graham. See also above vol. 1, p. 105.
7 Hancock, *Smuts*, vol. 1, p. 215, and generally; see above vol. 1, pp. 97–9.
8 Merriman Papers.
9 The papers of the Right Hon. Sir Patrick Duncan. Letter to Lady Selborne from the South African National Convention, Cape Town, 28 January 1909.
10 Hancock, *Smuts*, vol. 1, p. 159.
11 Duncan Papers.
12 Hancock, *Smuts*, vol. 1, p. 301.
13 *Ibid*, chapter 21.
14 Hancock, *Smuts*, vol. 2, pp. 10 and 324.
15 J. van der Poel (ed.) *Selections from the Smuts Papers*, vols V–VII, Cambridge, 1973, vol. V, nos. 1–3 and 13.
16 *Ibid.*, vol. VII, no. 712.
17 Albert Luthuli, *Let My People Go*, London, 1962, p. 197.
18 Speech to the Empire Parliamentary Association, 25 November 1943, reprinted N. Mansergh, *Documents and Speeches on British Commonwealth Affairs, 1931–52*, London, 1953, vol. 1, p. 569.
19 J. van de Poel, op. cit., vol. VI, no. 376.
20 *Ibid.*, vol. VI, no. 436.

21 Hancock, *Smuts*, vol. 2, p. 412.
22 Alan Paton, *Hofmeyr*, Cape Town, 1964, chapters 29–40 *passim*.
23 President de Valera's judgment was the more telling, because he felt he had also been a victim of Smuts' 'slimness'. Professor Hancock's account in *Smuts*, vol. 2, pp. 56–61, makes clear the limits of Smuts' understanding of Irish nationalist sentiments. For quotations above, see *ibid.*, p. 325.
24 The three volumes of the biography are R. MacGregor Dawson's *William Lyon Mackenzie King*, vol. 1, 1874–1923, Toronto, 1958; H. B. Neatby's *William Lyon Mackenzie King*, vol. II, 1924–1932, Toronto, 1963 and vol. III, 1932–1939, 1976.
25 J. English and J. O. Stubbs (eds) *Mackenzie King, Widening the Debate,* Toronto, 1977, p. 16.
26 Neatby, op. cit., vol. II, pp. 355–6. For earlier quotations, see pp. 29 and 207.
27 *Ibid.*, p. 44 and see generally chapter 3, entitled 'Educating Downing Street'.
28 *Ibid.*, chapter 9.
29 English and Stubbs, op. cit., p. 21.
30 *What's Past is Prologue, The Memoirs of the Right Hon. Vincent Massey,* Toronto, 1963, p. 112 and Neatby, op. cit., vol. II, pp. 190–1.
31 See above, pp. 276–7; James Eayrs, *In Defence of Canada: Appeasement and Rearmament*, Toronto, 1965, p. 63, and document 3 in appendices; Neatby, op. cit., vol. III, p. 223. For Eden's subsequent comments, see N. Mansergh, *Survey of British Commonwealth Affairs, 1931–1939*, Oxford, 1952, pp. 124–5.
32 Neatby, *ibid.*, vol. III, pp. 287–8 and 316.
33 J. W. Pickersgill, *The Mackenzie King Record* (4 vols), vol. I, Toronto, 1960; with D. F. Forster, vols. 2–4, Toronto, 1968–70.
34 *Ibid.*, vol. 1, p. 150.
35 *Ibid.*, vol. 1, p. 301.
36 English and Stubbs, op. cit., p. 30.
37 Pickersgill, op. cit., vol. 1, pp. 72–3.
38 *Cf.* R. T. Shannon, *Gladstone and the Bulgarian Agitation, 1876*, London, 1963, chapter 1.
39 Pickersgill, *The Mackenzie King Record*, vol. 1, p. 681.
40 *Ibid.*, p. 687.
41 *Ibid.*, p. 680–1.
42 *Ibid.*, p. 234.
43 *Ibid.*, p. 436.
44 *Ibid.*, p. 247.
45 *Ibid.*, pp. 233–4.
46 *Ibid.*, p. 318.
47 C. C. Lingard and R. G. Trotter, *Canada in World Affairs, 1941–1944*, Toronto, 1950.
48 Pickersgill, op. cit., vol. I., pp. 530–1.
49 English and Stubbs, op. cit., pp. 9–10.
50 The Earl of Birkenhead, *Halifax: The Life of Lord Halifax*, London, 1965, pp. 220 and 243.
51 Mansergh and Lumby (eds), *India. The Transfer of Power 1942–47*, vols. I–IV, London, 1970–, vol. I, no. 148.
Mansergh and Moon (eds) *India, The Transfer of Power*, vols. V–VII, Appendix; vol. VIII, no. 493.
52 The Rt. Hon. Lord Butler, *Jawaharlal Nehru: The Struggle for Independence*, Cambridge, 1966, pp. 8–11.

53 Jawaharlal Nehru, *The Unity of India*, London, 1941, pp. 290–3, and Mansergh, *Survey of British Commonwealth Affairs 1931–39*, pp. 359–60.
54 Jawaharlal Nehru, *The Unity of India*, p. 397.
55 Sapru Papers, Letter dated 22 April 1948.
56 Pickersgill and Forster, op. cit., vol. IV, p. 404.
57 Pandit Nehru told the author in 1947 that he never went on any speaking tour without a second microphone by way of reinsurance. The quotations are from Marie Seton, *Panditji. A Portrait of Jawaharlal Nehru*, London, 1967, p. 174.
58 S. Gopal, *Jawaharlal Nehru. A Biography*, London, 1979, vol. II, pp. 167–8.
59 Jawaharlal Nehru, *An Autobiography*, London, 1936, pp. 597–8.
60 *Jawaharlal Nehru's Speeches, 1949–1953* (2nd imp.), Ministry of Information and Broadcasting, Delhi, 1957, pp. 159, 189 and generally 158–60, 179–93.
61 *Ibid.*, pp. 127 and 124.
62 India, *Lok Sabha Debates*, 2nd ser., 1959, pt 2, vol. xxxiv, coll. 8006–12, and reprinted N. Mansergh, *Documents and Speeches on Commonwealth Affairs, 1952–62*, pp. 590–4.
63 *Annual Register*, 1962, p. 66 and Gopal, op. cit., vol. II, p. 181 and generally pp. 176–81 and 243.
64 Nehru' Speeches, p. 124.
65 *Ibid.*, p. 126.
66 *Ibid.*, p. 272.
67 *Ibid.*, pp. 223–5.
68 *Ibid.*, pp. 225 and 272–3.
69 Gopal, op. cit., vol. II, p. 288.
70 Mansergh, *Documents and Speeches*, 1952–62, pp. 762–4.
71 Gopal, op. cit., vol. II, p. 288.

THE HISTORICAL EXPERIENCE

1 Quoted in C. V. Wedgwood, *Truth and Opinion*, London, 1960, p. 157.
2 *Parl. Deb.* (Commons), 14 May 1900, vol. lxxxiii, col. 102.
3 J. P. Plamenatz, *On Alien Rule and Self-Government*, London, 1960, p. 17.
4 India, *Lok Sabha Deb.* 3rd series, vol. xlvi–, no. 29 (24 Sept. 1965), col. 7528.
5 *The Times of Malta*, 15 November 1967.
6 Reprinted in N. Mansergh, *Documents and Speeches on Commonwealth Affairs, 1952–1962*, London, 1963, pp. 276–8.
7 Sir George Gilbert Scott, *Personal and Professional Recollections*, London, 1879, chapter 4.
8 André Siegfried, *The Race Question in Canada*, London, 1907, pp. 178–9.
9 N. Mansergh, *The Multi-Racial Commonwealth*, London, 1955, pp. 132 and 142.
10 CAB. 32. E. 37. No. 12 paras 40–2.
11 Cmd. 6677. Reprinted in N. Mansergh, *Documents and Speeches on British Commonwealth Affairs, 1931–1952* (2 vols), Oxford, 1954, vol. 2, pp. 718–19.
12 Quoted in Sir Charles Webster, *The Art and Practice of Diplomacy*, London, 1961.
13 For the relevant Reports see Mansergh, *Documents and Speeches, 1952–1962*, pp. 692–9 and 702–14.
14 R. Hyam, *Britain's Imperial Century 1815–1914*, London, 1976, pp. 92–103.
15 For a contrary view, see W. D. McIntyre, *The Commonwealth of Nations. Origins and Impact 1869–1971*, University of Minnesota Press/OUP, 1977, p. 9.

16 W. K. Hancock, *Survey of British Commonwealth Affairs*, 2 vols, Oxford, 1937, vol. 1, pp. 1–5.
17 Seeley, pp. 1–2.
18 *The Sunday Times of Malta*, 12 November 1967. The delegate was Dr Guildo de Marco, Nationalist Member of the House of Representatives.
19 Sir R. Menzies, *The British Commonwealth of Nations in International Affairs. A Lecture* (Adelaide, 1950).
20 *The Times*, 2 April 1964.
21 *Le Figaro*, 5 November 1967.
22 The phrase was used by Dr Ramsay, Archbishop of Canterbury, preaching at the University Church of Great St Mary's, Cambridge.

Bibliography

The subject and the literature upon it are so vast that even a selective bibliography must necessarily run into many pages. There is furthermore the problem of the frontiers, on the one side dividing Commonwealth from imperial history and on the other side from the national histories of the member-states. Bibliographies tend to fall into two principal categories – the comprehensive Empire-Commonwealth and the more specifically Commonwealth. In the first category, Professor V. T. Harlow's *The Historiography of the British Empire and Commonwealth since 1945* submitted to *XIth Congrès International des Sciences Historiques* at Stockholm, 1960, and published in *Rapport V. Histoire Contemporaine*, Uppsala, 1960, *The Historiography of the British Empire-Commonwealth*, Durham N. C., 1966, edited by Robin W. Winks and Professor J. E. Flint's *Books on the British Empire and Commonwealth*, London, 1968, are most useful, while in great detail but for an earlier period only, there is *The Cambridge History of the British Empire*, vol. 3, *The Empire-Commonwealth*, 1870–1919, pp. 769–907. For a general historiographical essay on both Empire and Commonwealth the reader may be referred to Philip Curtin's 'The British Empire and Commonwealth in Recent Historiography', *American Historical Review*, vol. lxv, October 1959. The Historical Association's pamphlet, *Notes on the Teaching of Empire and Commonwealth History*, London, 1967, by G. M. D. Howat, offers a commentary with a book list. The second more specifically Commonwealth category is rather less well served though A. R. Hewitt's *Guide to Resources for Commonwealth Studies*, London, 1957, admirably fulfils its mainly research purposes. There are also more general guides in A. J. Horne, *The Commonwealth Today*, Library Association, 1965, and *Commonwealth History*, National Book League, 1965.

General histories are also apt to fall into the same two categories – those which are primarily histories of the British Empire, carrying over in some cases into the Commonwealth period but with their emphasis and perspective predominantly imperial; and those which focus their attention chiefly on Commonwealth. On Empire C. E. Carrington's lively *The British Overseas: Exploits of a Nation of Shopkeepers*, Cambridge, 1950, and D. K. Fieldhouse, *The Colonial Empires, a Comparative Survey from the Eighteenth Century*, London, 1966, provide general and, in the second case, comparative overall studies. Among more specialised works, chief place in respect of comprehensiveness is to be given to *The Cambridge History of the British Empire* in eight volumes. The first three, published over a wide spread of years, with the second appearing in 1940 and the third in 1959, relate the general history of British overseas expansion and imperial policy and the remaining five deal with the history of British India (2 vols), Canada and Newfoundland, Australia and New Zealand, and South Africa (2nd ed. 1963). Some of the regional volumes, however, are now so dated as to rank as works chiefly of historiographical interest. In the predominantly imperial category are also to be included Lord Elton, *Imperial Commonwealth*, London, 1945; some

274

mainly narrative histories, of which Professor E. A. Walker's *The British Empire: Its Structure and Spirit* (2nd ed.), Cambridge, 1953; Paul Knaplund, *The British Empire 1815–1939*, London, 1942; A. P. Newton, *A Hundred Years of the British Empire*, London, 1940, B. Porter, *The Lion's Share. A Short History of British Imperialism, 1850–1970*, London, 1975, should be mentioned, and also works devoted either mainly or in some considerable part to analysis of ideas notably Sir Ernest Barker, *Ideas and Ideals of the British Empire*, Cambridge, 1951; John Strachey's *End of Empire*, London, 1959; A. P. Thornton's *The Imperial Idea and its Enemies* (2nd ed.), London, 1966; R. Koebner and H. D. Schmidt's *Imperialism, The Story and Significance of a Political Word, 1840–1960*, Cambridge, 1964, a study in semantics not limited to 'Empire' in British history; C. A. Bodelsen's *Studies in Mid-Victorian Imperialism*, Copenhagen, 1924; B. Porter, *Critics of Empire*, London, 1968; M. Beloff, *Imperial Sunset*, vol. 1, *Britain's Liberal Empire 1897–1921*, London, 1969 and R. Hyam, *Britain's Imperial Century 1815–1914*, London, 1976 and to these may be added four articles, D. G. Creighton, 'The Victorians and the Empire' in *The Canadian Historical Review*, vol. xix (1938); John Gallagher and Ronald Robinson, 'The Imperialism of Free Trade' in *The Economic History Review*, vol. vi, no. 1 (1953); W. K. Hancock, 'Agenda for the Study of British Imperial Economy 1850–1950' in *The Journal of Economic History*, vol. xiii no. 3 (1953); and D. K. Fieldhouse, ' "Imperialism": An Historiographical Revision' in *The Economic History Review*, vol. xiv (1961).

In the second, and more immediately relevant Commonwealth category, there is Professor F. H. Underhill's brief but incisive lecture review in *The British Commonwealth, An Experiment in Cooperation among Nations*, Durham N. C., 1956 and W. D. McIntyre's comprehensive *The Commonwealth of Nations. Origins and Impact 1869–1971*, Minneapolis, 1977, its value enhanced by its distinctive antipodean perspective. For the earlier, formative years there are studies of historical and historiographical significance which, in whole or more often in part, throw light upon the developments which ultimately led to the emergence by name of a British Commonwealth of Nations. Among the more importance of these, taking Sir C. P. Lucas (ed.), *Lord Durham's Report on the Affairs of British North America* (3 vols), Oxford, 1912, or Sir R. Coupland, *The Durham Report*, Oxford, 1945, as a starting-point, were Charles Buller, *Responsible Government for Colonies*, London, 1840; E. G. Wakefield, *A View of the Art of Colonization*, London, 1849; Goldwin Smith, *The Empire: A Series of Letters 1862–3*, London, 1863; J. R. Seeley, *The Expansion of England*, London, 1883 (with which D. Wormell, *Sir John Seeley and the Uses of History*, Cambridge, 1980, may usefully be read); J. A. Froude, *Oceana: Or, England and Her Colonies*, London, 1886; C. W. Dilke, *Problems of Greater Britain*, London 1890; J. A. Hobson, *Imperialism: A Study*, London, 1902 (5th imp. 1954); R. Jebb, *Studies in Colonial Nationalism*, London, 1905; L. C. Curtis, *The Problem of Commonwealth*, London, 1916; H. Bourassa, *Independence or Imperial Partnership? A Study of the 'Problems of the Commonwealth'*, Montreal, 1916. Of later date, but still relevant to the earlier period are J. E. Kendle, *The Round Table Movement and Imperial Union*, Toronto, 1975; H. Duncan Hall, *The British Commonwealth of Nations*, London, 1920; and A. Zimmern, *The Third British Empire*, London, 1926.

For the Commonwealth in being, the publication of Professor W. K. Hancock's *Survey of British Commonwealth Affairs*, vol. 1, *Problems of Nationality, 1918–1936*, Oxford, 1937, heralded a new phase in Commonwealth historiography. It was followed by the same author's *Survey*, vol. 2 (in two parts), Oxford, 1942, on *Problems of Economic Policy*. The series was continued first with N. Mansergh's two volumes subtitled, *Problems of External Policy 1931–1939* and *Problems of Wartime*

Cooperation and Post-War Change 1939–1952 (Oxford, 1952 and 1958 respectively) and then with J. D. B. Miller's *Survey of Commonwealth Affairs, Problems of Expansion and Attrition 1953–1969* (Oxford, 1974) covering the later period. To these should be added H. D. Hall's *The Commonwealth: The History of the British Commonwealth of Nations*, New York and London, 1971, a study in depth of the development of the old dominions and N. Hillmer and P. Wigley, editors, *The First British Commonwealth*, London, 1980. Imperial preferences, the reason for their adoption at the Ottawa Conference and some of their consequences are analysed in I. M. Drummond, *British Economic Policy and the Empire, 1919–1939*, London, 1972. In more recent years there has been evidence of lively appraisal and reappraisal of familiar themes or topics. For the period as a whole there is to be noted a series of critical essays by R. Hyam and G. W. Martin entitled *Reappraisals in British Imperial History*, London, 1975, while on the opening phase there is Martin's *critique* of Durham, *The Durham Report and British Policy*, London, 1972, and J. M. Ward's widely ranging revisionist study of *Colonial Self-Government*, London, 1976.

There has also been some shift in emphasis from comprehensive to regional, national and local studies, for which, however, the Commonwealth has continued to provide the setting. A selection of these works may be conveniently listed later under their regional or national headings.

The principal printed source material for the study of the history of the Commonwealth is to be found in the Reports of Colonial and Imperial Conferences and of Meetings of Commonwealth Prime Ministers and Heads of State; in the Parliamentary Debates and State Papers of Commonwealth member-states and in the Reports of particular Constitutional Conferences, and in selected series of official documents on external policy published by individual Commonwealth governments – e.g. by the Australian government on *Australian Foreign Policy* and the British government on the *Transfer of Power in India* the details of which are listed under the countries with which they are chiefly concerned. Unpublished sources are rich and varied. On the British side are the official records of the relevant departments of state: the Colonial Office, the India Office (where those relating to the 'transfer' years 1942–7 are however being published), the Dominions Office, later renamed the Commonwealth Relations and the Commonwealth Office and by 1966, responsible for relations with all member-states or territories of the Commonwealth, the Minutes of the Committee of Imperial Defence from its inception and Cabinet Papers and Minutes relating to Commonwealth issues. To these should be added Minutes of Imperial Conferences and, for the period 1917–9, those of the Imperial War Cabinet and British Empire Delegation to Paris. *The Records of the Cabinet Office to 1922*, Public Record Office Handbooks, no. 11, London, H.M.S.O., 1966, provides a valuable guide to Cabinet, Imperial War Cabinet, Imperial Conference and C.I.D. papers. The records of the inter-war Imperial Conferences down to and including those of the 1937 Conference have been consulted on important issues in the writing of this book, and are listed with the Cabinet Papers in the Public Record Office in London. These British official records, now available for inspection after thirty years, have their counterpart in the records of the dominions, of the Government of India down to 1947 and of member states of the Commonwealth. There is no uniformity in respect of the 'closed' period. Dominion records on Commonwealth relations in the earlier period are usually on the files of Prime Ministers' Offices, since even after the creation of departments of external affairs, the more important or delicate issues of Commonwealth policy remained under prime ministerial control. This unpublished official material is supplemented by collections of Private Papers, published or unpublished, among those consulted in the writing of this book being the papers of Sir Wilfrid Laurier, Sir Robert Borden and W. L. Mackenzie King (down to 1922), together with the published *The Mackenzie King Record 1939–1948*, Toronto, 1960–1970, 4 volumes edited by J. W. Pickersgill and D. F. Forster and based on Mackenzie King's diary entries, in Canada; those of J. X. Merriman, J. C. Smuts, as edited by W. K. Hancock and J. van der Poel and published in *Selections from the Smuts Papers* (7 vols), Cambridge 1966–73 and Sir Patrick Duncan in South Africa; of the Viscount Bruce of Melbourne, for the years 1939–45 and of Sir Tej Bahadur Sapru, on particular points; on the British side, those of W. E. Gladstone, Sir Henry Campbell-Bannerman and C. R. Attlee.

Especially welcome in comparatively recent years has been the publication of autobiographies and biographies of outstanding Commonwealth interest. Among the former may be mentioned W. M. Hughes, *The Splendid Adventure*, London, 1929; Jawaharlal Nehru, *Autobiography*, London, 1936; Wavell, *The Viceroy's Journal*, edited by Penderel Moon, Oxford, 1973; Maulana Azad, *India Wins Freedom*, Bombay, 1959; Vincent Massey, *What's Past is Prologue*, Toronto, 1963, with its account, by no means uncritical, of diplomatic service under Mackenzie King's suspicious eye; Sir Robert Menzies, *Afternoon Light*, London, 1967; L. S. Amery, *My Political Life* (2 vols), vol. 2, *War and Peace*, London, 1953; Lester Pearson, '*Mike' The Memoirs of the Right Honourable Lester Pearson* (3 vols), vol. I, 1897–1948, vol. II, 1948–57, vol. III, 1957–68, London, 1973–5, the second volume being of the greatest interest in a Commonwealth context; and, from a distinctive standpoint, Sir Roy Welensky, *Welensky's 4000 Days*, London, 1964. Among the biographies should be listed D. G. Creighton, *John A. Macdonald* (2 vols), Toronto, 1952 and 1955; J. Schull, *Laurier*, Toronto, 1965; J. A. La Nauze, *Alfred Deakin* (2 vols), Melbourne, 1965; L. F. Fitzhardinge, *William Morris Hughes*, 2 vols., Sydney 1964 and 1979; C. M. van den Heever, *General J. B. M. Hertzog*, Johannesburg, 1946; W. K. Hancock, *Smuts* (2 vols), Cambridge, 1962 and 1968 and 7 volumes of Papers, the first four edited by W. K. Hancock and J. van der Poel and the last three by Dr van der Poel alone, all under the title of *Selections from the Smuts Papers* (Cambridge, 1966 and 1973 respectively); Alan Paton, *Hofmeyr*, Cape Town, 1964, movingly illustrative of the problems of a liberal in a racially divided society; R. MacGregor Dawson and H. B. Neatby, *William Lyon Mackenzie King* (3 vols), Toronto, 1958, 1963 and 1976, Dawson's volume covering the years 1874–1923, Neatby's two volumes 1924–39 and already mentioned, J. W. Pickersgill, *The Mackenzie King Record 1939–49* (4 vols in all); Dale Thomson, *Louis St Laurent*, Toronto, 1967; J. English and J. O. Stubbs, eds, *Mackenzie King. Widening the Debate*, Toronto, 1971, with its comprehensive bibliography; K. Sinclair, *Biography of Walter Nash*, Auckland, 1976; T. de V. White, *Kevin O'Higgins*, London, 1948; Earl of Longford and J. P. O'Neill, *Eamon de Valera*, London, 1970; B. R. Nanda, *Gokhale. The Indian Moderates and the British Raj*, Delhi, 1977; S. Gopal, *The Viceroyalty of Lord Irwin 1926–1931*, Oxford, 1957; Lord Glendevon, *The Viceroy at Bay. Lord Linlithgow in India 1936–43*, London, 1971; M. Brecher, *Nehru, A Political Biography*, London, 1959, B. N. Pandey, *Nehru*, London, 1976; S. Gopal, *Jawaharlal Nehru. A Biography*, vol. 1, 1889–1947, vol. II, 1947–1956, 1975 & 1979; M. A. H. Ispahani, *Qaid-E-Azam Jinnah, As I Knew Him* (2nd ed.), Karachi, 1967; and in a rather different category with the Commonwealth seen, so to speak, from its symbolic apex, Harold Nicolson's *King George V*, London, 1952, especially chapters 21, 28 and 29, and Sir John Wheeler-Bennett's *King George VI*, London, 1958, especially chapter 11. Au-

tobiographies, or biographies, of leading British statesmen, Churchill very much
included with them, usually contain material of Commonwealth interest. Of major
importance and full of insights into the actual working of the British-dominion
relationship is S. W. Roskill's biography of *Hankey – Man of Secrets*, 3 vols, London,
1970–74.

There are three periodicals devoted mainly or wholly to Commonwealth
affairs – *The Journal of Imperial and Commonwealth History*, *The Round Table*
(1910–81) and *The Journal of Commonwealth and Comparative Politics*. The *Annual
Register* year by year provides a near-contemporary record of Commonwealth
developments.

Selections of the more important documents and speeches of general Commonwealth interest have been published in a number of volumes. G. Bennett, *The
Concept of Empire, From Burke to Attlee* (2nd ed.), London, 1962, provides with
convenient compactness an historical documentary background to changing
ideas. The more important texts of Commonwealth interest are to be found in:-

K. N. Bell and W. P. Morrell, *Select Documents on British Colonial Policy, 1830–1860*,
Oxford, 1953.
A. B. Keith, *Speeches and Documents on British Colonial Policy 1763–1917*, Oxford,
1948.
A. B. Keith, *Speeches and Documents on the British Dominions 1918–31*, Oxford, 1932.
I. M. Cumpston (ed.), *The Growth of the British Commonwealth*, London, 1973.
A. F. Madden, *Imperial Constitutional Documents 1756–1952. A Supplement*, Oxford,
1953.
M. Ollivier, *The Colonial and Imperial Conferences from 1887–1937* (3 vols),
Ottawa, 1954.
N. Mansergh, *Speeches and Documents on British Commonwealth Affairs 1931–1952*
(2 vols), Oxford, 1953, and *Speeches and Documents on Commonwealth Affairs
1952–62*, Oxford, 1963.
J. Eayrs, *The Commonwealth and Suez*, Oxford, 1964.

There are also collections of more general interest relating to particular
countries. Mention may be made of:

Canada   *Historical Documents of Canada*. General Editor, C. P. Stacey, to be
published in six volumes, vol. v *The Arts of Peace and War*, Parts I & VIII especially,
(edited by C. P. Stacey), published Toronto, 1972.
Australia   *Documents on Australian Foreign Policy 1939–49*, (eds) R. G. Neale *et al.*
Canberra, 1975.
India   C. H. Philips, *The Evolution of India and Pakistan 1858–1945*, Select
Documents, London, 1962.
Sir M. Gwyer and A. Appadorai, *Speeches and Documents on the Indian Constitution
1921–47*, (2 vols), Bombay, 1957.
Constitutional Relations between Britain and India, The Transfer of Power 1942–7,
London, 1970–   , the first four volumes edited by N. Mansergh and E. W. R.
Lumby, Vol. v–   by N. Mansergh and Sir Penderel Moon.
Burma   A documentary series on Burma's attainment of independence, edited by
Professor H. Tinker is to be published by HMSO, 1982–

The working and constitutional development of the Commonwealth has
attracted the interest of students of administration and more especially of
constitutional historians and lawyers. On both there is much useful information to
be found in the annual official publication known successively, in accord with

changes in departmental nomenclature, as *The Dominions Office List, The Commonwealth Relations Office Year Book*, and from 1967, with the absorption of the Colonial Office, *The Commonwealth Office Year Book*, recent and much expanded issues being especially valuable. On the working of the system, H. J. Harvey, *Consultation and Co-operation*, London, 1951, is useful for reference. J. A. Cross, *Whitehall and the Commonwealth*, London, 1967, sets out concisely the history of departmental responsibility in London for relations with the Commonwealth overseas, while R. Hyam in *Elgin and Churchill at the Colonial office 1905–8: The Watershed of Empire-Commonwealth*, London, 1968, provides a study in depth of the outlook and working of the Colonial Office in some critical years. J. E. Kendle has made a recent study of *The Colonial and Imperial Conferences 1887–1911*, London, 1967. A full, authoritative and also first comprehensive account of the role of the Dominions, later the Commonwealth Relations Office, which became a separate Department of State in 1925, carrying responsibility for relations with the Dominion governments from that date until 1968 and for the organisation of Imperial Conferences and Prime Minister-Heads of State Meetings until the creation of a Commonwealth Secretariat in 1965, has been written by Lord Garner, who served in the Office for the greater part of the period and as Permanent Under-Secretary at the Commonwealth Office and Head of the Diplomatic Service 1965–8, prepared the way for the merger of the Commonwealth and Foreign Office in 1968, under the title *The Commonwealth Office, 1925–68*, London 1978. On the constitutional side, reflected as it was apt to be in working practice, Professor A. B. Keith, whose Minutes, as a Colonial Office official, on the restoration of self-government to the former Boer republics and on other constitutional questions may be read with difficulty but studied with profit, later made a formidable contribution in a number of books, his *Responsible Government in the Dominions* (2nd ed., 2 vols), London, 1928, being the standard work of the period. Also useful is R. MacG. Dawson (ed.), *The Development of Dominion Status 1900–1936*, London, 1937, a constitutional history in the form of a commentary upon documents reprinted in the second half of the book. For the later period the authoritative study is K. C. Wheare's *The Statute of Westminster and Dominion Status* (5th ed.), Oxford, 1953. The same author's *The Constitutional Structure of the Commonwealth*, Oxford, 1960, treats of developments in the post-Statute of Westminster period, as does S. A. de Smith's *The New Commonwealth and its Constitutions*, London, 1964, in the more particular context indicated by the title. W. I. Jennings and C. M. Young, *Constitutional Laws of the Commonwealth* (3rd ed.), London, 1957, vol. 1, *The Monarchies* (vol. 2, on *The Republics* has not been published) provides commentary and essential texts, while G. Marshall, *Parliamentary Sovereignty and the Commonwealth*, Oxford, 1957, uses South Africa as a test case, in a legal-constitutional enquiry into the effects of the enactment of the Statute of Westminster on the authority of the British and dominion parliaments. There is further G. W. Keeton's (ed.), *The British Commonwealth, The Development of its Laws and Constitutions*, London, 1951–, of which fourteen volumes have been published and which was intended as a series, to be comprehensive on a national basis – an intention which in view of the rapid constitutional changes, or transformations, in some member-states must seem more difficult of satisfactory fulfilment now than when first adopted. *Commonwealth and Colonial Law*, London, 1966, by Sir Kenneth Roberts-Wray, the former legal adviser to the Commonwealth Relations and Colonial Offices pronounces, with the authority of experience, on many matters at once complex and important. Of continuing interest is the last chapter in L. S. Amery's *Thoughts on the Constitution*, Oxford, 1953.

Government in the Commonwealth has inspired a number of comparative studies. Outstanding among them are Alexander Brady's *Democracy in the Dominions* (3rd ed.), Toronto, 1958; and K. C. Wheare's *Federal Government* (4th ed.) London, 1968, which, while analysing federalism in general, pays much attention to federations within the Commonwealth, as was in some degree the case in a paper prepared by J. Bardach in collaboration with H. Izdebski on *L'état fédéral et le principe fédératif en histoire* for the xvth International Congress of Historical Sciences 1980 (Rapports pp. 237–91). To these should be added A. H. Birch, *Federalism, Finance and Social Legislation in Canada, Australia and the United States*, Oxford, 1955; and W. S. Livingston's cogently argued *Federalism and Constitutional Change*, Oxford, 1956. Reference should be made also to two works by Sir Ivor Jennings, *The Commonwealth in Asia*, Oxford, 1951, and *The Dominion of Ceylon – The Development of its Laws and Constitution*, Oxford, 1952, compiled from the vantage point of the vice-chancellor's residence in Colombo and with personal contribution to Ceylon's advance to independence.

War and international relations have much preoccupied the Commonwealth since the coming of the first world war and have received due attention from its historians. In respect of defence policies three general works may be mentioned: D. C. Gordon, *The Dominion Partnership in Imperial Defence 1870–1914*, Johns Hopkins, 1965; F. A. Johnson, *Defence by Committee*, London, 1960; and R. A. Preston, *Canada and 'Imperial Defense'*, Durham N. C., 1967; with Lord Hankey's *The Supreme Command 1914–18* (2 vols), London, 1961, written with authority and great discretion which no doubt is how he became a 'man of secrets', and now in part outdated by S. W. Roskill's biographical study to which reference has already been made. Like the United Kingdom, both Australia and New Zealand have published official histories, both civil and military, of the second world war. The Australian Civil Series comprised five volumes, with two of broad historical interest by PaulHasluck on *The Government and the People 1939–41*, Canberra, 1952 and 1970; F. L. W. Wood in *The New Zealand People at War: Political and External Affairs*, Wellington, 1958, provided the New Zealand counterpart to Hasluck's volumes. Both authors wrote with unrestricted access to official records, including War Cabinet papers. Among publications on Commonwealth and international affairs. G. M. Carter's *The British Commonwealth and International Security*, Toronto, 1947, and R. F. Holland's *Britain and the Commonwealth Alliance 1918–1939*, London, 1981, analysing policies in the light of official records, are to be noted, while of a more recent period Professor J. D. B. Miller's *The Commonwealth in the World* (2nd ed.), London, 1965, which provides a readable, general conspectus, may be supplemented by reference to individual national series, pioneered by the Canadian Institute of International Affairs, with their biennial reviews of *Canada in World Affairs*, and creating a precedent that has been followed with profit by the Australian Institute and by the Indian Council of World Affairs. These series reflect the expanding rôle of the Commonwealth states, other than Britain, in international affairs since the second world war. In *Commonwealth D'Abord*, Paris, 1955, Y. G. Brissonnière considered British Commonwealth relations with Europe from a continental standpoint and with regard to the possibility of association as distinct from membership.

The transfer of power in India and in the Colonial Empire attracted much attention, possibly overmuch in respect of its technical and ephemeral aspects, and apart from works of regional interest, some books may be mentioned as providing contemporary or near-contemporary background: H. V. Hodson, *Twentieth Century Empire*, London, 1948; R. Hinden, *Empire and After*, London, 1949;

N. Mansergh, *The Commonwealth and the Nations*, London, 1948; Sir Ivor Jennings, *The Approach of Self-Government*, Cambridge 1956, Sir Charles Jeffries, *Transfer of Power*, London, 1960; and W. B. Hamilton (ed.), *The Transfer of Institutions*, Duke, 1964. In respect of India, on British party attitudes there is Georges Fischer's *Le Parti travailliste et la décolonization de l'Inde*, Paris, 1966, and K. Veerathappa on *The British Conservative Party and Indian Independence*, Delhi, 1976. On the I.C.S. there is Philip Mason, *The Men who ruled India* (2 vols), London, 1953–54, especially vol. 2. On the conditions and circumstances of the transfer there is Sir Penderel Moon, *Divide and Quit*, London, 1962; I. M. Stephens, *Monsoon Morning*, London, 1966; A. Campbell-Johnson, *Mission with Mountbatten*, London, 1951; V. P. Menon (at the time Reforms Commissioner of the Government of India), *The Transfer of Power in India*, London, 1957; E. W. R. Lumby, *The Transfer of Power in India*, London, 1954 and H. V. Hodson, *The Great Divide; Britain – India – Pakistan*, London, 1969, all written in the light of personal experience and knowledge and Hodson's with access to the papers of Earl Mountbatten of Burma. The government and administration of former Colonial territories lies outside the scope of this bibliography, but useful for background to self-government and independence. M. Wight, *The Development of the Legislative Council, 1606–1945*, London, 1946, and *British Colonial Constitutions*, Oxford, 1952; Kenneth Robinson, *The Dilemmas of Trusteeship*, London, 1965 (a highly compressed and valuable review); R. Heussler, *Yesterday's Rulers*, Oxford, 1963; Margery Perham, *The Colonial Reckoning*, London, 1961; and, for the first-hand impressions of the last phase as seen by *The Times* correspondent in Africa, W. P. Kirkman's, *Unscrambling an Empire*, London, 1966.

Professor J. D. B. Miller's volume in the *Survey of Commonwealth Affairs* series, already alluded to, provides a comprehensive and critical analysis of the later period. Among other works on it a notable place is to be given to *The Commonwealth*, London, 1962, by Patrick Gordon Walker, a former Labour Secretary of State for Commonwealth Relations and a committed supporter of the Commonwealth connection. A popular exposition is to be found in Sir Kenneth Bradley, *The Living Commonwealth*, London, 1961. There are also two collections of specialised studies by divers hands from the Commonwealth Studies Center at Duke University: N. Mansergh *et al, Commonwealth Perspectives*, Durham N. C., 1959; and W. B. Hamilton, K. Robinson and C. D. W. Goodwin (eds), *A Decade of the Commonwealth, 1955–64*, Durham N. C., 1966 and a general review by M. M. Ball, *The 'Open' Commonwealth*, Durham, N. C., 1971. The Proceedings of the Fourth Unofficial Commonwealth Relations Conference at Bigwin Inn, Ontario, 1949, provide the material for F. H. Soward's *The Changing Commonwealth*, Oxford, 1950, and the Fifth, held at Lahore in 1954, for N. Mansergh's *The Multi-Racial Commonwealth*, London, 1955. J. D. B. Miller has contributed a study of *Britain and the Old Dominions*, London, 1966, in the period of decolonisation and consequent Commonwealth expansion, and H. V. Wiseman one of *Britain and the Commonwealth*, London, 1967. Mention may also be made of three prime ministerial Smuts Memorial Lectures, Sir Robert Menzies, *The Changing Commonwealth*, Lee Kwan Yew, *The Commonwealth, a continuity of association after Empire* and Lester Pearson, *The Commonwealth 1970*, Cambridge, 1960, 1969 and 1971 respectively.

Finally a small selection from works of regional or national interest may be listed as providing an all-important counterbalance to more widely ranging over-all Commonwealth studies and also as an indication of the contemporary and often remarkable growth of historical studies in many parts of the Commonwealth overseas. Each list is prefaced by one or two general works and some include studies read by the author, but not yet published. Other books which have been consulted are listed in the footnotes to each chapter.

CANADA

G. S. Graham, *Canada*, London, 1950.
J. M. S. Careless, *Canada. A Story of Challenge*, Cambridge, 1953.
D. G. Creighton, *Dominion of the North* (2nd ed.), Toronto, 1965.
A. R. M. Lower, *Colony to Nation* (4th ed.), Toronto, 1964.
P. Burroughs, *The Colonial Reformers and Canada, 1830–1849*, Toronto, 1969.
P. Burroughs, *The Canadian Crisis 1828–1841*, London, 1972.
Chester New, *Lord Durham's Mission to Canada*, Oxford, 1929 rpt. Toronto, 1963.
D. G. Creighton, *The Road to Confederation 1863–67*, Toronto, 1964.
P. B. Waite (ed.), *The Confederation Debates on the Province of Canada 1865*, Toronto, 1968.
D. M. L. Farr, *The Colonial Office and Canada, 1867–1887*, Toronto, 1956.
G. P. de T. Glazebrook, *A History of Canadian External Relations*, Toronto, 1950.
P. G. Wigley, *Canada and the Transition to Commonwealth, British–Canadian Relations, 1917–1926*, Cambridge, 1977.
James Eayrs, *In Defense of Canada* (2 vols), Toronto, 1964; vol. 2, especially throws light on Commonwealth international policies in the period of appeasement.
F. M. Wade, *The French Canadians, 1760–1945*, Toronto, 1956.

AUSTRALIA AND NEW ZEALAND

C. M. H. Clark (ed.), *Select Documents in Australian History* (2 vols), Sydney, 1950 and 1955.
J. M. Ward, *Empire in the Antipodes*, London, 1966.
A. G. L. Shaw, *Convicts and the Colonies*, 1966.
G. Greenwood (ed.), *Australia: A Social and Political History*, Sydney, 1955.
T. R. Reese, *Australia in the Twentieth Century*, London, 1964.
D. Pike, *Australia: The Quiet Continent*, Cambridge, 1962.
Alfred Deakin, *The Federal Story* (revised ed. by J. A. La Nauze), Melbourne, 1963.
J. D. B. Miller, *Australian Government and Politics* (2nd ed.), London, 1965.
L. F. Crisp, *The Parliamentary Government of the Commonwealth of Australia* (rev. ed.), London, 1961.
L. F. Crisp, *Australian National Government*, 4th ed. Melbourne, 1978.
P. Hasluck, *The Office of Governor-General*, Melbourne, 1979.
G. Sawer, *Australian Government Today* (revised ed.), Melbourne, 1964.
J. C. Beaglehole, *New Zealand*, London, 1936.
W. P. Reeves, *The Long White Cloud*, London, 1898.
F. L. W. Wood, *Understanding New Zealand*, New York, 1949.
H. Miller, *New Zealand*, London, 1950.
K. Sinclair, *A History of New Zealand* (2nd ed.), London, 1961.
K. Sinclair, *The Origins of the Maori Wars*, Wellington, 1957, and *Imperial Federation. A Study of New Zealand Policy and Opinion 1880–1914*, London, 1955.
Angus Ross, *New Zealand Aspirations in the Pacific in the Nineteenth-Century*, Oxford, 1964.

A. Siegfried, *Democracy in New Zealand*, London, 1914.
C. G. F. Simkin, *The Instability of a Dependent Economy 1840–1914*, Oxford, 1951.

AFRICA

J. Gallagher and R. E. Robinson, *Africa and the Victorians*, London, 1961.
C. W. de Kiewiet, *A History of South Africa: Social and Economic*, Oxford, 1946.
E. A. Walker, *A History of Southern Africa* (3rd ed.), London, 1957.
L. M. Thompson and M. Wilson (eds.), *The Oxford History of South Africa* (2 vols.), Oxford, 1969–71.
J. S. Galbraith, *Reluctant Empire: British Policy on the South African Frontier, 1834–1854*, Berkeley, 1963.
F. A. van Jaarsveld, *The Awakening of Afrikaner Nationalism 1868–1881*, Cape Town, 1961.
C. W. de Kiewiet, *The Imperial Factor in South Africa*, Cambridge, 1937.
C. F. Goodfellow, *Great Britain and South African Confederation*, Cape Town, 1966.
G. H. Le May, *British Supremacy in South Africa, 1899–1907*, Oxford, 1965.
Jean van der Poel, *The Jameson Raid*, Cape Town, 1951.*
Elizabeth Pakenham, *Jameson's Raid*, London, 1960.*
T. Pakenham, *The Boer War*, London, 1979.
J. S. Marais, *The Fall of Kruger's Republic*, Oxford, 1961.
G. B. Pyrah, *Imperial Policy and South Africa, 1902–1910*, Oxford, 1955.
D. Denoon, *A Grand Illusion. The Failure of Imperial Policy in the Transvaal Colony during the Period of Reconstruction 1900–1905*, London, 1973.
N. Mansergh, *South Africa 1906–1961; The Price of Magnanimity*, London, 1962.
L. M. Thompson, *The Unification of South Africa 1902–1910*, Oxford, 1960.
G. M. Carter, *The Politics of Inequality*, New York, 1958.
D. W. Krüger, *South African Parties and Policies, 1910–1960*, Cape Town, 1960.
Albert Luthuli, *Let my People Go*, London, 1962.
Frank Hayes, 'South Africa's Departure from the Commonwealth 1960–61', in *The International History Review*, vol. II, no. 3 (July 1980) describes the development of Canadian attitudes and policies.
Dennis Austin, *Britain and South Africa*, London, 1966.
R. Hyam, *The Failure of South African Expansion 1908–1948*, London, 1972.
A. J. Hanna, *The Beginnings of Nyasaland and North-Eastern Rhodesia 1859–95*, Oxford, 1956.
P. Mason, *Birth of a Dilemma*, London, 1958.
M. Chanock, *Unconsummated Union. Britain, Rhodesia and South Africa 1900–1945*, Manchester, 1977.
Colin Leys, *European Politics in Southern Rhodesia*, Oxford, 1959.
L. H. Gann, *The Birth of a Plural Society*, Manchester, 1958.
C. Palley, *The Constitutional History and Law of Southern Rhodesia*, Oxford, 1966.
D. A. Low and A. Smith, editors, *History of East Africa*, Vol. 111, Oxford, 1976.
J. Iliffe, *A Modern History of Tanganyika*, Cambridge, 1979.

---

* To these two books should be added Dr Ethel M. Drus' articles in the Bulletin of the Institute of Historical Research 1952, vol. XXV and in the E.H.R. October 1953 vol. lxviii, *A Report on the Papers of Joseph Chamberlain, relating to the Jameson Raid, and the Inquiry* and *The Question of Imperial Complicity in the Jameson Raid* respectively. It is a curious fact that the Jameson raid, which on any reckoning was an altogether manly affair should have attracted so much attention from women historians.

J. D. Fage, *An Introduction to the History of West Africa* (3rd ed.), Cambridge, 1962.
J. E. Flint, *Nigeria and Ghana*, New York, 1966.
C. W. Newbury, *The West African Commonwealth*, Duke, N. C., 1964.
Dennis Austin *Politics in Ghana, 1946–1960*, London, 1964.

IRELAND

J. C. Beckett, *The Making of Modern Ireland 1603–1923*, London, 1966.
F. S. L. Lyons, *Ireland since the Famine*, London, 1971.
N. Mansergh, *The Irish Question, 1840–1921*, London, 1965.
J. A. Murphy, *Ireland in the Twentieth Century*, Dublin, 1975.
D. G. Boyce, *Englishmen and Irish Troubles, 1918–1922*, Cambridge, Mass., 1972.
Charles Townshend, *The British Campaign in Ireland, 1919–1921*, Oxford, 1975.
Thomas Jones, *Whitehall Diary*, edited by K. Middlemas, 3 vols, Oxford, 1969–71,
  vol. III, *Ireland*.
F. A. Pakenham, *Peace by Ordeal*, London, 1935.
D. Williams (ed.), *The Irish Struggle 1916–1922*, London, 1966.
D. Harkness, *The Irish Free State and the British Commonwealth of Nations, 1921–32*,
  London, 1968.
J. J. Carroll, *Ireland in the War Years and After*, New York, 1973.
Irish Historiography 1936–70, edited by T. W. Moody, Dublin, 1971 for the Irish
  Committee of Historical Sciences, provides a critical record of publications for
  the modern as well as earlier periods.

SOUTH AND SOUTH-EAST ASIA

C. H. Philips, *India*, London, 1949.
T. G. P. Spear, *India*, Michigan, 1961.
K. M. Panikkar, *Asia and Western Dominance*, London, 1953.
E. Stokes, *The English Utilitarians and India*, Oxford, 1959.
S. Gopal, *British Policy in India 1858–1905*, Cambridge, 1965.
R. J. Moore, *Liberalism and Indian Politics 1872–1922*, London, 1966.
S. R. Mehrotra, *The Emergence of the Indian National Congress*, Delhi, 1971.
J. M. Brown, *Gandhi and Civil Disobedience. The Mahatma in Indian Politics*,
  Cambridge, 1977.
B. R. Tomlinson, *The Indian National Congress and the Raj 1929–42*, London, 1976.
J. Gallagher, G. Johnson and A. Seal, *Locality, Province, Nation. Essays on Indian
  Politics 1870–1940*, Cambridge, 1973.
R. J. Moore, *The Crisis of Indian Unity, 1917–1940*, Oxford, 1974.
R. J. Moore, *Churchill, Cripps and India 1939–1945*, Oxford, 1979.
C. H. Philips and M. D. Wainwright, editors, *The Partition of India: Policies and
  Perspectives 1935–1947*, London, 1970.
N. Mansergh, *The Prelude to Partition: Concepts and Aims in Ireland and India*,
  Cambridge, 1978 (Smuts Memorial Lecture).
R. J. Moore, Recent Historical Writing on the Modern British Empire and
  Commonwealth. Later Imperial India, *Journal of Imperial and Commonwealth
  History*, vol. 4, no. 1, 1975 comments on the 'explosive' volume of writing in this
  field.
Sir R. Coupland, *India: A Restatement*, Oxford, 1945.
Sir P. Griffith, *The British Impact on India*, London, 1952.

J. Nehru, *The Discovery of India*, London, 1946.
H. Tinker, *Experiment with Freedom: India and Pakistan 1947*, London, 1967.
W. H. Morris-Jones, *Parliament in India* (2nd ed.), London, 1965.
R. Symonds, *The Making of Pakistan* (3rd ed.), London, 1951.
G. W. Choudhury, *Pakistan's Relations with India 1947–1966*, London, 1968.
I. M. Stephens, *Pakistan*, London, 1963.
S. R. Mehrotra, *India and the Commonwealth, 1885–1929*, London, 1965.
B. H. Farmer, *Ceylon: A Divided Nation*, London, 1963.
H. Tinker, *The Union of Burma* (4th ed.), Oxford, 1967.

UNPUBLISHED CAMBRIDGE UNIVERSITY PH.D DISSERTATIONS

M. N. Lettice, *Anglo–Australian Relations 1901–1914. A Study at the Official Level.*
M. Hasan, *The Transfer of Power to Pakistan and its Consequences.*
N. Hillmer, *Anglo–Canadian Relations*, 1926–1937. See also Dr Hillmer's articles within this theme: 'A British High Commissioner for Canada 1927–8' in the *Journal of Imperial and Commonwealth History*, vol. 1, no. 3 (May 1973) and 'The Anglo–Dominion Alliance 1919–1939' in *Rapports II, Chronologie*, XVᵉ Congrès International des Sciences Historiques, pp. 538–551.
D. McMahon, *Anglo–Irish Relations 1932–38.*

Index

Abyssinia, 74; Anglo-Dominion policies in crisis (1935), 76–80; 93
Accra, see Commonwealth Economic Consultative Council
Adams, Sir Grantley, 179
Addison, Lord, 150
Adefobe, Major General, 199
Africa: avoidance of war in, 72, 75; 97, 146; Commonwealth membership in, 144, 162, 169; political transformation of, 173–5, 177–8; 'wind of change in', 176; 181–2; underlying dilemma for British policy – making in, 183; the African Commonwealth and Rhodesia, 190–1, 193–4, 198–9; 240–1; suitability of British parliamentary institutions in, 244–5; 247, 249–50
Africa, Central, the Federation of, 179–83, 187; see also Rhodesia
Africa, East, 80, 93, 239, 242
Africa, North, 93
Africa, South, 12; and Locarno, 20; and defining of Commonwealth relations, 21–2, 23–5; Hertzog's initiative in 1926, 25–7; and Balfour Report and Statue of Westminster, 28, 32–3; Status of the Union Act (1934), 33–4, 37; 43, 65; concern to keep European warfare out of Africa, 72–5; Fusion government and policy of 'South Africa first', 82–3; the Smuts–Hertzog compact on non-belligerency, September 1938, 86–7; divided on participation in war, 91–3; casualties in second world war 94; 97–8, 112, 135, 144, 146, 157–8; 'the wind of change' in Africa, 175–6; republican membership and withdrawal from Commonwealth of,

184–7; 193, 195, 198, 217, 238–9, 246
Africa, South-West, 212, 239
Africa, West, 194–5, 239
Afrikaners, the, 18, 33, 43–4, 181
Ahmadnagar Fort, 227
Alexander, A. V. (later earl), 109
Alexander of Tunis (1st earl), Field Marshal, 140
Ali Mohammad, 43–4
Ambedkar, B. R., 130
American War of Independence, 188
Amery, L. S., colonial secretary (1924–9, also dominions secretary from 1925), 19, 21, 23; and Imperial Conference (1926), 24, 26; 31, 39, 46, 89, 94; secretary of state for India (1940–5), 107; 202, 210
Aney, M. S., 147
Anglo–Irish Treaty (1921), 9, 34, 65, 201
Angola, 199
Anti–Fascist People's Freedom League, 149
appeasement, policy of, 76, 79–80, 82–3, 86, 88–90, 210, 218, 228
Asia, 44, 53; Inter-Asian Conference (1947), 145–6; 'Asia for the Asiatics', 148–9; first attendance of prime ministers of Asian dominions at Commonwealth Conference (1948), 151; 155–6, 162–5; regional alliances extended to, 168; policy of non-alignment in, 169; Asian reactions to Suez crisis, 171; Asian membership of Commonwealth precedes African, 173–4; decolonisation in south-east Asia, 175–8, 183; influence of Asian membership, 239–41; 244, 247, 249

286

Asquith, H. H. (1st earl of Oxford and Asquith), 7, 122, 218, 220
Assam, 122
Athlone, earl of, 224
Attlee, Clement (later first earl), appeal to Durham and Canadian precedent (1942), 107; introduces Indian Independence Act (1947), 111–12; 129, 140, 146; and Indian republican membership, 152–3, 155
'August offer', 106–7, 116, 120
Aung San, 148–9
Australia: and Chanak incident, 10–12; 22, 24; first Australian-born governor-general, 30; and Balfour Report and Statue of Westminster, 32; 34; and abdication of Edward VIII, 36–7; and Ottawa agreements, 40–2, 43, 65; sense of vulnerability in and attitude to sanctions of, 72–3, 75, 78–9; her faith in British naval supremacy shaken, 80–1; and Sudeten and Czech crises, 83–4, 86–8; and second world war 91, 93, casualties in, 94; representation of, in British war cabinet, 98–100; drawn into US strategic orbit after Pearl Harbour, 100–1; 135; attitude to republican Ireland, 143; and India's republican membership, 155, 157–8; relations with USA and SEATO (1954), 165, 168; and Suez crisis, 172–3; 179–80; and Rhodesia, 191–2, 199; and Britain's membership of EEC, 195; 217, 237–9; Sir Robert Menzies' vision of Empire and Commonwealth, 253
Austria – Hungary, the *Ausgleich* of 1867, 46
Azad, Maulana A. K., 118; challenges formation of one-party provincial governments (1937), 119; 122; favours deferment of independence in interests of unity, 126–7

Baghdad Pact (1955), 168
Baldev Singh, 111
Baldwin, Stanley (1st earl), 19; and abdication crisis, 36–7; and imperial trade, 38–9; 65, 89, 160
Balewa, Sir Abubakar Tafawa, 190, 202

Balfour, A. J., 1st earl of, presides over Imperial Conference (1926), 24, 27–8; 47, 49, 72, 202
Balfour of Burleigh, Lord, 38
Balfour Report, the, 27–9; 'took stock of everything', 32; 43, 64, 66, 72, 93, 137, 154–5
Baluchistan, 122
Balzac, Honoré de, quoted, 55
Bandaranaike, Mrs, 186, 202
Bandung Conference (1954), 231
Bangladesh, 131
Barbados, 175
Basutoland (Lesotho), independence (1966), 174
Bechuanaland (Botswana), independence (1966), 174
Belgium, 210
Benes, President E., 84
Bengal, 56; first partition of (1905–11), 60–1; the transfer of power and, 118, 122–3, 125; East Bengal becomes Bangladesh, 131; 153
Bennett, R. B., (later Lord), 39–40, 42, 220
Berlin, 81
Bihar, 147
Birkenhead, 2nd earl of, 225
Boers, the, 112, 207, 238–9
Bombay, 45, 115, 148
Borden, Sir Robert, 7, 202
Botha, General Louis, 103, 208
Botswana, *see* Bechuanaland
Bright, John, 207, 220
British Commonwealth Air Training plan, 93
British North America, 237
British North America Act, 31–3; and patriation, 33, 43
British South Africa Company, 180
Bruce, Stanley (Viscount Bruce of Melbourne), 20, 32, 78–9, 84–5, 88, 100, 138
Brussels, 42; Five Power Brussels Pact (1948), 166; Edward Heath signs Treaty of Accession in, 197
Bryce, James, 52
Burke, Edmund, 237
Burma, 146; transfer of power in, secession of, 148–9; precedent created by, 150, 160, 164

Byng, General Viscount, 14; King-Byng controversy, 22–3; 30, 32, 216

Cabinet Mission (1946), 58, 123, 126–7
Calcutta, 48; 'Great Calcutta Killing', 121
Campbell-Bannerman, Sir Henry, 56, 112, 202, 205
Canada, 5, 6; and Chanak incident, 10–12; treaty making by, 12–16; and Imperial Conference (1923) and challenge to centralising tendencies, 17–18, 38; and separateness in foreign policy of, 20–1; King-Byng controversy in, 22–3; and Imperial Conference (1926), 23, 26; and exclusion of BNA Acts under Section 7 of Statute of Westminster and patriation of constitution, 31–3; analogy of Canadian status for Ireland, 34; and abdication crisis, 36–7; and Ottawa agreements, 39–42; 43–4, 65, 72–4; and discussion of foreign affairs at Imperial Conference (1937), 78–9; and sovereignty of Parliament, 81, 91; visit of President Roosevelt to, 81–2; and Czech crisis, 83–5; attitude to participation in war of (1938), 87–8; and second world war, 91, 93 (casualties in, 94); the 'continuing conference of cabinets', 96–8; and methods of post-war cooperation, 102–3; 107; Canadian Citizenship Act (1946), 136–7; and Irish secession, 140, 142–3; and India's republican membership, 155–8; 164–7; signature of North Atlantic Treaty (1949), 167–8; and Suez crisis, 171; and republican membership of South Africa, 185; 192; and Britain's membership of EEC, 195; 238–9; André Siegfried on the Westminster model in Ottawa, 244; diplomatic representation of, 248
Canberra, 32, 75, 91, 95
Cape Colony, 34, 237
Cape Town, 175, 184
Carrington, Lord, 200
Casey, R. G. (later Lord), 131
Ceylon, 146; dominion status (1947),

149–50; 157–8, 165, 168, 170, 175, 184, 186, 192; and Soulbury Report (1945), 245–6
Chamberlain, Sir Austen, 19
Chamberlain, Joseph, 38, 44–5, 49, 202, 207, 237
Chamberlain, Neville, 39, 78, 85–6, 89–90, 95, 211, 218, 227–8
Chanak incident, the (1922), 9–12, 19, 90
Chanock, Dr M., *Unconsummated Union – Britain, Rhodesia and South Africa, 1900–45*, 181, 183
Chelmsford, Lord, 50, 63–4
Chifley, J. B., 143
China, 73, 164; Indo – Chinese Treaty on Tibet (1954), 169; 170, 179; invasions across Indian border (1962), 231
Chittagong, 56
Chou En-lai, 231
Churchill W. S. (later Sir Winston): opposed to self-government for India, 54, 68, 116; and Statute of Westminster, 71–2; on Polish guarantee (March 1939), 90; 95–7; and wartime consultation with Dominions, 97–100; and Cripps Mission to India, 107–9; 126, 163, 168, 173, 202, 221; Atlantic Meeting with President Roosevelt, 222–3
Clark, Sir William, 86, 92
Clemenceau, G., 5
Clutterbuck, Sir Alexander, 137
Cold War, the, 166
Colombo Plan, the, 249
Colonial Development and Welfare Acts, 163
Colonial Laws Validity Act (1865), 4, 23, 29
Colonial Office, the, 4; cabinet paper, *A Common Imperial Policy in Foreign Affairs* (1921), 7–9; 16; reorganisation of (1925), 19, 21; 23, 151; wound up, 176; 181, 243; and government of colonies, 244–5
Common Market, the, 144; and new economic departures, 172; 197; *see also* European Economic Community
Commonwealth Economic Consultative Council, 195–6

Commonwealth Prime Ministers' and Heads of Government Meetings: character of Meetings changed by increase in numbers, 247–8; 250; 1944, 'marked the apotheosis of Mackenzie King and all that he stood for', 102–3, 220–1; 1946, 103; 1948, and Irish secession, 142–3; representation of the three new dominions of Asia at, 151–3; 1949, settles Indian republican membership, 156–8; 1955, 173; 1961, and South African withdrawal, 184–8; 1962 and 1964, Britain assailed by African leaders on Rhodesia 188–9, 196; 1965, Commonwealth Secretariat (established 1965), 189, 247, 250; 1966, two meetings on Rhodesia (January) at Lagos, first Meeting held outside Britain, 190–1, 194; (September), 191–2

Commonwealth Relations Office, 136
Commonwealth Secretariat (established 1965), 189, 247, 250
Constantinople, 10
Corfield, Sir Conrad, 114
Corneille, Pierre, quoted, 240
Cornwallis, Lord, 49
Cosgrave, W. T., 18, 35
Costello, J. A., 140–3
Council of Europe, 145
Cranborne, Lord, 222
Creech-Jones, Arthur, 150
Cripps, Sir Stafford, his Mission to India (1942), 53, 107–9, 120, 225
Cromer, 1st earl of, 44
Crown, position of, in 1921, 3–5; 19; common allegiance and equal access to, 26–8; 30; succession to, 30–1, 34; doctrine of divisible crown, 33; oath of allegiance abolished in Irish Free State (1933), 34–6; abdication crisis, 36–7; External Relations Act (1936) and, 37; 108, 135, 137–41, 144, 147; devising new form of relationship with, 152–7; 'symbol of the free association ... Head of the Commonwealth', 158–9; variety of royal titles (1953), 160–1; 183–4
Curtin, John, 99, 102–3, 202
Curtis, Lionel, *Civitas Dei*, 71, 202, 243
Curzon, 1st Marquis of, foreign secret-ary (1920–4), 16; 44; Viceroy of India (1899–1905), 49–50, 53–4, 60–1

Cyprus, independence (1960), 175, 178, 192, 242
Czechoslovakia, 78; crisis in (1938), 83–90; 218

Dafoe, John, 102, 202
Dáil Éireann, 34, 139–41
Dalhousie, 1st Marquis of, 49, 60
Danzig, 84
Dar-es-Salaam, 242
Dawson, Geoffrey, 85, 88, 202
Dawson, Professor R. MacGregor, *William Lyon Mackenzie King 1874–1923*, 17–18
Deakin, Alfred, 189, 202
Delhi, Durbars (1903) and (1911) in, 46, 60; 56, 64, 66–7, 108, 112, 124–5, 128, 145, 159, 169
Derby, 17th earl of, 17
Devlin Commission, the, 182
Diefenbaker, John, 185–6
Dillon, James, 139
Disraeli, Benjamin (afterwards earl of Beaconsfield), 252
Dixon, Sir Charles, 152
dominion status, 3, 25; defined in Balfour Report (1926), 27–9; 'the root principle of equality' and Imperial Conference (1926), 30–1; legal effect given to, by Statute of Westminster (1931), 31–5; 43, 61–3, 66–7, 71–2; impact of, in foreign affairs, *see* foreign policy; for India, 104, 106; Cripps mission to India (1942), Cabinet mission to India (1946) and, 107–10, 116; V. P. Menon's plan and, 125–6; 'common allegiance' and republican membership, 137–40; interim expedient to ease transfer of power, 146–7, 149, 151, 154; for Ceylon, 149–50; 213, 216
Dominions Office, 19, 243
Drummond, Dr I. M., *British Economic Policy and the Empire 1919–1939*, 38
Dublin, 48
Dulanty, J. W., 76, 84–5
Dumbarton Oaks Conference, the, 135
Duncan, Sir Patrick, 92, 205–6
Durham, J. G. Lambton, 1st earl of, 107

Durham Report, the, 55, 63
Dutt, R. C., 56

East India Company, 47
Easter Rising (1916), 147
Economist, The, 171
Eden, Sir Anthony, 171–2, 227
Edward VIII, abdication of, 36–7, 138
Edwardes, Michael, quoted, 125
Egypt, 170–2
Elgin, 9th earl of, 189
Elizabeth II, 160, 199, 242
Elphinstone, Mountstuart, 53, 111–12
Empire Marketing Board, 39
European Economic Community
(EEC), 145; Commonwealth misgivings
as Britain draws closer to
Europe, 166–7, 188, 195; and reaction
to General de Gaulle's exercise
of veto (January 1963), 196; and
acquiescence by time of Britain's
entry (January 1972), 197
Evatt, Dr H. V., 135, 137
External association, formula of, 27;
precedent of, 115, 144, 149
External Relations Act (1936), 138–41

Fadden, Sir Arthur, 98–9
Federation, Central African, 179–80;
established (1953), characteristics of,
181–2; Devlin and Monckton Commissions,
182; dismantling of (1963)
and mistrust sown between settlers
and British Government, 182–3; 187
Federation, Imperial, 28
Federation, Indian, 54; attitude of
Muslim leadership to, 59, 117;
change in Muslim sentiment after
1937, 119; federation contemplated
by Government of India Act (1935),
position of princes in, federal provisions
of Act never applied, 68–9, 105
Federation, Malaysian, 177; survival of,
secession of Singapore from, 179–80
Federation, West Indian, causes of failure
of, 179
Finland, 95
first world war, 5, 8, 24, 38, 53, 62, 94,
161, 163, 240, 247
force, rôle of, legacy of Indian mutiny/
rebellion, 56–7; 72, 75, 77–9, 83;

pressure for use of in Rhodesia, 188,
190–3; Nehru and, 229–32; 'the
sword' in imperial government,
236–9
foreign policy, the rôle of the dominions
in, 7–8; concept of joint responsibility,
9; significance of Chanak incident,
10–12, 19; Canadian attitude
to, 12, 15–16; and Imperial Conference
(1923), 16–18; separate dominion
control of, 20–1, 28, 72, 93; and
the Abyssinian crisis, 76; and Imperial
Conference (1937), failure of the
League and collective security, 78–9;
Fusion government and, 82–3;
dominion attitudes to appeasement
and war, 83–9; for the post-war
world, 101–3; aims of India and
Pakistan, 146; 150; variety of postwar
problems, 165–6; meeting of
Commonwealth foreign ministers in
Colombo (1950), 167; defence pacts
(1949–54) and non-alignment,
167–70; failure to consult in Suez
crisis, 170–3
France, 55; alliance of, with Britain,
and dominions' fear of involvement
in war, 77, 82, 88; Anglo-French
guarantees (1939), 90; 93, 95, 106,
146; Anglo-French intervention at
Suez, 170–1; 210
Fraser, Malcolm, 199
Fraser, Peter, 137, 143, 202
free trade, 37–9, 145
French-Canadians, 43, 74, 238, 244
Fusion government, the, 33, 82–3,
86–7, 92, 209

Gambia, 174
Gandhi, Mrs Indira, 202
Gandhi, Mahatma M. K.: and non-violent
non-cooperation, transformation
of Congress into a mass
movement, 57; and *Swaraj* and equality,
65–6; and Government of India
Act (1935), 68; 105–6; silent acquiescence
in 'the vivisection of Mother
India', 111–13, 126–7; and the
communal problem, 114–16, 122;
125, 129, 202, 228, 230; his teaching
and the manner of achievement of

India's republican membership, 232–3

Garner, Lord, *The Commonwealth Office*, 103, 189

Garson, S. G., 33

Gaulle, General Charles de, 134, 196–7, 352

General Agreement on Trade and Tariffs GATT (1947), 142, 167

George V, 23, 30, 253

George VI, 37, 108–9, 112, 155

Germany, 62, 77, 81–5, 89–90, 95, 101, 105, 239

Ghana (Gold Coast), first African member of Commonwealth (1957), 174–5; 178, 184, 186–7; breaks off relations with Britain on Rhodesian issue, 191–2; President Nkrumah ejected by army revolt, 195; 239

Gladstone, W. E., 142, 219–20, 237, 252

Godley, Sir Alexander, 60

Gokhale, G. K., 50–1, 54, 56

Gopal, Dr S., *British Policy in India, 1885–1905*, 44; *Jawaharlal Nehru, A Biography*, 153, 231–2, 235

Governor-General: legislative rôle of, 3–4; appointment of, 5; and exercise of discretionary authority in dissolution (Canada, 1925), 22–3, 216; (1926) separation of his functions, 24, 26; redefinition of his functions, 30; 34; office abolished in Irish Free State (1936), 35; 36, 47; reasons of, for refusing dissolution in South Africa (1939), 92–3; 184, 224

Greece, 10, 90, 242

Greenwood, Anthony, 176

Guyana, independence (1966), 175–6, 192

Gwyer, Sir Maurice, 125

Hailey, Sir Malcolm (later Lord), 65

Haldane, R. B., 237

Halifax, 1st earl of, 53; as Lord Irwin, Viceroy of India (1926–31) and dominion status for India (1929), 64, 66–7, 125, 225; *Fulness of Days*, 77; foreign secretary (1938–40), 83–5, 87–8; ambassador to United States (1941–6), 101, 220; 202

Hamilton, Lord George, 49

Hancock, Professor Sir Keith, *Survey of British Commonwealth Affairs*, 29, 41, 250; *Smuts*, 205, 207–8, 211

Hardinge, Lord, 49

Harijans, the, 57

Hastings, Warren, 49

Heath, Edward, 197

Henderson, Sir Nevile, 84

Hertzog, General J. B. M., prime minister 1924–39: against European involvements and centralising policies, 18, 20; and international recognition of dominions, 21–3; submits his draft declaration to Imperial Conference (1926), 25–7; and Statute of Westminster, 31–4; attitude to collective security and appeasement (1937), 78–80; prime minister of Fusion government (1934–9), and the 'monster treaty', 82–3; secret compact with Smuts (1938), 86–8, 90, 210–11; issue of peace or war, 91–2; 137–8, 202

high commissioners, system of, 24, 26; meetings of, with secretary of state for dominion affairs, 76; and Czech crisis, 83–6, 88–9; and second world war, 95, 99

Hindu, the, 112

Hindus, the, 51, 55, 58, 60–1, 110, 116–17, 120–2, 127

Hindustan, 70, 121–2, 128, 148

Hitler, Adolf, 62, 81–3, 85–7, 89, 92, 95

Hoare-Laval Pact, the (1935), 76

Hoare, Sir Samuel (later Lord Templewood), 74, 87

Hobhouse, Emily, 207

Hobson, J. A., *Imperialism: A Study*, 44

Hofmeyr, J. H., 92, 212

Holland, 95, 146, 252

Home, Douglas, Sir Alec (earl of), UN speech on colonialism (1963), 177–8; 189, 194

Home Rule (Ireland), 176

Honduras, British, 179

Hopkinson, H., 178

Hughes, W. M., 22, 32

Hungary (1956), 172

Hyderabad, 58, 115

Imperial Conferences, 21, 38, 247; 1921, 3, 7–9; 1923, and challenge to centralising tendencies, 13–18; 38; 1926, 17; Balfour Report and definition of dominion status and inter imperial relations, 20–30; 1930, 29–31, 33; 1937, discussion of foreign affairs, 78–80, 82, 88; and Irish constitutional developments, 138; and colonial government, 244–5

Imperial Economic Conference (Ottawa 1932), 39–42

Imperial Economic Council (1924), 39

imperial preferences, 37–42

Imperial War Conferences and Cabinet, first world war, 7, 16, 38, 63–4, 97, 247

imperialism, imperialists, imperial policies and purposes, and Chanak incident, 10; concept of a single imperial foreign policy, 15–17; 29; imperial system demolished (1931), 34; 44, 48, 91, 102, 119, 122, 146, 174; problems connected with liquidation of imperial rule, 180; 207, 238–9, 241; and 'the frontiers of fear', 250; 252

India, 5, 8, 20, 24, 44; East India Company rule ended, provisions of Government of India Act (1858), 47–50; first session of Indian National Congress (1885) and demand for British parliamentary institutions, 45–6, 61–2; composition and outlook of Indian Civil Service (ICS), 50–3; British ambivalence, threat of violence, Congress claim to represent all India, 53–8; position of the Princely States, safeguards for Muslims, 58–9; partition of Bengal, 59–61; Montagu declaration, responsible government and dominion status, 61–8; Government of India Act (1935), 68–70; and second world war, 94; viceroy's declaration of war, Congress and League reactions, 104–6; attempts to end constitutional deadlock (1940–6), 106–11; interim government and Constituent Assembly (1946), Mountbatten and the transfer of power, 111–12; analysis of partition, 109–31; time limit and transfer plans, 124–6; acquiescence of Congress leaders in partition, risks of delay, 126–7; the successor states, 127–9, 138–9, 145–8; republican commonwealth membership of, 151–62, 164–5; and non-alignment, 169; and Suez crisis, 171–2; 173, 175, 177, 184, 186, 192, 225–35, 238–9, 241, 248, 251

India, Government of, Act (1858), 47; (1919), 63–4; (1935), 68–70, 105, 129, 148

India Office, the, 49, 55, 114

Indian Independence Act (1947), 111, 128, 137

Indian mutiny-rebellion (1857), 47, 55–6, 121

Indian National Congress: first session of (1885), 45; claim of, to represent all India, 56–8, 128, 130; draft constitution for India (1929), 59; 60–1; and responsible government and dominion status, 64–5; and Government of India Act (1935), 68–70; attitude to war-time cooperation, resignations of provincial governments (December 1939), 105–7; rejects August (1940) and Cripps (1942) offers, endorses 'Quit India' resolution, 107–9; and Cabinet Mission, 110–11; resigned to partition, 111–13, 118, 126; 114–17; effects of formation of one-party provincial governments (1937) and their resignations (December 1939), 118–20; contests Muslim League's claim to parity, 121–2; and interim government (1946), 123; 125, 127; and republican membership, 147, 151, 153; Jaipur resolution of (1948), 154; 238

Indo-Chinese Treaty (1954), 169

Indonesia, 177

Inter-Asian (Asian Relations) Conference (1947), 145

Ireland, Irish, 44, 47, 56, 121–2, 238, 241

Irish Free State, Eire, Republic of Ireland, 3–4; first dominion diplomatic appointments, Washington (1924), 6; League of Nations (1923), 18; and

Imperial Conference (1926), 20–1, 23, 26–7, 30; and Statute of Westminster (1931), 32–7; Removal of the Oath Act (1933), 36; External Relations Act (1936), 37; 65, 73–4; and sanctions against Italy, 75–6; 84–5; neutrality of, 83, 86, 93, 95, 105; nature of Irish association after 1936, 138–9; J. A., Costello and repeal of External Relations Act (1948), 140; Republic of Ireland Act (1948) and effect on citizenship and trade preferences, 141–2; Commonwealth response to secession, 142–4; rapprochement with Europe, 144–5; 147; precedent of republican association, 148–9, 151–2, 154; 160, 180, 238–9

Irwin, Lord, *see* Halifax

Italy, 74, 80, 95

Jaipur Resolution, the (1948), 154

Jamaica, independence (1962), 175, 192

James I, 236–7

Japan, 41; attack upon Manchuria, 73–4; Australian attitude to, 81; irruption into south-east Asia, 93–4; attack on Pearl Harbour and Australian reactions, 100–1; 106; impact of entry into war on India, 107; 148, 163, 168, 196, 239

Jebb, Richard, 202

Jinnah, Mohammed Ali, 58, 69; and the interim government (1946), 111; 112–14; Lahore meeting of Muslim League (1940) and claim for Muslim nationhood, 117–19, 121–2; protests at 'moth-eaten Pakistan', 122–3; 126, 128, 147, 202

Jordan, W. J., 84–5

Jowitt, Lord, 142

Kampala, 251

Karachi, 112

Kashmir, 58, 115, 129, 226, 229–31

Kaunda, President Kenneth, 193, 199

Kawawa, R. M., 161

Keith, Professor A. B., 22–3, 70

Kenya, independence (1963), 174, 176–8, 183, 229, 239

Kenyatta, Jomo, 202, 242

Khan, Liaquat Ali, 111, 123, 202

Kimberley, 1st earl of, quoted, 45

Kingston (Ontario), 81

Korea, 169–70

Kripalani, Acharya, 129, 231

Lagos, 190–1, 194–5

Lahore: meeting of Muslim League (1940) at, 104, 112–13, 117–18; unofficial Commonwealth Conference (1954) at, 183

Lancaster House Conferences, the, 179; on Rhodesia (1979), 199–200

Lapointe, Ernest, 20, 22, 74, 220

Laurier, Sir Wilfrid, 18, 202, 228

Lawrence, Sir Henry, 53

League of Nations, the, 5, 12, 18–20, 64, 72; authority of, challenged in Manchuria and Abyssinia, 73–4; dominion reactions to failure of, 75–82; 161, 210, 248

Le Figaro, 253

Liesching, Sir Percivale, 84

Lindsay, A. D. (later Lord), *The Essentials of Democracy*, 247

Linlithgow, 2nd marquess of, viceroy of India (1936–43) 104–5, 116, 225

Lloyd George, David (1st earl), 5, 39; and Chanak incident, 9–11, 90; 137

Lobengula, 253

Locarno Treaty of (1925), 12, 19–21, 77, 210

Long, B. K., 92

Lothian, 11th marquess of, 18

Lucknow: district jail, 227; Pact (1916), 258

Lusaka, 199

Luthuli, Albert, 209–10

Lyons, J. A., 36, 87, 95, 138

Lytton Report, 73–4

Macaulay, Thomas Babington, 53–5

MacBride, Sean, 140

MacDonald Malcolm, 85, 87, 102, 138, 222

MacDonald, Ramsay, 216

McGilligan, Patrick, 34

Mackenzie King, W. L.: and Chanak incident, 10–12; on sovereignty of Parliament, 10–12, 74, 81, 91; inter-

Mackenzie King (*Contd.*)
  national relations, treaty-making and decentralisation, 12–18, 20; and Byng controversy, 23, 216–17; and rôle at Imperial Conference (1926), 23, 26, 30, 32, 217; 36–7; and trade preferences, 38, 40; 70; and sanctions against Italy (1935), 74–5; 76–7; his fear of European involvements, 78–9; 81–2; and Czech crisis (1938),'83, 87, 89, 218; and preservation of Canadian unity (September 1939), 91; wartime cooperation, and the 'continuing conference of cabinets', 96–8; and 'the apotheosis of ... all that he stood for' (1944), 102–3; 137–8, 155, 165; man of commonwealth, 213–25; mastery of the techniques of politics, singlemindedness and attention to detail, 213–15; the cause of Canadian unity, central political position, 215–16; and wartime leadership, 218–20; concept of decentralised Commonwealth and Canadian interests, 220–2; influence on Commonwealth development, 222; 223–6, 228, 235
Macmillan, Harold: and 'the wind of change' (1960), 175–6; 186; and EEC, 195–6; 202; in Delhi (1958), 234
Malan, Dr Daniel François, 156–7
Malawi (Nyasaland), independence (1964), 174; and Central African Federation, 181–3, 187; 192, 199
Malaya, 175
Malaysia, independence (1957), 175, 177, 179–80, 192
Malta, independence (1967), 175, 242; Independence Conference (1963), 176; 192, 251
Manchester Guardian, the, 112
Manchuria, 73–4
Manila Pact (1954), 168–9
Manley, Michael, 199
Marais, Professor J. I., 204
Martin, Paul, 219
Masani, M., quoted 153
Massey, Vincent, 18, 75–6, 84–6, 88
Mau Mau, the, 229–30, 239
Mauritius, 175

Meighen, Arthur, 11, 22, 216
Menon, V. K. Krishna, 153
Menon, V. P., *The Transfer of Power in India*, 120; and transfer by way of dominion status (1947), 125; 126, 128
Menzies, Sir Robert: his criticism of Statute of Westminster, 32; and Empire preference, 41; and Czech crisis, 83–4, 86; his declaration of war (1939), 91; 98, 144; and Suez crisis, 172; and South African withdrawal, 185–6; 191, 202, 222; his vision of Empire and Commonwealth, 253
Merriman, J. X., 205
Mill, James, 44, 53
Mill, John Stuart, 53, 56
Miller, Professor J. D. B.: *Britain and the Old Dominions*, 143–4; *The Commonwealth in the World*, 173; *Survey of Commonwealth Affairs*, 197
Milner, Alfred (later viscount), 44
Minto, 4th earl of, viceroy of India (1905–10), 45, 50, 54, 60–1
Monckton, Sir Walter (later viscount), 115, 182
Montagu, Edwin, 50, 53, 61; declaration (1917), 62–5; 202
Moon, Sir Penderel, *Divide and Quit*, 119
Morley, John (later viscount), secretary of state for India (1905–10), 45; Morley-Minto reforms (1909), 50, 59–60; and Gokhale, 54, 56
Mountbatten of Burma, Louis, 1st earl, 46; last viceroy of India (1947), 111, 113–14; and Jinnah's case for partition, 123; 124; his first transfer plan retracted, 125; 126, 130–1, 148–9, 152, 155, 202, 226
Mozambique, 199
Mugabe, Robert, 200–1
Mughal emperors, 46, 147
Munich, dominion policies in the crisis (1938), 86–9, 95
Munro, Thomas, 53
Muslim League, the: and rejection of Congress claim to represent all India, 57, 118–19, 122; Lucknow Pact (1916) with Congress, 58; 68; Lahore meeting of, (1940) and demand for

separate homelands, 104, 112–13, 117–18; attitude to wartime cooperation, 104–6; constitutional proposals and new concept of non-accession, 107–11, 120–1; and participation in interim government and boycott of Constituent Assembly (1946), 111, 123; 115; reactions to formation of one-party provincial governments (1937), 118–20, 234; claim to parity with Congress, 121–2; and the attainment of Pakistan, 122–7; 128

Muslims, the, 51, 57–60, 104, 107, 110, 112–14, 116–23, 126, 130

Mussolini, B., 74

Muzorewa Bishop Abel, 198

Nadan's case, 4, 23

Nairobi, 242

Nasser, President, 170

National Convention, the (1908–9), 205–6

nationalism, nationalists, nationality, 238–9, 251; African, 162, 164, 174–6, 178; Afrikaner, 18, 25–6, 28, 33, 92–3; Asian, 149–50, 162, 164–5; Dominion, 21, 87–8; German, 89; Indian, 56–8, 60–2, 68, 108, 118–19, 145; Irish, 34, 141, 144, 238–9

naval defence, and Australian vulnerability to attack, 73–5, 80–1, 93–4, 168

Nazis, the, 77, 95, 100, 168, 218

Neatby, Dr H. B., *William Lyon Mackenzie King*, 215–16

Nehru, Jawaharlal, 57, 68–9, 105, 109; 'tryst with destiny', 112, 146; 114; discounts Muslim nationalism, 119; 122–3; 'devastating effect' of first Mountbatten plan on, 125; and partition, 113, 126–7, 130; 'strong winds over Asia' (1947), 145–6; and republican Commonwealth membership, 147–8, 151–7; statement on and credit for settlement reached, 159–60; representative figure of his times, 165, 229–30; and defence pacts in Asia and non-alignment, 168–9; and Suez crisis, 171–2; 186, 221; man of commonwealth, 225–35; personal

qualities and natural leadership, 225–9; and Kashmir, Goa and Chinese disillusionment (1962), 230–2; reinterpretation of Commonwealth and republican membership, 232–4; architect of the multiracial Commonwealth, 235

Nehru, Motilal, and draft constitution (1929), 59; and dominion status, 65–6

New Zealand: satisfaction with 'status quo', 4, 6, 22, (1926, 24, 28); response to Chanak appeal, 10; 12; Statute of Westminster not adopted until 1947, 31–2, 36–7; 34; and Ottawa Conference (1932), 40; 43–4, 65; support for League and sanctions, 75, 79–80; and Czech crisis, 84–5, 87; and second world war, 91, 94, 99; and Irish secession, 143; and India's republican membership, 155, 157–8; 165; misgivings as Britain draws closer to Europe, 166; joins SEATO (1954), 168; 179, 192, 197, 217, 238, 251

Newfoundland, 20, 25

Nicholls, G. Heaton, 92

Nigeria, independence (1960), 174–5; Willink Commission report on, 178; 187; Commonwealth meeting (1966) in, 190–1; 192; army revolt in, 194–5, 246, 251

Nkomo, Joshua, 198, 200

Nkrumah, President Kwame, 187, 189, 195, 202

North Atlantic Treaty (1949), 167–8; North Atlantic community, 252

North-West Frontier Province, 114, 122

Norway, 95

Nyasaland, *see* Malawi

Nyerere, President Julius, 161, 186, 199, 202, 242

Observer, the, 186

O'Higgins, Kevin, 26–7, 202

Olivier, Dr Borg, 242

Ollivier, Lord, 65

Organisation of African Unity (OAU), 198

Orissa, 119

Ottawa, 6, 10, 13; Ottawa Conference (1932) and agreements, 39–42; 74, 95–6, 140, 244

Pacific, the, 74, 81; Pacific War Council (1941) 94; 97–8, 100–1, 163, 238–9
Pacific Security Agreement 168
Page, Sir Earle, 83–4, 99–100
Pakistan, 43, 70, 110; goal of (March 1940), 'Day of Deliverance' proclaimed December, 1939, 118; and two-nation theory, 117–19, 121–2, 128; and principle of non-accession and importance of Cabinet Mission's proposals, 120–1; 'Direct Action Day' and 'Great Calcutta Killing' (August 1946), 113, 121; and partition of Punjab and Bengal, 122–3; time limit too short for, 124; truncated form of, 123, 125–6; Sikh threats against, 127; international status of, 127–9; partition of and independence of Bangladesh (1971–2), 131; 139; foreign policy and Commonwealth membership of, 146–8, 150; 157–9, 165; joins SEATO, 179; 192, 197, 217, 238, 251
Pan–African Congress (1960), 184
Pandit, Mrs V., 242
Panikkar, K. M., *Asia and Western Dominance*, 53; 108, 202, 231
Parnell, Charles Stewart, 176
Partition: India, 109–31; first partition of Bengal, 60–1; Punjab and Bengal, 118, 123; Ireland, 75, 142; Pakistan, 131
Patel, Sardar Vallabhbhai, 110–11, 113, 118, 123, 126, 153; on 'Headship' of Commonwealth, 157
Patriotic Front, the, 198–200
Pearl Harbour, 100
Pearson, Lester, and 1949 Commonwealth Meeting, 156–7; 171, 202
Peking, 195, 231
Pethick-Lawrence, Lord, 109
Pickersgill, J. W., 215, 217; *The Mackenzie King Record* (ed.), 223
Plamenatz, Professor J. P., *On Alien Rule and Self-Government*, 240
Poland, 77; Anglo–French guarantee

(March, 1939), 78; and Churchill and Smuts on guarantee, 90; 95
Port Kembla, 81
Prague, 83, 89
Prasad, Rajendra, 119
Pretoria, 95, 209
princes, Indian, 106, 110, 113–15, 117, 127
Privy Council, Judicial Committee of the, 4, 23, 26–7, 32–3, 36
Punjab, the, 56, 114, 118, 123, 127

Quebec, 74, 82, 218, 238, 244

racial questions, 44–5, 51, 75, 146, 165–6, 239; multi-racial Commonwealth membership, implications of, 43, 183–4, 191, 235, 238, 246; Rhodesia, 180–4, 187–94 South Africa, 135, 184–6, 246
Rajagopalachari, Chakravarti, 148, 171
Rajan, Professor M. S., *The Post-War Transformation of the Commonwealth*, 178
Ramphal, Shridath, 199
Reading, 1st marquess of, 65
republics, republicanism, 22, 183, 235; Burma, 149; Cyprus, 242; India, 138, 147, 151–60, 235; Ireland, 27, 34, 138–44, 147; South Africa, 184–7; Tanganyika, 161–2
Rhineland, the, 77–8, 80
Rhodes, Cecil John, 180, 200, 204, 207, 253
Rhodesia, Southern (Rhodesia–Zimbabwe, Zimbabwe), 144, 172, 174, 176, 180; and Central African Federation, 181–3, 187; unilateral declaration of independence (UDI) (1965), 188, Commonwealth reactions to and pressure for use of force against, 188–94; conditions for independence, the Five (later Six) Principles, 189–90; sanctions imposed against, 188, 190–4, 198; and majority rule, 189–90, 192–4, 200; British ultimatum, HMS *Tiger* talks (1967), commitment to NIBMAR, 193–4; HMS *Fearless* talks (1968), fresh proposals (1976), 194; combination of circumstances leading to

formation of transitional government (1978), 197–8; elections under new constitution, Lusaka and Lancaster House Conferences, 199–200; transfer of power, Robert Mugabe first Prime Minister of Republic of Zimbabwe, 200–1; 239, 246, 251, 253; *see also* Zimbabwe

Riddell, Walter, 74–5

Ripon, 1st marquess of, 6

Robinson, Professor R., 201

Roosevelt, President F. D., 81–2

Round Table, the, 88, 202

Round Table Conferences, the (1930–1), 57, 68, 117

Rumania, 90

Runciman, Walter (later viscount), 42, 83

Russell, Lord John, 236

Russia, 62, 81, 164; *see also* Soviet Union

St Laurent, Louis, 13, 168, 202

Salisbury, 3rd marquess of, 49

Salisbury (Rhodesia), 193–4, 200

San Francisco, 135

sanctions: against Italy, 74–6, 78–9, 95; against Rhodesia, 188, 190–4, 198, 251

Sandys, Duncan, 176

Sapru, Sir Tej Bahadur: appeal to British prime minister following Japanese entry into war, 107; and republican forms not inconsistent with Commonwealth ties, 147–8; 228

Scullin, J. H., 30

secession, dominion right of, 108, 147; republicanism and, 158; of Burma, 149, 152, 160, 164; of Ireland, 144–5, 160; of South Africa, 185–6

Second world war, 91–103; casualties in, 94; reactions in India to Viceroy's declaration, 104–6; 116, 163, 179, 240, 247

Seeley, Sir John, 237, 252

Shanghai, 73

Sharpeville, 184

Shaw, George Bernard, 141

Siegfried, André, 244

Sierra Leone, independence (1961), 174, 192

Sikhs, the, 55, 114, 127

Simla, Conference, the, (1945), 109, 122; 125

Simon Commission, the, 45–6, 66, 129

Simpson, Mrs W., 36–7

Sind, 122, 129

Singapore, 163, 175, 179–80, 192

Singh, Master Tara, 127

Sinn Féin, 27, 65

Skelton, Dr O. D., 15, 18

Smith, Arnold, 189

Smith, Ian: and UDI, 188; takes part in H. M. S. *Tiger* talks, 193; member of transitional government, 198

Smuts, General J. C., 11–12; and defining dominion relations, 19, 21, 24–5, 31, 33–4; and occupation of Rhineland, 77; and Fusion government 82–3; and secret compact with Hertzog (1938), 86–8; on Polish guarantee, 90, 211; brings South Africa into second world war, 91–2, 211; opposed to imperial cabinet, 97; suggestion of Commonwealth-West European grouping (1943), 101, 166; on Cripps offer (1942), 109; 135, 137, 165; man of Commonwealth, 203–13; reaction to defeat, range of experience and gifts, 203–7; reconciliation of Europeans his priority, peace-making, neglect of native question, 206–10, 212; debts to Botha and J. H. Hofmeyr, faith in Commonwealth, 212–13; 226–7, 235

Snowden, Philip (afterwards Lord), 39

Soames, Christopher (Lord), 200

Somalia, 177

Soulbury, Lord, 150; Soulbury Report (1945), 245–6; and Constitution (1946), 150

South Africa Act, the (1909), 34

South African War, the (1899–1902), 238

South-East Asian Treaty Organisation (SEATO), 168–70

Soward, Professor F. H., *Some Aspects of Canadian Foreign Policy in the Last Quarter Century*, 18

Soviet Union, the, 81, 95, 101, 150, 164

Status of the Union Act (1934), 33, 37

Statesman, the, (Calcutta), 137
Sudetenland, the 83–4, 86, 89
Suez, 166, 180; Canal, 48, 170; crisis (1956), 170–3, 249, 251
Swaziland, independence (1968), 174
Sweden, 95, 252
Switzerland, 46

Talleyrand, C. -M. de, Prince, 247
Tanganyika, independence (1961), republic (1962), 160–2, 174, 176, 186
Tanzania, 349, 360, 363–4, 368
tariffs and tariff reform, 37–40; General Agreement on Trade and (1947), 142
Taylor, A. J. P., *English History, 1914–1945*, 163
Templewood, Lord, *see* Sir Samuel Hoare
Thatcher, Mrs Margaret, 199–200
Thomas, J. H., 35–6
Tibet, 169
Tilak, B. G., 56
Times, The, 32, 85, 88, 117, 253
Tobago, independence (1962), 175, 178, 192
trade, 6, 12–13, 37–42, 142, 195–7, 251–2; preferences, 37–42, 142; *see also* treaties and agreements, commercial
Travancore 58, 115
treaties and agreements, commercial: Anglo-Irish Free Trade Agreement, 145; Canadian-United States Halibut Fisheries Treaty (1923), 12; United Kingdom, United States, Canadian agreements (1928), 41; United States-Canadian Reciprocity Treaty (1854), 6
Treaty of Lausanne, the (1924), 12, 14–15, 19
Treaty of Rome, the, 145
Treaty of Versailles: 'a landmark' in constitutional development of Commonwealth, 7–8, 13–14; 64; German defiance of (1936), 77; 78; Hertzog on the 'monster treaty', 82; dominions consider war to uphold territorial provisions of, unjustified, 88; Smuts on 'Carthaginian' peace, 210; 239

Trinidad, independence (1962), 175, 178, 192
Trudeau, Pierre, and patriation of constitution, 33; 202
Tuker, General Sir Francis, *While Memory Serves*, 121
Turkey, and Chanak incident, 9–10, 13–15, 17

Uganda, independence (1962), 174, 192, 251
Unilateral Declaration of Independence (UDI), 188, *see* Rhodesia
United Nations, the, 93, 128; Smuts and Charter of, 135; 150; and ending of colonialism and Lord Home's speech on, 174, 177; and sanctions against Rhodesia, 193, 198; 248
United Provinces, 56
United States of America, 6, 12–13, 20, 41, 46, 62, 73, 81–2, 91, 93; naval victories of, 94; after Pearl Harbour, Australia 'looks to America', 100–1; commercial treaty with Ireland (1950), 142; 153, 162, 164, 166; relations with Australia and New Zealand, Atlantic and Pacific pacts, 165, 167–9; 177, 196

Valera, Eamon de, and Oath of Allegiance, 34–6; and sanctions against Italy, 75; 76; and 'external association', 139; falls from office (1948), 140; 202, 213
Vereeniging, peace of (1902), 208
Verwoerd, Dr Hendrik, 185–6
Vietnam, 168

Walker, Patrick Gordon, 139, 153; *The Commonwealth*, republican membership and Headship, 155, 157
Washington, 6, 13, 18, 74, 88, 94
Water, C. te, 75–6
Watt, D. C., 89
Wavell, Field-Marshal, Viscount, viceroy of India (1943–7), 112–14, 123, 148
Webster, Professor Sir Charles, 135
Wedderburn, Sir William, 52
Welensky, Sir Roy, *Welensky's 4000 Days, The Life and Death of the Federation of Rhodesia and Nyasaland*, 182–3

West Indies, the, 175–6; federation in, 179; 197, 241, 251

Westminster, Parliament at, 3–4, 33, 111, 139, 170; Westminster model, 162, 243–5

Westminster, Statute of (1931), 29; gives legal effect to Balfour Report on dominion status, 31–5; not adopted by Australia till 1942 and New Zealand till 1947, 32; and Oath of Allegiance in Irish Free State, 35–6; 37, 39, 43, 71, 92; and incompatibility of allegiance with republican membership, 137, 154, 158, 160

Wheare, Professor Sir K. C., *The Statute of Westminster and Dominion Status*, 29, 37

Wigley, Dr P. G., *Canada and the Transition to Commonwealth. British Canadian Relations 1917–1926*, 18

Willink Commission, 178

Wilson, Sir Harold: his warning to Rhodesian rebels, 187–8; assailed by African leaders, 189; talks on HMS *Tiger* and HMS *Fearless*, 193–4; 196

Wilson, Thomas Woodrow, President, 5

Yalta, 135

Zafrullah Khan, Chaudhuri Sir Muhammad, 157

Zetland, 2nd marquess of, 106, 116

Zimbabwe, 200–1, 253; *see also* Rhodesia, Southern

45 Buc